Attracting Birds:
from the Prairies
to the Atlantic

Attracting Birds:
from the Prairies
to the Atlantic

VERNE E. DAVISON

Thomas Y. Crowell Company

NEW YORK   ESTABLISHED 1834

Contents

Figures

Tables

Preface

This book is a guide to the favorite foods, nesting habits, and water needs of more than 400 species of birds that live in or migrate to eastern North America, from the prairies to the Atlantic. It is a guide for those people who want to attract, observe, and study birds in the pastime known as "birding" or "birdwatching." It will also help those who seek outdoor recreation hunting game birds and those who want to support and increase flocks of eastern North American birds on farms and fields, along streams and shores, at ponds and marshes, and in woodlands, backyards, and gardens.

What makes this book especially useful is the author's new classification of the food preferences of birds. The conclusions it presents are derived largely from thousands of carefully recorded observations made over the past 30 years during experiments to determine which foods birds select when they are offered a variety of different foods. The results of these studies have been supplemented by data accumulated over the years by direct analysis of stomach contents. Most of the author's findings were published from 1940 to 1965 in the *Journal of Wildlife Management, Proceedings of the North American and Southeastern Wildlife Conferences, Audubon Magazine,* and the Wildlife Society's *Investigational Research Techniques* (2d ed., 1963); this is however, the first full-length book to make extensive use of his modern methods.

This book does not describe birds for purposes of identification. If you cannot recognize each bird on sight, you need one of the up-to-date field guides or a book that illustrates and fully describes species that live in your state. Some of these books are listed in the Bibliography.

To make the most efficient use of *Attracting Birds*, you should know how it is arranged so that you can readily find the information you seek. The book is divided into seven sections, the most important of which are sections 4 and 5.

Section 4 contains entries for more than 400 species of birds, with information about where they may be found in the East, their food and nesting habits, and successful ways of attracting them. The "choice" and "fair" foods of each species are given in separate classifications.

The entries are arranged in alphabetical order by the common names established in the *A.O.U. Check-List of North American Birds* (5th ed., Baltimore, Md.: American Ornithologists' Union, Lord Baltimore Press, 1957). For each of the birds, the technical (Latin) name is given; commonly used, but no longer correct, variant names of each bird are also noted. Laymen birdwatchers, students, and ornithologists will all find this format useful, though professionals often prefer a taxonomic arrangement.

Section 5 contains entries for over 700 plants and other foods. It names alphabetically the birds to which each is most important, and tells how birds use it. By consulting this section, the reader can select a combination of agricultural and ornamental plants that are attractive to a wide variety of birds. He can also plan an exclusive feeding program by selecting only those foods that are attractive and nutritious for a chosen few.

The plant and food entries are arranged in alphabetical order, the plants by their common rather than scientific names. The approved common names for trees and grasses are drawn for the most part from the *Check List of Native and Naturalized Trees of the United States,* by Elbert J. Little, Jr. (Washington, D.C.: U.S. Department of Agriculture, Forest Service, Agricultural Handbook No. 41, 1953); and *Manual of the Grasses of the United States,* by A. S. Hitchcock (2d ed., revised by Agnes Chase; Washington, D.C.: U.S. Department of Agriculture, Miscellaneous Publication No. 200, 1950). For other plants, the common names are usually those established by *Standardized Plant Names,* prepared by the editorial committee of the American Joint Committee on Horticultural Nomenclature (2d ed.; Harrisburg, Pa.: J. Horace McFarland Co., 1942).

In a few cases the author took exception to names that seemed confusing, and used instead the technical name or a widely accepted common name. For example, the words "pondweed" and "waterweed" are widely used to designate all weeds that infest ponds, so the author uses "potamogeton" and "anacharis," respectively, instead. "Chufa" seemed better than "nutgrass" or "southern wild rice," as it is neither a grass nor a kind of rice. Alternate plant names that are widely used are also listed in alphabetical order, with a reference to the common name used throughout the book. This permits the reader to find a plant by the name he has used and helps to establish a single "common" name for each plant, an objective not yet fully realized in the botanical field.

Sections 6 and 7 list alphabetically the scientific names of birds and plants, respectively, for the convenience of those who are familiar with technical names of either birds or plants. Each entry directs the reader to the common name used throughout this book.

Section 1 defines the terms "choice," "fair," and "unimportant," as used in this book to designate a food's attractiveness to each kind of bird. It explains how to study food preferences by the new and interesting method which is based on "free-choice comparison between two or more foods when they are equally available."

Section 2 discusses the significance of foods and tells how to feed birds by natural, agricultural, and artificial means. It includes lists of birds that eat similar types of foods such as nuts, seeds, fruits, green forage, and various animals. It also lists bird foods that are commercially available.

Section 3 deals with nests and birdhouses, listing in groups the birds that nest in birdhouses, holes, and crevices; on the ground; in upland trees, shrubs, and vines; or in aquatic habitats. Specifications for birdhouse dimensions, and related information, are given in its birdhouse table.

Acknowledgments

If the dedicated agriculturists, botanists, and ornithologists of past genera-
tions had failed to publish the results of their research and experience, this
book could not have been written. I am deeply indebted to them for their
pioneering work in plant taxonomy and culture, their classification and naming of birds, and their rich legacy of bird-food studies.

I am particularly grateful for the help of three twentieth-century scientists
who were formerly with the Biological Survey Food-Habits Division: Drs.
Clarence Cottam, Alexander C. Martin, and W. L. McAtee. They identified
many bird foods in my field collection, reviewed and often criticized my
field-study techniques and the resulting manuscripts, and willingly made
their own hypotheses and principles known to me.

The editors of the *Journal of Wildlife Management* encouraged my contin-
uing bird-food studies by editing and publishing 15 manuscripts. I am indebted to Drs. W. L. McAtee, Tracy I. Storer, Oliver H. Hewitt, J. J. Hickey,
C. M. Kirkpatrick, and Thomas G. Scott.

I am similarly appreciative of the help of *Audubon Magazine* editors John
K. Terres and John Vosburgh, and Mason C. Russell, editor of *Florida Nat-
uralist*, who published my series of nongame-bird studies (1959–1965).

I received much-needed help with writing the manuscript for this book
from Lawrence V. Compton, Head Biologist, Soil Conservation Service,
Washington, D.C., and from Patrick Barrett and Edward Tripp of the
Thomas Y. Crowell Company.

A great amount of work went into the free-choice bird-food appraisals that
contributed so significantly to the contents of this book. Many people helped
in one way or another, collecting seeds and fruits and recording their own
feeding observations for me, especially the following biologists and plant-
materials technicians of the Soil Conservation Service: V. E. Ahlrich, Philip
F. Allan, Howard R. Bissland, C. B. Blickensderfer, Adrey E. Borell, Morris
E. Byrd, Olan W. Dillon, Floyd R. Fessler, Karl E. Graetz, Edward H. Gra-
ham, Roy A. Grizzell, Wade H. Hamor, Harry J. Haynsworth, John A. Johnson, W. W. Neely, Lloyd E. Partain, John D. Powell, W. Hancell Rhodes,

Paul M. Scheffer, Walter E. Shrader, E. Ray Smith, Edward G. Sullivan, Paul Tabor, Wm. R. Van Dersal, and W. C. Young.

Dr. T. S. Buie, Spartanburg, South Carolina—and the state conservationists of the 11 southeastern states with whom I worked 26 years—kindly welcomed my efforts to understand each bird's relationship to agricultural lands and people.

A large number of land managers established the practical proof that choice foods dependably attract and support birds in fields, ponds, marshes, and woodlands that are managed favorably. Although they are too numerous to name, they thoroughly confirmed a lesson my father, George E. Davison of Arnett, Oklahoma, taught me 50 years ago: "Wildlife will come wherever you feed them well."

W. E. Freeborn of the Hastings Seed Company in Atlanta, Georgia, often provided feeds for my experiments, as did the Bruce Pennington Seed Company of Madison, Georgia.

An enormous amount of secretarial work went into the preparation, frequent revisions, and cross-checking of the details in this book and the several manuscripts involved in the previous publications. Those patient helpers— Ruth Bennett, Martha Bonner, Ruth P. Higgins, Helen Johnson, and Lorraine Stanelle—have my utmost thanks.

I am grateful to Harry E. Schmidt of Portland, Oregon, for his patience and skill in preparing the book's illustrations.

Without being facetious, I must also mention the contributions that the birds themselves made consistently and patiently—and sometimes impatiently—as I manipulated their diet and feeding habits for the sake of my experiments.

Mildred Lashley Davison, my wife, kept my work going with her encouraging patience, observations, and feeding chores during the 40-odd years that we have bird-studied together. My brothers, "Dr. Gus" and Francis, aided my studies with contributions from Arkansas, Louisiana, and Oklahoma. Our son Meredith of Spartanburg, South Carolina, made bird feeders and birdhouses for experimental studies, and our daughter Barbara, now Mrs. S. M. Craft of Jackson, Mississippi, fed her birds and faithfully informed me of their behavior.

Introduction

Ornithologists estimate that an acre of land in the eastern United States supports only from one to ten birds, an average of four. Bird enthusiasts, however, have learned that they can attract far more birds than nature alone can support, by means of artificial supplements. Those interested in increasing flocks of game birds improve undeveloped lands by growing better fields, strips, or plots of food than nature does, and they are rewarded with larger populations of bobwhites, doves, ducks, geese, pheasants, snipe, and wild turkeys. Owners of suburban and rural homes bring delightful birds to their picture windows by installing interesting feeding devices and increase nesting sites by erecting birdhouses that blend into the beauty of natural settings. They bring more birds into the landscape around their homes by raising shrubs and trees that offer choice foods and suitable nesting areas. The same plants usually provide the birds with adequate shade and the protective cover they need to escape from cats, dogs, predatory birds, and storms.

By using methods such as these, my wife and I might be visited by over 60 birds, far above the average, on a typical summer day at our one-acre suburban homes, first in Alabama and later in Georgia. Our backyard guests might include a pair of bluebirds and their young, five or more pairs of cardinals and a dozen young, one or two pairs of Carolina chickadees, ten to a dozen mourning doves, two to four yellow-shafted flickers, two to ten common grackles, a like number of blue jays, a pair of ruby-throated hummingbirds, a pair of mockingbirds, two to four brown-headed nuthatches, several robins, two pairs of summer tanagers, at least one pair each of chipping sparrows, brown thrashers, wood thrushes, and tufted titmice, two pairs of rufous-sided towhees and their young, a nesting pair of wood pewees, and one pair of Carolina wrens. They weren't exclusively ours, of course, but we had their delightful company for our own satisfaction every day.

In winter we kept the same birds, except the migratory hummingbirds, tanagers, and wood thrushes, and our feathered population increased gratifyingly as foods became scarce elsewhere. Our cardinals increased to around 50; the bluebirds numbered from three to six.

The winter residents that immigrated from the North always included 12 to 15 white-throated sparrows, an equal number of slate-colored juncoes and purple finches, more doves, a dozen myrtle and pine warblers, one or two song sparrows, and sometimes fox sparrows, evening grosbeaks, and flocks of cedar waxwings. Each day of the winter season, then, we enjoyed the company of more than 100 birds, and we supported them with attractive and nutritious foods to each one's liking. We lost no bluebirds of our little flock during the storms of March 1960 that decimated more than half of the eastern population. Our birds reached the spring nesting seasons in robust health, ready to reproduce successfully.

We disagree with the theory that artificial feeding weakens a bird's ability to make a living naturally or to withstand the rigors of weather and periods of food shortages. Our birds survived when we would be gone a week or a month without leaving them their usual supply of choice foods. A female red-bellied woodpecker, handicapped by complete blindness of the left eye, survived and successfully raised young every year of the six we lived in Athens, Georgia.

Bird lovers who have been feeding birds for many years have surprised us by asking: "How do you get the bluebirds to come so easily? They never come to our feeders." Our stock answer always includes a question: "You probably do not feed them what bluebirds like. Do you offer them fruits such as currants and raisins?"

Few people seem to realize that different kinds of birds have decided peculiarities about the foods they like best. Bluebirds don't like grain mixtures, suet, peanutbutter, biscuits, or table scraps; they like insects and fruits. Cardinals are happy with at least 76 choice foods and 25 fair items that include many seeds, grains, fruits, and nuts. Chickadees, nuthatches, and titmice substantially agree on the choice foods that they eat; their tastes run to nuts, sunflower seeds, suet, and (except nuthatches) peanutbutter—mostly oily foods—and bread, cookies, and cake. Attracting birds with food is accomplished most successfully when you know the likes and dislikes of each species. Conversely, a thoughtful study of each species' food preferences and feeding habits reveals ways of feeding selectively, ways which discourage birds that are unwelcome.

Accomplished birdwatchers have more immediate ways of attracting birds when they want merely to identify or count them, or to observe them in the wild. A mimicked mating call or cry of distress is often used to lure birds from hiding places. They come to the site of the disturbance out of curiosity, perhaps, or to defend their mating territory, or to help the sufferer.

During the nesting season, a supply of choice nesting material—thin strips of soft cloth, string, unraveled rope, excelsior, shredded cellophane or paper, and feathers or down—will prove attractive. The string should be cut into short bits, no longer than 8 inches, for birds often become entangled in longer pieces and have been known to hang themselves. Even if the birds in your community do not "need" your nest-material offerings, they will delight you by coming repeatedly for the handouts.

Once birds have come to depend upon your generosity, you can expect them to return year after year. For ornithologists know from records of banded birds and countless careful observations, that many adult birds, even migratory species, come back to the same feeding and nesting areas—often to the same field or pond, and even to a particular tree, nesting box, or feeding station. Since most birds live from three to ten years, it is possible that in time you will recognize some of your visitors as old acquaintances.

It is difficult to generalize briefly about the nesting territories of birds, the ways younger birds select their first mating areas, and the behavior of older birds toward their newly matured offspring. Most birds evidently remember well the favorite feeding and nesting places of yesteryear, and return seasonally to continue their life habits in the same places.

The male bird selects his mating territory early in the mating season. A few species such as the pheasant, ruffed grouse, and prairie chicken select only a crowing or drumming ground; they then mate with hens that come into the general area and leave the ne.t building and rearing of the young to the hens alone. Most birds, however, live throughout a nesting season with a single mate, and the male selects the nest site and helps with the rearing of the young. (In a few species, such as the mourning dove, the male also takes his turn at incubating the eggs.)

Although a few species, such as boobies, gulls, murres, and terns, nest together in rather densely packed colonies, most of our backyard birds make strenuous efforts to keep other nesting pairs of the same species out of the small domain which they stake out for their exclusive use during the rearing season. An older male, as long as he is physically able to do so, permits no young from his own or any other's last-year brood to set up housekeeping in the old home place. Birds just reaching sexual maturity, therefore, must establish a home territory wherever they can find and defend suitable sites.

Each year, then, you may expect the return of old acquaintances to former nesting sites, or a new tenant in case the old one has died of old age or some accident. This will not occur, however, if last year's bluebird house or the dead tree with the woodpecker's nesting hole is gone. Nor will the winter resident remain long at last year's field or feeding table if the food is missing. On the other hand, you can make room for additional birds by increasing nesting sites and choice foods.

Attracting Birds:
from the Prairies
to the Atlantic

Food Preferences

If you are familiar with other bird books, either technical or popular, you will quickly observe that this book presents a new and more comprehensive classification of the food preferences of each species. You may want to know how this new system was developed, and why it is valuable.

Background of earlier studies

The first published studies of the food habits of American birds were based on the observations of Indians and European explorers. In the latter half of the nineteenth century ornithologists and agriculturists recorded the feeding patterns of individual species more intensively and supplemented their findings by examining stomachs of dead birds.

In 1885, at the request of the American Ornithologists' Union, Congress established a unit of the U.S. Department of Agriculture to study "economic ornithology or the study of the interrelation of birds and agriculture." First known as the Biological Survey, it later became part of the Fish and Wildlife Service established in 1940 in the Department of the Interior. While it was affiliated with the Department of Agriculture, it conducted extensive research into the food habits of birds, but considerable controversy arose between biologists who favored field observation and those who believed that laboratory analysis and measurement of stomach contents provided more accurate and dependable information about bird feeding habits. The stomach-analysis technique became the standard procedure and was used as the basis of hundreds of published reports. The most comprehensive summary of these Biological Survey records was written by Alexander C. Martin, H. Zim, and Arnold L. Nelson and appeared in their *American Wildlife and Plants* (New York: McGraw-Hill, 1951).* My copy is worn, torn, and extensively marked with use.

---

* The original publication was reprinted in paperback cover by Dover Publishing Company (New York, 1961).

Both methods of studying the food habits of birds—observation and stomach analysis—have their limitations, and neither is sufficient alone. The procedures used in each case and the aims of the examiner strongly influence interpretations of the data and the amount of time required to complete a study. Not unexpectedly, the original methods were refined and improved with experience, and some of the earlier hypotheses were corrected.

One cause of error in earlier studies of many birds was that insufficient attention was paid to the structure of their stomachs. Most nongame birds have only a single stomach in which to keep foods that are to be digested. Upland game birds such as bobwhite, doves, grouse, pheasants, and turkeys have an enlarged area of the gullet, called a "crop," which holds quickly swallowed foods until the muscular stomach, or "gizzard," has time to digest them; a similar but less pronounced enlargement of the gullet is also found in waterfowl such as coot, ducks, and geese. (More technically, a glandular organ called the "proventriculus" is considered the true stomach in birds. Located at the entrance to the gizzard, it secretes acids for digestion.)

In determining the kind and quantity of food consumed by birds it was the standard practice of Biological Survey experts to assign equal importance to the contents of the crop and gizzard if both contained identifiable food items; if the crop were empty, as often happened it was assumed that the gizzard contained all the food that had been consumed.

Using methods approved by the Biological Survey, I began careful studies of birds' foods in the early 1930's, working with bobwhites, lesser prairie chickens, crows, and white-necked ravens on our ranch in western Oklahoma. In 1935 my employment by the Soil Conservation Service in South Dakota afforded me an opportunity to analyze the crops and gizzards of about 300 ring-necked pheasants killed during the open hunting seasons. My measurements of the freshly swallowed food in their crops, compared with the food materials in matching gizzards, indicated that measurement of the contents of gizzards give seriously misleading results. Hard seeds which are slowly or negligibly digestible remain in the gizzard for hours and days, and both frequency-of-occurrence and volumetric measurements grossly exaggerate their importance. The crop contents, however, accurately represented all of the foods that had been eaten a few minutes earlier, digestion having consumed none of the softer food items.

Opportunity to explore the subject further came with my transfer in 1937 to the Southeastern States Region of the Soil Conservation Service, headquartered in Spartanburg, South Carolina. With the help of soil conservationists and biologists, I collected and examined crops and gizzards from more than 6,000 bobwhites and mourning doves during the three hunting seasons of 1937–1938, 1938–1939, and 1939–1940. These studies confirmed my earlier observations. After I had published my conclusions, and changes in stomach-analysis methods had been suggested, the Biological Survey accepted the proposition that crop contents are more reliable than gizzard contents. Though this change corrected one obvious flaw in food-preference studies, some other faults remained.

To understand, document, and interpret food preferences properly, bird biologists needed some further information:

1. For dependable conclusions regarding "preferences," the examiner must know what foods were actually available to the bird when it chose a feeding area. What foods were available but ignored? Most of the crops, stomachs, and gizzards subjected to laboratory analysis had been obtained from hunters several weeks or months earlier, and seldom, if ever, yielded this information. Nevertheless, published results always listed foods in numerical order of "preference" according to the amount of each item identified and measured. It was commonly though erroneously stated that "preferences reflected availability," despite the fact that scores of food items such as the seeds of morningglories, redbud, mimosas, verbenas, Mexican clover, sweet clover, waterlilies, Scotchbroom, and perennial grasses were often abundantly available but left uneaten by seed-eating birds.

2. Biologists, even today, are likely to argue that a food which has been listed frequently among the food items found in gizzards is therefore important because "birds eat it," regardless of the amounts eaten. Many foods appear frequently, but only in minor quantities in the stomachs of birds examined. We call them "trace items," as they usually amount to less than one-thousandth part of the foods eaten. The accepted theory was that seeds found frequently but in small amounts probably contain "highly essential minor nutrients" that meet some physiological need of the birds. That hypothesis has never been proved by research or otherwise.

3. A most important barrier to the understanding of bird-food preferences was the widely accepted professional belief that birds have little or no sense of taste and few if any taste buds. It was assumed, therefore, that birds choose their foods by color, size, shape, texture, or "what they are used to." Ornithologists generally rejected any hypothesis that stated or implied selection by "taste."

In the mid-1950's in Alabama, Georgia, Mississippi, and elsewhere, I began to seek more dependable evidence regarding the questionable theories described in the three foregoing paragraphs. In the natural setting of our wooded backyard in Athens, Georgia, I repeatedly offered to wild, unpenned birds their free choice of several foods, a total of over 300 kinds of seeds, fruits, nuts, and other items. Without repeating here the numerous details of method, procedure, and resulting behavior of the various birds, I will state that the following facts emerged:

1. Each of the more than 40 species of birds that fed regularly or fre-

quently in our yard exhibited consistent preferences for some foods over other equally available foods of the same general type. They maintained the same preferences over a period of four years. They steadfastly ignored many kinds of foods that were offered, leaving them to rot or germinate. Their eager and consistent acceptance of the most preferred foods, stubborn reluctance to consume less attractive items, and nearly absolute refusal to eat others, gave convincing evidence of definite likes and dislikes. Their behavior made it obvious that the contents of a bird's stomach usually represent some undetermined compromise between "preference" and "availability."

2. My observations of bird behavior convinced me that the "trace items" were swallowed sparingly, even when abundantly available, in the birds' process of tasting or sampling items to determine their palatability, especially when preferred foods were scarce or unavailable. This behavior was repeated hundreds of times by every species of bird in my experiments. I had examined hundreds of bird stomachs that evidenced ingestion of the same food items in trace amounts. The proper way to prove that food items taken only in trace amounts have nutritional values in excess of their quantitative occurrences is by feeding each bird species under conditions of rigid control and examining the effects on its physical well-being, a common procedure in studying nutritional values of foods in human beings and domestic animals. This has not been done with trace items and wild birds.

3. Having arrived at the hypothesis that our birds were sampling each food before they consumed much of it, I became intrigued by the long-held assumption that birds were unable to select their foods by taste. From January 1960 to January 1964, I studied the feeding behavior of 43 species of birds that fed in our yard at Athens, Georgia. I concentrated my studies on three species—eastern bluebirds, cardinals, and mourning doves—whose foods and eating habits differ markedly. The bluebirds were attracted only to fruits, which they swallowed whole, the cardinals ate fruit, seeds, and grain; they chewed all of their foods, and discarded the covering. The mourning doves ate nothing but seeds, and swallowed them whole, never removing the covering. I repeatedly tested the validity of the theories that birds might select their foods by color, size, shape, texture, or what they were accustomed to.

The bluebirds in the tests eagerly ate the red fruits of flowering dogwood, Carolina snailseed, and amur honeysuckle; but they ate the red chokeberry and nandina fruits sparingly and reluctantly. Although they readily ate the black fruits of blackgum, black cherry, and laurelcherry and the blue fruits of blueberries and eastern redcedar, they demonstrated less liking for the blue fruits of privets and silky dogwood. They absolutely refused the blue fruits of wintergreen barberry. They ate orange-colored pyracantha in obvious preference to red-fruited pyracantha. (The red fruit was noticeably puckery to my taste.) The bluebirds ate the white fruits of Russianolive, but rejected the white fruits of Christmas mistletoe.

Mockingbirds, robins, and cedar waxwings seemed to agree that color made no difference. They eagerly ate some red, blue, white, orange, and black fruits, but rejected other kinds of fruit in similar colors. The doves selected 64 kinds of seeds that they liked consistently at all times of the year. They disregarded color, eating black, brown, yellow, white, orange, red, and various shades of gray seeds. They reluctantly ate 20 kinds of seeds in similar colors.

Hoping for a still clearer indication that birds ignore color in choosing food, I dyed separate lots of one favorite food (browntop millet) with a tasteless cake coloring—dark red, light red, dark green, light green, a rich blue, and dark yellow. The doves ate them all readily. On the other hand, when I colored the same seeds with a green enamel-like material, the doves rejected them. Cardinals agreed with the doves that the colored browntop millet seeds were all attractive. The cardinals, however, also ate the green enamel-covered seeds, as they discard all hulls anyhow.

Except for the doves' rejection of the enameled seeds, the behavior of none of our birds supported the idea that foods are chosen by shape or surface texture. The preferred, or choice, foods of the doves ranged from smooth corn seeds and crotons to the rougher hulls of browntop millet; on the other hand, they ate reluctantly or refused many seeds of similar textures and shapes, such as rice or safflower seeds.

Size affected bluebirds and doves, of course, since they swallow fruits or seeds whole. Bluebirds could not swallow attractive berries that were ⅜ inch in diameter—but they tried. Doves could hardly swallow unusually large grains of field corn and had to turn the average or smaller grains lengthwise to swallow them easily. They readily ate the tiny seeds of amaranth, chickweed, and switchgrass, and the intermediate-size seeds of croton, browntop millet, pines, and grain sorghums.

I concluded from my experiments that the birds selected their foods chiefly on the basis of taste and that color, shape, and texture were not significant factors under the conditions of these experiments. Size was a significant factor only when the seed or fruit was too large to be swallowed. I drew additional confirmation for my hypothesis by the behavior of the birds when they approached the feeding area. A dove, for example, usually stopped at a placement of food and sampled a seed or two deliberately, hesitating between "bites." If it was attractive, the dove would squat and feed rapidly, eating many seeds. If it was unpalatable, he walked around hunting something better. I watched this consistent behavior carefully, hundreds of times, as I offered them more than 200 kinds of food repeatedly in lots of 2 to 20 at a time. More than 100 of the foods offered were never consumed by the doves after they had sampled them.

The bluebirds behaved similarly, as did all the other species that visited the testing site. It is my opinion that their sampling procedure provides a sound hypothesis for explaining the frequent occurrence of trace items in birds' stomachs. My conclusions were published in an article "Taste, Not Color, Draws Birds to Berries and Seeds," *Audubon Magazine* (November–December 1962), 64(6):346–350.

As a result of their research at Cornell University in 1957, M. R. Kare and P. Lindemaier found that a "sense of taste" existed in chickens. They later discovered taste buds on the tongue of the domestic chicken and used electronic and chemical stimulation techniques to confirm that chickens have sensory responses to flavors. Of course, there is still uncertainty whether taste buds are the only receptors of the sense of taste in chickens and other birds.

This is the first book to use these new hypotheses as an aid to classifying the food preferences of birds. Without them it could not have been so conclusive. Perhaps it makes no practical difference whether it is taste, color, size, or some mysterious factor as yet unknown to man that determines why birds select some foods and reject many others. The fact remains that each species displays preferences among the animal and plant foods in eastern North America.

Improved Classification of Bird Foods

The terms used in this book must be defined as they relate to each individual bird species. All of the foods known to be eaten by a species can be classified in three categories—"choice," "fair," and "unimportant."

The terms "choice" and "fair" are used to express degrees of acceptance. The third category, "unimportant," includes "trace" items, which should be ignored as insignificant. In a complex experiment, proved unimportance will necessarily be part of the data and subsequent report, but unimportant items have no place in a summary publication such as this book.

The terms "choice" and "fair" are not new, having been used by biologists in many bird publications that also used terms such as "excellent," "highly preferred," "preferred," "very good," "good," "staple," "poor," "emergency," and "starvation." Unfortunately these terms were seldom defined. I found that the two terms "choice" and "fair" are generally adequate. From the following definitions it will be apparent that both choice and fair foods are "important" in the lives of birds in the wild.

Choice foods are foods that regularly attract a species, are eaten readily and eagerly in substantial quantities, are easily digestible, and evidently are nutritionally adequate to maintain good health, alertness, and reproductive ability. Fortunately, the foods that each species likes best are readily digestible, and I have found reasonable evidence that such foods meet their dietary requirements. I have expressed this conclusion in several published papers, but it may need further confirmation through intensive feeding experiments in which individual birds are confined in pens where the foods available are completely controlled, and their physical condition can be determined over extensive periods of time. A similar procedure is used in nutritional research with domestic livestock, poultry, human beings, plants, and other living organisms. The contention that a bird cannot long maintain proper health on the nutrients provided by a single food item does not negate the value of choice foods. Birds that live in the wild usually have a variety of choice and fair foods available.

I occasionally find it useful to employ the term "extra-choice" to designate an item that is exceptionally attractive. Commercial sunflower seeds, for example, are preferred above most of their other choice foods by birds such as cardinal, chickadee, purple finch, evening grosbeak, and tufted titmouse. On the other hand, the sunflower seed is not the only choice food of these species.

Fair foods are foods that are eaten in substantial quantity only when choice foods are not available. Although fair foods are nutritious enough to maintain life for at least short periods, they evidently are deficient in some way, permitting loss in weight, delay or prevention of reproduction, and general decline in physical well-being. Certainly foods which are rated as "fair" for a given species are not especially attractive to them; they can be important, however, because they offer sustenance to birds during periods of temporary privation, such as deep snows, when choice foods are not available.

You too can study food habits

The study of birds' food preferences need not be left entirely to scientists. You can discover for yourself the pleasure and excitement of attracting the more exotic birds that occasionally visit your community and learn by experience, when you have tested a wide variety of foods, which items attract each species best. By offering the same foods in different kinds of feeders, you can become familiar with the method of segregating your feathered visitors through the use of devices which favor their respective feeding habits.

You might begin by obtaining food items that you can buy at grocery stores, meat markets, or seed and feed stores. Section 2 provides a list of such food items from which to choose, or you may turn to section 4 to find the foods known to be preferred as "choice" by any bird that you want to attract. Or turn to section 5 if you want a list of birds that are known to eat the kind of food you'd like to try.

The fruits and berries that your own yard does not supply can be gathered from wild plants or bought when they are plentiful and inexpensive. Feed them immediately, keep them in a cool place for a few days, or quick-freeze them to make out-of-season treats, weeks or months later. Weed seeds, acorns, and nuts can be gathered and held in dry storage or refrigeration for any length of time.

HOW TO FEED. The simplest place to feed is on bare ground where you can see the birds and each food easily from a window. Or you can place the foods on a window feeder in plastic dishes or wooden trays that have dividers to separate the food items. Since the type of feeder is important to some birds, you will want to read section 2 about "feeders and feeding" and the "attracting" data in section 4 for the species that live in your neighborhood.

Arrange each food item separately—a few inches or a few feet apart—so you can distinguish its placement. If necessary, make a rough sketch showing the arrangement of each food offered at one time. There is nothing to be gained with changes in pattern, since the birds can see much better than humans and they will find the foods that each one likes best.

Birds usually feed first each day between daybreak and sunup, but a display of foods will often tempt them at any hour of the day. They come to feeders most readily in winter and early spring when their natural supply of food is wanting. You may feed them the year around or only in winter and spring, as you wish.

OBSERVATION TECHNIQUES. Your appraisal will be based on what you actually see of the birds' behavior and the records you keep. Binoculars are useful and generally needed if the food is more than 25 feet away. I usually list the foods available at one time on a sheet of paper or a card, and record each species that repeatedly eats an item—and sometimes the fact that a species consistently says "No" to a food item.

At a window feeder you can even count and record the number of raisins a bluebird, mockingbird, or robin eats at one "sitting," or you can make a story of how one species behaves, accepting and rejecting food items as it chooses.

If you want to make written records of foods which you observe your birds eating, the sample records below may help you get started. You could begin by studying one interesting species such as the cardinal, or any other bird that feeds regularly around your home. Sample 1 illustrates a simple system of daily recordings, over a period of a week or less. It is easier at first to offer birds a choice of only five or six foods for comparison. Later you can handle a dozen or more at the same time. There is no value in making a seed mixture part of your study. Commercial mixtures contain at least half a dozen different seeds and grains, and it is impossible to recognize which items a feeding bird is selecting.

Sample 2 is useful as a beginning to study the response to a food item that you have not previously offered.

Sample 3, which may be used when you have gained confidence in your ability to identify each species and make quick judgments about feeding behavior, combines the two approaches. I find it adequate in most cases, as most of the observed bird species may be feeding at the stations at the same time. Of course you cannot see them all at one time, or record every one's behavior each minute; but you can firmly and quickly classify most of their feeding responses in a few minutes.

In the samples an xc, for "extra choice," means that the bird eats a great deal of one food with obvious relish, scattering seeds or bits in its excitement. A c, for "choice," is used for a food which is eaten in lesser amounts and with no apparent excitement; an f, for "fair," denotes a food at which the bird has fed only briefly. A food at which the bird merely pecks before passing on to some other item is marked with a t for "tasted." When a food is no longer available, this fact is noted with a dash, a mark which can also be used to indicate days when no observations are made. A blank square means the food was on hand, but ignored completely. A zero, or a circle around the abbreviation for the day, means the species did not visit the feeder during the observation period.

Each of the individual notes about feeding behavior, of course, must be regarded as a tentative judgment. Your findings will become progressively more conclusive as you summarize and evaluate the results of successive observations. After a season, or even better, several seasons, you can make a quite dependable summary of the food preferences of each bird species, or you can classify each food as "choice," "fair," or unimportant (those merely tasted) for all the species you have regularly observed.

You can determine seasonal use by summarizing your recorded data. Furthermore, you can compare consumption of the foods you feed with that of wild fruits, nuts, and seeds available nearby. For example, your cardinals may abandon your feeding station for a month or more in the fall when pines are opening their cones and scattering the seeds, which are extra-choice items in the cardinal diet.

If your records also contain notes about the type of feeder used for each food, you can learn to favor the feeding habits of birds you want to attract, and to discourage or segregate the unwanted species.

Sample feeding records

SAMPLE 1

Cardinal
January 3–9, 1965

	S	M	T	W	T	F	S
wh. bread	c	c	—	—		c	c
whole corn	c	c	c	c		—	—
raisins		t					
sunflower	xe	xe	xe	—		—	xe
wheat	c	c	c	c		c	c
peanut butter	—	—	t	f		—	—
corn bread	—	—	—	t		c	e
suet						f	f

(the second T column is circled)

SAMPLE 2

Sunflower Seed
January 10–16, 1965

	S	M	T	W	T	F	S
junco		c	c	o	no observation	o	c
m. dove		t	n	n	no observation	t	n
cardinal	xc	xc	xe	xe	no observation	xe	xc
bluebird	n	n	n	n	no observation	n	n
p. finch	xe	xe	o	xe	no observation	xe	o
myrtle warbler ⎫	Appeared to be gleaning bits from seed						
pine " ⎬	hulls on the ground						
wh. br.							
nuthatch	first time seen → c?						o

SAMPLE 3

Feeding Record
Jan. 16, 1965

	wh. bread	whole corn	peanut butter	raisins	suet	sun- flower	wheat
robin	e	n	n	c	n	n	n
finch						xe	t
chickadee	c	n	c	n	c	xe	n
pine warbler	e	n	c	n	c	?	n
sparrows	c	NOTE					c
myrtle warbler	c	n	c	n	c	?	
wh. br. nuthatch						c	
junco	c	n			?	e	c
bluebird	f?	n	n	e	t	n	n
cardinal	c	e				xc	c
br. hd. nuthatch	c	n		n	c	xc	n
mourning dove	n	e	n	n	n	n	e

NOTE: Sparrows followed cardinals and grabbed bits of corn they dropped

Food, Feeders, and Feeding

Food is by far the most significant influence in a bird's life. It is the all-important element that governs bird populations. Upon food depends the vitality of the species, its energy to feed, reproduce, and withstand the hardships and dangers of life—storms, injury, and old age. It is food that provides heat to combat cold rains, snows, and the low temperatures of winter. Food gives strength to overcome disease and the life-sucking drain of parasites.

Eggs in the nest must be produced by food. Chicks grow to maturity only if they get enough food to supply their growing needs.

Section 1 explained a modern concept of food sufficiency, emphasizing the quality of choiceness.

Section 2 will explain the concept of food availability and how it can be assured in various dependable and interesting ways—natural, agricultural, and artificial.

Nature's food supplies

When eastern North America was settled, the landscape was heavily covered in most areas by dense growths of trees and perennial grasses. From diaries and chronicles of America's pioneer explorers and early travelers, it is evident that the large numbers of birds observed most often were concentrated in limited areas where foods abounded. For many species, however, nature offered "too much cover and not enough food." The bird populations today in wilderness areas, extensive forests, vast marshes and swamps, and wide expanses of native range and grasslands are scarce.

Agriculture produces foods

The American Indian cultivated relatively few acres, but as the European settlers moved westward and north, they opened the forest canopy and greatly extended agriculture. Grains became available, annual grasses and weeds were released from the competition of perennial grasses and trees, and many species of birds began to expand their territories and to increase their numbers. The ricelands of the Carolina-Georgia coastal areas became famous to hunters as the wintering grounds of vast numbers of brants, canvasbacks, geese, mallards, pintails, and black ducks. The bobwhite and mourning dove prospered with man's cropland production of choice foods. The ring-necked pheasant, introduced from the Old World, spread with cropland foods. The prairie chicken flocked from prairies to grain fields. Blackbirds, bobolinks, and grackles moved back and forth between nesting marshes and grain fields.

But while some species prospered, others fell prey to market hunters, or suffered when their wetland habitats were drained. Many, such as hawks, declined because of campaigns against "predators." Some species made a comeback; ibises and turkey are examples of overhunted birds that thrive with the combined blessings of restricted gunnery and purposefully managed habitat. It is certain that the population of many species of birds can be increased again with adequate food, water, and shelter.

Land management in eastern North America is producing better feeding conditions and increased supplies of food for bobwhite, doves, ducks, geese, snipe, and turkey. The bulbul and spotted-breasted oriole are now established in Florida's Miami area as a result of cultivated ornamental plants that provide them adequate food supplies. Mockingbirds spread northward, and robins extended their range southward, as civilization incidentally fed them better. Still other species will prosper more as we ascertain their food preferences and manage them to meet the birds' needs.

On the other hand, the prevention of fires in American forest lands has significantly reduced the food supply of ground-feeding birds, such as the bobwhite, cardinal, mourning dove, and wild turkey. While occasional fires improve the seeds, fruits, and insects preferred by these birds, unburned woods produce fewer foods, cover them too deeply with needles and leaves, maintain excessively high summer temperatures, and are infested with hordes of parasitic redbugs (chiggers), lice, and ticks. The practice of "controlled burning" or "prescribed burning" will probably be used to aid ground-feeding birds in the future.

Foods such as weed and annual grass seeds have also declined as a result of intensive row-crop cultivation and the use of weed burners and chemicals for weed control. Since the change from horses and mules to tractors, farmers have been growing fewer feed grains. Silage and mixed feeds have replaced corn in many areas, thereby reducing supplies of this excellent bird-food grain.

It is well that we know and understand the meaning of these economic advancements and their effects on the birds we wish to preserve. No useful purpose can be served by deploring human progress, but we can do something about the birds' situation by replacing the lost foods. One way is to save or grow choice foods again, whether they be plants long considered undesirable (such as ragweed, crotons, and bristlegrasses), wild fruits and nuts, or ornamentals that we can raise around homes and in parks, fence rows, and idle corners of farmlands. For nongame species, landscaping offers additional shelter. Game birds for hunting and birdwatching can also be aided by the management of food patches, plots, fields, woodlands, ponds, and wetlands on both private and public lands.

Artificial feeding

While the fortunes of American birds ebb and flow in wilderness areas, parks, forests, farm and ranch lands, anyone interested in better birding can improve the habitat for the species he wants around his home. He can attract many birds and increase their numbers by using feeding devices of many kinds and by providing the foods most preferred by the species he wants most. Selective feeding can also be employed to deny food to unwelcome species. In fact, the ultimate art of feeding birds is the ability to feed them selectively.

SCATTERING FOOD ON THE GROUND. This is an easy and interesting way to attract bobwhite, cardinal, mourning dove, blue jay, junco, sparrow, starling, brown thrasher, towhee, and several other species which feed readily on the ground. Although the ground-feeding method is not very selective, you can attract or discourage certain birds by the choice of foods offered. Starlings, for example, don't like grains, preferring table scraps; blue jays don't like millet seeds. By varying the foods or eliminating some of them, you can keep the numbers of these pests—if that's how you feel about them—at a minimum.

Most books discourage ground feeding by warning that food put directly on the ground may spoil, get wet, or become contaminated by bird droppings. They say that seed on the ground may attract field mice and rats, cats, dogs, and other unwanted animals, and that in winter the feed may be covered with snow and wasted. One author recommends that canvas or a burlap bag be spread on the ground before the food is scattered. Another says that grain should be spread only on rock or cement to prevent sprouting; he adds that wet food more than a day old and spoiled food should be discarded, because it may sour and get moldy.

The facts are: Birds eat wet foods regularly in the wild, eat them from the ground, and do not eat moldy or otherwise-spoiled foods. Grains do not spoil quickly; most of them last several days without deterioration. Snow-covered foods are not wasted, just held in cold storage until the snow melts. Mice and rats can be controlled easily with warfarin. Cats and dogs don't eat many grains, but they are attracted by table scraps. In any event, you can scatter the feed in different areas while the sun, wind, and rain cleanse the former sites. During several years of experimental feeding on the ground, I often swept a feeding area with a broom when seed hulls obscured my observations or rains had intermingled the various seeds that had been offered individually near each other; you can do the same.

FEEDERS OFF THE GROUND. Platform feeders are quite simple in construction and may be placed at any point of vantage. A tablelike platform can be placed in the yard; a shelflike feeder at a windowsill. Wood is the best material for such feeders; plastic, glass, or tile have surfaces that are too slick for a steady foothold.

A platform feeder may consist merely of a plain board set on horses or swung from the branches of a tree, but you can add anything you think might be interesting to yourself or to the birds: a rim, dividers to keep foods in place, adornments such as perches, suet nooks, or pockets for grit. A rim around the edge is useful and is often recommended to prevent waste. However, you'll note with experience that birds waste almost nothing; some feed on the shelf or platform while others clean up grains that are blown off by wind or dislodged by the birds themselves.

The chief advantage of a windowsill feeder is that it brings the birds very close for observation, especially smaller birds such as bluebirds, chickadees, nuthatches, titmice, myrtle, and pine warblers. If you live in a far-northern area, you would do well to choose a site on the sunny side of the house for your platform feeder. In milder climates, almost any site will do.

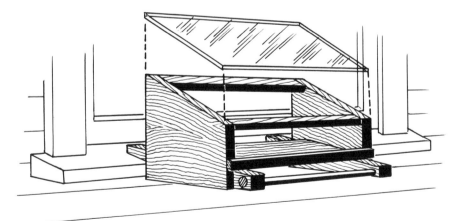

Figure 2.1 Window-sill feeder. This is a simple shelf that can be attached to the sill with screws. Its back is open, so you can service the feeder through the open window. To keep the food dry, you may add a glass cover.

SUET FEEDERS. Suet is one of the choice foods of about 45 species. It is an in-expensive food, sometimes free. Two types of suet feeders are commonly used: a stationary box with a wire-mesh front, usually fastened to a tree trunk about 5 feet above ground, and the suet-log feeder, having 1¼-inch holes bored for the suet, and hung from a tree limb (or from a wire, to frus-trate squirrels). The tree site is particularly attractive to woodpeckers, chick-adees, nuthatches, tufted titmice, and warblers, but it has the disadvantage of making the trunk unsightly when weather is warm enough to melt the suet. Most people feed suet only in winter.

Suet can be melted and made into cakes with nut bits, cornmeal, seeds, or syrup added. Cakes are also commercially available. Suet mixes are discussed in section 5.

HOPPER FEEDERS. This type of feeder offers scores of opportunities for designs in which wood, glass, and metal can be combined. All are designed to hold a supply of feed for several days. Most people fill them with a bird-food mix-ture consisting of cracked corn, millets (foxtail and proso), wheat, grain sorghum, and sometimes sunflower seeds. The chief disadvantage of hoppers is that timid birds have to wait their turns while more aggressive species satisfy their appetites. Mixtures, however, offer the birds various choices at a single feeder.

Hopper feeders may be placed at a window, on a pole, on or near the ground, or hung from a tree limb. The metal "quail feeders" manufactured in the South and usually filled with scratch-feed (cracked corn, sorghum, and wheat) are placed so that the slots are only 6 to 10 inches from the ground. Of course, the birds that like these foods will be joined at the feeder by rab-bits, squirrels, mice and rats, and snakes that feed on the mice and rats.

SWINGING FEEDERS. These are somewhat selective, depending on their size and weight and the the kind of food placed in them. A freely swinging station discourages the blue jay and house sparrow from feeding. Figure 2.4 illus-trates a free-swinging, whirling feeder of light weight. It is simply a half grapefruit skin, hung by three light strings that form a triangular pyramid, and can be attached to a limb, eave of a building, or a horizontal wire. When filled with sunflower seeds it is especially attractive to cardinal, chickadee, purple finch, nuthatch, and tufted titmouse. Employing the same basic prin-ciple you can substitute a half-coconut bowl, using wire or chain instead of string. You can also place the other half of the coconut an inch above the lower half to exclude the cardinal and finch.

You will have discerned that the discussion of swinging feeders introduces three selective features: (1) an extra-choice but expensive food—sunflower seed; (2) the swinging action that frightens some species; and (3) modified design that further discourages the species which feed greedily.

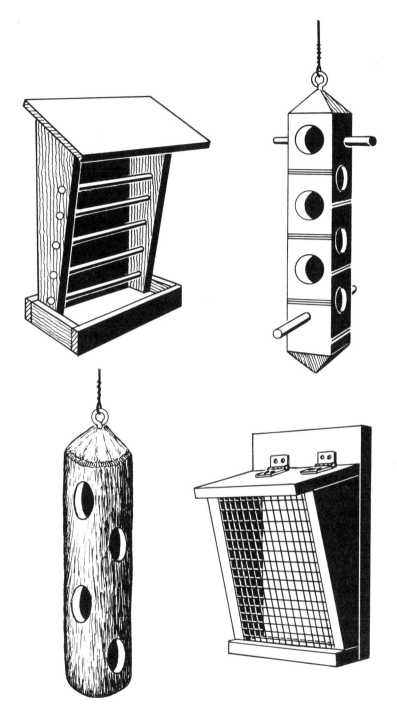

Figure 2.2 Suet feeders. The bark of the suet-log feeder at lower left provides a toe hold for the birds; deep grooves serve the same purpose on a stick feeder with smooth sides.

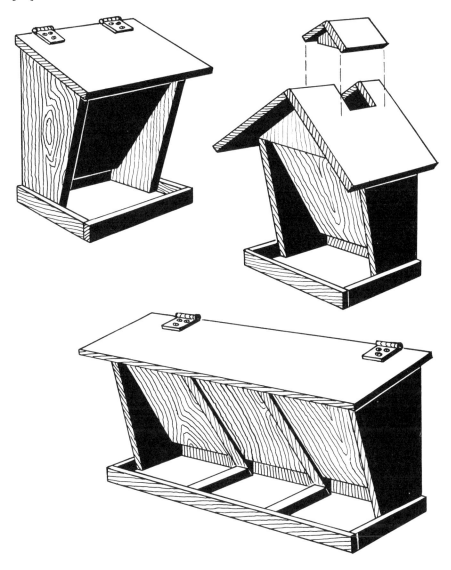

Figure 2.3 **Hopper-feeders.** These hold several days' supply of food. The single feeders may be used for seed mixtures; multisectioned hoppers, for experimental study of separate foods.

PEANUTBUTTER IN A SWINGING FEEDER. This is one of my favorite feeders because cardinal, chickadee, mockingbird, summer tanager, brown thrasher, tufted titmouse, and myrtle and pine warblers visit it regularly. This feeder, shown at right in figure 2.4, is a variation of the coconut-shell or grapefruit-

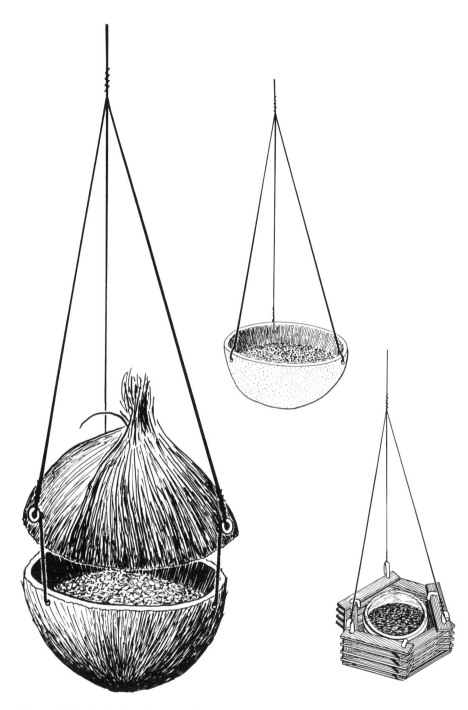

Figure 2.4   Swinging feeders. Blue jays, sparrows, and starlings will shun such devices. Simple forms may be made from the halves of a coconut shell or a grapefruit rind. They may also be made to hold a shallow, removable dish, which is especially useful as a container for peanutbutter.

rind. A receptacle of wood or tin is attached to the wires, and a small plastic or glass dish is nestled into it for easy removal when the peanutbutter needs restocking. Peanutbutter smeared on a tree trunk is unsightly but is taken by brown creeper and other birds.

Although peanutbutter is expensive by the pound, a small amount packs a lot of nutrition. Several authors warn that birds may choke on peanutbutter but I never saw this happen. Other foods, such as cornmeal and suet, can be added to peanutbutter if you desire; but there is little, if any, advantage in adding sunflower, millet, and other seeds.

HUMMINGBIRD FEEDERS. Many styles of hummingbird feeders are commercially available. They dispense sweetened liquids similar to the natural nectar of many flowers which hummingbirds drink. The liquids also attract small insects which these birds relish.

EXCLUSIVE BLUEBIRD FEEDER. Figure 2.5 shows a gable-house feeder for bluebirds only. It has 1½-inch entrance holes in the gable ends and glass sides so that the bluebirds can be observed while feeding. This type of feeder is selective because it is designed to protect bluebirds and their extra-choice foods, currants and raisins, from mockingbirds and robins. These and other fruit eaters do not go into holes; bluebirds, of course, nest in holes. Other hole-nesting birds, such as chickadees, nuthatches, and titmice, will use the feeder if you provide sunflower seeds or nuts, but not if feed is limited to fruits. The feeder need not be protected from squirrels as long as only fruits are fed.

Figure 2.5   Exclusive bluebird feeder. Stocked with raisins or dried currants, this type of feeder will be used only by bluebirds; with sunflower seeds and nuts, it will attract chickadees, nuthatches, and titmice. It has entrance holes at both ends, a hinged roof, and glass sides so you can watch the birds feeding.

With ingenuity other feeder-and-food combinations can be developed to feed birds more selectively. It is a fascinating problem for the inventive person who also knows something about each bird's food preferences.

Following is a list of commercially available foods that are attractive to one or more species of birds. To learn which birds are attracted to each food, consult the plant entries in section 5.

Commercially available bird foods

almonds	filberts	rape
apples	hemp (sterile)	rice (broken)
barley	honey	rye
bird feed[a]	millet, browntop	safflower
brazilnut	foxtail	scratch-feed[c]
bread	pearl	sorghum, grain
buckwheat	proso	suet[d]
canarygrass	oatmeal	sugar
cantaloupe seed	oats	sunflower seed
cheese	peanutbutter[b]	syrup
corn	peanuts	walnuts
cornmeal	pecans	wheat
crackers	pumpkin seed	
currants	raisins	

[a] Wild-bird-feed mixtures often include varied portions of canarygrass, cracked corn, foxtail millet, proso, grain sorghum, sunflower, and wheat. Other foods sometimes included are barley, buckwheat, hemp, oat groats, peanut hearts, rape, and safflower.

[b] Cornmeal, suet, or both may be mixed with peanutbutter.

[c] Scratch-feed sold for poultry usually is a mixture of cracked corn, grain sorghum, and wheat.

[d] "Suet cakes" usually include one or more of the following: cornmeal, proso millet, peanut hearts, peanutbutter, pecan bits, sunflower or other seeds.

Birds that eat similar foods

Some general groupings of bird and food relationships are interesting and useful. From them you can learn quickly which birds you are likely to attract to the various types of food you offer. In the lists that follow, the birds which eat significant amounts of similar foods are listed alphabetically by their common names.

Birds that eat nut meats as choice foods

bobwhite	catbird	crossbills
cardinal	chickadees	crows

Birds that eat nut meats as choice foods (*continued*)

finch	nuthatches	towhee
goldfinch	sapsucker	turkey
grackle, common	siskin	warbler (myrtle, orange-
grosbeaks	starling	crowned, pine, yellow-
jays	thrasher	throated)
junco	thrush, hermit	woodpeckers (all species)
mockingbird	titmouse	wren (Bewick's, Carolina)

Birds that eat dry seeds such as corn, grasses, weeds

blackbirds	finch	pipits
bobolink	geese	prairie chicken
bobwhite	goldfinch	redpolls
brant	grackles	siskin
buntings	grosbeak, blue	sora
cardinal	jays	sparrows (all)
coot	junco	swans
cowbird	lark	thrasher
crows	longspurs	towhee
dickcissel	meadowlarks	turkey
doves	partridge, gray	
ducks (most species)	pheasant	

Birds that eat berries and fruits in significant amounts[a]

blackbirds (3 species)	grosbeaks (except blue)	sparrows (fox, house, song,
bluebird	grouses	white-throated)
bobwhite	gull, ring-billed	starling
bulbul	jays (3 species)	swallow, tree
cardinal	junco	tanagers
catbird	kingbirds (3 species)	thrasher
chat	mockingbird	thrushes
crows	orioles	towhee
dove, rock	ptarmigan (2 species)	turkey
finch	redstart	veery
flicker	robin	vireos
flycatchers (some species)	sapsucker	warbler, myrtle
goldfinch (American)	solitaire	waxwings
grackles		woodpeckers (most species)

[a] Most of these birds (except the rock dove) prefer insects or other animal matter when it is readily available; a few prefer seeds. See the entries in section 4 for details.

Birds that eat upland green forage—leaves of clover, grains, etc.

bobwhite	grouse	swans
coot	prairie chicken	turkey
cranes	ptarmigan (2 species)	widgeon
geese		

Birds that eat aquatic-plant forage—widgeongrass, etc.

brant	coot	ducks (several)
bufflehead		

Birds that feed on rodents and other small mammals

caracara	hawks (most species)	roadrunner
eagles	kite, white-tailed	shrikes
goshawk	owls	

Birds that feed chiefly on flying insects

chuck-will's-widow	kites (except Everglades)	swallows
flycatchers	martin	swift
gnatcatcher	nighthawk	whip-poor-will
kingbirds	phoebe	wood pewee

Birds that eat terrestrial insects, earthworms, grubs, etc.

anis	curlew	mockingbird
avocet	dickcissel	nuthatches
blackbirds	egret, cattle	orioles
bluebird	flicker	ovenbird
bobolink	flycatchers (most)	owls
bobwhite	grackles	partridge, gray
buntings	grouse, sharp-tailed	pheasant
cardinal	gulls	pipits
catbird	hawk, sparrow	plover (American,
chat	junco	golden upland)
chickadees	killdeer	prairie chicken
cowbird	kingbirds	ptarmigan (2 species)
creeper	kinglets	raven
crossbills	lark	redstart
crows	longspurs	roadrunner
cuckoos	meadowlarks	robin

Birds that eat terrestrial insects, earthworms, grubs, etc. (*continued*)

sandpiper	thrasher	vireos
shrikes	thrushes	warblers (all species)
siskin	titmouse	woodcock
solitaire	towhee	woodpeckers (all species)
sparrows (all)	turkey	wrens
starling	veery	yellowthroat

Birds that eat aquatic animals such as fish and crustaceans

anhinga	guillemot	rails
bitterns	gulls	raven
booby	herons	razorbill
bufflehead	ibises	sanderling
coot	jaegers	sandpiper
cormorants	kingfisher	scoters
cranes	kite (Everglades, swallow-	skimmer
crows	tailed)	snipe
dovekie	kittiwake	solitaire
dowitchers	knot	sora
ducks (most species)	limpkin	spoonbill
dunlin	loons	stilt
eagle, bald	mergansers	swans
egrets (except cattle)	murres	terns
eiders	oldsquaw	turnstone
frigate-bird	osprey	waterthrushes
gallinules	owl, snowy	whimbrel
gannet	oystercatcher	willet
godwits	pelicans	wrens (marsh)
goldeneyes	phalaropes	yellowlegs
grackle, boat-tailed	plovers (most species)	
grebes	puffin	

Birds that often prey upon other birds

caracara	gulls (herring, ring-billed)	jaegers
eagles (both)	gyrfalcon	owls (all species)
falcon	hawks (Cooper's, pigeon,	shrike (both species)
goshawk	and sharp-shinned; and	
grackle, boat-tailed	others less significantly)	

Nests and Birdhouses

To reproduce successfully and properly take care of their young, birds must have suitable nesting sites. This element of their habitat is second in importance only to food, and unfortunately, like wild-food supplies, nesting sites are often destroyed as man preempts the countryside for his own houses and farms, his roads and recreation areas. The increasing scarcity of natural nesting sites makes it more and more important to manage wisely the remaining wilderness. It should also encourage bird lovers to protect such sites on their own property, for, with intelligent planning, most rural and suburban areas can be made to shelter, and feed, many more birds than nature herself supports.

As the tables on the succeeding pages make clear, the choice of nesting sites varies greatly from species to species. Some birds nest on the ground, others in shrubs and trees; some float their homes on water, still others build them high on craggy cliffs. Happily, many species will adopt a man-made home quite readily, and most of them can be helped in other ways during the nesting season by the willing bird enthusiast who understands their preferences and needs.

Ground-nesting birds

The first table below lists 201 species that usually nest on the ground—under tufts of grass, on bare beaches, in underground burrows, or on rocky cliffs. A few of these sometimes nest in trees and shrubs, too. Man usually can do little to help ground-nesting birds with nesting habitat on farms and ranches, except to avoid unnecessary mowing or burning during the nesting months.

Tree and shrub-nesting birds

The second table below lists 132 species that usually nest off the ground in trees and shrubs of upland habitat. It includes many of the birds that inhabit farms, ranches, parks, and the landscape around our homes. In these places we can attract birds by means of shrubs and trees such as apple, blackberry, camellia, elm, hawthorn, live and post oaks, osageorange, pines, redcedar, and roses. More specific references to attractive nesting plants are mentioned in discussions of individual birds and plants in sections 4 and 5, respectively.

The third table below lists 73 species that usually nest off the ground in wetland habitat, notably in shrubs, trees, and other plants of swamps, marshes, and ponds. Many waterfowl refuges and wading-bird sanctuaries have been established to provide protected nesting sites. Similar habitat on farms and ranches is also important and can be saved or developed by the interested landowner.

Birds that nest on ground, cliffs, or beaches

avocet	junco	razorbill
bobolink	killdeer	sanderling
bobwhite	kingfisher	sandpipers (11 species
booby (2 species)	kittiwake	except solitary)
brant	knot	scoters (3 species)
bunting (lark, snow)	lark	skimmer
chuck-will's-widow	longspurs (4 species)	snipe
cormorants (3 species)	loons (2 species)	solitaire
cranes (2 species)	meadowlarks (2 species)	sparrows (18 species)
curlew	mergansers (common, red-	stilt
dickcissel	breasted)	swallows (4 species)
dove (ground, mourning)	murres (2 species)	swans (3 species)
dovekie	nighthawk	swift
dowitchers (2 species)	oldsquaw	terns (11 species)
ducks (20 species)	ovenbird	towhee (sometimes)
dunlin	owls (5 species)	turkey
eagle, golden	oystercatcher	turnstone
eiders (2 species)	partridge, gray	vultures (2 species)
gannet	pelican, white	warblers (14 species)
geese (4 species)	phalaropes (3 species)	waterthrushes (2 species)
godwits (2 species)	pheasant	whimbrel
grouse (3 species)	pipits (2 species)	whip-poor-will
guillemot, black	plovers (7 species)	willet
gulls (8 species)	prairie chicken	woodcock
gyrfalcon	ptarmigan (2 species)	yellowlegs (2 species)
hawks (2 species)	puffin	yellowthroat
jaegers (3 species)	raven	

Birds that nest off the ground in upland habitat—in trees, shrubs and vines

anis (2 species)	bunting (indigo, painted)	chat
blackbird (Brewer's,	caracara	cowbird
rusty)	cardinal	crossbills (2 species)
bulbul	catbird	crows (2 species)

Birds that nest off the ground—in upland habitat (*continued*)

cuckoos (3 species)
dove (mourning, white-
  winged)
eagles (2 species)
falcon
finch
flycatchers (8 species)
gnatcatcher
goldfinch
goshawk
grosbeaks (5 species)
gull, Bonaparte's
hawks (13 species)
hummingbirds

jays (3 species)
kingbirds (3 species)
kinglets (2 species)
kites (3 species)
mockingbird
orioles (3 species)
osprey
owls (4 species)
raven
redpolls (2 species)
redstart
roadrunner
robin
sandpiper, solitary

shrikes (2 species)
siskin
sparrows (10 species)
tanagers (2 species)
thrasher
thrushes (4 species)
towhee (usually)
veery
vireos (7 species)
warblers (17 species)
waxwings (2 species)
wood pewee

Birds that nest in aquatic habitats—swamps, marsh plants, or floating nests

anhinga
bitterns (2 species)
blackbird (red-winged,
  yellow-headed)
coot
cormorants (3 species)
ducks (21 species)
egrets (4 species)

gallinules (2 species)
grackle, boat-tailed
grebes (6 species)
gull, Franklin's
herons (7 species)
ibises (4 species)
kite, Everglades
limpkin

pelican, brown
rails (5 species)
sora
sparrows (4 species)
spoonbill
tern, black
vireo, black-whiskered
wren (2 species)

Birds that nest in natural or artificial cavities

The birdhouse table, below, lists 44 species of eastern birds that left to their own devices, would nest in some natural cavity in a tree or stump. Eight of these species seldom if ever nest in artificial situations, but the remainder can be attracted readily to a sturdily built birdhouse, gourd, or nesting box, if the size and design please them.

The table gives the inside dimensions of cavities and prescribes the heights that are suitable for each of the 44 species. If you are interested in attracting a particular species, it is important to (1) make the entrance hole the right size, (2) provide the correct interior depth, (3) mount the house at a favorable height above ground, and (4) place it in an attractive location. The floor sizes and the diameter of the openings given are near the minimum sizes for each bird.

The table also provides columns that show the number of broods produced annually by each species, the usual number of eggs laid at each nesting, the incubation period, and the number of days that young remain in the nest.

Birds that will nest in birdhouses and natural cavities and crevices

BIRDHOUSE SPECIFICATIONS (INCHES)

SPECIES	Entrance diameter	Entrance above floor	Floor dimensions	House depth	Nest above ground (feet)	Number of broods annually	Usual number of eggs	Incubation period	Number of days young in nest
bluebird	1½	6–7	5x5	8–9	5–10	2–3	3–5	13–15	15–18
chickadee, black-capped[a,b]	1⅛	6–8	4x4	8–10	5–15	1–2	5–6	11–13	
boreal	1⅛	6–8	4x4	8–10	5–15		5–6		
Carolina	1⅛	6–8	4x4	8–10	6–15	2	4–5	11–13	12–16
creeper	crevices in tree trunks					1–2	4–8	15±	
dove, rock	nesting houses		12x12	9	10–15	2–3	2	15–16	app. 28
duck, wood: metal cyl.[a,b]	4	18–19	12 diam.	24	8–15	1	10–15	28–30	1
wooden[a,b]	3x4 oval	18–19	12x12	24	8–15				
flicker[a,b]	3	14–16	7x7	16–24	6–20	1	4–8	11–16	25–28
flycatcher, great crested[b]	2	6–8	6x6	8–10	8–20	1–2	4–8	13–15	15–18
goldeneye, Barrow's	cavities in trees				up to 50	1			
common	see wood-duck specifications					1	6–19	20	1
hawk, sparrow	3	9–12	8x8	12–15	10–30	1	3–7	29–30	3 wks.
martin, purple[d]	2½	1	6x6	6	15	1	3–8	12–16	28–36

SPECIES	Entrance diameter	Entrance above floor	Floor dimensions	House depth	Nest above ground (feet)	Number of broods annually	Usual number of eggs	Incubation period	Number of days young in nest
merganser, common	hollow trees					1	6–17	28	1
hooded	see wood-duck specifications					1	5–12	31	1
nuthatch, brown-headed[b]	1	6–8	2x3	8–10	5–20	1	5	14	18–20
red-breasted[b]	1				5–20	1	5	12±	
white-breasted	1¼	6–8	4x4	8–10	5–20	1	4–6	12–13	
owl, barn	6	4	10x18	15–18	12–18	1–2	5–8	21–24 (to 11 wks.)	
barred	tree cavities				15–40	1	2–4	28±	
boreal	woodpecker holes in trees					1	4–7		
hawk	cavities and woodpecker holes					1	4–7	app. 21	
saw-whet	2½	8–10	6x6	10–12	12–20	1	3–7	21	
screech	3	9–12	8x8	12–15	10–30	1	4–5	21–25	25–30
phoebe	open front & sides		7x7	8	8–12	2	3–8	12–16	16–19
robin	open front & sides		7x7	8	8–12	2–3	3–5	11–14	12–14
sapsucker[a,b]	1¾	12–16	6x6	14–18	12–40	1	5–7	14	
sparrow, European tree	1½	6–8	4x4	8–10	4–12	2–3	5–6		
house	1½	6–8	4x4	8–10	4–12	3	4–8	12–14	14–16
starling	2	6–8	6x6	8–10	8–20	1–3	5–8	11–14	14–20

BIRDHOUSE SPECIFICATIONS (INCHES)

SPECIES	Entrance diameter	Entrance above floor	Floor dimensions	House depth	Nest above ground (feet)	Number of broods annually	Usual number of eggs	Incubation period	Number of days young in nest
swallow, barn	open front & sides		6x6	6	8–12	2	4–5	11–13	18–23
tree[d]	1½	1–5	5x5	6	3–6	1	4–5	14±	15–26
titmouse, tufted	1¼	6–8	4x4	8–10	4–5	1–2	5–6	12	16
warbler, prothonotary	1½	5	4x4	8	4–7	1–2	3–7	14	
woodpecker, downy[a,b]	1¼	6–8	4x4	8–10	6–20	1	4–5	12	21±
hairy[a,b]	1½	9–12	6x6	12–16	12–20	1	3–5	14	21
pileated[a,b]	3–4	10–12	8x8	12–30	12–60	1	3–5	18±	26
red-bellied[a,b]	2½	10–12	6x6	12–14	12–20	1–2	3–5	14±	
red-cockaded	holes in live trees (with "red-heart")				15–50		3–5		
red-headed[a,b]	2	9–12	6x6	12–15	12–20	2	4–6	14±	27±
wren, Bewick's	1x2½	4–6	4x4	6–8	5–10	2–3	4–6	13–15	14
Carolina	1¼x2½	4–6	4x4	6–8	5–10	2–3	4–6	12	12–14
house	1x2½	4–6	4x4	6–8	5–10	2	5–7	11–13	12–18
winter	1x2½	4–6	4x4	6–8	5–10	2	4–6		12–18

a Add wood shavings or sawdust to 2- or 3-inch depth.
b Prefer hollow-log-type houses.
c Wood-duck boxes must be predator-proof (especially from raccoons) to be safe. See the entry for wood duck in section 4.
d Also use gourds for nesting.

Birdhouse types

Human ingenuity has produced a wide variety of birdhouse designs, all aimed at satisfying man's aesthetic sensibilities as well as the practical needs of birds. Most styles, however, are clever variations of a few basic principles of construction.

Perhaps the simplest birdhouse is a boxlike structure made of lumber with rectangular bottom, sides, back, front with entrance, and a sloping lean-to roof as shown below in figure 3.1. It may also be built with a gable roof, as shown at right.

Usually it is more interesting to build a birdhouse that can be used by two or more species. A house 8 inches high, with 5x5 or 4x6 inches of floor space and a 1½-inch opening placed 6 inches above the floor, is suitable for such smaller birds as the bluebird, chickadee, nuthatch, tree swallow, titmouse, prothonotary warbler, downy woodpecker, and wren. Thus you may enjoy a change of tenants within a single nesting season and from year to year.

Similarly a 6x6-inch house, 14 inches high, with a 2-inch opening placed 9 or 10 inches above the floor, may be appropriated by a pair of great crested flycatchers, starlings, or woodpeckers (red-bellied or red-headed).

Flickers, sparrow hawks, saw-whet and screech owls, starlings, and red-

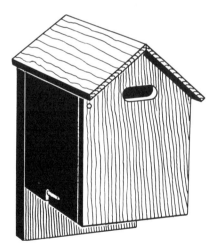

Figure 3.1 Simple birdhouses. The design at left will be used by practically all hole-nesting birds; the birdhouse table in section 3 contains appropriate dimensions for each species. The gabled house at right has an elongated hole that is used for wrens. The houses are shown with hinged panels that swing open to permit cleaning. They may also be designed with a glass pane inside the hinged panel, to permit brief observations of nesting progress when the parent birds are away.

bellied and red-headed woodpeckers will use a house 8x8 inches, 16 inches high, with a 3-inch opening placed about 14 inches above the floor.

A few additional designs for rather simple bird boxes with gabled roofs are shown in figure 3.2. The roof of the A-frame house at upper left extends an inch or two beyond a level floor. A two-piece roof may be substituted for the overlapping shingles on the house at upper right. The house with the V-shaped bottom is equipped with a panel which may be swung open when you want to remove old nesting materials.

Figure 3.2   Other simple designs. These houses have features which make cleaning quick and easy. With an elliptical hole, they make ideal wren houses.

HOLLOW-LOG HOUSES. Inexpensive houses like those shown in figure 3.3 are made from pieces of logs 6 to 8 inches in diameter and 10 to 14 inches long, depending on the species for which they are built. To make the house at left, cut a slab 2 or 3 inches thick from the length of the log. With a saw, make 3 or 4 pie-shaped cuts into the core of the wood and knock them out with a chisel, leaving a wall about an inch thick. The roof is a slab, which should hang beyond the wall on all sides so that rainwater will not drip into the house. A more quickly made house, to be set on a shelf or atop a post, can be fashioned from a log sawed in half lengthwise, hollowed out, and the halves bound together with stout wire. The houses should be anchored with a couple of thin nails driven at a slant through the lower wall into the bottom board, or with a pair of small angle brackets.

Elm, hemlock, pine, or spruce are suitably soft woods for making log houses; gouging the core from harder woods, such as hickory, oak, maple, or fruit woods, is quite a laborious task.

The log-type birdhouse is especially attractive to chickadees, flickers, crested flycatchers, nuthatches, sapsuckers, titmice, and woodpeckers. Further details are suggested for each species in section 4.

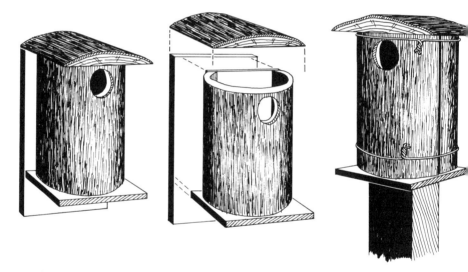

Figure 3.3   Hollow-log houses. Birds that normally nest in wooded locations may more readily attracted by the rustic appearance of a log house. Any other design, course, may be fashioned of rough lumber or given a façade of bark.

SHELVES AND BRACKETS. These designs, shown in figure 3.4, are used by phoebes, robins, and barn swallows. Any one of these species will be attracted to a design that has a 7x7-inch shelflike bottom, lean-to roof, open front, and rudimentary sides. The roofed styles may be nailed to a tree or the side of a building, from 8 to 12 feet from the ground. Unroofed platforms or brackets, which may also be used by cliff swallows, should be placed under the eaves of a building, or beneath some other protective overhang.

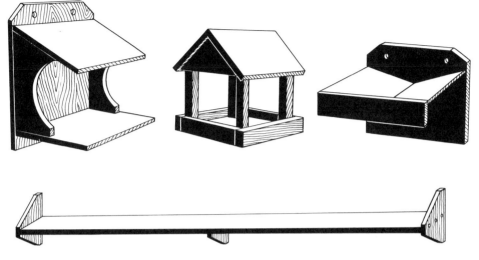

Figure 3.4   Shelves and brackets. Phoebes, robins, and barn swallows will use these designs. The unroofed versions should be placed under eaves or some other protective overhang.

MARTIN HOUSES. The most elaborate housing structures are built for colonies of purple martins, following basic designs first published by the U.S. Department of Agriculture. Though the original publication is out of print, you can find detailed designs in Thomas P. McElroy, Jr., *The New Handbook of Attracting Birds* (rev. ed.; New York: Alfred A. Knopf, 1961). Mr. McElroy states that he has had 100 percent success with his variation of the USDA martin plan. Walter E. Schutz, *Bird Watching, Housing and Feeding* (Milwaukee: Bruce Publishing Co., 1963), gives detailed drawings, instructions, and bills of materials for three types of houses that accommodate 14 or 24 families of martins.

Single pairs of martins will also nest in gourds or in one-room houses which meet the specifications given in the birdhouse table above. Before you build the apartment-type house, which can be a rather expensive project, you would do well to find out if martins have customarily nested in your neighborhood. If you are not near water and an open field, you are not likely to have much luck attracting them. At any rate, it would be wise to begin with just one floor of the multiple-unit house; you can add additional floors when these rooms are all tenanted.

MATERIALS. Most birdhouses are made of wood. It is important, however, that you use well-seasoned wood; green lumber or freshly cut logs will warp and crack as they dry out. The more durable woods are baldcypress, redcedar,

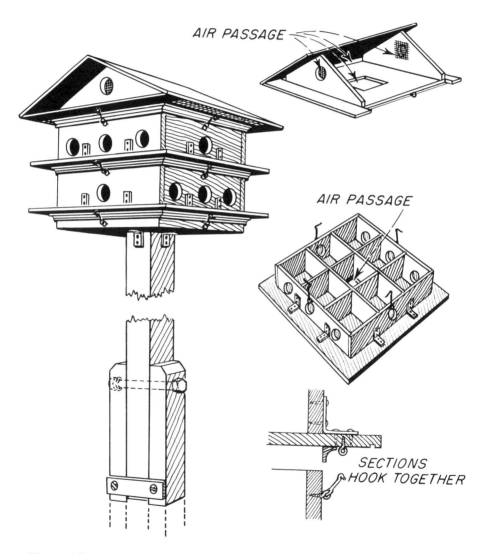

Figure 3.5   Martin house. Before erecting this rather expensive apartment-type house, it would be well to establish that martins have customarily nested in your neighborhood.

or redwood, which do not need stain or paint to preserve them against warping and weathering. Birdhouses made of spruce, whitecedar or white pine will last longer if they are treated with stain or paint. Green or brown colors are attractive and serviceable, but white is used to reduce heat in martin houses, which are always placed in direct sunlight.

You can use finished boards, roughly sawed lumber, slabs with bark on the rounded side, or a section of a small log that has been hollowed out to the proper size. For most birdhouses, boards ¾-inch thick are suitable, but ½-inch boards are better for the lighter weight needed for martin houses. An entrance hole in a board or slab more than ½ inch thick should be beveled a little, inside and out, or it may be too small.

Cement or stucco houses are desirable because of their durability and appearance. They are fashioned of wooden lathing or wire-mesh framing and are described in detail by Walter E. Schutz in his little book, *Bird Watching, Housing and Feeding*. He also provides detailed information on designs and materials that can be used in 20 wooden birdhouses, with handy suggestions for cutting and assembling the pieces.

Rust-proof hardware should be used in house construction—galvanized nails and hooks, brass or aluminum screws, and brass hinges.

VENTILATION AND DRAIN HOLES. Two or more ¼-inch holes are needed in each side a little below the roof for ventilation, and others should be drilled through the floor for drainage of any water that may get into the house. Without these features, baby birds may suffocate on hot days or catch a chill from dampness on cold days. The sides of any rectangular birdbox should extend about ⅛ inch below the bottom so the moisture that drains down the sides of the birdhouse will not seep into the floor.

Cleats (strips of wood nailed horizontally) or similar toeholds on the inside wall below the entrance help the young birds when they are ready to leave the nest. This is especially important for flickers, wood ducks, woodpeckers, and other birds that use nests with entrances more than 8 inches above the floor. See the birdhouse table, above, for the species which make their homes in deep cavities.

NESTING MATERIALS. Hole-nesting ducks, flickers, sapsuckers, and wood-peckers need 1 or 2 inches of wood shavings, soft chips, or sawdust in the bottom of their nest boxes, and these materials may be used also for chicka-dees, nuthatches, and tufted titmice. Other species fashion their nests from pieces of grass, twigs, excelsior, strips of soft cloth, paper, cellophane, string, feathers, and down. Baltimore orioles, in particular, like to weave their nests with colored string, according to Dr. Henry S. Williams, *Private Lives of Birds* (New York: McBride & Co., 1939). The string, he warns, should be cut in strands of not more than 8 inches, because birds occasionally become entangled in longer pieces.

You may offer the nesting materials on a windowsill, in a pile on the lawn, strung from the branches of bushes and trees, or in a box like either of the roofed suet feeders shown in figure 2.2, which will help keep the materials dry. If you nail the box in view of a window, you may spend many enjoyable hours watching the birds make their selections, and you can tell at a glance when the supply should be replenished.

CLEANING. You should clean your birdhouse after each nesting, soon after the young fledglings have left the nest. This is a sanitary measure, to remove any remaining bird droppings and to get rid of mites or other parasites that may be left in the old nesting materials. So be sure the house you construct or buy is designed for easy cleaning. Many houses have a hinged top, or bottom, or nail or screw pivots that allow a side or bottom to be opened. These swinging tops, sides, or bottoms require a fastener to hold them tight during the period of egg laying, incubation, and fledging. An L-shaped screw or a screen-door hook-and-eye are commonly used for fastening.

GOURDS. Some people have good luck with gourds made into birdhouses. Whole colonies of purple martins have been known to make their homes in them, and pairs of bluebirds, crested flycatchers, white-breasted nuthatches, house sparrows, starlings, tree swallows, tufted titmice, downy woodpeckers, and (especially) wrens will also use them for nesting. For martins, the gourds should be strung in direct sunlight, at least 15 feet from the ground and far enough apart so the wind will not knock them together. See the entry on "gourds" in section 5, for more details about their use for nesting birds.

COMMERCIAL BIRDHOUSES. You can buy a variety of birdboxes at most seed, feed, and nursery houses. They are also sold by the Service Department of the National Audubon Society, 1130 Fifth Avenue, New York, N.Y. 10028. You may obtain the Society's free catalog by writing to its Service Department.

PREDATORS. Occasionally, a squirrel will gnaw at the entrance hole of a birdbox and make it large enough so he can enter and make the premises his own. Such an invader can be readily discouraged by nailing a metal shield, at least an inch wide, around the hole. This guard may be fashioned from sheet metal. Before you nail it on, however, be sure that the edge which circles the hole is filed smooth to remove any barbs or sharp edges that might injure birds.

Cats, of course, are the chief annoyance to birds. A birdhouse erected less than 5 feet high puts the parent bird in danger of being caught by a cat who may be sitting beneath the box waiting to leap to the entrance. Young birds in the nest may be taken by a cat unless the house is tightly built, with a secure fastener to hold any hinged side, bottom, or top.

An effective, though unsightly, deterrent to climbing cats and squirrels is a cone-shaped guard.

Perhaps a birdhouse should not be placed close to a board fence or other object from which a cat might spring upon a parent bird entering its home;

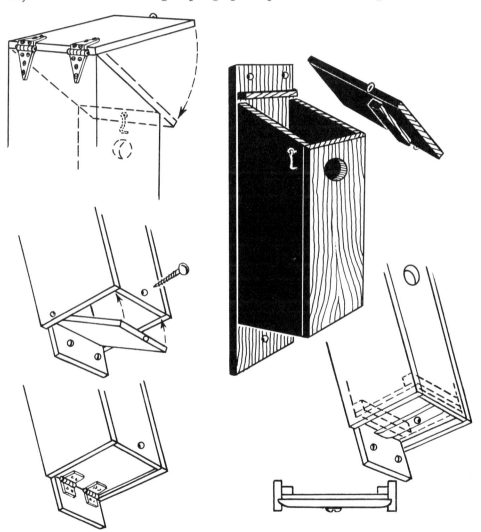

Figure 3.6   Access for cleaning and inspection. The simple box shown at right can be fashioned with a hinged roof, or one that is removable; its bottom can be hinged or pivoted and held shut with a screw, or adapted with a turn button that allows the entire floor to drop out.

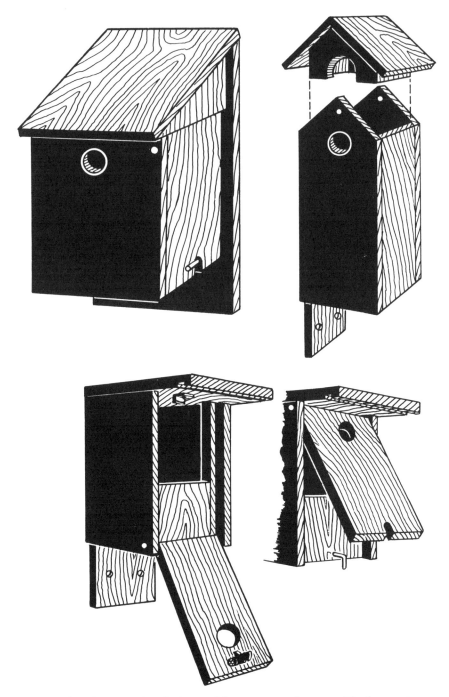

Figure 3.7   More complex designs, with easy-access features. The house at upper left has a pivoted side wall that is held with an L screw. The box at upper right has a removable roofed section which drops into main portion of the house. The birdhouse at bottom is shown with a front that pivots from either top or bottom.

however, I have had houses built into board fences without any trouble. A sturdy box placed on a tree trunk usually is safe; the bird can see the cat, and in any case the cat cannot spring far when clinging to the tree.

Your own or a neighbor's cat may cause the occasional loss of a bird, but it is not of sufficient importance to warrant long grieving.

WEATHER. Since a well-built birdhouse protects the birds from wind, rain, storms, and sun, the direction that a birdbox faces is not important. Drain and ventilation holes, however, are important. Remember that rain may run down into a box with a sloping roof through the entrance hole unless you extend the roof an inch or more beyond the entrance side.

WHEN TO ERECT BIRDHOUSES? The answer, broadly speaking, is: "Whenever you have one ready." If you put it up in the summer or fall, it is not likely to be used until the following year; but it will be ready and properly weathered when the birds begin their house hunting. On the other hand, if you wish to be rewarded by quick occupancy, put the birdhouse up by January in the deep South, February in mideastern United States, and before the end of March in the northern United States and Canada. The male bird selects the nest site early, but both sexes do a great deal of house hunting each spring; those who raise two or three broods annually hunt later as well.

WHERE TO PLACE BIRDHOUSES. Birds that usually nest in deep woods—chickadees, nuthatches, and woodpeckers—will take more readily to a birdhouse placed in similar environment, or at least on the edge of woodlands. Most house-nesting birds, however, will nest in boxes around the backyard or attached to a building. For details, read the "attracting" information for the bird under consideration in section 4.

ROOSTING BOXES. In the winter, birds such as the bluebird and wren sometimes suffer and die in periods of extremely low temperatures and scarce food supplies. A warm, dry roost will help to protect them.

Two basic types are in use: one is a "single-story" box with open front and one or more roosting perches made of ¼-to-½-inch doweling; the other is a deep box with an escalated series of perches, staggered so that one bird does not roost above another. It has a 2- or 3-inch entrance hole, cut into the base of the wall to conserve the heat of birds' bodies. The closed box may be placed 8 to 10 feet high on a tree or building; the open-faced design should be used in more sheltered locations, such as the ell of a building.

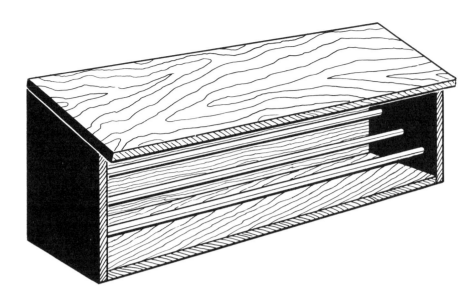

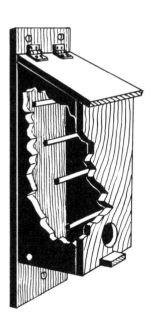

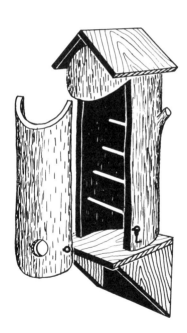

Figure 3.8   Roosts. A warm, dry roost may save the lives of wintering birds during cold and stormy nights. The open-faced design should be used only in sheltered locations, such as the ell of a building. The completely closed box may be placed on trees. Because its entrance hole is on the bottom, it retains much of the body heat of the birds.

NESTING TIME. In general, nesting time is an anxious one for birds and their human friends, since high winds and hail, cats, dogs, snakes, squirrels, ants, and mites destroy a moderate number of nests, eggs, and nestlings every year. Don't let these losses cause chronic unhappiness, however. Only one or two birds from a nest that began with three or four eggs may see maturity, but that is more than enough to maintain a species' population. Also, birds usually nest again if their eggs or young are destroyed. Fortunately most birds' nesting periods are short—3–7 days to build a nest, 2–15 days for laying, 9–28 days for incubation, and 10–28 days for the young to reach independent maturity. Thus the nesting period is less than 5 weeks for bluebirds, cardinals, catbirds, doves, and most small birds, and some of these birds raise a second brood, or more rarely, a third, in one season. Others, such as bobwhite, ducks, geese, grouse, pheasants, prairie chicken, and turkey, require 12–18 weeks to nest and raise their young to maturity. Of course, they raise but one brood annually.

Birds—What They Eat, Where They Nest, How to Attract Them

The most successful way of attracting birds and increasing their number is to satisfy their most basic needs—good food, favorable nesting sites, and water. Though a bird may survive for a while in conditions of privation, he will live longer and reproduce better if his foods and home site are of superior quality. This is what section 4 is about.

In order to use this section effectively, you should understand its style, contents, and arrangement. There are entries for more than 400 bird species, alphabetized by their official common names. These names are printed in **boldface type,** and when they contain several elements, the more important is put in first place. This means, for example, that you should look for "Baltimore oriole" at "oriole," and "Ipswich sparrow" at "sparrow." In parentheses following the bird's common name, you will find outdated names by which the species is also known, as well as its scientific name, printed in *italic type*. The spellings of both common and scientific names of birds in this book are identical with those in *The A.O.U. Check-List of North American Birds* (5th ed.; Baltimore, Md.: American Ornithologists' Union, Lord Baltimore Press, 1957). The information given about each species also applies without significant variation to subspecies.

It is hoped that this book will increase the acceptance and use of the common names officially established for each species. You may have grown up calling a yellow-shafted flicker by the name "yellowhammer," a rufous-sided towhee a "joree," a ring-necked pheasant a "Chinese pheasant" or "chink," and an American widgeon a "baldpate." Perhaps you'd rather not change, but you'll want to know what names are universal now, since your children and grandchildren are likely to use them.

The outdated vernacular names of birds will also be found in their alphabetical places with a cross-reference to the correct name—for example, "yellowhammer. See flicker, yellow-shafted."

A general idea of the population of each species and its distribution is given after the bird's name. More exact information can be obtained from local bird-club lists or the books on birds of various states. It should be noted that the data on the distribution of each species refer only to eastern North America, from the prairies to the Atlantic, though the bird may be found elsewhere as well.

Since birds are more likely to be attracted by food than by any other means, all of the important foods known to be eaten by each species are named under "plant food" and "animal food." The more important category is always given first. In practically all entries, the plant foods have been further classified as either "choice" or "fair," but these designations have been omitted occasionally when plant foods constitute only a minor part of the diet of a species. Remember that "choice foods" are more attractive and nutritious than "fair foods," as explained in section 1, "Food Preferences." When a percentage figure is given, it is only approximate; for example, "100% animal food" does not exclude a trace amount or even 1 or 2 percent of a plant material swallowed by a bird in the "tasting" process or by accident.

The significant food items are arranged alphabetically in each category—not in the order of importance, which may change with seasonal availability or the birds' physiological needs. The "fruiting" part of a plant—the acorn, berry, fruit, nut, seed, or tuber—is usually the part eaten. Tender forage, however, is also eaten by a few birds, such as geese, grouse, prairie chicken, and turkey. To avoid complexity, the part eaten is usually not specified in section 4 but is noted in section 5, in the individual entries for plants.

The information that follows the word "nest" often contains the terms "frequently," meaning commonly, and "occasionally," denoting uncommonly. Very unusual nesting sites are ignored.

The better-known ways to attract each kind of bird are briefly summarized after the heading "attracting." You will find here mention of extra-choice foods and special attracting devices, such as feeders and birdhouses designed for specific species. A bird's special use or need of water may be noted. If water is not mentioned, you can assume that the bird drinks water, or gets it with its food. Its bathing needs will be met wherever it drinks, or in the dry dust baths that a few species often prefer. Where the "attracting" information is lacking, you may assume one of two reasons: (1) the habitat needs are obvious from the food and nest paragraphs, or (2) methods have not been developed to improve natural habitat or supplement it with feeding stations and artificial nesting sites. In the latter case, we usually must visit the birds' natural homes and feeding area to see them, and we should support all efforts to conserve their natural habitats.

anhinga (also called snakebird and waterturkey; *Anhinga anhinga*). Common resident of swamp and pond habitats from Arkansas, Tennessee, and North Carolina southward to Louisiana, Florida, and Central America. *Animal food* (100%). Chiefly fish (catfish, mullets, pickerel, suckers, sunfish); also crabs, crayfish, aquatic insects, shrimp, snakes, tadpoles, terrapin. *Nest.* Frequently in baldcypress, buttonbush, mangrove, maple (red), willow.

ani, groove-billed (*Crotophaga sulcirostris*). Uncommon in Louisiana and Mississippi; accidental in Arkansas, Florida, and northward. *Animal food* (nearly 100%). Mostly insects flushed by grazing cattle; also lizards. Feed occasionally in orchards. *Nest.* Frequently in lemon, orange, and royalpalm in Mexico and Central America.

ani, smooth-billed (*Crotophaga ani*). Established and breeding in south Florida; rare in south Louisiana. *Animal food* (nearly 100%). Chiefly beetles, bugs, caterpillars, chameleons, crickets, frogs, grasshoppers, locusts, moths. Usually seen feeding beside cattle or in sugarcane fields. *Nest.* Frequently in bamboo, devils-walkingstick, lemon, mistletoe, and orange in tropical Americas.

auk, little. See dovekie.

auk, razor-billed. See razorbill.

avocet, American (*Recurvirostra americana*). Common summer resident of marshes and mudflats north and west of Iowa; rare east of the Mississippi River. Winters from southern Texas to Central America. *Animal food* (65%). Aquatic insects, billbugs, grasshoppers, snails, marine worms. Feeds in shallow water at pond edges. *Plant food.* CHOICE: potamogeton seeds. *Nest.* On the ground, near water.

baldpate. See widgeon, American.

bee bird or **bee martin.** See kingbird, eastern and western.

bird of paradise. See flycatcher, scissor-tailed.

birds of prey. See buzzards, caracara, eagles, falcons, gyrfalcon, hawks, kites, osprey, and owls.

bittern, American (also called stake driver, thunder pumper; *Botaurus lentiginosus*). Fairly common resident in marshes and ponds of eastern North America. *Animal food* (100%). Crayfish, dragonflies, grasshoppers, fish, frogs, lizards, mice, salamanders, shrews, snakes. *Nest.* Frequently in bulrush, cattail, or on a platform of stems and grasses.

bittern, green. See heron, green.

bittern, least (*Ixobrychus exilis*). Fairly common summer resident in marshes from U.S.-Canadian border southward. *Animal food* (100%). Crustaceans, fish, frogs, insects, tadpoles. *Nest.* Frequently in bulrush, cattail, reed, rush, sawgrass, willow, or on a platform of stems and grasses.

blackbird, Brewer's (*Euphagus cyanocephalus*). Common summer resident around marshes, ponds, and streams in states north and westward from Kansas, Wisconsin, and Ontario. Winters south and westward from Kansas, occasionally eastward to South Carolina. *Animal food* (80% summer, 25% winter). Chiefly beetles, cankerworms, caterpillars; also aphids, centipedes, crickets, grasshoppers, snails, sowbugs, spiders. *Plant food.* CHOICE: bread (white), cherry (cultivated), corn, junglerice, oat (common, wild), rice, sorghum (grain), wheat. FAIR: barley (cultivated), barnyardgrass, blackberry, bristlegrass, crabgrass, croton, panicum, ragweed, rye, signalgrass, smartweed, spikerush, strawberry, sunflower. *Nest.* Frequently in shrubs and trees, occasionally on the ground.

blackbird, crow. See grackle, common.

\blackbird, red-winged (also called redwing; *Agelaius phoeniceus*). *Includes* eastern, Florida, Maynard's, Gulf Coast, Rio Grande, giant, and thick-billed subspecies. Common summer resident around marshes, ponds, and streams throughout eastern North America; winters in grain fields in southern half of United States. *Plant food* (50% summer, 95% winter). CHOICE: ash (white), barley (cultivated), barnyardgrass, bread (white), bristlegrass, canarygrass, cockspur (coast), corn, cornbread, junglerice, millet (browntop, pearl), mulberry, oat (common), paspalum (bull, Florida), peanut, pine (loblolly, longleaf, shortleaf, slash), ragweed (common, giant), rice, seaoats, signalgrass (broadleaf), smartweed (dotted), sorghum (grain), sweetgum, wheat, wildrice. FAIR: beech, birdeye, cherry (black), crabgrass, croton (woolly), fig, goosegrass, palmetto (cabbage), sesame, sunflower (common, cultivated), tallowtree, witchgrass (common). *Animal food.* Chiefly ants, beetles, cankerworms, caterpillars, grasshoppers, grubs, weevils; also crustaceans, snails, spiders. *Nest.* Frequently in marshes, or in shrubs and trees near ponds and water courses—in alder, blackmangrove, bulrush, buttonbush, cattail, forestiera, hawthorn, orange, peach, rose (multiflora), rush (needlegrass), willow. *Attracting.* Red-winged blackbirds eat seeds readily on the ground, or from pine cones and sweetgum balls in trees. They will also eat from platform feeders. Mulberries attract them in early summer. Shrubs and marsh plants bring nesting pairs to ponds, streams, and canals. Blackbirds are beneficial insect feeders in summer but damage corn, rice, and grain sorghums in late summer and fall. The practical protection of such farm crops is the obvious one—harvest the grains as soon as they have ripened.

blackbird, rusty (*Euphagus carolinus*). Common summer resident of brushy swamps from central Ontario and New York northward to the limit of trees in Canada. Winters from Ohio and Delaware valleys southward to the Gulf coast. *Animal food* (70% spring to fall, 20% winter). Chiefly beetles, caterpillars, grasshopers; also ants, aquatic insects, centipedes, crustaceans, flies, salamanders, snails, spiders. *Plant food.* CHOICE: ash (white), bristlegrass, corn, hackberry, oak, oat (common), ragweed (common), rice, wheat, wildrice. FAIR. beech, blackberry, elder, grape, panicum, signalgrass. *Nest.* Frequently in alder, fir (balsam), spruce (red), willow. *Attracting.* Waste grain attracts them to fields.

blackbird, white-winged. See bunting, lark.

blackbird, yellow-headed (*Xanthocephalus xanthocephalus*). Common summer resident of marshes from central Manitoba and Hudson Bay southward to northern Indiana, southern Wisconsin, northern Minnesota. Winters uncommonly from western Louisiana through southern Texas; occasionally east of Mississippi River. *Plant food* (60% summer, 85% winter). CHOICE: bristlegrass, corn, oat (common), sorghum (grain), wheat. FAIR: barley (cultivated), ragweed (common, western), sunflower. *Animal food.* Chiefly beetles, caterpillars, grasshoppers, mayfly. *Nest.* Frequently in bulrush, cattail, reed, willow. *Attracting.* Grain on the ground.

blackheads. See scaups.

black-poll. See warbler, blackpoll.

blatherskite. See duck, ruddy.

bluebills. See scaups.

bluebird, eastern (also called red-breasted bluebird; *Sialia sialis*). Common summer resident of orchards and open woods from southern Canada to the Gulf of Mexico; rare in winter north of the Ohio valley and New Jersey. State bird of Missouri and New York. *Animal food* (90% summer, 60% winter). Chiefly beetles and their larvae, caterpillars, crickets, grasshoppers, weevils; also ants, centipedes, earthworms, moth larvae (cutworms), snails, sowbugs, spiders, wasps. Suet is a fair food. *Plant food.* CHOICE: blackberry, blackgum, blueberry, cake, camphortree, cherry (black, choke, mahaleb, mazzard, pin, sour), cotoneaster, creeper (Virginia), currants (dried), dahoon, dogwood (alternateleaf, flowering, gray, roughleaf), elaeagnus (autumn, cherry, thorny), elder (American), honeysuckle (Amur, Japanese), laurelcherry, liriope, mountainash (American), mulberry, pokeberry (common), possumhaw, pyracantha, raisins, redbay, redcedar (eastern), sassafras, snailseed (Carolina), sumac (smooth), viburnum (arrowwood, mapleleaf). FAIR: asparagus (garden), bittersweet, bread, chokeberry (red), cornmeal, date (pitted), euonymus (brook), fig (dried), gallberry, holly (Chinese, Japanese), huckleberry (black), mistletoe (Christmas), partridgeberry, peanut, peanutbutter, pecan, photinia (Chinese), poisonivy, privet (Amur, Chinese, glossy, Japanese), prune, raspberry, rose (multiflora), serviceberry, sumac (shining, staghorn), waxmyrtle (northern). *Nest.* Frequently in birdhouses or holes in posts and trees; occasionally in tin cans, cliff swallows' nests, crevices in rocks. *Attracting.* Bluebirds like a shallow birdbath and eat the insects on fertile and mowed lawns and pastures.

Currants, raisins, and other choice fruits, attract them to various types of stationary feeders; they will not come to swinging feeders. A feeder that excludes all other birds when only choice fruits are offered, is illustrated in figure 2.5. (The same feeder, if filled with sunflower seeds or nut meats, exclusively feeds chickadees, nuthatches, and tufted titmice.) Bluebirds like, and need, nesting homes that are provided best by birdhouses. See the birdhouse table (section 3), for specifications. These specifications also attract chickadees, nuthatches, house sparrows, tree swallows, titmice, prothonotary warbler, downy woodpecker, and wrens; but you can favor bluebirds by placing the house only 5 feet above ground and providing two or three birdhouses of this size within one "territory." Since they select their nesting site earlier than most birds, and raise two or three broods annually, you should clean the birdhouses in midwinter and after each nesting. They may nest alternately in two or three birdhouses during a single summer. Bluebirds usually compete successfully for housing with other species but, if necessary, an aggressive pair of house sparrows can be removed.

bluebird, indigo. See bunting, indigo.

bluebird, red-breasted. See bluebird, eastern.

blue peter. See coot.

boatswainbird. See frigate-bird.

bobolink (also called butterbird, reedbird, ricebird, and Robert; (*Dolichonyx oryzivorus*). Abundant summer resident of meadows and fields from Pennsylvania to Iowa, and northward into southern Canadian provinces. Migratory visitor in southern states; winters in South America. *Animal food* (90% summer, 20% winter). Chiefly ants, beetles, caterpillars, centipedes, cutworms, grasshoppers, spiders, weevils. *Plant food.* CHOICE: barley (cultivated), barnyardgrass, bristlegrass (yellow), junglerice, millet (Japanese), oat (common), panicum, rice, wheat, and wildrice. FAIR: knotgrass, ragweed (common), signalgrass, smartweed, and sunflower. *Nest.* On the ground in meadows; in a nest of leaves, stems, and grasses.

bobwhite (also called quail and bobwhite quail; *Colinus virginianus*). Common game bird, yearlong resident of farms and open woods in all states from Minnesota and Pennsylvania southward. *Plant food* (nearly 100% winter, 75%–90% spring to fall). CHOICE: aneilema (keisak), beech, beggarweed (Florida), blackberry, bristlegrass (green, yellow), canarygrass, cherry (black), chickweed, clover (crimson, white), corn, cowpeas, croton (gulf, linear, oneseed, Texas, tropic, woolly), dogwood (flowering), Hardinggrass, hemp, lespedeza (bicolor, common, japonica, Kobe, Korean, Thunberg), lupine (bicolor), milkpea (erect, hoary), millet (browntop, foxtail, Japanese, pearl, proso, Texas), mulberry, nutrush (fringed, sloughgrass), oak (Arkansas, bluejack, live, northern red, pin, post, runner, sawtooth, Shumard, southern red, water, white, willow), oat (common), panicum (browntop, fusiform), partridgepea (sensitive, showy), paspalum (barestem, bull), pecan, pine (loblolly, longleaf, pitch, shortleaf, slash, spruce, Virginia), plum (American), ragweed (common, lanceleaf, western), rape, rye, sassafras (common), signalgrass, snapweed (spotted), sorghum (grain), strawberry, sudangrass, sunflower (common), sweetgum, switchgrass, tickclover (diamondleaf, Dillen, panicled), vetch (hairy, flowering, narrowleaf), wheat. FAIR: amaranth (prostrate, redroot, spiny), ash (white), bean (mung), beautyberry (American), blackgum, blueberry (ground), buckwheat (common), bumelia (gum), butterflypea (coastal), carpetgrass (big, common, tropical), crotonopsis, deerplum, elaeagnus (autumn), four-o'clock, gallberry, goldstargrass, hackberry (common), hogpeanut (southern), Johnsongrass, locust (black), lovevine, osageorange, palmetto (cabbage), panicum (beaked, Dominican, fall, flexile, hiddenseed, longleaf, *neuranthum, oligosanthes*, roundseed, Tennessee, velvet, warty, woolly), paspalum (Florida), peanut, pokeberry (common), potatobean, privet (Chinese), pyracantha, raspberry, redbay, rhynchosia (dollarleaf, erect), rice, sesame, sesbania (hemp), soybean, sparkleberry, stillingia (corkwood, dentate, queen's-delight), sumac (smooth), sumpweed (seacoast), treadsoftly (risky), waxmyrtle (northern, southern), wildbean (pink, small, trailing). *Animal food.* Chiefly beetles, bugs, caterpillars, centipedes, crickets, grasshoppers, katydids, leafhoppers, snails, spiders, walkingsticks. *Nest.* On the ground, usually sheltered by a clump of grass or weeds. *Attracting.* Provide an adequate supply of choice foods for a covey. A food patch of ¼ acre or larger feeds a covey of 12 or more birds. They also come to a feeder on the ground near cover in a moderately grazed pasture, at the edge of a field, in an open-type woodland, or around suburban homes. Bobwhites do not require surface water, but sometimes drink from a birdbath on the ground. Lespedeza, though only an average-choice food, is especially important to bobwhites because its seed is not a choice food of any other bird. Thus, when competing species have seriously reduced most of the winter foods, lespedeza remains available to the bobwhite covey.

booby, blue-faced (also called masked and white booby; *Sula dactylatra*) and **brown booby** (also called white-bellied booby; *S. leucogaster*). Both boobies are rare but regular visitors to Gulf and Atlantic coasts from South Carolina south; accidental northward to Massachusetts. *Animal food* (100%). Fish (flying, mullet), and other marine life. *Nest.* On the ground in bare sand, occasionally in bushes, on Caribbean islands.

brant (also called American or Atlantic brant, and brent goose; *Branta bernicla*). Fairly common winter visitor in Atlantic coast areas from Massachusetts to South Carolina; rarely to Florida. *Plant food* (95%). CHOICE: barley (cultivated), cordgrass, corn, eelgrass, sealettuce, widgeongrass. *Ani-

mal food. Bivalves, crustaceans, marine worms. *Nest.* On the ground in marshy areas of arctic islands and Greenland.

brant, blue. See goose, blue.

brent goose. See brant.

buffalo bird. See cowbird, brown-headed.

bufflehead (also called bufflehead duck and butterball; *Bucephala albeola*). A diving duck; rather uncommon visitor to lakes, salt bays, and rivers of the eastern states from the Great Lakes southward in winter. *Animal food* (80%). Chiefly aquatic insects 40%, crayfish and shrimp 17%, mollusks 16%, fishes 4%; also grasshoppers, leeches, snails. *Plant food.* CHOICE: bulrush (water), naiad (northern), panicum (fall), potamogeton (sago, thorowort), widgeongrass. FAIR: bulrush (American), duckweed, hornwort, smartweed (Pennsylvania), spikerush, stonewort, watershield, wildcelery, wildrice. *Nest.* Usually in a tree cavity near water, in western Canada and Alaska.

bulbul, red-whiskered (*Pycnonotus jocosus*). Naturalized resident at Miami, Florida. *Plant food* (predominant). CHOICE: barbadoscherry, beautyberry (American), bottlebrush, carissa (natalplum), chinalaurel, dewdrop (golden), lily (Easter), loquat, mango, mulberry, orange, papaya, peach, pitanga, sapodilla, shrimp-plant. FAIR: lady-of-the-night. *Animal food.* Insects. *Nest.* An open cup, woven of grasses and fibers, in the branches of a shrub or tree. *Attracting.* Grow their choice fruits. A birdbath is very attractive.

bullbat. See nighthawk.

bullfinch, pine. See grosbeak, pine.

bull peep. See sanderling; sandpiper, white rumped.

bunting, black-throated. See dickcissel.

bunting, common. See bunting, snow.

bunting, indigo (also called indigo bird, indigo bluebird, indigo finch, blue finch, and blue canary; *Passerina cyanea*). Fairly common summer resident of brushy and open wooded areas in all eastern states except Florida; common migrant in Florida; winters in Caribbean islands and Central America, rarely on the Gulf coast. *Plant food* (80%). CHOICE: blackberry, bluestem (big), bristlegrass, corn, crabgrass (hairy), dandelion, elder, hemp, Johnsongrass, millet (browntop, Japanese, Texas), mulberry, oat (common), peanut, ragweed, rye, sorghum (grain), wheat. *Animal food.* Beetles, cankerworms, caterpillars, grasshoppers. *Nest.* Frequently in blackberry, cane, coralberry, maple (red), raspberry, rose, tungoiltree. *Attracting.* They sometimes comes to feeders to eat cracked corn, peanuts and other nut meats, and wheat. A birdbath attracts them, too. They come to oat and wheat fields, feeding on the grain in the "dough" stage, and to browntop millet in the fall.

bunting, lark (also called white-winged blackbird and prairie bird; *Cal-*

amospiza melanocorys). Rare winter visitor in eastern U.S. State bird of Colorado. *Animal food* (100% winter and spring, 75% summer, 50% fall). Chiefly beetles (weevils), grasshoppers, truebugs (stinkbugs); also ants, bees. *Plant food.* CHOICE: amaranth, needlegrass, oat (common), portulaca, sorghum (grain), sunflower, wheat. *Nest.* On prairie ground, under grass tussock in western states and southwestern Canada.

bunting, painted (also called nonpareil and Mexican canary; *Passerina ciris*). An uncommon summer resident of brushy areas from North Carolina to Kansas and southward to the Gulf; winters from Florida and the Louisiana coast to Caribbean areas and Panama. *Plant food* (85%). Bread crumbs, bristlegrass, cornmeal, junglerice, panicum, millet (proso), rice, vaseygrass. Bristlegrass is the chief summer food. *Animal food.* Chiefly beetles (weevils), caterpillars, grasshoppers; also snails, spiders. *Nest.* Frequently in blackberry, blackgum, elm, greenbrier, oak (live, post, scarlet), osageorange. *Attracting.* Painted buntings are attracted to cracked grain and bread crumbs at home feeders in Florida.

bunting, snow (also called common bunting, snowbird, and snowflake; *Plectrophenax nivalis*). Common winter visitor of fields and prairies from Virginia and Kansas northward into Canada. *Plant food* (100% in winter). CHOICE: amaranth (redroot), barley (cultivated), bristlegrass, corn, goosefoot, oat (common), ragweed (common), sandgrass, sedge, wheat. FAIR: alder, beachgrass, buttercup, dropseed, panicum, wildrye. *Animal food.* Beetles, caterpillars, cranefly. *Nest.* On barren ground, among rocks or grass tussocks in the arctic region, farther north than any other land bird.

burgomaster. See gull, glaucous.

butcherbird. See shrike.

buteos. See hawks.

butterball. See bufflehead.

butterbird. See bobolink.

buzzards. See vultures.

calico bird, calico plover. See turnstone, ruddy.

camp robber. See jay, gray.

Canada bird, Canada white-throat. See sparrow, white-throated.

canary, blue. See bunting, indigo.

canary, Mexican. See bunting, painted.

canary, wild. See goldfinch, American; warbler, yellow.

canvasback (*Aythya valisineria*). Fairly common diving duck; winters in ponds and marshes of the Atlantic and Gulf coasts and lower Mississippi valley. *Plant food* (80%). CHOICE: arrowhead (common, delta), barley, corn, potamogeton (leafy, longleaf, sago, thorowort), waterlily (yellow Mexican), wildcelery, wildrice. FAIR: barnyardgrass, bristlegrass, bulrush, burreed (giant), hornwort, naiad (northern, southern), parrotfeather, smartweed, stonewort, watershield, widgeongrass. *Animal food.* Aquatic insects, crustaceans, fish. *Nest.* Frequently in bulrush or other marsh plants in northwestern United States, western Canada, and Alaska. *Attracting.* Grow choice foods in ponds and marshes.

caracara (also called Mexican eagle; *Caracara cheriway*). Uncommon resident in southern half of Florida; occasional in Louisiana. *Animal food* (100%). Chiefly carrion; also beetles, birds, cottontail, crayfish, fish, frogs, grasshoppers, lizards, mice, rabbits, rats, skunks, snakes, squirrels, turtle eggs, turtles. *Nest.* Frequently cliffs, or in trees—elm, live oak, cabbage palmetto; occasionally in hackberry, pine, sawpalmetto. Nest mostly in arid country from western Texas into Mexico.

cardinal (also called cardinal grosbeak, and redbird or winter redbird; *Richmondena cardinalis*). Common yearlong resident in all of eastern United States, except New England. State bird of Illinois, Indiana, Kentucky, North Carolina, Ohio, Virginia, and West Virginia. *Plant food* (90% fall and winter, 40%–60% spring and summer). CHOICE: almond, arborvitae (oriental), barley, barnyardgrass, beautyberry (American, Japanese), birdeye, blackberry, brazilnut, bread (white), bristlegrass (green, yellow), buckwheat (common), camphortree, canarygrass, cantaloup seed, cherry (black, mazzard, sour), Columbusgrass, corn (chick-feed, cracked, whole), cornbread, croton (gulf, oneseed, Texas, tropic, woolly), dogwood (flowering, roughleaf), elaeagnus (autumn, cherry), elder (American), filbert (commercial), grape (cultivated, frost, muscadine, summer), hackberry (common, sugar), Hardinggrass, hemp, hickory meats (mockernut, nutmeg, sand, shagbark, shellbark), hornbeam (American), Johnsongrass, millet (browntop, foxtail, Japanese, pearl, proso, Texas), mulberry, nettlespurge (bellyache), nightshade (black), oat (common), panicum (hiddenseed), papermulberry, pea (garden), peanut, peanutbutter, pecan, pine (eastern white, loblolly, longleaf, shortleaf, slash, Virginia), pistachionut, pokeberry (common, stiff), pumpkin seed, ragweed (common, giant), raspberry, rice, safflower, seaoats, serviceberry (downy), sorghum (grain, reed), squash seed, strawberry, sudangrass, sunflower (common, cultivated, prairie), sweetgum, walnut (black Persian), watermelon seed, wheat, witchhazel. FAIR: apple (dried), ash (white), bahiagrass, birch (river), bittersweet, blueberry, chickencorn, chickweed, cockspur, coralberry, cowpeas, crabgrass, dodder, elm (American), fig, flax (common), four-o'clock, goosegrass, greenbrier, hawthorn, holly (American), magnolia (southern), plum (garden), privet (Chinese, glossy, Japanese), pyracantha, ragimillet, raisins, redcedar (eastern), rose (multiflora), rye, sage (lyreleaf), sesame, sorgo, sowthistle, sumac, switchgrass, tallowtree, verbena, viburnum, yellow-poplar. *Animal food.* Ants, beetles, caterpillars, grasshoppers, scale insects, weevils; also butter, cheese, pork fat, and suet are fair. *Nest.* Frequently in abelia, camellia, grape, holly, honeysuckle (Amur, Japanese, tatarian), orange, privet (Chinese, Japanese), red-cedar, rose (multiflora), willow, yaupon. *Attracting.* The cardinal is one of the easiest birds to attract because it likes more than 100 foods. It comes readily to swinging feeders for bread, corn, grass seeds, nut meats, peanut-butter, safflower, scratch-feed, grain sorghum, and sunflower seed. Plant choice nesting shrubs for cover and food.

    catbird (*Dumetella carolinensis*). Common summer suburban resident in eastern United States and southern Canada; winters from South Carolina to Florida and Texas. *Plant food* (20% spring, 60% summer, 80% winter). CHOICE: apple (sliced), blackberry, blackgum, blueberry (highbush), bread (white), cake (sweet), cherry (black, mahaleb, mazzard, sour), creeper (Japanese, Virginia), currant (dried), dogwood (alternateleaf, silky, tatarian), elaeagnus (autumn, cherry), elder (American, European red), fig, gooseberry, grape (cultivated, frost, summer), holly, honey syrup, honeysuckle (Belle, tatarian, winter), huckleberry (black), magnolia (southern), mountainash (American, European), mulberry, papermulberry, peach, peanut, pear, pecan, peppervine, plum (garden), poisonivy, pokeberry (common), raisins, raspberry, sassafras, serviceberry (Allegheny), strawberry, sugar, sumac (shining, smooth), walnut (black). FAIR: alder, beautyberry (American), bittersweet, greenbrier, hackberry, honeysuckle (Japanese), persimmon, pyracantha, redcedar, spicebush (common), sumac (staghorn), waxmyrtle (northern). *Animal food.* Chiefly ants, beetles, caterpillars, grasshoppers; also bugs, cheese, spiders, suet. *Nest.* Frequently in apple, blackberry, chokeberry, elder, elm, grape, hawthorn, honeysuckle (Amur, Japanese, Morrow, tatarian), lilac, mockorange, osageorange, privet (Chinese, Japanese), redcedar, spirea, willow. *Attracting.* Catbirds will eat white bread, cheese, grapes, peanuts, raisins, suet, and walnut meats at feeders, but their chief foods are fleshy fruits of many wild plants, such as the pokeberry.

    cathedral bird. See veery.

    cedar bird. See waxwing, cedar.

    chad. See woodpecker, red-bellied.

    chat, long-tailed. See chat, yellow-breasted.

    chat, yellow-breasted (also called long-tailed chat; *Icteria virens*). Member of the wood warbler family; uncommon, but noisy, summer resident of brier thickets from southern Minnesota and New Hampshire southward to the Gulf, except southern Florida; winters in Central America, and rarely in its summer range. *Animal food* (65% summer, 98% winter). Chiefly ants, beetles (ground, weevils), caterpillars, grasshoppers, spiders, truebugs. *Plant food.* CHOICE: blackberry, blueberry, elaeagnus (cherry), elder (American), thimbleberry. FAIR: dogwood, grape (wild), strawberry (wild), sumac. *Nest.* Frequently in blackberry, dogwood, greenbrier, hawthorn, redcedar, spirea, viburnum, willow. *Attracting.* Leave brier patches for nesting in swamps.

chatterer, wandering. See waxwing, Bohemian.

chebec. See flycatcher, least.

cherry bird. See waxwing, cedar.

chewink. See towhee, rufous-sided.

chickadee, Acadian. See chickadee, boreal.

chickadee, black-capped (also called long-tailed chickadee; *Parus atricapillus*). Common resident of orchards, parks, and woods from Missouri and North Carolina mountains northward to northern Ontario and Newfoundland. State bird of Maine and Massachusetts. *Animal food* (90% summer, 50% winter). Ants, beetles, caterpillars, flies, insect eggs (katydid, moths, plantlice, spiders), leafhoppers, moths, plantlice, scale insects, spiders, suet, treehoppers, wasps. Lard is a fair food. *Plant food.* CHOICE: bread (white), butternut, doughnuts, hemp, honey syrup, peanut, peanutbutter, pine (pitch), pumpkin seed, squash seed, sunflower (cultivated), walnut (Persian). FAIR: blueberry, birch, creeper (Virginia), elaeagnus (autumn), elm, fir, hemlock (eastern), oak, poisonivy, ragweed, serviceberry, spruce, sumac (staghorn), sweetgum, waxmyrtle (northern). *Nest.* Frequently in birdboxes, holes and natural cavities in fence posts, old stumps, and trees. *Attracting.* Chickadees will come readily to windowsill feeders and to other stationary or swinging feeders for peanutbutter, suet, sunflower seeds, and other choice foods. They will nest in man-made birdhouses which are placed 5–15 feet from the ground on a tree at the edge of woods or in a shaded area of gardens and orchards. (See the birdhouse table, section 3, for specifications.) They prefer the natural appearance of the hollow-log house, and like to nest in 2 or 3 inches of wood shavings or sawdust. Nuthatches and wrens use houses of the same dimensions, with a 1⅛-inch entrance hole.

chickadee, boreal (also called Acadian, brown-capped, Columbian, and Hudsonian chickadee; *Parus hudsonicus*). Fairly common resident from Great Lakes and New England northward; casual farther south in winter. *Animal food* (probably 90% summer, 50% or less winter). Chiefly aphids, beetles, bugs, caterpillars, moths, spiders; also ants, bees, wasps. *Plant food.* CHOICE: fir, hemlock, pine, spruce, sunflower. *Nest.* Usually in a cavity of a post, tree, or stump. *Attracting.* Use feeders with suet and suet mixtures. Birdhouse specifications are similar to those for black-capped chickadee.

chickadee, brown-capped. See chickadee, boreal.

chickadee, Carolina (also called Florida and plumeous chickadee; *Parus carolinensis*). Common yearlong resident of woodlands and groves in eastern United States, southward from Missouri, Ohio, and New Jersey to the Gulf coast. *Animal food* (90% summer, 45% winter). Chiefly caterpillars, moths, suet. Also ants, beetles, bugs, cheese, katydids, leafhoppers, plantlice, scales, spiders, treehoppers, wasps. *Plant food.* CHOICE: almond, brazilnut, bread (white), butternut, cashew, cookie crumbs, doughnuts, filbert (commercial), hickory (mockernut, shagbark), peanut, peanutbutter, pecan, pie crust, pine (eastern white, loblolly, shortleaf, Virginia), pistachionut, poisonivy wax, pumpkinseed, squash seeds, sunflower (common, cultivated), walnut (black, Persian). FAIR: hemp, locust (black), sweetgum. *Nest.* Frequently in birdhouses, holes in fence posts, stumps, and trees. *Attracting.* Feed bread, cracked nuts, peanutbutter, pumpkin and squash seeds, suet, and/or sunflower seeds in swinging or stationary feeders. Erect birdhouses as for black-capped chickadee.

chickadee, Columbian. See chickadee, boreal.

chickadee, Florida. See chickadee, Carolina.

chickadee, Hudsonian. See chickadee, boreal.

chickadee, long-tailed. See chickadee, black-capped.

chickadee, plumeous. See chickadee, Carolina.

chock. See grackle, boat-tailed.

chuck-will's-widow (also called great bat and goatsucker; *Caprimulgus carolinensis*). Common summer resident of woodlands in southern United States from Missouri, Indiana, and Maryland to the Gulf of Mexico; winters occasionally in Florida and Louisiana, mostly in Mexico and Central America. *Animal food* (100%). Chiefly ants (flying), beetles, flies, grasshoppers, mosquitoes, moths; occasionally small birds. *Nest.* On the ground, lined with leaves.

cock of the wood. See woodpecker, pileated.

coot, American (also called mudhen, blue peter, and pulldoo; *Fulica americana*). Abundant in winter on ponds, marshes, and lakes of southern United States. *Plant food* (nearly 100% winter, 55% summer). CHOICE: alfalfa, barley, bulrush (tule), clover (white), corn, duckweed (common, star), millet (proso), naiad (northern, southern), oat (common), potamogeton (sago), rice, rye, ryegrass (Italian), sorghum (grain), stonewort, wheat, widgeongrass, wildcelery, wildrice. FAIR: algae (filamentous), anacharis, arrowarum, beet (sugar), bladderwort (common), bulrush (American, California, river, softstem), burreed (giant), eelgrass, hornwort, parrotfeather, potamogeton (leafy, longleaf), St. Augustinegrass, saltgrass (seashore), sedge, spikerush (squarestem). *Animal food.* Chiefly aquatic insects, fish, snails, tadpoles. *Nest.* Frequently in marsh growth, especially bulrush or cattail, throughout western United States, upper Mississippi, New England, and southern Canada. Nest of plant stems floats on water.

coot, sea. See scoters.

coot, white-winged. See scoter, white-winged.

cormorant, double-crested (also called shag, water turkey, and nigger goose; *Phalacrocorax auritus*). Common around lakes and coastal waters in eastern North America. *Animal food* (100%). Catfish, crabs, eels, fish (drum, herring, parrotfish, sculpins, etc.), marine worms. *Nest.* Frequently on the ground, on rock islands in western states and the North Atlantic coast; in trees in the southern states—baldcypress, birch, blackmangrove, mangrove (American), oak, pine (longleaf).

cormorant, great (also called shag, water turkey, and niggergoose; *Phalacrocorax carbo*). Winters commonly from Long Island, New York, northward; rarely southward. *Animal food* (100%). Chiefly fish. *Nest.* On the ground, among rocks, Nova Scotia to Greenland.

cormorant, olivaceous (also called shag, water turkey, and niggergoose; *Phalacrocorax olivaceus*). Uncommon to rare on the Atlantic coast from Newfoundland to South Carolina. *Animal food* (100%). Crustaceans, fish, marine worms. *Nest.* In bushes or trees over water, Gulf of St. Lawrence to Greenland.

cowbird, brown-headed (also called buffalo bird, and common or eastern cowbird; *Molothrus ater*). Includes four subspecies. Common resident in eastern North America. *Plant food* (95% winter, 50% summer). CHOICE: bahiagrass, barnyardgrass, bristlegrass (yellow), chickencorn, corn, cutgrass (rice), junglerice, millet (browntop, Japanese, proso, Texas), oat (common), panicum (browntop), paspalum (bull, Florida), sorghum (grain), wheat. FAIR: crabgrass, croton (woolly), ragweed (common), rice, switchgrass, timothy. *Animal food.* Beetles, caterpillars, grasshoppers, spiders. *Nest.* Lays its eggs in the nests of other birds—at least 158 different species. It is the only bird in eastern North America that displays this behavior, which is called "nest parasitism." *Attracting.* Little is needed to encourage and little can be done to discourage cowbirds. To save crops from them, harvest as soon as ripe. They come frequently in pairs to eat scratch-feed and small grains from the ground or low platforms.

crane, blue. See heron, great blue.

crane, brown. See crane, sandhill.

crane, Florida. See crane, sandhill.

crane, sandhill (*Grus canadensis*). Includes two subspecies of eastern United States: the Florida or southern subspecies, which is a yearlong resident in Florida and southern Georgia; the northern or brown sandhill crane, which winters in southern Texas and nests northwestward from Michigan. *Plant food* (90%). CHOICE: arrowhead, barley (cultivated), bulrush, chufa, clover (white), corn, oat (common), potato, rice, sorghum (grain), sweetpotato, wheat. FAIR: alfalfa, blueberry, crowberry (black), waterlily. *Animal food.* Chiefly beetles, caterpillars, crickets, earthworms, frogs, grasshoppers, snails, toads; also fish, lizards, mice, snakes. *Nest.* Usually on marsh ground. *Attracting.* Grain fields attract flocks in winter.

crane, whooping (*Grus americana*). A rare species of less than 50 birds. They breed in a muskeg area, Wood Buffalo Park, Alberta, Canada; winter on the Aransas National Wildlife Refuge, Aransas, Texas. *Plant food* (probably predominant). CHOICE: bulrush (Olney), cordgrass, corn, crinum (Florida), falsegarlic (yellow), oak (blackjack, live, pin), oat, sorghum (grain), sweetpotato. FAIR: wheat. *Animal food.* Chiefly crabs, crayfish, and fish; also aquatic insects, frogs, small mammals. *Nest.* On marsh ground, lined with grass.

creeper, black-and-white. See warbler, black-and-white.

creeper, brown (also called tree creeper and common creeper; *Certhia familiaris*). Common in summer in coniferous forests of southern Canadian provinces southward to mountains of North Carolina; winters throughout its breeding range and southward to the Gulf coast, Florida to Texas. *Animal food* (90%). Ants, beetles, bugs (scales, plantlice), caterpillars, insect eggs, moths, spiders, truebugs, wasps; also suet. *Plant food.* CHOICE: bread (white), peanutbutter, pine. FAIR: corn. *Nest.* In holes or under loose bark of trees, often in balsam fir. *Attracting.* Smear peanutbutter, suet, or a mixture of the two on a tree trunk for these tree-creeping birds.

creeper, common or tree. See creeper, brown.

crossbill, American and common. See crossbill, red.

crossbill, red (also called American and common crossbill; *Loxia curvirostra*). Fairly common resident of coniferous forests from Minnesota eastward to Nova Scotia, and south in Appalachians to West Virginia; rare farther south. *Plant food* (100% winter, 85% summer). CHOICE: almond, birch (paper), fir (balsam), hemlock, pine (eastern white, pitch, Scotch, shortleaf, Virginia), ragweed (common), spruce (Norway, red, white), sunflower (cultivated), tamarack. FAIR: apple seeds, beech nuts, crabapple (Japanese flowering). *Animal food.* Chiefly beetles (including larvae), caterpillars, fly larvae, plantlice, spiders, and spittlebugs, mostly obtained from conifer trees. *Nest.* Frequently in conifer trees—fir, hemlock, pine, spruce (red). *Attracting.* Sunflower seed is the most attractive food at a feeder.

crossbill, white-winged (*Loxia leucoptera*). Resident of evergreen forests from the New England states and eastern Canadian provinces to Alaska; rare winter visitor in eastern United States south of Minnesota, Michigan, and New England. *Plant food* (nearly 100% winter, 75% summer). CHOICE: fir, hemlock, pine (eastern white), spruce (red, white), sunflower (cultivated), tamarack, teasel (venuscup). FAIR: ragweed, redcedar. *Animal food.* Chiefly caterpillars and other insect larvae. *Nest.* Frequently in spruce.

crow, common (*Corvus brachyrhynchos*). Common throughout all of eastern North America. *Plant food* (85% winter, 55% summer). CHOICE: almond, apricot, barley (cultivated), beech, buckwheat (common), cantaloup, cherry (black, mazzard), corn, creeper (Virginia), mulberry, oak, oat (common), pea (garden), peanut, pecan, pokeberry (common), service-berry, sorghum (grain), strawberry, sumac (smooth), walnut, watermelon, wheat. FAIR: apple, blackberry, cherry (choke), chufa, cottonseed cake, cranberry, dogwood (alternateleaf, flowering, redosier), fig, grape, hack-berry, nightshade (bitter), poisonivy, poisonsumac, raspberry, redcedar (eastern), sumac (staghorn), sunflower, winterberry (common). *Animal food.* Amphibians, beetles, bugs, carrion, caterpillars, crayfish, eggs (domes-tic poultry, duck, prairie chicken), grasshoppers, snails, snakes, turtles; also frogs, gophers, mice, rabbits, salamanders, spiders, toads; suet is a choice food. *Nest.* Frequently in alder, beech, cottonwood, fir, maple, oak (live), osageorange, pine (jack, loblolly, longleaf, shortleaf), poplar, redcedar, spruce, willow. *Attracting.* Corn, grain sorghum, and other choice foods occasionally bring them to a feeding station, but crows usually are wary of people.

crow, fish (*Corvus ossifragus*). Common yearlong resident along stream and bay shores of the Gulf and Atlantic coasts and large southern rivers. *Plant food* (75% fall and winter, 30%–60% summer). CHOICE: blackberry, camphortree, corn, fig, magnolia (southern), mulberry, peanut, wheat. FAIR: blueberry, dahoon, dogwood, grape, greenbrier, hackberry, huckleberry, mistletoe, oat (common), palmetto, pawpaw, redcedar, sawpalmetto, sumac, tallowtree, wildrice. *Animal food.* Beetles, birds' eggs, carrion, clams, crabs, crayfish, fish, grasshoppers, weevils. *Nest.* Frequently in holly (American), oak (black, live, pin), pine (loblolly, pitch, slash), redcedar.

crying bird. See limpkin.

cuckoo, black-billed (also called rain crow; *Coccyzus erythropthalmus*). Fairly common summer resident of woodland groves from Arkansas to North Carolina and from Minnesota to Nova Scotia; winters in South America. *Animal food* (nearly 100%). Chiefly caterpillars (tent, hairy, and bristly species not eaten by most birds); also beetles, bugs, grasshoppers, sawflies, spiders; occasionally birds' eggs. *Plant food.* Mulberry. *Nest.* Frequently in beech, blackberry, boxelder, hemlock, kalmia (mountainlaurel), pine (east-ern white), redcedar; occasionally in chokeberry, elder, hawthorn, larch, maple (sugar), rose, viburnum, willow; also on old logs or on the ground— usually in thickets and groves.

cuckoo, mangrove (also called Maynard's cuckoo; *Coccyzus minor*). Un-common resident from Florida Keys to Tampa Bay. *Animal food* (100%). Chiefly caterpillars, flies, grasshoppers, moths, spiders. *Nest.* Frequently in mangrove swamps.

cuckoo, yellow-billed (also called rain crow; *Coccyzus americanus*). Com-mon summer resident of orchards, swamps, and woods in eastern United States and southern Canada. *Animal food* (nearly 100%). Chiefly caterpillars; also beetles, grasshoppers, locusts, moths. *Plant food.* Elder, grape, mulberry. *Nest.* Frequently in alder, apple, cottonwood, crabapple, elm (Siberian, Chinese), hawthorn, oak (live, water), osageorange, pine, red-cedar, rose, willow; occasionally in other shrubs and trees along streams and in thickets.

curlew, black. See ibis, glossy.

curlew, Eskimo (*Numenius borealis*). This species in 1929 was considered to be "probably extinct," but it has since been recorded five times on the Texas coast and five times on the Atlantic coast, including sightings in 1959, 1960, and 1962. So this "nearly extinct" curlew might yet be seen some fall on the Atlantic coast migrating southward, or on the Texas coast in April on its return northward. (Weston and Williams, *Auk* (1965), 82(3):493–496).

curlew, Hudsonian or jack. See whimbrel.

curlew, long-billed (*Numenius americanus*). Common to abundant winter visitor of shores and prairies on the Louisiana and Texas (Aransas) coast; rare elsewhere in eastern North America. *Animal food* (nearly 100%). Beetles, caterpillars, crabs, crayfish, crickets, crustaceans, flies, grasshoppers, larvae, locusts, mollusks, periwinkle, snails, spiders, toads, and worms. *Plant food.* Blueberry. *Nest.* Grass-lined, on ground in open prairies of northwestern United States and southwestern Canada.

curlew, pink. See spoonbill, roseate.

curlew, Spanish, stone, or white. See ibis, white.

dabchick. See grebe, pied-billed.

darter, big blue. See hawk, Cooper's.

darter, blue. See goshawk.

darter, little blue. See hawk, sharp-shinned.

dickcissel (also called black-throated bunting and little meadowlark; *Spiza americana*). Common summer resident of prairies from Texas and Mississippi to Minnesota, rarely eastward; winters in Central and South America. *Animal food* (80%). Chiefly crickets, grasshoppers, katydids; also ants, beetles, bugs, caterpillars, flies, snails, weevils. *Plant food.* CHOICE: bristlegrass, millet (proso), oat (common), peanutbutter. FAIR: corn, panicum, wheat. *Nest.* Frequently on the ground, sheltered by tuft of grass, and in shrubs or trees—elm, hackberry, mulberry, osageorange.

didapper or divedapper. See grebe, pied-billed.

dove, ground (*Columbigallina passerina*). Common resident of open lands from South Carolina to Florida and Texas in Lower Coastal plain. *Plant food* (100%). CHOICE: amaranth, beefwood, bristlegrass, chickweed, corn, croton (tropic), panicum, paspalum, rice, sorghum (grain). FAIR: birdeye, crabgrass, flatsedge (poorland), goosefoot, nutrush, portulaca, ragweed, violet, wheat. *Nest.* Frequently on the ground, a rotting stump, or in shrubs or trees—baccharis, blackberry, cottonwood, grape, orange, palmetto (cabbage), pear, willow. *Attracting.* Ground doves are seldom hunted for sport. They often come to feeders in open pastures, and even dooryards, for small seeds and cracked grains. They need surface water to drink.

dove, mourning (also called turtle dove; *Zenaidura macroura*). Common to abundant resident of farms, towns, and open woods from southern Canada throughout United States. *Plant food* (100%). CHOICE: amaranth (prostrate, redroot, slim), *Aneilema nudiflorum*, barnyardgrass, birdeye, bluegrass (annual), bristlegrass (Faber's, giant, green, knotroot, yellow), canarygrass (canariensis, reed), chickweed, Columbusgrass, corn, croton (gulf, oneseed, Texas, tropic, woolly), euphorbia (Brazil, painted), geranium (Carolina), Hardinggrass, hemp, knotgrass, millet (browntop, foxtail, Japanese, pearl, proso, Texas), nettlespurge (bellyache), nutrush (sloughgrass), panicum (Dominican, fall, hiddenseed, shoredune, velvet), paspalum (bull, giant), pine (eastern white, loblolly, longleaf, pond, shortleaf, slash, spruce, Virginia), pokeberry (common, stiff), poppy (Mexican prickly, white prickly), ragweed (common), rape, signalgrass (broadleaf), sorgo, sorghum (grain, reed), sudangrass, sunflower (common, prairie), sweetgum, switchgrass, watermelon, wheat. FAIR: bahiagrass, barley (cultivated), buckwheat (common), cantaloup, chickencorn, copperleaf (hophornbeam, Virginia), cornflower, cowpea, crabgrass (hairy, smooth), dayflower (erect), flatsedge (poorland), flax (common), goosefoot, goosegrass, Johnsongrass, lespedeza (Kobe, Korean), oat (common), orange seed, panicum (beaked), portulaca (common), ragimillet, rice, rushfoil (narrowleaf), rye, safflower, sage (lyreleaf), seaoats, sesame, soybean, spiderflower, spruce (white), treadsoftly (risky), vetch (lana, showy), wildbean (pink, small, trailing), witchgrass (common). *Nest.* Frequently on the ground, or in apple, boxelder, elm, hackberry, locust (black), maple, mulberry, oak (bur, live, post), osageorange, peach, pecan, pine (Austrian, eastern white, loblolly, longleaf, red, Scotch, shortleaf, slash, Virginia), redcedar, spruce (Norway, white), willow. *Attracting.* Mourning doves feed only on the ground, preferring little or no cover. Landowners can plant small food patches of millets, pokeberry, or wheat. Doves come to feeding stations where choice foods are available on the ground, and they drink daily from surface waters, chiefly ponds, streams, and rain puddles.

dove, ring. See dove, ringed-turtle.

dove, ringed turtle (also called ring dove; *Streptopelia risoria*). Domesticated throughout the world. Naturalized (but uncommon) in Florida. *Plant food* (100%). Chiefly seeds. *Nest.* In trees.

dove, rock (usually known as "domestic pigeon"; *Columba livia*). Common to abundant in most cities and towns. *Plant food* (100%). CHOICE: birdeye, bread, camphortree, corn, lespedeza (common), millet (brown

top), oat (common), peanut, pine (eastern white, loblolly), rice, rye, sweetgum, wheat. FAIR: hackberry (sugar), soybean, vetch (common). *Nest.*
Usually on ledges of buildings; occasionally in rock quarries or recesses in
cliffs.

dove, sea. See dovekie.

dove, singing. See dove, white-winged.

dove, turtle. See dove, mourning.

dove, white-winged (also called singing dove; *Zenaida asiatica*). Common in farmed areas from San Antonio, Texas, into Mexico; rare east and
north of central Texas. *Plant food* (100%). CHOICE: barley, bristlegrass,
cantaloup, corn, croton (woolly), hemp, millet (browntop, proso), nettlespurge, oat, orange, panicum, poppy (Mexican prickly), safflower, sorghum
(grain), sunflower, watermelon, wheat. *Nest.* In trees, cactus, and large
shrubs. *Attracting.* Provide surface water for daily drinking. Plant or otherwise manage its choice foods, or provide scratch-feed and other choice foods
at feeding stations.

dovekie (also called little auk and sea dove; *Plautus alle*). Abundant
breeder along the coasts of Greenland and other islands of the North Atlantic coast. Winters to New Jersey, usually in the open sea; rare inland.
Animal food (nearly 100%). Crustaceans, fish. *Plant food.* Seaweed. *Nest.*
On cliffs, exposed rocks, on islands and coasts of the arctic region.

dowitcher, eastern. See dowitcher, short-billed.

dowitcher, long-billed (also called red-bellied snipe, greater gray-back,
and greater long-beak; *Limnodromus scolopaceus*). Common winter visitor
of shallow waters and mudflats on the Gulf coast from Florida to Texas, rare
in fall migration on the Atlantic coast as far north as Maine. Breeds in the
arctic. *Animal food* (nearly 100% winter). Chiefly fly larvae, grasshoppers,
leeches, marine worms, mollusks, and water beetles; also small crustaceans.
Plant food. Bogbean (common), bulrush, potamogeton. *Nest.* On the ground
around marshy lakes and ponds.

dowitcher, short-billed (also called eastern dowitcher, and gray, red-
breasted, or robin snipe; *Limnodromus griseus*). Winters regularly, in lesser
numbers than the long-billed dowitcher, along mudflats and shores of the
Gulf coast from Texas to Florida and casually to South Carolina. Breeds from
southern Alaska to northern Ontario, and probably Quebec. The short-billed
and long-billed dowitchers are so similar (they were once considered a single
species) that their names, foods, and nesting places are confused in the
literature.

duck. The 27 species of ducks that reside or visit regularly in eastern North
America have a common feeding preference which influences the best
means of attracting them. Although they will feed occasionally on dry land,
they prefer to obtain their food from the water. They have wide, flat bills

with comblike edges by which they strain food. Most ducks are important game birds and they are, in the main, plant feeders. Since pollution and drainage and land-fill projects often destroy their source of foods, it is becoming increasingly important that sportsmen and landowners learn how they can flood fields and manage wetlands to replace the lost supplies. Much valuable advice in these matters is to be found in Farmers' Bulletin No. 2218, "Wild Ducks on Farmland in the South," issued in 1966 by the U.S. Department of Agriculture.

The species listed throughout this section include 10 "surface-feeding" ducks, 16 "diving" species, and the fulvous tree duck, a gooselike bird which also dives for food.

The surface-feeding ducks are known variously as "dabbling," "marsh," "pond," "puddle," "river," "shoal," and "tipping" or "tip-up" ducks. They are the black, mottled, and wood ducks, and the gadwall, mallard, pintail, shoveler, teal (blue- and green-winged), and American widgeon. These species prefer water shallow enough for them to reach food without diving; to reach deep food they flip head-down, the tail poking straight out of the water. The maneuver is called "tipping," and the head-down attitude is maintained by paddling. The hind toe of these ducks is little more than a nail.

The diving ducks (known variously as "bay," "deep-water," or "sea" ducks) include the harlequin, ring-necked, and ruddy ducks, and the bufflehead, canvasback, eider (common and king), goldeneye (Barrow's and common), oldsquaw, redhead, scaup (greater and lesser), and scoter (common, surf, and white-winged). These birds feed deeply, their dive assisted by a wide lobe or flap on the hind toe.

Three species of mergansers, often called fish ducks, also dive for their food.

duck, American tufted. See duck, ring-necked.

duck, baldpate. See widgeon, American.

duck, black (also called black mallard; *Anas rubripes*). Surface-feeding duck; common in marshes and ponds throughout eastern North America. Breeds in northern states and Canada; winters from Indiana, New York, and Newfoundland southward to the Gulf coast, Florida to Texas. *Plant food* (80%). CHOICE: aneilema (keisak), arrowhead (common), barley, beech, bread (white), buckwheat (common), bulrush (saltmarsh, water), corn, cutgrass (rice), eelgrass, flatsedge (redroot), millet (browntop, Japanese), naiad (southern), oak (pin, white), oat (common), panicum (fall, warty), pipewort, podgrass (shore), poolmat, potamogeton (baby, floatingleaf, largeleaf, longleaf, ribbonleaf), rice, ryegrass (Italian), smartweed (bigroot, dotted, marshpepper, Pennsylvania), tearthumb (arrowleaf), waterelm, waterhemp (tidemarsh), waterlily (yellow Mexican), widgeongrass, wildcelery, wildrice. FAIR: arrowarum, barnyardgrass, beakrush (horned), beggartick, bulrush (American, river, Smith's, softstem, Torrey, tule, wool-grass), burreed, chufa, cordgrass, cowlily (painted), duckweed, hornwort, naiad (northern), sedge, spikerush, stonewort, waterhemp (tall), water-shield, winterberry (common). *Animal food.* Chiefly mollusks (mostly bivalves); also aquatic insects, crustaceans, earthworms, fish, frogs, snails, tadpoles. *Nest.* On the ground in reedy bogs, bushy swamps, and meadows. *Attracting.* Manage southern duck fields and ponds with choice foods, and maintain suitable nesting marshes in northern areas.

duck, blackhead. See scaup, greater and lesser.

duck, blue-bill. See scaup, greater and lesser.

duck, bristletail. See duck, ruddy.

duck, bufflehead. See bufflehead.

duck, canvasback. See canvasback.

duck, eider. See eider, common and king.

duck, fiddler. See duck, fulvous tree.

duck, Florida. See duck, mottled.

duck, fool. See duck, ruddy.

duck, fulvous tree (also called fiddler duck and whistling or fulvous whistling duck; *Dendrocygna bicolor*). Uncommon resident of Louisiana and east Texas marshes. *Plant food* (100%). CHOICE: alfalfa, cockspur (coast), corn, junglerice, knotgrass, oak, paspalum (bull), rice, signalgrass (broadleaf). FAIR: barnyardgrass, smartweed, spikerush, watershield. *Nest.* Frequently in rice fields, the nest attached to rice or signalgrass in shallow water; also bulrush and marsh grasses; occasionally in cavity of trees.

duck, fulvous whistling. See duck, fulvous tree.

duck, gadwall. See gadwall.

duck, goldeneye. See goldeneye, Barrow's and common.

duck, gray. See gadwall.

duck, greenhead. See mallard.

duck, harlequin (*Histrionicus histrionicus*). Diving duck; winters casually on Atlantic coast from Labrador to Long Island. *Animal food* (nearly 100%). Chiefly aquatic insects, crabs, fish, frogs, mussels, tadpoles. *Plant food.* Bread, potato, raisins. *Nest.* Frequently on the ground under logs and drift-wood or among rocks; occasionally on stumps near water, from Newfound-land to Greenland.

duck, long-tailed. See oldsquaw.

duck, mallard. See mallard.

duck, mottled (also called Florida duck and Florida mallard; *Anas ful-vigula*). Surface-feeding duck; fairly common resident of Florida, Louisiana, and Texas marshes. *Plant food* (75% summer, 100% winter). CHOICE: bristle-grass (knotroot), bulrush (Olney, saltmarsh), chufa, clover (white), corn, junglerice, millet (browntop), naiad (southern), panicum (Bartow, fall,

redtop), paspalum (fringeleaf, mudbank), ragweed (common), rice, smartweed (dotted, Puerto Rico, swamp), tearthumb (arrowleaf). FAIR: arrowhead (delta), barnyardgrass, beakrush (horned), cockspur (coast), cowlily
(spatterdock), duckweed, fanwort (Carolina), guava, hornwort, potamogeton (longleaf), spadeleaf, spikerush, waterlily (yellow Mexican), watershield, widgeongrass. *Animal food.* Chiefly aquatic insects, crayfish, crustaceans, snails, *Nest.* On the ground.
  duck, pintail. See pintail.
  duck, raft. See scaup, greater and lesser.
  duck, redhead. See redhead.
  duck, ring-billed. See duck, ring-necked.
  duck, ring-billed scaup. See scaup, greater and lesser.
  duck, ring-necked (also called ring-billed duck, American tufted duck,
black jack, and ring-necked scaup; *Aythya collaris*). Small diving duck;
common winter resident of ponds in southeastern states. *Plant food* (85%
winter, 60% summer). CHOICE: arrowhead (common, delta), bulrush (American, Torrey, water), buttercup, corn, cowlily (spatterdock), millet (browntop, Japanese), naiad (northern), oak, potamogeton (baby, floatingleaf,
Illinois, largeleaf, leafy, longleaf, ribbonleaf, sago, thorowort, variableleaf),
ragweed (common), rush (brown-fruited), smartweed (bigroot, dotted,
marshpepper, swamp), stonewort, waterelm, waterlily (yellow Mexican),
wheat, widgeongrass, wildcelery, wildrice. FAIR: barnyardgrass, burreed
(American, giant, green-fruited), chufa, cockspur, duckweed, flatsedge (redroot), hornwort, lovegrass (teal), pipewort, rice, sedge, spikerush, watershield. *Animal food.* Aquatic insects, fish, mollusks, snails. *Nest.* On the
ground in marshes, west of Great Lakes and in southern Canada. *Attracting.*
Provide choice foods in southern ponds and flooded fields, and maintain
northern marshes for nesting.
  duck, ruddy (also called stiff-tailed, fool, sleepy, or bristletail duck,
blatherskite, and at least 60 other names; *Oxyura jamaicensis*). Uncommon
diving duck of lakes and ponds, wintering from Illinois and Pennsylvania
southward; breeds westward from Illinois. *Plant food* (70%). CHOICE: bulrush (American, softstem), corn, naiad (northern, southern), potamogeton
(sago, thorowort), stonewort, widgeongrass, wildcelery. FAIR: arrowhead,
duckweed, eelgrass, naiad (spiny), sedge, smartweed (Pennsylvania),
watershield. *Animal food.* Crustaceans, insects, mollusks. *Nest.* On shores
of lakes, ponds, and streams—in bulrush, cattail, rivergrass, sedge.
  duck, scaup. See scaup, greater and lesser.
  duck, shoveler. See shoveler.
  duck, sleepy. See duck, ruddy.
  duck, stiff-tailed. See duck, ruddy.
  duck, summer. See duck, wood.

duck, teal. See teal, blue-winged and green-winged.
duck, whistling. See duck, fulvous tree.
duck, widgeon. See widgeon, American.
duck, wood (also called summer duck; *Aix sponsa*). Common surface-feeding duck of swamps and woodland streams, breeding from southern Canada to Gulf of Mexico; winters southward from Missouri, Illinois, and Maryland. *Plant food* (90%). CHOICE: aneilema (keisak), arrowhead (common), barley, beech, buckwheat (common), bulrush (Cuban, water), chestnut, corn, flatsedge (redroot), millet (browntop, foxtail, proso), oak (blackjack, bur, pin, southern red, water, white), oat, pecan, potamogeton (floatingleaf), redroot (blood), rye, ryegrass, smartweed (swamp, water), sorghum (grain), swamp-privet, waterelm, wheat, wildrice. FAIR: arrowarum, ash (white), barnyardgrass, beggarticks (Becks), burreed (giant, greenfruited), chufa, duckweed, elm, hickory (water), hornwort, mannagrass (fowl), millet (Japanese), panicum (redtop), rice, stonewort, waterlily (yellow Mexican), watershield, wildcelery. *Animal food.* Ants, beetles, crustaceans, mollusks, spiders, truebugs. *Nest.* Frequently in cavities and holes in trees, and in nesting boxes. *Attracting.* Grow any of their choice foods in ponds, flooded fields, and woodlands. Farmers' Bulletin No. 2218 (see **duck**) explains practical ways to establish and maintain good duck habitats. To attract wood ducks in the nesting season, save trees with nesting crevices, or erect nesting boxes (see the birdhouse table, section 3, for specifications). A nest box in a pond or stream may be placed 2 or 3 feet above high water, so it will not be flooded, and may be reached easily from a boat for inspection and maintenance. On solid ground, the boxes should be set at least 8 feet high, beyond the reach of curious humans; the entrance hole should be clearly visible to ducks on the water. Treat wooden boxes with a preservative; paint metal boxes with aluminum to help keep them cool. The box should be made safe from predators, especially raccoons. A flaring, cone-shaped piece of sheet metal can be used beneath boxes set on posts or small trees; on large trees, a 3-foot band of sheet metal is effective. Boxes on thin posts or metal poles can be guarded with soft sheet aluminum folded over the post into a thin-edged "sandwich," 9 inches wide and 3 feet high. The entrance of a wooden box may be guarded by masking it with a 6-inch square of sheet metal with a 3x4-inch elliptical hole. A 4x4x10-inch wooden entrance tunnel has been found an effective deterrent in Massachusetts, but not in Maryland, where raccoons evidently are smaller. Additional details may be found in "Improved Nest Structures for Wood Ducks" U.S. Department of Interior Wildlife Leaflet No. 458.

dunlin (also known as red-backed sandpiper, and American and red-backed dunlin; *Erolia alpina*). The compact flocks are fairly common during the winter months on the Atlantic and Gulf coasts from Massachusetts to

Florida and Texas. *Animal food* (nearly 100%). Crustaceans, insects, and worms are the chief food supply. *Plant food.* Eelgrass. *Nest.* On the ground, in saltmarshes or near freshwater lakes and ponds in the arctic.

eagle, American. See eagle, bald.

eagle, bald (also called American eagle; *Haliaeetus leucocephalus*). Uncommon in much of eastern North America. Resident in southeast and Gulf states but the population is limited. Emblem of the United States. *Animal food* (100%). Chiefly carrion and fish; also birds (crippled ducks), domestic fowl, mice, muskrats, rabbits, snakes, squirrels, and rarely a lamb. *Nest.* Frequently in baldcypress, pine (longleaf); occasionally in blackmangrove, elm, hickory, maple, oak (white), pine (eastern white, loblolly, red, shortleaf), poplar, sycamore, and on rocky cliffs. Leave large nesting trees, especially those with used nests, as eagles return to the same nest year after year.

eagle, brown. See eagle, golden.

eagle, golden (also called brown eagle; *Aquila chrysaetos*). Uncommon resident from New York northward to northern Ontario and Labrador; casual elsewhere in the East and South. *Animal food* (100%). Birds, rodents, and other small mammals. *Nest.* Frequently in cliffs or large oaks (white), pine, poplar, spruce, sycamore.

eagle, Mexican. See caracara.

egret, American. See egret, common.

egret, blue. See heron, little blue.

egret, cattle (*Bubulcus ibis*). Common resident of swamps and pastures in Gulf and south Atlantic coast areas. *Animal food* (100%). Feed chiefly on insects flushed by grazing cattle. *Nest.* Frequently in buttonbush, maple (red), oak (live), redcedar, willow, yaupon.

egret, common (also called American and white egret; *Casmerodius albus*). Common summer resident of marshes, ponds, lakes, and swamps southward from Minnesota and New Jersey; winters in southern states. *Animal food* (100%). Chiefly crayfish, fish, frogs, snakes. *Nest.* Frequently in baldcypress, blackmangrove, bulrush, buttonbush, mangrove, maple, osageorange, privet, redcedar, willow, yaupon; occasionally in cottonwood, elm, hackberry, oak, and on plank platforms. *Attracting.* Fertile pasturelike edges of shallow ponds attract them to feed.

egret, little white. See egret, snowy.

egret, reddish (*Dichromanassa rufescens*). Rare, except on Florida Keys and Texas Gulf coast, in brackish-water areas. *Animal food* (100%). Chiefly fish, frogs, tadpoles. *Nest.* Frequently in mangrove, yucca; occasionally on the ground in grass or glasswort.

egret, snowy (also called little white egret, snowy heron, and little snowy; *Leucophoyx thula*). Common resident of ponds, lakes, marshes, and swamps in states from South Carolina southward. *Animal food* (100%). Chiefly crayfish, cutworms, fish, grasshoppers, lizards, moccasins; also aquatic insects, crabs, frogs. *Nest.* Frequently in baldcypress, bulrush, buttonbush, forestiera, mangrove, redcedar, willow, yaupon. *Attracting.* Provide shallow ponds and wet pasture areas for feeding.

egret, white. See egret, common.

eider, American. See eider, common.

eider, common (also called American eider and eider duck; *Somateria mollissima*). Diving duck; common resident on north Atlantic coast from Labrador to Maine; winters regularly as far south as Long Island, and casually to North Carolina. *Animal food* (nearly 100%). Mollusks 70%, crustaceans 15%, fishes 9%, echinoderms 3%. *Nest.* Frequently on rock ledges, on the ground, or in mosses, arctic region.

eider, king (*Somateria spectabilis*). Diving duck; breeds on arctic coasts; winters to Great Lakes and Long Island, occasionally farther south. *Animal food* (95%). Mollusks 45%, crustaceans 19%, echinoderms 17%, insects 5%. *Plant food.* Eelgrass, widgeongrass. *Nest.* On the ground or among rocks, lined with down, arctic region.

falcon. See caracara, peregrine falcon, gyrfalcon, and pigeon and sparrow hawk.

falcon, peregrine (also called duck hawk; *Falco peregrinus*). Uncommon resident from Tennessee and Kansas northward to arctic; winters to Gulf of Mexico and Panama. *Animal food* (100%). Chiefly birds. *Nest.* Frequently on rocky cliffs and bluffs, and in baldcypress and sycamore; occasionally on tall buildings.

finch, black shore. See sparrow, dusky seaside.

finch, blue. See bunting, indigo.

finch, indigo. See bunting, indigo.

finch, purple (*Carpodacus purpureus*). Common summer resident of orchards, towns, and woodlands in northern states and Canada; winters southward to northern Florida. State bird of New Hampshire. *Plant food* (nearly 100%). CHOICE: fruit, seeds, or nut meats of ash (white), birch, boxelder, butternut, canarygrass, corn, elm (American), fir (balsam), hemp, honeysuckle (Amur), millet (browntop, foxtail, proso), mulberry, oat, osage-orange, peach, peanut, pine (loblolly, shortleaf, slash), privet (Chinese, glossy, Japanese), pumpkin, ragweed (giant), redcedar, safflower, smoke-tree, spruce (white), sudangrass, sunflower (common, cultivated), sweet-gum, tamarack; also cornbread, honey syrup. FAIR: buds or flowers of apple, beech, buckwheat, cherry (mazzards, sour), elm, maple, peach, pear; also peanutbutter and fruits or seeds of blackgum, bulrush (saltmarsh), coral-berry, cotoneaster, elaeagnus (autumn), grape, hophornbeam, poplar, pos-sumhaw, pyracantha, rape, rye, sumac (smooth), sycamore, yellow-poplar. *Animal food.* Aphids, caterpillars, suet. *Nest.* Frequently in alder, spruce (red), willow; occasionally in apple, fir, pine, redcedar, and tamarack, in northern states and Canada. *Attracting.* Purple finches come readily to a feeder for hemp, nut meats, pumpkin, safflower, squash, and sunflower seeds.

finch, southern pine. See sparrow, Bachman's.

firebird. See tanager, scarlet.

fish duck. See merganser, (common, hooded, and red-breasted).

fish hawk. See osprey.

flicker, northern and southern. See flicker, yellow-shafted.

flicker, yellow-shafted (also called yellowhammer; *Colaptes auratus*). Includes two subspecies, northern and southern flicker. Species is a member of woodpecker family. Common summer resident of woods and lawns from tree limit in Canada to the Gulf, wintering as far north as the Great Lakes. "Yellowhammer" is the state bird of Alabama. *Animal food* (90% summer, 40% winter). Chiefly ants and beetles; also bugs, caterpillars, cockroaches, crickets, grasshoppers, and suet. *Plant food.* CHOICE: ampelopsis (heartleaf), beech, blackgum, blueberry, cherry (black, mahaleb, mazzard, pin), creeper (Virginia), dogwood (alternateleaf, flowering, pagoda, roughleaf, tatarian), hackberry (common, sugar), magnolia (southern), poisonivy, tupelo (water). FAIR: blackberry, cherry (choke), corn, dahoon, elder (American, scarlet), grape (frost), greenbrier (cat, laurel), hawthorn, holly (American), honeysuckle (woodbine), huckleberry, mulberry, oak, oat, plum (garden), poisonsumac, pokeberry (common), possumhaw, ragweed (common), raspberry, redcedar, rye, serviceberry (downy), spicebush (common), strawberry, tallowtree, waxmyrtle (northern), wheat, winterberry (common). *Nest.* Frequently in a birdhouse or a hole in a stub, tree, or building. *Attracting.* Flickers often live close to human habitation and feed extensively in gardens, cultivated land, orchards, pastures, and woods. They sometimes feed on peanutbutter and suet at feeders. The birdhouse table (section 3) shows specifications of birdboxes and hollow-log houses suitable for flickers. Two or 3 inches of wood shavings or sawdust should be placed in the bottom of the cavity. Sparrow hawk, saw-whet and screech owls, starling, and red-bellied and red-headed woodpeckers also may use the house designed for flickers.

flinthead. See ibis, wood.

flycatcher. Thirteen members of the family known as "tyrant flycatchers" (Tyrannidae) may be found east of the Mississippi. Eight are named flycatchers (Acadian, great crested, least, olive-sided, scissor-tailed, Traill's, vermilion, yellow-bellied); the other five are the kingbirds (eastern, gray, western) and the eastern phoebe and the eastern wood pewee. A few of these species eat fruit, but their chief foods are insects, which they catch in flight.

flycatcher, Acadian (*Empidonax virescens*). Uncommon summer resident, and generally unnoticed, in deciduous woods from the Great Lakes and New York to the Gulf of Mexico; winters in Central America. *Animal food* (about 97%). Chiefly ants, bees, beetles, bugs, flies, moths, spiders, wasps. *Plant food.* Blackberry, raspberry. *Nest.* Frequently in baldcypress, beech, dogwood, hemlock, hickory, maple (sugar), oak (post, water, white), sweetgum, witchhazel.

flycatcher, alder. See flycatcher, Traill's.

flycatcher, Canadian. See warbler, Canada.

flycatcher, crested. See flycatcher, great crested.

flycatcher, great crested (also called crested flycatcher; *Myiarchus crinitus*). Common summer resident of woodlands and near dwellings from southern Canada to Gulf of Mexico; winters in Central America and southern Florida. *Animal food* (90%). Chiefly beetles, caterpillars, crickets, grasshoppers, moths, spiders, wasps. *Plant food.* CHOICE: creeper (Virginia), mulberry, sassafras. FAIR: blackberry, blueberry, cherry (black, choke, pin), dogwood (roughleaf), elder (American), grape, pokeberry (common), raspberry, spicebush (common). *Nest.* Frequently in gourds or wooden birdhouses, and in natural cavities or woodpecker holes in a stump or tree. *Attracting.* Erect a birdhouse for them. (See the birdhouse table in section 3 for size.) Provide shrubs or trees that produce choice fruits.

flycatcher, least (also called chebec; *Empidonax minimus*). Common summer inhabitant of woodlands and orchards, north from Oklahoma and the North Carolina mountains to southern Canada; migrates through southern United States to winter quarters in Central America. *Animal food* (nearly 100%). Chiefly beetles, bugs, caterpillars, weevils. *Nest.* Frequently in alder, apple, aspen (quaking), birch, chokecherry, dogwood (redosier), fir, hemlock, larch, maple, mountainash, pine, poplar, spruce.

flycatcher, olive-sided (*Nuttallornis borealis*). Uncommon summer resident of coniferous forests from southern Canada to North Carolina mountains; winters in South America. *Animal food* (nearly 100%). Ants, bees, beetles, wasps. *Nest.* Frequently in fir, spruce (black); occasionally in alder, pine (eastern white).

flycatcher, pewee. See wood pewee, eastern.

flycatcher, scissor-tailed (also called bird of paradise; *Muscivora forficata*). Common summer resident of shade trees and prairies from Kansas to Louisiana; winters in Central America; occasional in Florida. State bird of Oklahoma. *Animal food* (nearly 100%). Chiefly crickets and grasshoppers; also beetles, wasps, weevils. *Plant food.* Pokeberry. *Nest.* Frequently in elm, hackberry, Jerusalemthorn, oak (live, post, water), pecan; occasionally in other trees, and iron or wooden framework. *Attracting.* Plant or protect their nesting trees along fencerows and about your home.

flycatcher, Traill's (also called alder flycatcher; *Empidonax traillii*). Common summer resident of thickets near streams from Kansas and West Virginia northward into Canada; winters in the tropics; migrates through southern states. *Animal food* (about 95%). Chiefly bees, beetles, caterpillars, flies, grasshoppers, moths, wasps. *Plant food.* Blackberry, dogwood (rough-leaf), elder (American), raspberry, redcedar. *Nest.* Frequently in valley or mountain thickets of alder, buttonbush, chokecherry, dogwood (gray, red-osier), elder (American), honeysuckle (tatarian), ninebark, osageorange, privet (European), rose, spirea, willow.

flycatcher, vermilion (*Pyrocephalus rubinus*). A southwestern flycatcher; occasional winter visitor of open woodlands and swamps in Arkansas, Louisiana, Mississippi, and Florida. *Animal food* (100%). Beetles, grasshoppers. *Nest.* Frequently in cottonwood, sycamore, willow.

flycatcher, Wilson's. See warbler, Wilson's.

flycatcher, yellow-bellied (*Empidonax flaviventris*). Uncommon summer resident from Canadian provinces to Minnesota and Pennsylvania; winters in Central America. *Animal food* (nearly 100%). Beetles, caterpillars, leaf-rollers, weevils. *Nest.* Frequently in upturned roots of a fallen tree trunk, in low bushes, or on ground in sphagnum moss.

foulmart. See frigate-bird.

frigate-bird, magnificent (also called foulmart, boatswain-bird, and man-o'-war bird; *Fregata magnificens*). Common sea bird over the Florida Keys and along the Gulf coast to Texas. *Animal food* (100%). Chiefly fish. *Nest.* Sticks and morningglory vines set on top of low bushes and sometimes on rocks, chiefly in West Indies.

gadwall (also called gray duck; *Anas strepera*). Surface-feeding duck; uncommon but regular breeder in northern states and Canada; winters in ponds and marshes of all southern states. *Plant food* (90%). CHOICE: arrow-head (delta), barley, barnyardgrass, bulrush (American, saltmarsh), corn, millet (foxtail, Japanese, proso), naiad (northern, southern), oat, panicum (fall), poolmat, potamogeton (baby), rice, rye, sorghum (grain), wheat, widgeongrass. FAIR: algae (filamentous), chufa, cutgrass (rice), duckweed, flatsedge (redroot), glasswort (woody), hornwort, lovegrass (teal), smart-weed (bigroot, curltop, Pennsylvania, swamp), stonewort. *Animal food.* Aquatic insects, mollusks, snails. *Nest.* On the ground in marshes, or among bushes and trees on higher ground, principally in western United States and Canada. *Attracting.* Gadwalls accompany other species of duck to ponds and duck fields for feeding.

gallinule common (also called Florida gallinule, moorhen, and water chicken; *Gallinula chloropus*). Common summer resident of large marshes from southern Ontario and Massachusetts southward to the Gulf of Mexico; winters in the Gulf region. *Animal food* (perhaps 60%). Insects, snails, worms. *Plant food.* Chiefly grasses, rootlets, seeds. *Nest.* A buoyant platform in cattail, cowlily, pickerelweed, or on a log or stump.

gallinule, Florida. See gallinule, common.

gallinule, purple (*Porphyrula martinica*). Common yearlong resident from Texas to South Carolina in swamps and ponds; winters widely in all eastern North America. *Plant food* (75%). CHOICE: banana, bread (white or raisin), cockspur (coast), duckweed, knotgrass, rice, signalgrass, wildmillgrass. FAIR: panicum, spikerush, widgeongrass. *Animal food.* Chiefly aquatic beetles and bugs; also ants, caterpillars, damselflies, dragonflies, flies, mollusks, spiders. *Nest.* A platform on floating islands, in swamps, ponds, and rice fields, especially in cattail, pickerelweed, rice, or willow.

gannet (*Morus bassanus*). The largest bird of the north Atlantic coast; breeds commonly on islands of the St. Lawrence River; winters along the Atlantic coast from Virginia to Florida, casual on Gulf of Mexico coast. *Animal food* (nearly 100%). Fish. *Nest.* On high ledges of rocky islands.

gnatcatcher, blue-gray (also called eastern blue-gray gnatcatcher; *Polioptila caerulea*). Seldom seen but fairly common summer resident of woodland habitat from the Great Lakes and New Jersey to the Gulf coast; winters from South Carolina and Texas coasts to Central America. *Animal food* (100%). Caddisflies, flies, gnats, locusts. *Nest.* Frequently in apple, elm, locust (black), oak (bear, bur, post, white), redcedar, sweetgum.

goatsucker. A family (Caprimulgidae) that includes the chuck-will's-widow, common nighthawk, poor-will (a western bird), and whip-poor-will. Their foods are insects caught on the wing and they are commonly seen in the evening or heard at night.

godwit, Hudsonian (*Limosa haemastica*). Migrant in fall on the Atlantic coast, and in the Mississippi valley in spring; arctic tundra breeder; winters in Argentina. *Animal food* (50%). Clamworms, crustaceans, fly larvae, mosquitoes, snails. *Plant food.* CHOICE: bulrush, cranberry (small). FAIR: bogbean, smartweed. *Nest.* On the ground, lined with grass and leaves, in arctic.

godwit, marbled (*Limosa fedoa*). Rare; seldom seen in eastern North America except on coasts from South Carolina to Texas. *Animal food* (50%). Chiefly beetles, fly larvae, grasshoppers; also crustaceans, mollusks (univalves). *Plant food.* CHOICE: potamogeton (sago). FAIR: bulrush. *Nest.* On the ground in dry fields from Minnesota northwestward into Canada.

gold-crest. See kinglet, golden-crowned.

goldeneye, Barrow's (also called goldeneye duck; *Bucephala islandica*). Diving duck; uncommon winter resident from Newfoundland to New England; breeds in northeast Canada. *Animal food* (80%). Crustaceans 18%, fish 1%, insects 36%, mollusks 19%. *Plant food.* Bulrush (water), potamogeton (sago). *Nest.* Frequently in cavities in trees, occasionally on the ground.

goldeneye, common (also called goldeneye duck, and whistler; *Bucephala clangula*). Uncommon diving duck of northern states and Canada; winters casually from southern Canada to the Gulf of Mexico. *Animal food* (75%). Chiefly crabs 30%, insects 28%, mollusks 10%, fish 3%; mussels and other shellfish. *Plant food.* CHOICE: bulrush (river, water), corn, cutgrass (rice), potamogeton (baby, floatingleaf, sago, thorowort), smartweed (bigroot, curltop, Pennsylvania), wildcelery. *Nest.* Frequently in cavities in trees; also in nesting boxes, as specified for wood ducks.

goldfinch, American (also called common and eastern goldfinch, wild canary, and thistlebird; *Spinus tristis*). Common summer resident of intermingled woods and open, weedy areas from southern Canada to the upper south, and to the southern end of the Appalachians. Winters throughout the east from the Gulf coast states to Canada. State bird of Washington; "eastern goldfinch" is the state bird of Iowa and New Jersey. *Plant food* (nearly 100%). CHOICE: alder, birch (gray, paper, river), burdock (smaller), canarygrass, catnip, chickweed, chicory, coreopsis, corn (cracked), cornbread, cornflower, cosmos, dandelion, elm (American, Siberian), fleabane (daisy), goosefoot, hemlock, hemp, hornbeam (American), joepyeweed (spotted), larch (European, Japanese), lettuce (blue), millet (foxtail, pearl), mulberry, nut meats, oat (common), osageorange, peanut, pecan meats, pine (loblolly, shortleaf, slash), ragweed (common), rape, salsify (meadow), serviceberry (Allegheny), smoketree, spruce, sudangrass, sunflower (blackhead, cultivated, prairie), sweetgum, thistle, turnip, velvetgrass (common), zinnia. FAIR: algae (filamentous), beggarticks, carrot (wild), coneflower, goldenrod, honeysuckle (tatarian), rose (multiflora), sorghum (grain), sourwood, sowthistle (common), sycamore (American), teasel (venuscup), trumpetcreeper (common). *Animal food.* Aphids, caterpillars. *Nest.* Frequently in apple, birch, blackberry, cottonwood, dogwood (gray, redosier, silky), elder, elm, hawthorn, maple, ninebark, pear, pine (shortleaf), poplar, rose, sunflower (cultivated), thistle, willow. *Attracting.* They sometimes come to feeders for hemp, millet, and nut meats, but prefer seeds of garden flowers and weeds.

goldfinch, common. See goldfinch, American.

goldfinch, eastern. See goldfinch, American.

goosander. See merganser, common.

goose, blue (sometimes miscalled "blue brant"; *Chen caerulescens*). Abundant winter resident of marshes and rice fields in coastal Louisiana, less abundant in east Texas. *Plant food* (100%). CHOICE: bulrush (American, Olney, saltmarsh), cattail (narrowleaf), cordgrass (gulf, marshhay, smooth), cutgrass (giant), horsetail, marshcress (bog), panicum (torpedo), rice, ryegrass, saltgrass (seashore). FAIR: bermudagrass, bluestem, bristlegrass, burreed (giant), cabbage, dropseed, fescue, lovegrass, panicum, paspalum (mudbank), podgrass (shore), reed, sedge, smartweed, spikerush (square-stem), spinach. *Nest.* On the ground, near water, in the Canadian arctic.

goose, brent. See brant.

goose, Canada (also called gray goose, honker, and outarde; *Branta canadensis*). Common winter resident of grain fields and sandy shores from Illinois to Texas, on the Atlantic seaboard from Maryland to northern Florida, and the Gulf coast; summer resident in marshes of northern states and Canada. *Plant food* (nearly 100%). CHOICE: alfalfa, barley (cultivated, wild), barnyardgrass, bilberry (bog), blueberries, brome, bulrush (alkali, American, tule), chufa, clover (crimson, white), cordgrass (marshhay), corn, crowberry (black), eelgrass, millet (foxtail, proso), oat (common, wild), peanut, potamogeton (sago), redroot (blood), rice, rye, ryegrass (Italian), saltgrass (seashore), sealettuce, shoalgrass (marine), sorghum (grain), timothy, wheat, widgeongrass. FAIR: bermudagrass, cabbage, fescue, glasswort, marshcress (bog), millet (browntop), naiad (southern), orchardgrass, panicum (fall), paspalum (bull), polypogon (rabbitfoot), smartweed (Pennsylvania), soybeans (sometimes the beans swell in the esophagus and cause death by impaction and pressure), spikerush, spinach. *Nest.* On the ground in marshes; also in captivity, in man-made nests of baskets and galvanized tubs. *Attracting.* Grow winter grazing crops (clovers, ryegrass, wheat); provide fall and winter grains (chufa tubers, corn, rice, grain sorghums). "Control burn" marshlands in fall and winter—but if you have never done this before, get advice from your local Soil Conservation Service technician. To decoy a wild flock until it gets accustomed to returning each winter (2 years), obtain tame decoys, preferably Canada geese.

goose, gray. See goose, Canada.

goose, snow (*Chen hyperborea*). Includes two subspecies: greater snow goose, which winters on the Atlantic coast, New Jersey to North Carolina; and lesser snow goose, a common winter resident of Louisiana and Texas Gulf coast fields; less abundant elsewhere. *Plant food* (nearly 100%). CHOICE: barley (wild), bulrush (American, saltmarsh), cattail (narrowleaf), cordgrass (gulf, marshhay, smooth), crowberry (black), horsetail, rice, saltgrass (seashore), wheat, wildrice. FAIR: bermudagrass, bluestem, bristlegrass, cabbage, dropseed, fescue, glasswort, lovegrass, panicum, reed, sedge, smartweed, spikerush (squarestem), spinach. *Animal food.* Negligible in winter. *Nest.* On the ground, in Canadian arctic.

goose, speckle-belly. See goose, white-fronted.

goose, white-fronted (also called speckle-belly and speckle-belly goose; *Anser albifrons*). Uncommon winter resident of grain fields and marshes west of Mississippi River—Louisiana and Texas Gulf coast, casual elsewhere in eastern North America. *Plant food* (nearly 100%). CHOICE: barley (cultivated), barnyardgrass, bulrush, cattail, cockspur, oat (common), panicum, rice, wheat. FAIR: cabbage, oat (wild), spinach. *Animal food.* Negligible in winter. *Nest.* A depression lined with grass, feathers, and down, usually near freshwater lakes, in arctic region.

goshawk (also called eastern and American goshawk and blue darter; *Accipiter gentilis*). Common summer resident of woodland and open country in northern states and Canada; winters in breeding range and, casually, farther southward. *Animal food* (100%). Birds (blackbird, crow, ruffed grouse, blue jay, and others), chipmunk, cottontail, squirrel (gray, red). *Nest.* Frequently in beech, pine (eastern white, jack).

goshawk, American and **eastern.** See goshawk.

gourdhead. See ibis, wood.

grackle, boat-tailed (also called chock, jackdaw, and great-tailed grackle; *Cassidix mexicanus*). Common resident of brushy tidal areas and in towns along the Atlantic and Gulf coasts from the Carolinas to Texas. *Animal food* (65% summer, 35% winter). Beetles, caterpillars, crabs, crayfish, crickets, dragonflies, fish, frogs, grasshoppers, lizards, tadpoles, toads, and other insects and mammals. *Plant food.* CHOICE: bread, corn, fig, pecan, rice. FAIR: bristlegrass, chufa, grape, oat (common), palmetto (cabbage), tallowtree. *Nest.* Frequently in colonies, in baccharis, bulrush, buttonbush, cattail, cordgrass, hawthorn, oak (live), pine, sawgrass, waxmyrtle, willow, yucca. *Attracting.* Bread, corn, or meat scraps often bring them to a feeding station.

grackle, bronzed. See grackle, common.

grackle, common (also called crow blackbird; *Quiscalus quiscula*). Includes bronzed, Florida, and purple varieties. Common summer resident of swamp thickets in eastern North America; winters southward from Kansas, Ohio, and New Jersey. *Plant food* (80% winter, 50% summer). CHOICE: beech, bread (white), chestnut (American), chinkapin (Allegheny), corn, cornbread, elaeagnus (cherry), grape (muscadine), mountainash (American, European), oak (Arkansas, black, blackjack, bur, laurel, northern pin, northern red, pin, post, runner, scarlet, shingle, southern red, water, willow), oat (common), pea (garden), peanutbutter, pecan, pine (eastern white), potato chips, rice, sorghum (grain), sunflower (cultivated), wheat. FAIR: apple, blackberry, bristlegrass, canarygrass, cherry (black), chickencorn, chokeberry (red), croton (woolly), dogwood (flowering), elder (American), fig, greenbrier, hackberry (common), hemp, millet (pearl, proso), mulberry, palmetto (cabbage), ragweed (common), rye, serviceberry (downy), sudangrass, waxmyrtle (southern). *Animal food.* Bees, crayfish, crickets, earthworms, grasshoppers, snails, sowbugs, spiders; also suet. *Nest.* Frequently in apple, arborvitae (eastern), baldcypress, birch, blackmangrove, buttonbush, fir, forestiera, honeylocust, honeysuckle (tatarian), oak (laurel, live, water), orange, pear, pine (eastern white, longleaf, red), redcedar, spruce (Norway), willow; occasionally in other trees, shrubs, and cattail. *Attracting.* Grackles come regularly to bird feeders to eat bread, corn (whole or cracked), nut meats, oats, grain sorghum, suet, sunflower seeds, wheat.

grackle, Florida. See grackle, common.

grackle, great-tailed. See grackle, boat-tailed.

grackle, purple. See grackle, common.

grassbird. See sandpiper, pectoral.

gray-back, greater. See dowitcher, long-billed.

grebe, eared. (*Podiceps caspicus*). Resident of ponds westward from Iowa and Minnesota; casual eastward. *Animal food* (100%). Chiefly fish; also aquatic insects, mollusks, small crustaceans. *Nest.* Frequently in bulrush and cattail marshes.

grebe, Holboell's. See grebe, red-necked.

grebe, horned (*Podiceps auritus*). Common in ponds of eastern North America in winter; breeds in northern states and Canada. *Animal food.* Same as eared grebe, above. *Nest.* Same as eared grebe, above.

grebe, least (*Podiceps dominicus*). Includes a subspecies called Mexican grebe. Resident in southern Texas. *Animal food.* Same as eared grebe, above. *Nest.* Same as eared grebe, above.

grebe, pied-billed. (also called dabchick, didapper, divedapper, hell diver, and water witch; *Podilymbus podiceps*). The common grebe of ponds in eastern North America; breeds from Canada southward; winters from Tennessee and Maryland to the Gulf coast. *Animal food* (100%). Chiefly crayfish; also aquatic insects, mollusks, small fish. *Nest.* Frequently in bulrush and cattail marshes.

grebe, red-necked (also called Holboell's grebe; *Podiceps grisegena*). Fairly common in winter in Atlantic coastal waters from Newfoundland to Florida; breeds occasionally in northern states, commonly in Canada. *Animal food* (100%). Chiefly fish; also aquatic insects, mollusks, small crustaceans. *Nest.* Frequently in bulrush and cattail marshes.

grebe, western (*Aechmophorus occidentalis*). Casual on lakes east of the Great Plains. *Animal food* (100%). Chiefly aquatic insects, crayfish, fish, mollusks. *Nest.* Frequently in bulrush, cattail, and reed in western states and Canada.

greenlets. See vireos.

grosbeak, American pine. See grosbeak, pine.

grosbeak, black-headed (*Pheucticus melanocephalus*). Casual in Alabama, Florida, Louisiana, and eastern Texas. *Animal food* (70%). Snails, spiders, and a great variety of insects; also butter. *Plant food.* CHOICE: apricot, blackberry, bread, cherry (mazzard, sour), crabapple (pearleaf), elder, fig, gooseberry, mulberry, pea (garden), plum (garden), raspberry, serviceberry, strawberry, sunflower, watermelon. FAIR: wheat. *Nest.* In trees or shrubs, in western states. *Attracting.* White bread and butter sometimes attracts black-headed grosbeaks to feeders.

grosbeak, blue (*Guiraca caerulea*). Fairly common summer resident of brushy areas and grain fields in southern states from Missouri and Maryland southward, except in Appalachian mountains; winters in Central America. *Plant food* (50%). CHOICE: blackberry, bristlegrass (green, yellow), corn, Johnsongrass, millet (Japanese, pearl), oats (common), panicum, sorghum (grain), sunflower, wheat, wildrice. FAIR: crabgrass, smartweed. *Animal food.* Ants, beetles, bugs, caterpillars, grasshoppers. *Nest.* Frequently in blackberry, rhododendron, tungoiltree; occasionally in about 20 other shrubs and trees. *Attracting.* Blue grosbeaks sometimes come to feeders for grain sorghum and sunflower seed. They are attracted regularly to fields of choice grains and grass seed, usually alighting directly on the seed head to feed.

grosbeak, Canadian pine. See grosbeak, pine.

grosbeak, cardinal. See cardinal.

grosbeak, evening (*Hesperiphona vespertina*). Common resident of woodland habitat and towns in Canadian provinces; usually winter also in northern states, occasionally as far south as Georgia. *Plant food* (95%). CHOICE: apple seeds, ash (black, white), beech, boxelder, buckwheat (common), cherry (black, choke, mazzard, pin, sour), dogwood (flowering), elder, elm (American), fir, hemp, honeysuckle (woodbine), hornbeam (American), mountainash, osageorange, peanut, pine (eastern white, loblolly, shortleaf, slash, Virginia), redcedar, safflower, serviceberry, spruce (white), strawberry, sunflower (cultivated), sweetgum. FAIR: blackberry, catalpa, corn, cottonwood (eastern), crabapple, hackberry, hawthorn, maple (sugar), oak (scarlet), poisonsumac, poplar buds, rose (multiflora), sumac (staghorn), willow buds, yellow-poplar. *Animal food.* Beetles, caterpillars, spiders. *Nest.* Frequently in fir, maple, pine (eastern white, jack, red), spruce (black); occasionally in birch, larch, oak (black). *Attracting.* They come to feeders to eat ravenously of peanuts, safflower, and sunflower seeds. They feed heavily, of course, on fruits and seeds of trees. The occasional visits of flocks into southern states is caused by exhaustion of winter foods in their normal northern habitats.

grosbeak, Newfoundland pine. See grosbeak, pine.

grosbeak, pine (also called pine bullfinch and American pine grosbeak; *Pinicola enucleator*). Includes Alaskan, Canadian, and Newfoundland subspecies. Summer resident in Canadian coniferous forests; uncommon winter visitor to Great Lakes and New England states. *Plant food* (95%). CHOICE: seeds, buds, or fruits of apple, ash (white), beggarticks (devils), bittersweet (American), blackberry, boxelder, cherry (mazzard, sour), crabapple (seed), dogwood (flowering), fir (balsam), grape, hemp, mountainash

(American, European), pine (jack), redcedar, spruce (Norway). FAIR: bittersweet, crowberry, hawthorn, hickory, huckleberry (black), maple (sugar), ragweed, strawberry, sumac (staghorn), viburnum (blackhaw, witherod), willow buds, yellow-poplar. *Animal food.* Includes beetles and caterpillars. *Nest.* Frequently in conifers and redcedar. *Attracting.* Pine grosbeaks are rarely attracted to feeding stations but feed readily from the plants that have their choice foods. They visit occasionally in northern states when alpine food supplies are unusually scarce.

grosbeak, rose-breasted (*Pheucticus ludovicianus*). Common summer resident of thickets, woods, farms, and gardens from the southern Canadian provinces southward to Missouri, Ohio, New Jersey, and Appalachian mountains to Georgia; migrates in fall and spring through southern states to and from Central American wintering areas. *Plant food* (50%). CHOICE: barberry (Japanese), beech, cherry (black, choke, mazzard, pin, sour), corn, elder (American, European red, scarlet), hemp, honey syrup, mulberry, oat (common), pea (garden), serviceberry (Allegheny, downy), strawberry, sunflower, wheat. FAIR: blackberry, blackgum, dogwood (flowering, roughleaf), elm, hickory, ragweed, smartweed. *Animal food.* Chiefly beetles; also ants, bees, caterpillars, scale insects, suet, wasps. *Nest.* Frequently in arborvitae, boxelder, elder, elm, rhododendron; occasionally in beech, birch, cherry, chokecherry, hawthorn, hemlock (eastern), pear. *Attracting.* Trees such as beech and mulberry are especially attractive when the nuts and fruit are ripe.

grouse, Canada. See grouse, spruce.

grouse, Hudsonian spruce. See grouse, spruce.

grouse, northern sharp-tailed. See grouse, sharp-tailed.

grouse, pinnated. See prairie chicken, greater.

grouse, pin-tail. See grouse, sharp-tailed.

grouse, ruffed (also called birch partridge and native pheasant; *Bonasa umbellus*). Includes Canada, Eastern, and Nova Scotia ruffed grouse subspecies. Resident woodland game bird of Appalachian mountains, northern states, and Canadian provinces. *Plant food* (nearly 100%). CHOICE: alder (European), apple, aspen (bigtooth, quaking), beadruby (Canada), beech, birch (paper, yellow), blackberry, blueberry (blueridge, lowbush), bluegrass (Kentucky), buckwheat (common), cherry (black, choke, mazzard, pin, sand, sour), chestnut, Christmasfern, clover (alsike, red, white), corn, dandelion, dogwood (redosier), elder (scarlet), elm (American), filbert (American, beaked), grape (frost, summer), greenbrier, hawthorn, hogpeanut (southern), hophornbeam, huckleberry, mountainash (American), mountainholly, mountainlaurel, mushroom, oak (bear, chestnut, northern, red, white), partridgeberry, raspberry, saxifrage (lettuce), selfheal (common), serviceberry (downy), snapweed (spotted), strawberry, trailing-arbutus, violet, willow (pussy), witchhazel. FAIR: barberry (Japanese), bittersweet, chokeberry (red), cottonwood (eastern), crowberry (black), currant, dogwood (roundleaf), elaeagnus (autumn), elm, foamflower (Allegheny), goldenrod (fragrant), goldthread (common), hepatica (roundlobe), maple, miterwort (common), oat (common), pear, redcedar leaves, rose (multiflora), sedge, sheepsorrel, sumac (smooth, staghorn), tickclover, viburnum (American cranberrybush, arrowwood, blackhaw, European cranberrybush, mapleleaf, nannyberry, witherod). *Animal food.* Insects, snails, spiders. *Nest.* On the ground in thick woods. *Attracting.* Ruffed-grouse populations are subject to unaccountable periodic declines that are thought to be cyclic. Attempts at management of their habitat have not been too successful. They are attracted to apples in abandoned orchards, and to green foliage such as clovers in woodland openings and tender plant shoots along streams.

grouse, sharp-tailed (also called pin-tail, sharp-tail, spike-tail, sprig-tail, or northern sharp-tailed, grouse; *Pedioecetes phasianellus*). Includes northern and prairie subspecies of sharp-tailed grouse. Fairly common game bird of prairie brushlands in Michigan, Minnesota, western Wisconsin, and the Canadian provinces of Manitoba and western Ontario. *Plant food* (100% winter, 40% summer). CHOICE: alfalfa, birch, blueberry, cherry (choke, pin), clover (sweet, white), corn, dandelion, filbert (beaked), mountainash, oak (scarlet), pasqueflower (American), poplar, sunflower, wheat, willow. FAIR: alder, aspen (quaking), bristlegrass, cherry (black), cranberry, dogwood (redosier), groundcherry, hawthorn, maple, oat (common), plum (American), poisonivy, raspberry, rose, sedge, serviceberry. *Animal food.* Beetles, crickets, grasshoppers. *Nest.* On the ground, in grassy cover. *Attracting.* Dependable methods of managing the habitat of sharp-tailed grouse have not been established. They need considerable brush-type cover which includes choice food plants. Controlled burning of woodlands helps increase supplies of buds, seeds, and fruits which are staples of their diet.

grouse, snow. See ptarmigan, willow.

grouse, spike-tail and **sprig-tail.** See grouse, sharp-tailed.

grouse, spruce (*Canachites canadensis*). Includes two subspecies, Canada grouse and Hudsonian spruce grouse. Resident game bird of wet coniferous forests in the Canadian provinces and adjoining eastern states of the United States. *Plant food* (nearly 100%). CHOICE: birch, blueberry, cowberry, crowberry (black), fir, mushroom, pine (jack), spruce (white), tamarack, thimbleberry, whortleberry (ovalleaf), willow. FAIR: beech, currant, raspberry, sedge, viburnum (American cranberrybush). *Nest.* On the ground, concealed by shrub or tree.

grouse, white. See ptarmigan, willow.

guillemot, black (also called sea pigeon; *Cepphus grylle*). Common resident of bays and coastal islands from Maine to Labrador; extends its range southward in winter to open waters off Massachusetts. *Animal food* (100%). Crustaceans, fish, and mollusks obtained by diving, sometimes deep. *Nest.* In a rock crevice, often in colonies.

gull, **Bonaparte's** (*Larus philadelphia*). Casual visitor in winter and spring along Atlantic and Gulf coasts, especially from South Carolina to Texas. *Animal food* (100%). Ants, fish, flies, marine worms, shrimp. *Nest.* Frequently in spruce, about lakes in wooded regions of Alaska and Canadian provinces.

gull, **Franklin's** (*Larus pipixcan*). Common summer resident of lakes and marshes from southern Minnesota westward; winters commonly on Louisiana and Texas Gulf coast. *Animal food* (95%). Bees, crickets, damselflies, dragonflies, fish, grasshoppers, spiders. *Plant food.* Duckweed, oat (common), wheat. *Nest.* In marshes from Minnesota westward.

gull, **glaucous** (also called burgomaster; *Larus hyperboreus*). Arctic breeder, fairly common in winter on the Atlantic coast southward to New Jersey, and occasional farther south and on the Great Lakes. *Animal food* (100%). Carrion, eggs of birds, fish, mollusks. *Nest.* On rocks and ledges, from Labrador northward.

gull, **gray-sea.** See gull, herring.

gull, **great black-backed** (*Larus marinus*). Common-to-abundant resident on Atlantic coast islands from Maine to the arctic; winters around the Great Lakes and on the Atlantic coast, to Delaware. *Animal food* (100%). Chiefly carrion, fish; also eggs of birds and young terns. *Nest.* On low rocky islands from Maine to the arctic.

gull, **herring** (also called gray-sea gull and Thayer's gull; *Larus argentatus*). The most common large sea gull in eastern United States. Winters on the Atlantic and Gulf coasts, about the Great Lakes, and other large inland lakes; breeds from Long Island to the arctic. *Animal food* (90%). Birds, carrion, crustaceans, fish, insects, mollusks, snails. *Plant food.* CHOICE: blueberry. FAIR: palmetto (cabbage). *Nest.* Usually on the ground, occasionally in trees (fir, spruce).

gull, **Iceland** (*Larus glaucoides*). Arctic breeder. Winters along the Atlantic from Newfoundland to Virginia; casual about the Great Lakes. *Animal food* (nearly 100%). Chiefly carrion, crustaceans, fish. *Plant food.* Crowberry (black). *Nest.* On rocky cliffs and sandy shores, in arctic.

gull, **ivory** (also called ice partridge; *Pagophila eburnea*). Rare south of the arctic, accidental in eastern United States. *Animal food* (100%). Chiefly carrion, lemmings. *Nest.* On rock cliffs in arctic, on a nest of green moss.

gull, **laughing** (*Larus atricilla*). Abundant summer resident on islands of the Atlantic and Gulf coasts from Maine to Texas. *Animal food* (100%). Chiefly fish and garbage. *Nest.* On the ground, on coastal islands.

gull, little (*Larus minutus*). Casual visitor from Maine to Pennsylvania. *Animal food* (100%). Chiefly fish; also insects. *Nest.* In Europe and Asia, on grassy knolls in marshes.

gull, mackerel. See tern, common.

gull, ring-billed (*Larus delawarensis*). With the exception of the herring gull, this is the most common North American gull. Breeds from Michigan to the St. Lawrence River and New York. Common winter visitor on large lakes throughout eastern United States and along the coast from Maine to Florida and Texas. *Animal food* (90%). Beetles, birds, crickets, eggs of birds, fish, grasshoppers, grubs, mice, mollusks. *Plant food.* CHOICE: camphortree, garbage, palmetto (cabbage). FAIR: laurelcherry, potamogeton (sago). *Nest.* On beaches and rocky ground.

gull, sea. See gulls.

gull, storm. See skimmer, black.

gull, Thayer's. See gull, herring.

gyrfalcon (also called black, gray, and McFarlane's gyrfalcon; *Falco rusticolus*). Arctic hawk (falcon); winters irregularly to northern states. *Animal food* (100%). Chiefly birds, especially auks but also snow buntings, guillemots, gulls, and others; also hares and lemmings. *Nest.* On ledges of cliffs, eastern arctic America to Labrador.

harrier. See hawk, marsh.

hawk. The group of birds generally recognized as "hawks" belongs to the family Accipitridae, which also includes the Old World vultures and eagles. Like eagles and vultures, hawks are raptors, that is, birds of prey; they subsist entirely on animal foods. Twenty-four species of hawks occur in eastern North America.

Four are named "kites" (Everglade, Mississippi, swallow-tailed, and white-tailed). Rather fearless birds, and especially graceful in flight, they eat insects, small reptiles, and rodents, and do not prey on other birds.

The goshawk, Cooper's hawk, and sharp-shinned hawk, members of the genus *Accipiter,* are sometimes called "bird hawks." Fast and wary, their principal prey is other birds (although they eat small animals as well).

The largest hawks, called "buteos" or "buzzard hawks," are heavy-bodied, with broad wings and tails. Individual species are the black, broadwinged, Harlan's, Harris', red-shouldered, red-tailed, rough-legged, Swainson's, and white-tailed hawks. They eat mice, rabbits, rats, snakes, and occasionally a few birds.

A fourth group, known collectively as "falcons," includes the caracara, which sometimes eats carrion; the peregrine falcon, pigeon hawk, and gyrfalcon, which prey chiefly on other birds; and the sparrow hawk, whose diet is chiefly insects, spiders, mice, and an occasional bird.

Also numbered among the hawks are the marsh hawk, a species of moderate size whose relentless hunting habits classifies him as a "harrier hawk"; and the osprey, whose diet is reflected in the epithet "fish hawk."

hawk, American rough-legged. See hawk, rough-legged.

hawk, bird. See hawk, Cooper's and sharp-shinned.

hawk, black (also called Mexican black hawk and crab hawk; *Buteogallus anthracines*). Casual visitor in lower Rio Grande valley, Texas. *Animal food* (100%). Crabs, fish, frogs, insects, lizards, rodents, snakes. *Nest.* In cottonwood and pine trees, in Mexico, central Arizona, and New Mexico.

hawk, broad-winged (*Buteo platypterus*). Common summer resident in all eastern Canadian provinces and states of United States; winters in Florida and in Central and northern South America; several usually seen together when migrating. *Animal food* (100%). Chiefly insects, lizards, rabbits, rodents, snakes; also small birds. *Nest.* In many kinds of large trees.

hawk, buzzard. See hawks.

hawk, Cooper's (also called big blue darter, bird hawk, and striker; *Accipiter cooperii*). Uncommon "bird hawk." Summer resident from southern Canada to the Gulf states; winters from Iowa and New York southward through Mexico. *Animal food* (100%). Birds (24 species including bobwhite, cowbird, dove, flicker, grackle, meadowlark, robin, starling), chipmunks, poultry, rabbits, squirrels (gray, red); also suet. *Nest.* Frequently in cottonwood, hackberry, hickory, oak (scarlet, southern red, swamp white), pine (eastern white, loblolly), sycamore, willow.

hawk, crab. See hawk, black.

hawk, duck. See falcon, peregrine.

hawk, fish. See osprey.

hawk, Harlan's (*Buteo harlani*). Winters from Arkansas and Missouri to Louisiana and Texas, occasionally eastward; summers in Alaska and western Canada. *Animal food* (100%). Chipmunks, ground-squirrels, mice, rabbits, rats. *Nest.* In spruce trees and possibly others.

hawk, harrier. See hawk, marsh.

hawk, Harris' (*Parabuteo unicinctus*). Resident from southern Texas westward; casual in Louisiana. *Animal food* (100%). Chiefly mice; also ground-squirrels, pocketgophers, rabbits, snakes. *Nest.* Frequently in cottonwood, elm, hackberry.

hawk, hen-harrier. See hawk, marsh.

hawk, killy. See hawk, sparrow.

hawk, Krider's. See hawk, red-tailed.

hawk, marsh (also called harrier hawk, hen-harrier hawk, and white-rumped hawk; *Circus cyaneus*). Common summer resident of prairie lands in Canadian provinces and eastern United States as far south as Oklahoma and Virginia; winters in the United States from Minnesota and Massachusetts southward. *Animal food* (100%). Amphibians, birds, reptiles, rodents. *Nest.* On the ground.

hawk, Mexican black. See hawk, black.

hawk-owl. See owl, hawk.

hawk, pigeon (also called merlin; *Falco columbarius*). Summers from tree limit in eastern Canadian provinces southward into the northern tier of states: winters in southern states from South Carolina to Texas and Mexico, occasionally northward. *Animal food* (100%). Chiefly birds. *Nest.* Frequently in pine (eastern white, jack), spruce (black, red, white), or on rock ledges; occasionally in linden, pine (Norway).

hawk, red-bellied. See hawk, red-shouldered.

hawk, red-shouldered (also called red-bellied hawk; *Buteo lineatus*). Yearlong resident or visitor in all states of eastern United States. *Animal food* (100%). Chiefly lizards, rabbits, rodents, snakes; also small birds, suet. *Nest.* Frequently in ash, baldcypress, beech, maple (red), oak, palmetto (cabbage), pine (eastern white, loblolly), sweetgum, sycamore, willow.

hawk, red-tailed (also called Krider's hawk and eastern red-tail; *Buteo jamaicensis*). Fairly common resident from Ontario, Quebec, and Maine southward to the Gulf of Mexico. *Animal food* (100%). Chiefly lizards, rabbits, rodents, snakes; also small birds and chickens. *Nest.* Frequently in beech, birch, cottonwood, elm, hickory, linden, maple (sugar), oak (black, live, white), pine (eastern white, loblolly, pitch, shortleaf), poplar.

hawk, rough-legged (also called American rough-legged hawk; *Buteo lagopus*). Summers in the arctic. Winters from Minnesota and Maine southward to central Oklahoma and Virginia; occasionally to Texas, Louisiana, and Georgia. *Animal food* (100%). Lemmings, mice. *Nest.* In large trees, and sometimes on ledges.

hawk, sea. See osprey.

hawk, sharp-shinned (also called bird hawk and little blue darter; *Accipiter striatus*). Uncommon summer resident in all eastern Canadian provinces and eastern United States except Florida; winters throughout eastern United States, including Florida. *Animal food* (100%). Doves, grouse, poultry, quail, rodents, small birds. *Nest.* Frequently in fir, pine (Virginia, eastern white), spruce.

hawk, short-tailed (*Buteo brachyurus*). Resident locally in Florida and Central and South America. *Animal food* (100%). Carrion (fresh), mice, rats. *Nest.* Frequently in baldcypress, magnolia, mangrove (American), palmetto (cabbage); occasionally in pine, tupelo.

hawk, snail. See kite, Everglade.

hawk, sparrow (also called killy hawk and American kestrel; *Falco sparverius*). The smallest "falcon" (hawk). Fairly common summer resident throughout eastern North America; winters commonly in open country of eastern United States, from Iowa and the New England states to the Gulf of Mexico. *Animal food* (nearly 100%). Chiefly beetles, caterpillars, crickets, dragonflies, grasshoppers, mice, spiders; occasionally birds. *Plant food.* bread. *Nest.* In natural cavities and woodpecker holes in trees. They will also occupy man-made birdhouses (see birdhouse table, section 3).

hawk, Swainson's (*Buteo swainsoni*). Casual or rare in eastern North America from southern Canada to Florida. *Animal food* (100%). Chiefly insects, lizards, rabbits, rodents, snakes; also small birds and suet. *Nest.* Frequently on the ground or ledges, or in ash, boxelder, cottonwood, poplar, sycamore, willow.

hawk, white-rumped. See hawk, marsh.

hawk, white-tailed (*Buteo albicaudatus*). Uncommon resident of southern Texas. The white-tailed hawk nests in low trees and shrubs. Its food habits are not well known.

hell diver. See grebe, pied-billed.

heron. The group of birds referred to collectively as "herons," includes the black-crowned, great blue, great white, green, little blue, Louisiana, and yellow-crowned night herons; also the egrets (cattle, common, reddish, and snowy). They feed only on animal foods—crayfish, fish, frogs and other aquatic animals, insects, mice, and snakes.

heron, black-crowned night (*Nycticorax nycticorax*). Fairly common summer resident of marshes and lakes in southern Canadian provinces; winters on the Atlantic and Gulf coasts from New York to Texas. *Animal food* (nearly 100%). Chiefly crabs, crayfish, fish (50%), frogs, shrimp; also aquatic insects, leeches, lizards, mice, mollusks. *Nest.* Frequently in apple, ash, bulrush, cane, cattail, cottonwood, elm, mangrove, maple (red), oak (bear, black, swamp white, water), pine (eastern white, pitch), redcedar, spruce (black), sycamore, willow, yaupon; occasionally in other trees, on the ground, and in shrubs.

heron, Florida. See heron, great white.

heron, great blue (also called blue crane; *Ardea herodias*). Common summer resident of marshes, swamps, and shallow ponds from southern Canadian provinces throughout eastern United States; winters from the Ohio valley and Massachusetts to the Gulf of Mexico. *Animal food* (nearly 100%). Chiefly fish but also crayfish, eels, frogs, grasshoppers, mice, snakes, tadpoles, turtles. *Nest.* Frequently in ash, baldcypress, beech, birch, bulrush, elm, fir, mangrove, maple, oak (bur, black, live, white), sycamore, tupelo, willow; occasionally other trees and on the ground, rocks, and plank platforms.

heron, great white (also called Florida heron; *Ardea occidentalis*). Common resident of Florida Keys; wanders casually northward on the Atlantic coast to North Carolina and along the Gulf coast. *Animal food* (100%). Chiefly fish. *Nest.* Frequently in blackmangrove, mangrove.

heron, green (also called green bittern and shitepoke; *Butorides virescens*). Uncommon summer resident of freshwater ponds and marshes from Minnesota to New England states and southward throughout eastern United States; winters along the coasts from South Carolina to Texas and southward. *Animal food* (100%). Chiefly crayfish, crickets, earthworms, fish, frogs, grasshoppers, lizards, snakes. *Nest.* Frequently in baccharis, buttonbush, forestiera, hackberry, oak (water), pine (pitch), spruce (Norway), willow; occasionally in other shrubs and trees; rarely on the ground.

heron, little blue (also called blue egret; *Florida caerulea*). Common summer resident of swamps, marshes, and lakes from central Oklahoma and Tennessee southward to the Gulf coast and from New York to Florida on the Atlantic coast; winters from South Carolina to Texas and southward in coastal areas. *Animal food* (100%). Chiefly crabs, crayfish, crickets, cutworms, fish, frogs, grasshoppers, lizards. *Nest.* Frequently in baldcypress, buttonbush, catalpa, forestiera, hackberry, honeylocust, maple (red), oak, redcedar, willow.

heron, Louisiana (also called tricolored heron; *Hydranassa tricolor*). Locally breeding resident of marshes and swamps in coastal areas from Maryland to Texas and Central America; wanders inland occasionally. *Animal food* (100%). Chiefly crayfish, fish, frogs, grasshoppers, lizards, snails; also leeches and tadpoles. *Nest.* Frequently in blackmangrove, mangrove, willow, yaupon; occasionally other trees and shrubs or on the ground in marshes.

heron, night. See heron, black-crowned and yellow-crowned.

heron, snowy. See egret, snowy.

heron, tricolored. See heron, Louisiana.

heron, yellow-crowned night (*Nyctanassa violacea*). Uncommon summer resident of swamps from Oklahoma to Massachusetts and southward in eastern United States; wanders northward occasionally; winters from Florida to Texas and Central America. *Animal food* (100%). Chiefly crabs, crayfish; also eels, fish, snails. *Nest.* Frequently in ash, baldcypress, blackmangrove, cottonwood, pine (loblolly), sweetgum, willow.

honker. See goose, Canada.

hummingbird, ruby-throated (*Archilochus colubris*). Common summer resident around nectar-producing plants in gardens and woodlands from southern Canada throughout eastern United States; winters in Mexico and Central America, and casually from Florida to Texas along the Gulf coast. *Plant food* (percentage unknown). CHOICE: nectar of albizzia (silktree), amaryllis, azalea, bean (scarlet runner), beebalm (oswego), buckeye, bugle (carpet), cardinalflower, chinaberry, columbine (American), coralberry, coralvine (mountain rose), dahlia, elaeagnus (cherry), eveningprimrose, fig (common), four-o'clock, fuchsia, gladiolus, hibiscus, honeysuckle (dwarf bush, Japanese, limber), honey syrup, horsechestnut, lily (tiger, turkscap), locust (black), milkweed (butterfly), morningglory, nasturtium, painted-cup, penstemon, petunia, phlox, sage (red garden, scarlet), snapdragon, snapweed (spotted), sugar, thistle, torchlily, tritonia, trumpetcreeper (common), verbena, weigela, yellow-poplar, zinnia. *Animal food.* Ants, bees, beetles, flies, and spiders form a considerable portion of the hummingbird's diet. *Nest.* Frequently in apple, beech, birch, hemlock, hickory, hophorn-beam, hornbeam, maple, oak (blackjack, live, post, southern red, water, white), pear, pine (loblolly, shortleaf, Virginia), sweetgum. *Attracting.* Hummingbirds can be attracted to water sweetened with honey or sugar and to the flowers named above. To make the syrup, use one part of honey to three parts of water, or one part of sugar to two parts of water. Boil the honey mixture for 2 or 3 minutes, to reduce the tendency to ferment. A syrup reddened with food coloring seems more attractive than colorless syrup. The syrup can be placed in various types of containers—a jar, cup, saucer, small bowl, or in any of the attractive hummingbird feeders that are sold at pet stores, and advertised in magazines such as *Audubon.* You may place the feeder a few feet from a window in a patio, hung from a tree limb, or a house eave, or anywhere you can see the birds easily.

hummingbird, rufous (*Selasphorus rufus*). Occasional winter visitor on the Gulf coast from Florida to Texas. Commonly winters in Mexico; nests in northwest states and western Canada. It feeds more heavily on insects than does the ruby-throated hummingbird, but its diet also includes nectar.

ibis, glossy (also called black curlew; *Plegadis falcinellus*). Uncommon summer resident of coastal marshes and swamps from Maryland to Texas; winters in southern Florida and Louisiana; wanders northward occasionally. *Animal food* (nearly 100%). Chiefly crayfish, cutworms, grasshoppers, snakes (moccasin); also aquatic insects, crabs, snails. *Nest.* In elder, wax-myrtle, willow.

ibis, white (also called Spanish, stone, or white curlew; *Eudocimus albus*). Common to abundant yearlong resident in coastal areas from South Carolina to Texas and to South America. Wanders casually northward to Missouri and New York. *Animal food* (nearly 100%). Aquatic insects, crabs, crayfish, cutworms, fish, grasshoppers, moccasins, snails. *Nest.* In colonies, in bald-cypress, buttonbush, elder, mangrove, maple (red), tupelo, willow.

ibis, white-faced (also called white-faced glossy ibis; *Plegadis chihi*). Uncommon resident of swamps in Florida and Louisiana; occasionally winters in southern Texas; main breeding area is South America. *Animal food* (nearly 100%). Chiefly aquatic insects, crayfish, earthworms, fish, frogs, leeches, mollusks, newts. *Nest.* On marshy ground, or in bulrush.

ibis, wood (also called American wood stork, and flinthead, gourdhead, or ironhead; *Mycteria americana*). Common resident of southern coastal swamps from Florida to Texas, Mexico, and Central America; wanders northward occasionally through eastern United States to southern Canada. *Animal food* (nearly 100%). Aquatic insects, crabs, crayfish, fish, frogs, snails, tadpoles, water snakes. *Nest.* Wood ibis nest in colonies of hundreds, in baldcypress and mangrove.

indigo bird. See bunting, indigo.

ironhead. See ibis, wood.

jack, black. See duck, ring-necked.

jack, whisky. See jay, gray.

jackdaw. See grackle, boat-tailed.

jacksnipe. See snipe, common.

jaeger (also called sea hawk and skua). Three species—long-tailed (also called long-tailed skua, *Stercorarius longicaudus*), parasitic (also called arctic skua, S. *parasiticus*), and pomarine (also called pomatorhine skua, S. *pomarinus*)—are common offshore water birds along the Atlantic coast from Greenland to Florida, and are occasionally seen ashore and inland in winter. They breed in the arctic region. Their food is carrion, fish, mollusks, and some birds and bird eggs. Jaegers are commonly seen feeding on fish over reefs offshore; they also harass gulls and other fish-eating birds and take the fish which they drop.

jay, blue (also called Semple's jay, Florida blue jay, and northern blue jay; *Cyanocitta cristata*). Common resident of farms and woodlands in eastern United States and southern Canada. *Plant food* (90% winter, 60% summer). CHOICE: beech, blueberry, bread (white), cherry (black, mahaleb, mazzard, sour), chestnut, chinkapin, corn (cracked, ground, whole), cornbread, crackers, doughnuts, elaeagnus (cherry), elder (American), fig, filbert (American, beaked), grape (cultivated, muscadine), huckleberry, mulberry, oak (blackjack, chinkapin, laurel, live, pine, post, scarlet, shingle, southern red, water, white, willow), peach, peanut, peanutbutter, pecan, persimmon (kaki), pine, plum (American, garden), pumpkin seed, sorghum (grain), squash seed, strawberries, sunflower (cultivated), walnut (black, Persian), wheat. FAIR: apple, blackberry, buckwheat (common), cherry (choke), chickencorn, hawthorn, millet (proso), oat, palmetto (cabbage), papermulberry, pear, pyracantha, rye, safflower, serviceberry, sudangrass, sugar water, sumac (smooth, staghorn), tallowtree, tupelo (water). *Animal food.* Chiefly ants, beetles, caterpillars, grasshoppers; also crustaceans, fish, frogs, mice, salamanders, snails. They will also eat pork fat, suet, and occasionally the eggs and young of other birds. *Nest.* Frequently in alder, cottonwood, elm, hackberry, hemlock, oak (black, blackjack, laurel, live, northern red, post, sawtooth, water, white, willow), orange, pecan, pine (eastern white,

loblolly, pitch, Scotch, shortleaf, slash), redcedar, tungoiltree. *Attracting.*
Blue jays come readily to feeders for bread, corn, peanuts, peanutbutter,
pecans and other nut meats, grain sorghum, sunflower seeds, and wheat.
They disdain small seeds such as millet.

jay, Canada. See jay, gray.

jay, Florida. See jay, scrub.

jay, Florida blue. See jay, blue.

jay, gray (also called camp robber, whisky jack, and Canada, Labrador,
or Newfoundland jay; *Perisoreus canadensis*). Common resident of northern
forests from Labrador and Ontario southward to northern Minnesota and
New York; winters at lower altitudes in the breeding area. *Plant food* (perhaps 50% or more). CHOICE: banana, bread, grape (cultivated), oak, oat
(common), oatmeal; also conifer seeds. FAIR: apple, elder, serviceberry,
sumac, viburnum. *Animal food.* Bees, caterpillars, fresh carrion, grasshoppers, meat (cooked or raw), wasps; also cheese and suet. *Nest.* In fir, hemlock, pine, spruce. *Attracting.* The gray jay is a bold "camp robber" of bread,
meats, fruits, potatoes, sandwiches, and suet—easily and quickly attracted
to foods on the ground or anywhere within a camper's area.

jay, Labrador or **Newfoundland.** See jay, gray.

jay, northern blue. See jay, blue.

jay, scrub (also called Florida jay; *Aphelocoma coerulescens*). Uncommon resident of shrub lands in Florida; also common resident in western
United States. *Plant food* (60% summer, 80% winter). CHOICE: bread
(white), cake, corn, elder, fig, oak (black, southern red), oat (common,
wild), palmetto (cabbage), peanut, peanutbutter, raspberry, sunflower,
wheat. FAIR: apple, barley (cultivated), blueberry, huckleberry, pear,
serviceberry, waxmyrtle (southern). *Animal food.* Chiefly bees, beetles,
bugs, carrion, caterpillars, flies, grasshoppers, wasps; also birds, bird-eggs,
frogs, lizards, mammals, snails, and suet. *Nest.* Frequently in blackberry,
currant, hawthorn, oak (live), osageorange, osmanthus, pine (sand), waxmyrtle, willow. *Attracting.* Scrub jays come to feeders for bread, corn,
cracked nuts, peanuts, and suet.

jay, Semple's. See jay, blue.

jenny wren. See wren, Carolina and house.

joree. See towhee, rufous-sided.

junco, eastern or **northern slate-colored.** See junco, slate-colored.

junco, slate-colored (also called black, blue, common, or slate-colored
snowbird, eastern junco, and northern slate-colored junco; *Junco hyemalis*).
Common summer resident of forests from northern Ontario and Labrador
southward to Minnesota and the southern Appalachian mountains; winters
in woodland, brushland, backyards and open fields from southern Canada
to northern Florida and the Gulf coast. *Plant food* (90% winter, 40% summer). CHOICE: amaranth (redroot), barnyardgrass, bread (white), bristle-

grass (Faber's, green, yellow), canarygrass (canariensis, reed), corn (cracked or meal), cornbread, crabgrass (smooth), doughnut, dropseed, filbert (commercial), goosefoot, Hardinggrass, hemp, millet (browntop, foxtail, Japanese, pearl, proso, Texas), oat, oatmeal, panicum (Dominican, hiddenseed, shoredune), peanut, petunia, pie crust, pine (eastern white, loblolly, longleaf, pitch, shortleaf, slash), pumpkin seed, ragweed (common), rice, sorghum (grain), sudangrass, sunflower (common, prairie), sweetgum, switchgrass, walnut meats (black), wheat. FAIR: barley (cultivated), bird-eye, blackberry, chickencorn, elaeagnus (autumn), lespedeza (Kobe, sericea), panicum, paspalum (bull), peanutbutter, rape, raspberry, rose (multiflora), rye, sesame, signalgrass (broadleaf), smartweed, sorgo, St. Johnswort (shrubby), timothy, violet. *Animal food.* Ants, beef suet, beetles, bugs, caterpillars, grasshopper, spiders, wasps. *Nest.* Frequently on the ground, under a tuft of grass, in a rock crevice, or upturned tree roots. *Attracting.* At feeders juncos will eat bread, cracked corn, grain sorghum, millet, peanuts, suet, sunflower seeds, and wheat.

kestrel, American. See hawk, sparrow.

killdee. See killdeer.

killdeer (also called killdee, kildeer plover, and noisy plover; *Charadrius vociferus*). Common summer resident of fields and shores from northern Ontario and Maine to the Gulf of Mexico, except southern Florida; winters southward from Oklahoma, Ohio, and New York. *Animal food* (almost 100%). Ants, beetles, caterpillars, grasshoppers. *Nest.* On bare ground in fields, usually near water.

kingbird, Arkansas. See kingbird, western.

kingbird, eastern (also called bee bird and bee martin; *Tyrannus tyrannus*). Common summer resident of orchards, groves, and woodland borders from Ontario and Quebec to the Gulf of Mexico. Winters in South America. *Animal food* (90% or less). Chiefly ants, bees, beetles, bugs, flies, grasshoppers. *Plant food.* CHOICE: blackberry, blackgum, blueberry, cherry (black, choke, mahaleb, mazzard, pin, sour), creeper (Virginia), dogwood (roughleaf), gallberry (large), grape (fox, frost), honeysuckle (dwarf bush), magnolia (southern), mulberry, pokeberry (common), sassafras, serviceberry (downy), spicebush (common), strawberry, sweetbay. FAIR: dogwood (alternateleaf, gray, silky), elder (American). *Nest.* Frequently in apple, boxelder, cottonwood, elm, oak (live, post, southern red, water), pear, pine (loblolly, longleaf, shortleaf), sassafras. *Attracting.* Leave food and nesting trees in odd corners, fence rows, and around cropland and pasture. Also leave dead trees or branches for perching, from which kingbirds watch for insect food.

kingbird, gray (*Tyrannus dominicensis*). Uncommon summer resident in coastal Alabama, Florida, Georgia, and South Carolina; winters in Caribbean area; casual elsewhere in the United States. *Animal food* (perhaps

90%). Bees, beetles, bugs, dragonflies, weevils. *Plant food.* Cordia and possibly other fruits. *Nest.* Frequently in mangrove (American), oak (live); occasionally in chinaberry, palmetto (cabbage), pine, poplar.

kingbird, western (also called bee bird, bee martin, and Arkansas kingbird; *Tyrannus verticalis*). Common summer resident of farms, pastures, and roadsides with scattered trees, from Minnesota and Indiana southwestward to northeastern Oklahoma; winters in small numbers on the Atlantic coast from Florida to South Carolina, and occasionally northward. *Animal food* (90%). Chiefly bees, beetles, bugs, flies, grasshoppers, wasps. *Plant food.* Creeper (Virginia), elder, mountainash. *Nest.* Frequently in boxes and on fenceposts and telephone poles, on ledges, stumps, windowsills; and in elm (American, Siberian), oak (white), sycamore, willow. See birdhouse table (section 3) for nest-box size.

kingfisher, belted (also called eastern belted kingfisher; *Megaceryle alcyon*). Common summer resident around lakes, ponds, and bays from Ontario and Labrador to the Gulf of Mexico; winters from Iowa and Massachusetts to the Gulf coast and Central America. *Animal food* (nearly 100%). Chiefly fish; also crabs, crayfish, crickets, frogs, grasshoppers, lizards, mussels, snakes, tadpoles. *Nest.* In a bank burrow, dug 18 inches to 4 feet or more horizontally into the bank. *Attracting.* Ponds, canals, or streams provide fish, crayfish, and frogs. A dead limb or wire provides a perch from which they scan the area for food.

kinglet, golden-crowned (also called eastern golden-crowned kinglet, gold-crest, and golden-crested kinglet; *Regulus satrapa*). Fairly common summer resident of coniferous forests from Ontario and Newfoundland southward to Minnesota and Massachusetts and southward in the Appalachian mountains to eastern Tennessee and western North Carolina; winters from the southern edge of its summer home to the Gulf coast and northern Florida. *Animal food* (nearly 100%). Chiefly insects. *Nest.* Frequently in fir, spruce (black); occasionally in hemlock, redcedar. *Attracting.* They come occasionally to a suet feeder.

kinglet, ruby-crowned (also called eastern ruby-crowned kinglet and ruby-crowned warbler; *Regulus calendula*). Summer resident of coniferous forests from Ontario and Newfoundland southward to northern Michigan and New York; winters from Kentucky and Maryland southward to Florida, the Gulf coast, and Mexico. *Animal food* (about 90%). Beetles, bugs, flies, insect eggs, plantlice, wasps; also suet. *Plant food.* Peanuts, syrup (sweetened water as for hummingbird), walnut (black). *Nest.* In fir (white), spruce. *Attracting.* Sometimes come to feeders for cracked nuts, peanuts, suet, and syrup.

kite, black-shouldered. See kite, white-tailed.

kite, blue. See kite, Mississippi.

kite, Everglade (also called snail hawk; *Rostrhamus sociabilis*). Summer resident, few in number, in the Everglades south from Lake Okeechobee, Florida. *Animal food* (100%). Freshwater snails. *Nest.* Frequently in clump of grass, reed, sawgrass, or small trees; occasionally in waxmyrtle.

kite, forked-tailed. See kite, swallow-tailed.

kite, Mississippi (also called blue kite; *Ictinia misisippiensis*). Common to uncommon summer resident of prairies and open woods from Kansas, Tennessee, and South Carolina to northern Florida and Texas; winters in Mexico and southward, rarely in Florida and southern Texas. *Animal food* (100%). Frogs, grasshoppers, lizards, locusts, snakes. *Nest.* Frequently in baldcypress, cottonwood, elm, oak (blackjack, pin), pine, sweetgum, sycamore, tuliptree.

kite, swallow-tailed (also called forked-tailed kite; *Elanoides forficatus*). Rare summer resident from South Carolina to Texas, accidental elsewhere in eastern United States; winters in South America. *Animal food* (100%). Frogs, grasshoppers, lizards, locusts, snakes. *Nest.* In baldcypress, hickory, oak (pin), pine.

kite, white-tailed (also called black-shouldered kite; *Elanus leucurus*). Casual from Florida to Texas; rare elsewhere in eastern United States. *Animal food* (100%). Chiefly mice; also grasshoppers, gophers, lizards, shrews, wood rats. *Nest.* In trees.

kittiwake, black-legged (also called common kittiwake; *Rissa tridactyla*). Common resident along the coast and at sea from Labrador to New Jersey, rarely to Florida; accidental elsewhere in eastern States. *Food.* Chiefly fish; but also eats other animal and vegetable refuse (garbage). *Nest.* On rocky ledges overlooking the water.

knot (also called American knot, robin snipe, red-breasted plover, and red-breasted sandpiper; *Calidris canutus*). Winters casually along the Atlantic coast from Florida to Massachusetts and to Texas on the Gulf coast. *Animal food* (100% winter to summer, 75% fall). Chiefly mollusks; also crustaceans and insects. *Plant food.* Widgeongrass. *Nest.* On ground, lined with grass.

krieker. See sandpiper, pectoral.

lark, field. Sea meadowlark, eastern and western.

lark, horned (also called northern horned and prairie horned lark; *Eremophila alpestris*). Includes 4 subspecies. Common summer resident of prairies, fields, and roadsides from arctic Canada southward to Kansas and North Carolina; winters from southern Canada to the Gulf states, rarely to Florida. *Plant food* (70% summer, 90% winter). CHOICE: amaranth (prostrate, redroot, slim), bilberry (bog), bristlegrass, brome, buckwheat (common), corn (cracked), goosefoot, oat (common, wild), panicum, quackgrass, ragweed (common), wheat. FAIR: portulaca, smartweed, sorghum (grain), sunflower. *Animal food.* Chiefly beetles, caterpillars, grasshoppers. *Nest.* On the ground.

lark, northern horned or **prairie horned.** See lark, horned.

limpkin (also called crying bird; *Aramus guarauna*). Common resident in Okefenokee Swamp (southern Georgia) and peninsular Florida. *Animal food* (nearly 100%). Clams and snails. *Nest.* In sawgrass and other marsh plants, on large stumps, and in vines and trees.

linnet or **redpoll linnet.** See redpoll, common.

logcock. See woodpecker, pileated.

loggerhead. See shrike, loggerhead.

long-beak, greater. See dowitcher, long-billed.

longspur, Alaska. See longspur, Lapland.

longspur, chestnut-collared (*Calcarius ornatus*). Winters uncommonly in prairie lands of eastern Texas and northern Louisiana; breeds in the Great Plains area. *Plant food* (90% winter, 30% summer). CHOICE: amaranth, bristlegrass, dropseed, needlegrass, panicum, sunflower, wheat. FAIR: goosefoot, threeawn. *Animal food.* Chiefly beetles, grasshoppers, spiders. *Nest.* On the ground.

longspur, common. See longspur, Lapland.

longspur, Lapland (also called Alaska and common longspur; *Calcarius lapponicus*). Breeds in northern Canadian provinces; winters in fields and prairies from Minnesota to Nova Scotia, southward to central Texas, Ohio, and along the Atlantic coast to Delaware. *Plant food* (nearly 100% in winter). Amaranth, bristlegrass (green, yellow), corn (cracked), crabgrass (hairy, smooth), dropseed, millet (foxtail), oat, panicum, portulaca, ragweed (common), sedge, wheat. *Animal food.* Beetles, grasshoppers, weevils. *Nest.* On the ground or in a tussock of grass.

longspur, McCown's (*Rhynchophanes mccownii*). Winters sparingly on the prairies of southern Texas (Corpus Christi and Galveston area), rarely eastward; breeds in northern plains states and Canada. *Plant food* (90% fall and winter, 65% summer). Bristlegrass, buffalograss, goosefoot, knotweed, needlegrass, sunflower, wheat. *Animal food.* Beetles, grasshoppers, other insects and spiders. *Nest.* On the ground.

longspur, painted. See longspur, Smith's.

longspur, Smith's (also called painted longspur; *Calcarius pictus*). Breeds in Canada and Alaska; winters in short-grass areas from Iowa south to central Texas and Louisiana. *Plant food* (nearly 100% winter). CHOICE: bristlegrass, dropseed, needlegrass, panicum, wheat. FAIR: barnyardgrass, bulrush, ragweed (common), threeawn, timothy. *Animal food.* Beetles, caterpillars, spiders. *Nest.* On the ground.

loon, common (*Gavia immer*). Common summer resident of lakes surrounded by conifer forest from northern Canada southward to Minnesota and Maine; winters about the Great Lakes, and along the Atlantic and Gulf coasts from Newfoundland to Florida and Texas. State bird of Minnesota. *Animal food* (100%). Chiefly fish; also frogs, insects, mollusks. *Nest.* On the ground, in sand, or on muskrat houses.

loon, red-throated (*Gavia stellata*). Common winter visitor from Maine to Florida and the Gulf coast; breeds in the arctic. *Animal food* (100%). Chiefly fish; also frogs, insects, mollusks. *Nest.* On the banks of small ponds.

mallard (also called common mallard, mallard duck, and greenhead duck; *Anas platyrhynchos*). Surface-feeding duck; common to abundant in marshes, ponds, and streams of North America; nests in fresh marshes of northern states and Canada; winters from the northern states to the Gulf of Mexico and westward to the Pacific. *Plant food* (90% winter, less summer). CHOICE: aneilema (keisak), arrowhead (common, delta), barley (cultivated), barnyardgrass, chufa, cockspur (coast), corn, cutgrass (rice), flatsedge (redroot), junglerice, knotgrass, millet (browntop, foxtail, Japanese, proso, Texas), oak (Nuttall, pin, water, white), oat (common, wild), paspalum (brownseed), pea (garden), podgrass (shore), poolmat, potamogeton (baby, floatingleaf, leafy, sago, stiffleaf, thorowort), redroot (blood), rice, rye, smartweed (bigroot, curltop, marshpepper, Pennsylvania, swamp, water), sorghum (grain), sudangrass, swamp-privet, tearthumb (arrowleaf), waterelm, wheat, wildrice. FAIR: alfalfa, arrowarum, beakrush (horned), beggartick, buckwheat (common), bulrush, (American, Cuban, flatstem, river, softstem), burreed (giant, greenfruited), buttonbush, cowlily (painted, spatterdock), duckweed, eelgrass (common), hickory (water), hornwort, marestail, naiad (northern, southern), panicum (bulb, fall, woolly), parrot-feather, paspalum (bull), potamogeton (flatstem, largeleaf, longleaf), sedge, signalgrass (broadleaf), smartweed (dotted, Puerto Rico, spotted), soybean, spikerush (squarestem), stonewort, sweetgum, watercress, waterhemp (tall), waterlily (yellow Mexican), waterprimrose (creeping), watershield, widgeongrass, wildcelery. *Animal food.* Aquatic insects, fish, snails (especially juvenile mallards). *Nest.* On the ground, in marsh or grassland. *Attracting.* Save marshy nesting areas in the north. In winter, flood fields and woodlands having choice food. For details, consult USDA Farmers' Bulletin No. 2218 (see **duck**).

mallard, black. See duck, black.

mallard, Florida. See duck, mottled.

man-o'-war bird. See frigate-bird, magnificent.

marsh hen. See rail, clapper, king, Virginia; sora.

martin, bee. See kingbird, eastern, and western.

martin, house. See martin, purple.

martin, purple (also called house martin; *Progne subis*). Common summer resident of open lands near water, from Minnesota to Nova Scotia and southward to Georgia and the Gulf of Mexico. Migratory in Florida in spring and early summer. Winters in South America. *Animal food* (100%). Chiefly ants, bees, beetles, bugs, flies, moths, wasps; also spiders. *Nest.* In man-made birdhouses, gourds, or buildings; occasionally in natural cavities of cliffs and trees. *Attracting.* Today most martins occupy man-made bird-houses, which may be a large gourd, a single-room box, or an expensive 200-compartment house like that illustrated in figure 3.5. A good house is an apartment-type dwelling with 4 to 24 rooms for the separate pairs. The size of each compartment is 6x6x6 inches, with a 2½-inch entrance hole cut 1 inch above the floor level. Extend the floor 2½–3 inches beyond the out-side wall for roosting ledges. The house should be placed on a pole about 15 feet high, in direct sunlight and in open situations within a few hundred feet of a pond or stream. To help keep the house cool in summer, paint the roof and sides white, and in multi-storied houses provide a central shaft which opens into a screened attic space. If you use gourds, space them so the wind will not knock one against another. To keep house sparrows, starlings, and bluebirds from nesting in your martin house, don't raise it until the week the martins return from South America. The same birds usually return each year at about the same dates. But martins are rather erratic settlers, and if they are not known to nest in your neighborhood and you are making your first attempt at housing them, it would be well to start modestly—with one or two single boxes. If you want to try an apartment house, make it a one-story structure; you can put up additional floors when the first rooms are tenanted.

meadowlark, eastern (also called field lark; *Sturnella magna*). Common resident of open fields, pastures, prairies, and towns from Minnesota and Nova Scotia southward to Texas and Florida. *Animal food* (95% summer, 50% winter). Chiefly beetles, caterpillars, crickets, grasshoppers; also ants, bugs, spiders, wasps. *Plant food.* CHOICE: barnyardgrass, bristlegrass, corn (cracked, whole), millet (browntop), peanut, pine, sorghum (grain), wheat. FAIR: oat, panicum, ragweed (common), rice, sunflower. *Nest.* On the ground, roofed over with grass. *Attracting.* Come to the feeders on the ground, where they eat cracked corn, wheat, and sorghum mixtures. Mead-owlarks like to bathe under sprinklers in the heat of summer.

meadowlark, little. See dickcissel.

meadowlark, western (also called field lark; *Sturnella neglecta*). Common resident of fields, pastures, and prairies from southern Ontario, Indiana, western Tennessee, and central Texas westward throughout the United States. State bird of Kansas, Montana, Nebraska, North Dakota, Oregon, and Wyoming. *Animal food* (95% summer, 45% winter). Ants, bees, beetles, bugs, caterpillars, crickets, grasshoppers, wasps. *Plant food.* CHOICE: bristlegrass, corn, oats, sorghum (grain), wheat. FAIR: sunflower. *Nest.* On the ground under tufts of grass.

medrick. See tern, common.

merganser, American. See merganser, common.

merganser, common (also called American merganser, and fish duck, goosander, and sawbill; *Mergus merganser*). Common "fish duck" of wooded lakes, ponds, and rivers; nests from Ontario and Newfoundland southward to Minnesota and New Hampshire; winters from the Great Lakes and St. Lawrence River southward to Texas and Florida. *Animal food* (nearly 100%). Chiefly fish and mussels; also crayfish, eels, frogs, insects (water), leeches, snails, worms. *Nest.* In hollow trees, on the ground, or in rock crevices.

merganser, hooded (also called fish duck and sawbill; *Lophodytes cucullatus*). Common "fish duck" of wooded lakes, ponds, and rivers; nests from Ontario and New Brunswick southward to Missouri and Tennessee; winters throughout eastern United States. *Animal food.* Chiefly crayfish, fish, frogs, insects (aquatic), snails, tadpoles. *Plant food.* CHOICE: corn. *Nest.* In hollow trees, in nesting boxes, or in marshy land near salt water. *Attracting.* Flooded corn fields attract hooded mergansers in winter. In summer in the New England states they nest frequently in nesting boxes erected for wood ducks.

merganser, red-breasted (also called fish duck and sawbill; *Mergus serrator*). Common 'fish duck," summer resident of lakes and rivers from arctic Canada southward to Minnesota and the New England states. Winters from the St. Lawrence River south and southwestward to Florida and Texas; often in bays or at sea. *Animal food* (100%). Chiefly crayfish, fish, frogs, insects, mussels. *Nest.* On the ground, in rock crevices or under fir and spruce.

merlin. See hawk, pigeon.

mocker. See mockingbird.

mockingbird (also called mocker; *Mimus polyglottos*). Common yearlong resident of farms, roadsides, and towns from Iowa, Ohio, and New Jersey southward to the Gulf coast and Florida; occasionally north to southern Canada. State bird of Arkansas, Florida, Mississippi, Tennessee, and Texas. *Plant food* (65% winter, 25% summer). CHOICE: asparagus, banana, beautyberry (American), blackberry, blackgum, bottletree, bread (white), cake, camphortree, cherry (black, mazzard, sour), corktree (Chinese), crabapple (Siberian), creeper (Virginia), currant, dogwood (flowering, roughleaf), elaeagnus (autumn, cherry, thorny), elder (American), fig, filbert (commercial), gallberry (large), grape (cultivated), hackberry (sugar), holly (American, Japanese), honeysuckle (Amur, winter), laurelcherry, loquat, magnolia (southern), mulberry, papermulberry, peaches (fresh), peanutbutter, peppertree (Brazil), peppervine, persimmon (common, kaki), plum (garden), pokeberry (common, stiff), pomegranate (if cut open), possumhaw, privet (Amur, Chinese, glossy, Japanese), pyracantha, raisins, raspberry, redcedar, rose (multiflora), serviceberry (downy), snailseed (Carolina), sparkleberry, strawberries, sugar, sumac (smooth), sweetbay, winterberry (common), yaupon. FAIR: apple (sliced), arborvitae (oriental), ardisia (Christmas), barberry (European, Japanese), bittersweet, chinaberry, cotoneaster, date, euonymus (spreading), gallberry, greenbrier, guava, hawthorn, holly (Chinese), hophornbeam, Jerusalemcherry, nandina, palmetto (cabbage), partridgeberry, peanut, pecan, photinia (Chinese), pitanga, poisonivy, sassafras, sumac (shining), supplejack (Alabama), trumpettree (silverleaf), viburnum (European cranberrybush). *Animal food.* Chiefly ants, bees, beetles, caterpillars, crickets, locusts, grasshoppers, wasps; also chinch bugs, cottonboll worms, crayfish, cucumber beetles, flies, lizards, millipedes, snails, snakes, sowbugs, spiders; also butter, cheese, pork fat, suet. *Nest.* In many species of trees, shrubs, and vines. *Attracting.* For nesting, plant or protect ornamental shrubs such as camellia, holly, laurelcherry, live oak, multiflora rose, pecan, privet pyracantha, redcedar, thorny elaeagnus, water oak, and yaupon. Save or plant their choice fruiting plants around homes, along streams, in fence rows, and wildlife areas. Mockingbirds come to feeders for cracked walnuts and other nut meats, dried currants, peanutbutter, raisins, suet.

moorhen. See gallinule, common.

mudhen. See coot, American.

mud peep. See sandpiper, Baird's and least.

murre, Atlantic. See murre, common.

murre, Brunnich's. See murre, thick-billed.

murre, common (also called Atlantic murre; *Uria aalge*). Abundant summer resident of rocky cliffs, islands, and bays of the north Atlantic coast from Greenland to Nova Scotia; winters offshore in its summer range and southward to Maine, casually as far south as New Jersey. *Animal food* (100%). Chiefly fish (herrings and pilchers); also crustaceans. *Nest.* On rock cliffs (rookeries), in dense colonies.

murre, thick-billed (also called Brunnich's murre; *Uria lomvia*). Common summer resident of cliffs, islands, and bays of north Atlantic arctic southward to Hudson Bay, Labrador, and Gulf of St. Lawrence; winters in open waters within its breeding range and southward to South Carolina, casually in the Great Lakes. *Animal food* (100%). Chiefly small fish; also crustaceans. *Nest.* On rock cliffs, in colonies.

niggergoose. See cormorants.

nighthawk, common (also called eastern nighthawk, and bullbat, goatsucker, and nightjar; *Chordeiles minor*). Common summer resident of open

lands and towns in eastern Canada and eastern United States; most notice-
able in the fall as the birds group and feed in the air during their migration
to South America. *Animal food* (100%). Ants, beetles, flies, grasshoppers,
leaf chafers, mosquitoes, moths. *Nest.* On the ground in gravel, on large
rocks, or on gravel roofs of city buildings.

nightjar. See nighthawk.

noddy or brown noddy. See tern, noddy.

nonpareil. See bunting, painted.

nuthatch, brown-headed (also called gray-headed nuthatch; *Sitta pusilla*).
Common resident of pine woodlands in Arkansas, northern Georgia, Maryland, and southward to the Gulf coast and Florida. *Plant food* (55%).
CHOICE: almond, brazilnut, butternut, cashew, cookies, filbert (commercial),
hickory nuts (cracked), peanut (chopped), pecan meat, pine (eastern white,
loblolly, longleaf, shortleaf, slash, Virginia), sunflower (cultivated), walnut
(black, Persian). FAIR: peanutbutter, pistachionut. *Animal food.* Ants, caterpillars, cocoons, moth eggs, scale insects. Suet is a choice food at feeders.
Also eats pork fat. *Nest.* In hole of a stump or tree, and in birdhouses; begins
nesting activities early in February. *Attracting.* Nuthatches will use either of
two selective feeders, one that swings freely or one that is enclosed (see fig-
ures 2.4 and 2.5), and are attracted to bread, nut meats, suet, sunflower
seeds, and occasionally peanutbutter. A birdhouse for the brown-headed
nuthatch should be rustic, preferably the hollow-log type (figure 3.3) placed
in an open woodland setting. It should have a 1-inch entrance hole placed
6 or 8 inches above the floor, the inside dimensions of which should be 2x3
or 3x3 inches.

nuthatch, Canada. See nuthatch, red-breasted.

nuthatch, gray-headed. See nuthatch, brown-headed.

nuthatch, red-bellied. See nuthatch, red-breasted.

nuthatch, red-breasted (also called Canada and red-bellied nuthatch;
Sitta canadensis). Common summer resident of conifer forests from Ontario
and Newfoundland southward to Minnesota, New York, Massachusetts and
southward in the Appalachian mountains to North Carolina and Tennessee;
winters southward to northern Florida and Texas. *Plant food* (perhaps 50%).
CHOICE: almond, birch (paper), butternut, cantaloup seed, doughnuts, peanut, pine (pitch), spruce (black), sunflower (cultivated), walnut (Persian).
FAIR: peanutbutter. *Animal food.* Bark insects; also beef suet. *Nest.* In a
hole or cavity in a stump or tree; also in birdhouses. *Attracting.* Come to
feeders for nut meats, suet, and sunflower seeds. A birdhouse similar to that
described for the brown-headed nuthatch is also attractive to the red-
breasted species, which usually coats its entrance with fir balsam or pitch.

nuthatch, white-breasted (also called eastern white-breasted, Florida
white-breasted, and white-bellied nuthatch; *Sitta carolinensis*). Common

resident of deciduous woodlands and groves from Minnesota and Maine southward to northern Louisiana, central Alabama, and northern Florida. *Plant food* (50% or more). CHOICE: beech, bread (white), butternut, cantaloup seed, chestnuts, doughnuts, hemp, hickory nuts (cracked), oak (pin), peanut, pecan, pumpkinseed, squash seed, sunflower (cultivated), walnut (Persian). FAIR: corn, dandelion, peanutbutter. *Animal food.* Ants, beetles, caterpillars, moths, spiders, weevils; also pork fat and beef suet. *Nest.* In a hole or cavity of a stump or tree; also in birdhouses. *Attracting.* They come to feeders for bread, cantaloup seed, cracked nuts, doughnuts, hemp, pumpkin and squash seeds, suet, and sunflower seeds. A birdhouse for the white-breasted nuthatch must be a bit larger than the one which suits the two smaller species. It should be 8–10 inches deep, with an entrance hole 1¼ inches in diameter situated 6–8 inches above a 4x4-inch floor (inside dimensions). A hollow-log type or bark-covered design seems most attractive. Place the birdhouse in a woodland site.

oldsquaw (also called long-tailed duck; *Clangula hyemalis*). A diving duck which breeds in the arctic. Winters chiefly at sea and along the Atlantic coast from Greenland to South Carolina (rarely to Florida), on the Great Lakes, and casually on large interior lakes in Kentucky, Tennessee, and Texas. *Animal food* (90%). Chiefly aquatic insects, crustaceans, with lesser amounts of fish (including silver minnow), and mollusks. *Plant food.* Barley, corn, crowberry (black), eelgrass, oat, poolmat, stonewort, wheat, widgeongrass. *Nest.* On the ground near water.

oriole, Baltimore (also called Lady, and Lord, Baltimore oriole; *Icterus galbula*). Common summer resident of open lands with shade trees or groves, from southern Canada southward to northern Texas, Louisiana, and Mississippi; in the east to northern Virginia and the western Carolinas. Commonly winters south of the United States, but occasionally in the eastern states from Ontario to Louisiana and Florida. State bird of Maryland. *Animal food* (50% or more). Chiefly caterpillars; also ants, beetles, bugs, grasshoppers, spiders, wasps; also suet. *Plant food.* CHOICE: blackberry, cherry (black, mazzard, sour), fig, honey syrup, mountainash (American, European), mulberry, nut meats, orange halves, serviceberry (Allegheny, downy). FAIR: apple, aspen leaves, blackgum, blueberry, bread, elder, grape, pear, sugar water. *Nest.* Frequently in apple, birch, boxelder, cottonwood, elm, maple, poplar, sycamore; occasionally in ash, aspen, buttonbush, cherry (black), forestiera, hickory, lespedeza (bicolor), locust (black), oak (bur, laurel, overcup, post, southern red, water, willow), peach, pear, pecan, privet, redbud, spruce, sweetgum, tuliptree, walnut (black), willow. *Attracting.* Come to feeders for nut meats, suet, sugar syrup; and to darning thread and string offered for nesting materials.

oriole, orchard (*Icterus spurius*). Fairly common summer resident of groves, orchards, and shade trees from Minnesota, New York, and Massachusetts southward to the Texas Gulf coast and northern Florida; winters in Central and South America. *Animal food* (95%). Chiefly ants, beetles, bugs, caterpillars, grasshoppers, spiders. *Plant food.* CHOICE: blackberry, blueberry, burclover, cherry (black, mazzard, sour), crotolaria (cape), elder, fig, honey syrup, mulberry, nectar from flowers, sugar syrup. FAIR: bread, grape, huckleberry. *Nest.* Frequently in apple, camphortree, cottonwood, elm, hackberry, magnolia, maple, oak (live), pear, pecan, persimmon, reed, sweetgum, sycamore, tuliptree, tungoiltree, willow; occasionally in albizzia (silktree), baldcypress, blackgum, boxelder, buttonbush, crabapple, elder, hawthorn, hickory, honeylocust, lespedeza (bicolor), locust (black), loquat, oak (overcup, southern red, water, white, willow), peach, pine (loblolly, longleaf, Scotch), prickly-ash, Spanishmoss, walnut. *Attracting.* Occasionally come to feeders for sugar syrup as fed to hummingbirds, and for bread, especially with jelly.

   oriole, spotted-breasted (*Icterus pectoralis*). Naturalized around Miami, Florida. *Plant food.* CHOICE: avocado, banana, Barbadoscherry, bottlebrush, bread (white), chinalaurel, orange halves, papaya, pitanga, shrimp-plant. Also fond of flower nectar. *Animal food.* Insects. *Nest.* Pendulous, swung on tree branches. *Attracting.* They come to feeders for avocado, banana, bread, orange halves, papaya, and other choice foods, and come regularly to birdbaths.

   osprey (also called fish hawk or sea hawk; *Pandion haliaetus*). Fairly common member of the hawk family, around lakes, rivers, and sea coasts; summer resident in southern Canada and all eastern United States; winters along the Gulf coast from Florida to Texas and southward. *Animal food* (100%). Fish. *Nest.* Frequently on rock pinnacles, or in baldcypress, blackmangrove, fir, pine (loblolly, pitch, Virginia), spruce; occasionally in cherry (black), oak (bear, live, white), in duck blinds, fence rails, and on the ground.

   outarde. See goose, Canada.

   ovenbird (also called teacher, golden-crowned thrush, wagtail, and wood wagtail; *Seiurus aurocapillus*). A member of the wood warbler family. Common summer resident from southern Canada to Kansas, and the Appalachian mountains from Virginia to Georgia. Winters in southern Florida and Louisiana southward. *Animal food* (nearly 100%). Beetles, earthworms, slugs, snails, spiders; also suet. *Plant food.* CHOICE: grapes, peanut, peanutbutter. *Nest.* On the ground, domed over with grass, in dry woods near trees. *Attracting.* Try peanutbutter and suet at feeders on the ground.

   owl. Twelve species of owls may be seen more or less regularly in the eastern half of the continent. They belong to two closely related families: Tytonidae, the barn owls, and Strigidae, the typical owls. Like hawks and eagles, they are birds of prey, and most species do their hunting chiefly at night. The arctic summer residents, of course, feed also by daylight, as does the hawk owl. Rodents of various sizes are the mainstays of most owls, but the dietary preferences of individual species are quite varied and may include insects, birds, lizards, crayfish, amphibians, and fish.

owl, Acadian. See owl, saw-whet.

owl, American hawk. See owl, hawk.

owl, arctic. See owl, snowy.

owl, arctic saw-whet. See owl, boreal.

owl, barn (also called monkey-faced owl; *Tyto alba*). Fairly common resident from Minnesota and Massachusetts southward to the Gulf of Mexico and Florida. *Animal food* (100%). Chiefly rodents (gophers, ground squirrels, mice and rats, rabbits); less frequently various birds and insects. *Nest.* In natural hollows in trees, in holes or cavities in clay banks and cliffs, in barns and abandoned buildings or seldom used sites such as towers and steeples. See the birdhouse table, section 3, for specifications of a nesting box for barn owls. It may be placed in the high supports of barns, water towers, and similar structures.

owl, barred (also called hoot owl; *Strix varia*). Includes Florida, northern, and Texas barred owl subspecies. Common resident of river woods and swamps from Ontario and Nova Scotia southward to Gulf of Mexico and Florida. *Animal food* (100%). Birds, crayfish, fish, frogs, insects, lizards, various mammals (mice, rabbits, rats, squirrels), snails, snakes, spiders. *Nest.* In hollows and cavities of trees and in old crow or hawk nests in trees.

owl, billy. See owl, burrowing.

owl, boreal (also called Richardson's, arctic saw-whet, and sparrow owl; *Aegolius funereus*). Rare summer resident of woodlands in the eastern Canadian provinces; winters in most of its summer range and extends southward in the United States to Iowa and Pennsylvania. *Animal food* (100%). Chiefly mice and moles; also birds. *Nest.* In dead stubs of trees, in old nesting holes made by flickers and pileated woodpeckers.

owl, burrowing (also called billy owl, ground owl, prairie-dog owl, and Florida burrowing owl; *Speotyto cunicularia*). Rather uncommon owl of prairie grasslands, resident in Florida, eastern Texas, Louisiana, and westward in the Great Plains; accidental in other eastern United States areas. *Animal food* (100%). Chiefly beetles, caterpillars, crickets, dragonflies, grasshoppers; also ground squirrels, lizards, mice, rabbits, rats, other mammals and amphibians; occasionally birds. *Nest.* In burrows dug by themselves or by armadillos, badgers, foxes, prairie-dogs, skunks, or woodchucks.

owl, Canadian. See owl, hawk.

owl, cat. See owl, long-eared.

owl, day. See owl, hawk.

owl, ermine. See owl, snowy.

owl, Florida burrowing. See owl, burrowing.

owl, great gray (also called spectral owl; *Strix nebulosa*). Fairly common yearlong resident of boreal forests from northern Ontario to Minnesota and westward; winters irregularly to central states in eastern United States. *Animal food* (100%). Chiefly mice, rabbits, rats, squirrels; occasionally various species of birds. *Nest.* In old hawk nests, well up in large trees, dead or alive.

owl, great horned (also called arctic horned and Labrador horned owl; *Bubo virginianus*). Common summer resident of forest and woodland throughout most of North America, from northern tree limit to Mexico. *Animal food* (100%). Mice, rabbits, rats, squirrels, and other mammals; also birds such as coot, grackles, grebes, martin, meadowlarks, pigeons, sparrows, starlings, and woodcock. *Nest.* Frequently in old nests of crows, bald eagles, and red-tailed hawks; in beech, hickory, maple, pine (eastern white, loblolly, longleaf, pitch, Virginia), sycamore, willow; also in rocky caves, crevices, and on the ground.

owl, great white. See owl, snowy.

owl, ground. See owl, burrowing.

owl, hawk (also called Canadian owl, day owl, Hudsonian owl, and American hawk owl; *Surnia ulula*). Uncommon summer resident of northern Canadian forests southward to northern Michigan and southern Quebec, New Brunswick, and Newfoundland; winters in same area but wanders casually both south and north of breeding range. A "day-flying" owl. *Animal food* (100%). Chiefly birds, fresh carrion, ground-squirrels, insects, lemmings, and mice. *Nest.* In natural cavities or enlarged woodpecker holes in trees.

owl, hoot. See owl, barred.

owl, horned (arctic and Labrador). See owl, great horned.

owl, Hudsonian. See owl, hawk.

owl, lesser horned. See owl, long-eared.

owl, long-eared (also called cat owl and lesser horned owl; *Asio otus*). Uncommon to rare resident from southern Ontario and Nova Scotia southward to Arkansas and Virginia; winters from Canada to Texas and Florida. *Animal food* (100%). Chiefly rodents (mice and rats); and less importantly, several species of birds, rabbits, and other rodents, snakes, and insects. *Nest.* In old nests of crows, hawks, and squirrels in trees; occasionally on the ground.

owl, marsh. See owl, short-eared.

owl, McCally's. See owl, screech.

owl, monkey-faced. See owl, barn.

owl, prairie. See owl, short-eared.

owl, prairie-dog. See owl, burrowing.

owl, Richardson's. See owl, boreal.

owl, saw-whet (also called Acadian owl; *Aegolius acadicus*). Fairly common resident of woods from northern Ontario and Nova Scotia southward to Maryland and eastern Oklahoma; winters throughout breeding range and southward to Louisiana and Florida. *Animal food* (100%). Chiefly mice, but also birds, flying squirrels, insects, rats. *Nest.* In old nests of flickers and woodpeckers in dead stubs of trees; also in birdhouses, as specified in the birdhouse table (section 3).

owl, screech (also called shivering owl and McCally's owl; *Otus asio*). Includes six subspecies: Aikin's, eastern, Florida, Hasbrook's, southern, and Texas screech owls. Common residents of farm woodlands and groves from southern Ontario, Quebec, and Maine southward throughout eastern United States. *Animal food* (nearly 100%). Chiefly crayfish, insects, mice, and various species of birds; also fish, lizards, rats. *Nest.* In holes made by flickers or woodpeckers in trees; also in birdhouses, as specified in the bird-house table (section 3). *Attracting.* Will come to suet. Place birdhouses for them if you wish; however, they are said to prey on smaller birds near feeding stations.

owl, shivering. See owl, screech.

owl, short-eared (also called marsh and prairie owl; *Asio flammeus*). Common summer resident of marshes, prairies, and irrigated agricultural lands from Missouri and Virginia northward to northern Canada; winters in all eastern United States. *Animal food* (100%). Chiefly mice and rats; also various birds, insects, and rodents. *Nest.* On the ground; occasionally in a burrow.

owl, snowy (also called great white owl and arctic or ermine owl; *Nyctea scandiaca*). Common yearlong resident of fields, marshes, bare mountains, prairies, and tundras from the arctic to southern Canada; winters irregularly in northern United States if its food supply becomes exhausted farther north. *Animal food* (100%). Chiefly carrion, fish, lemmings, and mice; also several species of birds, rabbits, and other rodents. *Nest.* On the ground, on a rocky ledge, cliff, tundra, or a slight knoll in tidal marsh.

owl, sparrow. See owl, boreal.

owl, spectral. See owl, great gray.

oystercatcher, American (also called sea crow; *Haematopus palliatus*). Common yearlong resident along the coasts from Virginia to Texas, usually abundant on oyster beds at low tide; rare in Florida and north of Virginia on the Atlantic coast. *Animal food* (100%). Clams, limpets, mussels oysters, sea worms, shrimp. *Nest.* On sandy beaches.

partridge, birch. See grouse, ruffed.

partridge, European. See partridge, gray.

partridge, gray (also called European or Hungarian partridge; *Perdix perdix*). Introduced gamebird now common resident in corn- and wheat-field areas from Ontario and Nova Scotia southward to northeast Iowa, Ohio, and New York. *Plant food* (100% winter, 10% summer). CHOICE: barley (cultivated), bristlegrass (green, yellow), buckwheat (common), corn, oat, ragweed (common), wheat, wheatgrass. FAIR: alfalfa, amaranth (redroot), brome, dandelion, lettuce (prickly), raspberry, springbeauty, sunflower. *Animal food.* Chiefly grasshoppers and moths; also ants. *Nest.* On the ground. *Attracting.* Grow choice foods in fields, leaving meadow or other grass cover.

partridge, Hungarian. See partridge, gray.

partridge, ice. See gull, ivory.

Peabody bird. See sparrow, white-throated.

peep; peeps; peet-weet; sandpeep (and many other combinations). Colloquial names (from their characteristics, repeated cry) variously given to the sanderling and six smaller sandpipers—Baird's, least, semipalmated, spotted, western, and white-rumped.

pelican, brown (also called eastern brown pelican; *Pelecanus occidentalis*). Common summer resident along the coasts from North Carolina to Texas; winters from Florida to Texas. "Eastern brown pelican" is the state bird of Louisiana. *Animal food* (100%). Fish (90% menhaden, 1% commercial fish). *Nest.* Frequently on the ground or in blackmangrove and mangrove; occasionally in palmetto (cabbage), yucca.

pelican, eastern brown. See pelican, brown.

pelican, white (*Pelecanus erythrorhynchos*). Fairly common winter visitor along the Gulf coast from Florida to Texas; rare elsewhere in eastern North America. *Animal food* (100%). Fish. *Nest.* On the ground in western states.

pewee. See wood pewee.

phalarope (also called swimming sandpiper). The phalaropes are shore birds, with webbed toes that make them excellent swimmers. The **northern phalarope** (*Lobipes lobatus*) and the **red phalarope** (called gray phalarope in Europe; *Phalaropus fulicarius*) breed in the arctic and are abundant migrants, chiefly offshore, along the Atlantic coast to South America. They are rarely seen in the eastern interior. **Wilson's phalarope** (*Steganopus tricolor*) breeds commonly west of the Mississippi; rarely eastward. After breeding it goes to sea, wintering southward to the Argentine pampas. In winter it is occasionally seen along the Atlantic and Gulf coasts when storms drive it in from the sea. All three species nest in small depressions on the ground, usually near pools of fresh water. Their diet is almost entirely animal, and includes aquatic insects, billbugs, brine shrimp, grasshoppers, mosquitoes, snails, and wireworms.

pheasant, Chinese or **chink.** See pheasant, ring-necked.

pheasant, native. See grouse, ruffed.

pheasant, ring-necked (also called Chinese and chink pheasant; *Phasianus colchicus*). An introduced game bird, now a common resident in northern

states from Minnesota and southern Canada southward to Kansas and New
Jersey, in grain-field areas. State bird of South Dakota. *Plant food* (85%
summer, 99% winter). CHOICE: barley (cultivated), blackberry, bristlegrass
(green, yellow), buckwheat (common), corn, crabapple (pearleaf), oat
(common), pea (garden), ragweed (common), sorghum (grain), wheat.
FAIR: alfalfa, amaranth, apple, asparagus, barberry (European, Japanese),
beggartick (leafybract), bread (white), cherry (bessey, black, choke, pin),
chokeberry (red), dandelion, dogwood, elaeagnus (autumn), grape, hawthorn, hemp, lettuce (prickly), locust (black), millet (proso), oat (wild),
plum (American), poisonsumac, potato, raspberry, rose (multiflora), rye,
safflower, smartweed (Pennsylvania), soybean, strawberry, sumac (smooth),
sunflower. *Animal food.* Ants, beetles, caterpillars, crickets, earthworms, fly
larvae, grasshoppers, snails, spiders, toads. *Nest.* On the ground hidden by
tufts of grass. *Attracting.* Grow grain in fields, or feed grain on the ground
at feeding stations.

   phoebe, eastern (*Sayornis phoebe*). A member of the flycatcher family.
Common summer resident of farms and towns from Ontario and New Brunswick southward to Oklahoma and South Carolina. Winters from Virginia
southward to Florida, Texas, and Mexico. *Animal food* (90%). Ants, bees,
beetles, bugs, caterpillars, crickets, flies, grasshoppers, spiders, wasps. *Plant
food.* Fruits, including blackberry, elder, poisonivy, pokeberry, sumac, waxmyrtle (southern). *Nest.* Built on a shelf under bridges, on rock ledges, or
on a homemade wooden shelf. *Attracting.* Phoebes will nest on a board
nailed under the eaves of a building, or on a nesting platform (see the birdhouse table in section 3). The platform may also be placed 8–12 feet above
the ground. If there is no overhead protection, the platform itself should
have a roof slanted forward to shed rain water, and the flooring should have
small drainage holes. The wood is better left unpainted, but it should be
treated with a preservative. Sites near water are especially attractive to
phoebes; they are often seen feeding on insects over farm ponds.

   pigeon, domestic. See dove, rock.

   pigeon, sea. See guillemot, black.

   pigeon, white-crowned (*Columba leucocephala*). Uncommon summer
resident in south Florida and Florida Keys; usually winters in the West
Indies. *Plant food* (nearly 100%). Incomplete information; includes tropical
fruits and berries such as cordia and cocoplums (*Chrysobalanus species*).
Nest. In shrubs or trees such as mangrove (American) at Cape Sable and
on islands offshore from Florida, and in Caribbean areas.

   pintail (also called American pintail, pintail duck, and sprig or sprig-tail;
Anas acuta). A surface-feeding duck; fairly common summer resident of
marshes, ponds, and prairies from Iowa northward and westward. Winters
in coastal areas from the Chesapeake Bay to Texas. *Plant food* (90%).

CHOICE: aneilema (keisak), arrowhead (common, delta), barley, barnyard-grass, bulrush (alkali, American, Olney, saltmarsh), chufa, cockspur (coast), corn, junglerice, knotgrass, lettuce, lovegrass (teal), millet (browntop, Japanese), panicum (fall), paspalum (brownseed, bull), peanut, podgrass (shore), polypogon (rabbitfoot), redroot (blood), rice, smartweed (bigroot, Pennsylvania, swamp, water), sorghum (grain), sudangrass, wheat, wildrice. FAIR: beakrush (horned), bristlegrass (yellow), buckwheat, bulrush, cowlily (spatterdock), cutgrass (rice), duckweed, eelgrass, flatsedge (redroot), glasswort (woody), hornwort, longtom, naiad (northern), oak, oat, parrotfeather, poolmat, potamogeton (longleaf, sago), saltbush (fathen), saltgrass (seashore), sedge, smartweed (curltop), soybean, spikerush, stonewort, tearthumb (arrowleaf), waterhemp (tall), waterlily, watershield, widgeongrass. *Animal food.* Crustaceans, fish, frogs, insects, mollusks, mosquito larvae, snails. *Nest.* On the ground, near water, in tall prairie grasses. *Attracting.* Manage choice foods such as browntop millet, coast cockspur, Japanese millet, redroot, and smartweed in marshes or fields that can be flooded in winter.

pipit, American. See pipit, water.

pipit, Sprague's (also called Missouri or prairie skylark; *Anthus spragueii*). Winters in fields of southeastern states on the Gulf coast. *Animal food* (75%). Chiefly ants, crickets, grasshoppers, and moths; also beetles, bugs, caterpillars, weevils. *Plant food.* CHOICE: croton, euphorbia. FAIR: panicum, ragweed (common). *Nest.* On the ground, northwestward from northwestern Minnesota.

pipit, water (also called titlark and American pipit; *Anthus spinoletta*). Common to abundant summer resident of fields and bogs in Canadian provinces. Winters from Arkansas and Maryland southward throughout United States. *Animal food* (100% summer, 70% winter). Ants, beetles, bugs, caterpillars, crickets, crustaceans, flies, grasshoppers, spiders. *Plant food.* CHOICE: amaranth, crabgrass (hairy, smooth), croton, euphorbia (thymeleaf), violet, wheat, witchgrass (common). FAIR: bristlegrass, canary-grass, chickweed, copperleaf, corn, crowberry (black), oat, ragweed (common), smartweed, *Nest.* In carpet of plants on the tundra, around and under low shrubs such as birch (dwarf arctic), crowberry (black), dogwood (bunchberry).

plover. Seven species of plovers (subfamily Charadriinae) occur in eastern North America: six of those listed below, which are named "plover," and the killdeer, which is also a true plover. The upland plover belongs to the Scolopacinae subfamily.

plover, American golden (*Pluvialis dominica*). Common migrant, gathering in Labrador and Nova Scotia in the early fall; occasional in eastern United States. Fairly common in Mississippi valley during northern migration in spring toward northwestern North America. *Animal food* (perhaps 90%). Beetles, crickets, cutworms, grasshoppers. *Plant food.* CHOICE: crowberry. *Nest.* In moss or on the ground in the arctic.

plover, Bartramian. See plover, upland.

plover, black-bellied (also called black-breasted plover; *Squatarola squatarola*). Arctic breeder; winters (and nonbreeders occur in summer) on the coasts of Louisiana and Texas. Also winters on Atlantic coast from New Jersey southward. *Animal food* (100%). Beetles, crabs, earthworms, grasshoppers, marine worms, shellfish, snails, spiders. *Nest.* On the ground, lined with grass.

plover, calico. See turnstone, ruddy.

plover, Kentish. See plover, snowy.

plover, killdeer or **noisy.** See killdeer.

plover, piping (*Charadrius melodus*). Common summer resident on lake and coastal beaches from Great Lakes and Virginia northward into southern Canada; winters along the Atlantic and Gulf coasts from South Carolina and Florida to Texas. *Animal food* (100%). Tiny marine animals. *Nest.* Among stones on beaches.

plover, red-breasted. See knot.

plover, ring or **ring-necked.** See plover, semipalmated.

plover, semipalmated (also called ring or ring-necked plover; *Charadrius semipalmatus*). Abundant summer resident of muddy tidal shores from arctic Canada to the Gulf of St. Lawrence; winters on the Atlantic and Gulf shores from South Carolina to Florida and Texas. *Animal food* (100%). Marine animals, grasshoppers, mosquitoes. *Nest.* On the ground, lined with leaves and grass.

plover, snowy (also called Kentish plover; *Charadrius alexandrinus*). Common yearlong resident of Gulf beaches from Texas and Louisiana to Florida; numbers are increased in winter by migrants from the western states. *Animal food* (100%). Marine crustaceans and worms. *Nest.* On sandy beaches.

plover, thick-billed. See plover, Wilson's.

plover, upland (also called Bartramian plover; *Bartramia longicauda*). Uncommon summer resident of prairies, fields, and pastures from Ontario and Maine southward to Missouri, Ohio, and Maryland; migrates across the United States to Argentina. *Animal food* (nearly 100%). Chiefly crickets, grasshoppers, weevils; also ants, beetles, bugs, earthworms, flies, moths, snails, spiders. *Nest.* On the ground, in open, dry prairies.

plover, Wilson's (also called thick-billed plover; *Charadrius wilsonia*). Common yearlong resident along the surf of the Atlantic and Gulf coasts from southern New Jersey to Florida and Texas. *Animal food* (100%). Marine animals and insects. *Nest.* Among loose pebbles on beaches.

pochard, American. See redhead.

prairie bird. See bunting, lark.

prairie chicken, greater (also called pinnated grouse; *Tympanuchus cupido*). A subspecies in Texas is called Attwater's prairie chicken. Fairly common resident of tall-grass prairie lands from Ontario and Michigan southward to eastern Texas and Missouri. *Plant food* (nearly 100% winter, 70% summer). CHOICE: barley, blackberry, brome, buckwheat (common), clover (white), corn, oak (scarlet), oat, ruellia, rye, sorghum (grain), soybean, wheat. FAIR: apple buds, aspen (quaking), birch (bog), bristlegrass, cherry (black, choke, pin, sand), croton, dogwood (gray, roughleaf), elm, euphorbia, filbert (beaked), goldenrod, lespedeza (Korean), millet (foxtail), poplar, ragweed (western), rose (multiflora), sedge, smartweed, sudangrass, sumac (smooth), sunflower. *Animal food.* Chiefly grasshoppers; also ants, beetles, bugs. *Nest.* On ground, hidden in tuft of grass. *Attracting.* Grow corn, grain sorghum, or wheat in fields. Protect prairie grassland for nesting and summer insect foods.

preacher bird. See vireo, red-eyed.

ptarmigan, rock (also called Welch's ptarmigan; *Lagopus mutus*). Fairly common resident from northern Quebec and Newfoundland northward to Greenland. *Food.* Berries, green leaves, and insects in summer and fall; buds such as blueberries, rhodora, and willows in winter. *Nest.* On the ground in arctic prairies (tundra).

ptarmigan, Welch's. See ptarmigan, rock.

ptarmigan, willow (also called snow or white grouse; *Lagopus lagopus*). Common yearlong resident of muskeg and tundra in Ontario, Quebec, Labrador, and Newfoundland; extends its range southward in winter to Minnesota, New York, and Maine. State bird of Alaska. *Plant food* (perhaps 90% or more). CHOICE: alder, birch (low), blueberry (cowberry, lowbush), cinquefoil (wineleaf), cranberry (small), crowberry (black), huckleberry (black), mushrooms, peavine, strawberry, sweetgale, willow buds. FAIR: andromeda (downy), leatherleaf, ledum (Labradortea), rhodora. *Animal food.* Insects and spiders. *Nest.* On the ground.

puffin, common (also called sea parrot and arctic puffin; *Fratercula arctica*). Abundant resident on cliffs, islands, and bays of the north Atlantic from Labrador to Maine; winters from the ice line southward to Massachusetts, casually to New Jersey. *Animal food* (100%). Chiefly fish. *Nest.* In a burrow in the ground.

pulldoo. See coot, American.

quail, bobwhite. See bobwhite.

quail, coturnix (*Coturnix coturnix*). Introduced in the United States many times, but apparently without success.

rail. Eight members of the rail subfamily (Rallinae) are found in eastern North America: the five species which follow below, the sora, and the common and purple gallinules. The American coot is a near-relative.

rail, black (*Laterallus jamaicensis*). Common, but seldom seen (because of its sparrow size and secretive habits) summer resident of tidal marshes from Connecticut to Florida and less commonly to Kansas, Iowa, and Minnesota. Winters on the coasts of Georgia, Florida, and Louisiana.

rail, Carolina. See sora.

rail, clapper (also called marsh hen, and Florida, Louisiana, mangrove, northern, and Wayne's clapper rail; *Rallus longirostris*). Common yearlong resident of Atlantic and Gulf coast saltmarshes from New York to Florida. *Animal food* (90% winter). Clams, clamworms, crabs, crayfish, fish, insects (aquatic), shrimp. *Plant food.* Cordgrass. *Nest.* Built on the ground, in or under saltmarsh vegetation; frequently in cordgrass, glasswort, gumweed, rush (needlegrass), saltgrass; occasionally in bulrush, sumpweed.

rail, common. See sora.

rail, king (also called marsh hen; *Rallus elegans*). Common summer resident of inland fresh marshes from Minnesota and Connecticut southward to Texas and Florida; winters commonly on coastal marshes of southern states from Texas to Georgia, occasional northward. *Animal food* (nearly 100%). Aquatic bugs, beetles, crayfish, dragonfly nymphs, frogs, grasshoppers, leeches, tadpoles. *Plant food.* Arrowhead, rice. *Nest.* In freshwater marsh, built on the ground or in vegetation; frequently in buttonbush, cattail, oat, rice, rush, sedge.

rail, Virginia (also called marsh hen; *Rallus limicola*). Common summer resident of freshwater marshes from southern Canada southward to Missouri, Alabama, and North Carolina. Winters commonly in fresh and salt marshes along the Atlantic coast from North Carolina to central Florida; uncommon on the Gulf coast and inland. *Animal food* (predominant). Ants, aquatic insects, beetles, caterpillars, crayfish, crickets, crustaceans, earthworms, fish, grasshoppers, snails, snakes, spiders. *Plant food.* CHOICE: wildrice. FAIR: bulrush, cordgrass, spikerush. *Nest.* In freshwater marsh vegetation such as cattails or grass; occasionally in salt marsh.

rail, yellow (*Coturnicops noveboracensis*). Rare summer resident of freshwater marshes in southern Canada and northern United States; winters in marshes from Cape Sable, Florida, to Louisiana. *Animal food* (predominant). Ants, beetles, bugs, crustaceans, fly larvae, freshwater snails, grasshoppers, spiders. *Plant food.* CHOICE: sedge, smartweed. FAIR: bristlegrass, bulrush, nutrush. *Nest.* On the ground among grasses in marsh.

rain crow. See cuckoo, black-billed and yellow-billed.

raven, common (*Corvus corax*). Common yearlong resident of boreal forests and mountains from northern Canada southward to Minnesota, Maine, and in the Appalachian mountains south to Georgia. *Animal food* (nearly 100%). Chiefly carrion; also birds, crayfish, eggs, fish, frogs, insects, mammals, pork, reptiles. *Plant food.* Bread, corn, oat. *Nest.* In cliffs or trees;

frequently in hemlock, pine (eastern white), spruce; occasionally in box-elder, locust, oak (white), poplar, whitecedar, willow, windmill towers, old buildings, under bridges, or on crossarm poles.

razorbill (also called tinker and razor-billed auk; *Alca torda*). Fairly common yearlong resident of Atlantic coastal waters and islands from Labrador to Maine; extends range in winter southward to New York, rarely to South Carolina. *Animal food* (100%). Chiefly fish. *Nest.* On bare rock of island cliffs.

redbird. See cardinal.

redbird, black-winged. See tanager, scarlet.

redbird, summer. See tanager, summer.

redbird, winter. See cardinal.

redhead (also called American pochard; *Aythya americana*). Common diving duck, summer resident of freshwater marshes in Iowa, Minnesota, Wisconsin, and westward. Winters from northern Arkansas, southern Illinois, and eastern Maryland southward to the Gulf states, Georgia, and South Carolina; rarely to Florida. *Plant food* (90%). CHOICE: barley, bulrush (alkali, American, river, softstem), corn, millet (foxtail, proso), oat (common), potamogeton (baby, leafy, longleaf, sago, thorowort), rye, smartweed (bigroot, curltop, Pennsylvania, swamp), sorghum (grain), stonewort, waterlily (yellow Mexican), wheat, widgeongrass, wildcelery, wildrice. FAIR: algae (filamentous), barnyardgrass, bristlegrass (yellow), burreed (American, giant), cockspur (coast), duckweed, hornwort, naiads, poolmat, sedge, spikerush, watershield. *Animal food.* Caddisflies, grasshoppers, midge larvae, mollusks, snails. *Nest.* On the ground near water, or over water in a clump of vegetation. *Attracting.* Grow choice foods in ponds or fields that can be flooded in winter.

redpoll, common (also called linnet, redpoll linnet, and greater redpoll; *Acanthis flammea*). Common yearlong resident of birch thickets and shrubby areas of arctic and subarctic Canada. Winters from breeding range southward to Iowa, Ohio, and New Jersey; rarely farther south. *Plant food* (nearly 100%). CHOICE: alder (American green, red, thinleaf), amaranth, birch (paper), catnip, corn, goosefoot, hemp, larch (European, Japanese), millet (foxtail), ragweed, rape, smartweed, sweetgum, timothy. FAIR: bristlegrass, elm. *Animal food* (possibly important in summer). Ants, flies, spiders. *Nest.* In trees, frequently in birch (paper), larch, spruce.

redpoll, greater. See redpoll, common.

redpoll, hoary (*Acanthis hornemanni*). Common arctic breeder; winters irregularly in brushy areas as far south as Minnesota, Indiana, and Maryland. *Plant food* (nearly 100%). Similar to common redpoll, above. *Animal food.* Insects. *Nest.* In trees and shrubs; frequently in spruce, willow.

redstart, American (*Setophaga ruticilla*). Common member of the "wood warbler" family; summer resident of brushy deciduous woodlands from northern Ontario and Newfoundland southward to southeastern Oklahoma, Georgia, and North Carolina. Winters mostly in Central America. *Animal food* (perhaps 95%). Chiefly insects; also suet and suet mix. *Plant food.* Grapes, serviceberry. *Nest.* Frequently in alder, beech, birch, elm, hawthorn, maple (red, sugar), willow; occasionally in apple, ash, blackgum, hophornbeam, oak (white), pear, plum, viburnum, or other shrubs.

   red-tail, eastern. See hawk, red-tailed.

   redwing. See blackbird, redwinged.

   reedbird. See bobolink.

   ricebird. See bobolink.

   ringdove. See dove, ringed-turtle.

   roadrunner (*Geococcyx californianus*). Uncommon yearlong resident of open brushy country in western Arkansas and Louisiana, and westward. State bird of New Mexico. *Animal food* (nearly 100%). Chiefly fresh carrion, grasshoppers, and lizards; also beetles, birds and bird eggs, crickets, mice, rats (cotton), snails, snakes, spiders, wireworms, and other insects. *Plant food.* Grapes. *Nest.* Frequently in redcedar; occasionally in hackberry, honeysuckle (winter), oak (live), osageorange, sycamore, willow, or on the ground.

   Robert. See bobolink.

   robin (also called eastern robin; *Turdus migratorius*). Common to abundant member of the "thrush" family; summer resident of towns, open woodlands, lawns, golf courses, and roadsides from northern Ontario and Newfoundland southward to south central Texas, central Alabama, and South Carolina. Some robins winter throughout the range; abundant flocks migrate to the Southern states (including Florida) to feed on berries and fruits and the earthworms of moist and unfrozen southern soils. State bird of Connecticut, Michigan, and Wisconsin. *Plant food* (75% fall, 60% winter and spring, 25% summer). CHOICE: apple, barberry (Japanese), blackberry (Allegheny), blackgum, blueberry (highbush), bread (white, including toast), camphortree, cherry (black, choke, European bird, mahaleb, mazzard, pin, sour), cornbread, cotoneaster, crabapple (Japanese flowering), cranberry (small), creeper (Virginia), currants, dogwood (alternateleaf, flowering, gray, roughleaf, silky, stiffcornel, tatarian), elaeagnus (autumn, cherry, thorny), elder (American, European red, scarlet), fig (dried), gallberry, gooseberry, grape (cultivated, fox, frost, summer), hackberry (common, sugar), holly (Japanese), honeysuckle (Amur, Belle, Manchurian, Morrow, tatarian), huckleberry (black), laurelcherry, magnolia (southern), matrimonyvine, mountainash (American, European), mulberry, papermulberry (common), peach (dried), plum (American, garden), pokeberry (common), possumhaw, privet (Japanese), prunes, raisins, raspberry, red-cedar, sassafras, serviceberry (Allegheny, downy), snailseed (Carolina), spicebush (common), strawberry, sumac (smooth), sweetbay, tupelo (water). FAIR: apricot, barberry (European), beautyberry (American), bittersweet, chinaberry, chokeberry (red), coralberry, corn, date, hawthorn (English), holly (American, Chinese), ivy (English), Jerusalemcherry, liriope, moonseed, nandina, nightshade (bitter), nut meats, palmetto (cab-bage), peanut, peanutbutter, pear, peppertree (Brazil), persimmon (com-mon), photinia (Chinese), privet (Amur, Chinese, glossy), pyracantha, rose (multiflora), seabuckthorn (common), serviceberry, sumac (shining, staghorn), supplejack, viburnum, waxmyrtle (northern), winterberry (com-mon). *Animal food.* Chiefly earthworms; also beetles, bugs, caterpillars, centipedes, crickets, cutworms, flies, grasshoppers, millipedes, slugs, snails, sowbugs, spiders, termites. Suet is a fair food. *Nest.* Frequently on platform-type birdhouses, and in trees: apple, arborvitae (eastern), ash, boxelder, elm, maple, oak (blackjack, live, pin, post, sawtooth, shingle, water, white, willow), pine (loblolly, red, shortleaf), poplar, redcedar, spruce (Norway), willow; occasionally in 50 other kinds of trees and shrubs. *Attracting.* Robins feed heavily on insects and earthworms on well-kept lawns, improved pas-tures, irrigated fields and other fertile lands. They will nest on a platform-type box with a 6x8-inch floor and a sloping roof, placed under eaves. They use mud in building their nests. They will come to bread, raisins, and other fruits at feeders or on the ground. Choice fruit plants such as blackgum, mulberry, and pokeberry are especially attractive.

sanderling (also called bull peep, and surf or white snipe; *Crocethia alba*). Common shore bird of beaches and lakes. An arctic breeder; common migrant or winter resident from Massachusetts southward along the Atlantic and Gulf coasts to South America, and migrant through the Great Lakes and Canada. *Animal food* (nearly 100%). Crustaceans, insects, marine worms, shellfish. *Nest.* In a depression on the ground, lined with grass or leaves.

sandpeeps. See sandpiper.

sandpiper. The sandpipers are members of the Scolopacidae, a family of shorebirds, 26 species of which occur in eastern North America—the sander-ling, 11 species with the name sandpiper, long-billed curlew, long- and short-billed dowitcher, dunlin, marbled and Hudsonian godwit, knot, upland plover, common snipe, whimbrel, willet, American woodcock, and greater and lesser yellowlegs. The diet of most species is invertebrate animal life, taken from shallow water and mud flats.

sandpiper, Baird's (also called peep, mud peep, or sandpeep; *Erolia bairdii*). An arctic breeder; fairly common migrant through the interior west of the Mississippi River, less common in spring; occasional on the Atlantic coast. *Animal food* (nearly 100%). Ants, caterpillars, earthworms, flies, grasshoppers, mosquitoes, snails, water-beetles, weevils, and various other larvae. *Nest.* A depression on the ground.

sandpiper, buff-breasted (*Tryngites subruficollis*). Common migrant from arctic America to Argentina, with spring concentrations on fields and prairies in Texas (Rockfort). Fall migrant through Louisiana and Missouri, and small numbers eastward to Florida (Leon County) and the New England states. *Animal food* (100%). Ants, crickets, grasshoppers, small mollusks. *Nest.* On the ground, in a depression lined with grass or leaves.

sandpiper, least (also called American stint, mud peep, and sandpeep; *Erolia minutilla*). Common winter resident of grassy tidal marshes and shores from North Carolina to Florida and Texas (nonbreeding birds also occur throughout this range in summer). Nests chiefly in Alaska. *Animal food* (100%). Crustaceans, earthworms, insects, mollusks. *Nest.* A depression in the ground lined with grass and leaves, near water.

sandpiper, pectoral (also called grassbird and krieker; *Erolia melanotos*). Common fall migrant about ponds and tidal waters on the Atlantic coast and Hudson Bay area, and through the Mississippi River valley enroute from South America to arctic breeding grounds. *Animal food* (nearly 100%). Chiefly crustaceans, earthworms, insects, mollusks. *Nest.* On the ground, in a depression lined sparsely with grass.

sandpiper, purple (*Erolia maritima*). Arctic breeder; winters sparingly from Nova Scotia along the Atlantic coast to Maryland. Casual migrant through inland United States and Canada. *Animal food* (probably 100%). Clams, mussels. *Nest.* On the ground, in a slight depression thinly lined with grass.

sandpiper, red-backed. See dunlin.

sandpiper, red-breasted. See knot.

sandpiper, semipalmated (also called peep, black-legged peep, little peep, and sandpeep; *Ereunetes pusillus*). Common summer resident of beaches and shores from Labrador to Quebec. Winters from South Carolina to the Gulf of Mexico; migrates along the Atlantic coast and interior waters of United States and Canada. *Animal food* (nearly 100%). Ants, beetles, caddisflies, clamworms, crustaceans, mollusks *Nest.* On the ground, in a hollow lined with grass.

sandpiper, solitary (*Tringa solitaria*) Common summer resident of marshes, ponds, and swamps from Ontario to Labrador and Quebec. Winters from Georgia and Florida southward to Texas and South America. *Animal food* (probably 100%). Caddisfly nymphs, fish (shiners), grasshoppers, hellgramites, snails, tadoples. *Nest.* Frequently in birch, spruce; and in old nests of other birds (rusty blackbird, robin).

sandpiper, spotted (also called peep, peet-weet, sandpeep, tip-up, teeter, teeterer, and teeter-tail; *Actitis macularia*). Common summer resident of lakes, ponds, and shores from northern Ontario and Labrador southward to central Texas and Virginia. Winters along the Atlantic coast of South Carolina to Florida, the Gulf coast to Texas, and southward to South America. Migrates along the Atlantic coast and through interior United States in spring and fall. *Animal food* (probably 100%). Ants, beetles, caddisfly nymphs, dragonfly nymphs. *Nest*. On the ground near water, in a depression lined with grass and leaves.

sandpiper, stilt (*Micropalama himantopus*). Breeds in marshes and shallow ponds of American arctic south to northern Ontario; winters in South America. Migrates in spring along the western Mississippi valley, and in fall regularly (in small numbers) through the Great Lakes and Atlantic coastal states south of Maine. *Animal food* (more than 90%). Clamworms, crustaceans, fly larvae, grasshoppers, other insects, and mollusks. *Nest*. On the ground, in a depression.

sandpiper, swimming. See phalarope.

sandpiper, western (also called peep, black-legged peep, little peep, and sandpeep; *Ereunetes mauri*). Common to abundant winter resident or visitor of beaches, mudflats, and shores from the North Carolina coast to Florida, along the Gulf coast to Texas and southward. Breeds in Alaska, and migrates regularly in small numbers on the south Atlantic coast as far north as New York. *Animal food* (perhaps 100%). Aquatic and shore invertebrates. *Nest*. On the ground, in a depression.

sandpiper, white-rumped (also called bull peep; *Erolia fuscicollis*). Migrant between arctic America and South America, chiefly on interior plains in the spring and along the north Atlantic coastal states in the fall. *Animal food* (nearly 100%). Clamworms, crustaceans, fish, insects, mollusks. *Nest*. On the ground around marshy lakes and ponds.

sapsucker, yellow-bellied (also called common, red-breasted, red-naped, or red-throated sapsucker, and yellow-bellied woodpecker; *Sphyrapicus varius*). Fairly common member of the woodpecker family. Summer resident of orchard and open woodland habitat from Ontario and Newfoundland, southward to Missouri and Virginia. Winters from Missouri, Ohio valley, and New Jersey southward to the Gulf of Mexico and Florida. *Plant food* (about 50%). CHOICE: apple, cherry (black), creeper (Virginia), dogwood (flowering), elder (American), hackberry (common), honeysuckle (Amur), nut meats, peanutbutter, poisonivy, strawberry; also the sap of many tree species. FAIR: apricot, blackgum, grape (frost), hawthorn, holly (American), nandina, plum (garden), pokeberry (common), redcedar, sassafras. *Animal food*. Chiefly ants; also beetles, caterpillars, centipedes, katydid eggs, locust eggs, spiders. Also suet. *Nest.* In a hole in a dead or decaying tree. *Attracting.* They often come to feeders for their choice fruits, and occasionally for nut meats and suet.

sawbills. See mergansers.

scaup, greater (also called raft or scaup duck, ring-billed scaup duck, blackhead, and bluebill; *Aythya marila*). Common diving duck; summer resident of lakes, ponds, and rivers from Ontario and Quebec southward to Michigan. Winters in salt bays and estuaries of the Atlantic and Gulf coasts from Quebec to Florida and Texas, and on Lakes Erie and Ontario. *Animal food* (about 50%). Chiefly aquatic insects, clams, crabs, gastropods, mussels, oysters. *Plant food.* CHOICE: corn, naiad (northern), pea (garden), potamogeton (baby, sago), rice, sealettuce, stonewort, wheat, widgeongrass, wildcelery, wildrice. FAIR: arrowhead, bristlegrass (green), bulrush (American, river, saltmarsh), burreed, eelgrass, hornwort, marestail, naiad (southern), parrotfeather, sedge, smartweed (spotted, water), waterlily (yellow Mexican), watershield. *Nest.* In marshy ground, made of weeds and grass.

scaup, lesser (also called raft or scaup duck, ring-billed scaup duck, little bluebill, and blackhead; *Aythya affinis*). Common diving duck, summer resident from Iowa north and westward. Winter resident of freshwater and saltwater bays, lakes, marshes, and ponds from Arkansas, Illinois, and Maryland southward to the Gulf of Mexico and Florida; less common in Northern states to Canada. *Plant food* (60%). CHOICE: arrowhead (common), bulrush (American, river, saltmarsh), corn, naiad (northern), oak, poolmat, potamogeton (floatingleaf, sago), sealettuce, sorghum (grain), stonewort, widgeongrass, wildcelery, wildrice. FAIR: barnyardgrass, bogbean (common), bristlegrass, bulrush (water), burreed (American, giant), buttonbush, chufa, cutgrass (rice), duckweed, eelgrass, flatsedge (redroot), hornwort, naiad (southern), sedge, smartweed (curltop, dotted, marshpepper, Pennsylvania, swamp), spikerush, waterlily (American, yellow Mexican), watershield. *Animal food.* Chiefly clams and aquatic insects. *Nest.* In marshy grounds, made of weeds and grass.

scaup, ring-necked. See duck, ring-necked.

scissorbill. See skimmer, black.

scoter, American. See scoter, common.

scoter, American velvet. See scoter, white-winged.

scoter, common (also called American scoter and often miscalled black or sea coot and black duck; *Oidemia nigra*). Fairly common diving duck. Breeds in arctic tundra; winters on the Great Lakes and the Atlantic coast from Newfoundland to South Carolina, and rarely or irregularly to inland states and Florida. *Animal food* (nearly 100%). Chiefly clams, mussels, scallops and other mollusks; also crustaceans, echinoderms, fishes, insects. *Nest.* On ground, near water.

scoter, surf (often miscalled sea coot; *Melanitta perspicillata*). Fairly common diving duck. Breeds in northwest Canada and Alaska; winters in ocean and coastal salt bays from Bay of Fundy to Florida, and on the Great Lakes; rarely in the interior from Iowa and Kentucky to the Gulf of Mexico. *Animal food* (nearly 100%). Chiefly clams, crayfish, mussels, scallops; and echinoderms, fishes, insects. *Nest.* On the ground, usually in marsh grass.

scoter, white-winged (also called American velvet scoter, and miscalled sea coot and white-winged coot; *Melanitta deglandi*). Common summer diving duck in large lakes from Ontario and Newfoundland southward to Massachusetts. Winters sporadically from Nebraska, the Great Lakes, and Gulf of St. Lawrence southward to the Tennessee Valley and South Carolina Atlantic coast. *Animal food* (nearly 100%). Chiefly clams and mussels; also crustaceans, fishes, insects, mollusks. *Nest.* In a depression on the ground, usually under small shrubs.

sea coots. See scoters.

sea crow. See oystercatcher, American.

sea dove. See dovekie.

sea gull. See gull species.

sea hawk. See jaeger; osprey.

sea parrot. See puffin, common.

sea pigeon. See guillemot, black.

shag. See cormorants.

shitepoke. See heron, green.

shoveler (also called spoonbill or spooney; *Spatula clypeata*). Common to abundant surface-feeding duck of freshwater marshes and shallow ponds. Summer resident from southern Ontario and Pennsylvania southward to Iowa and North Carolina, occasionally in other northern states. Winters along the Gulf of Mexico from Texas to Florida and the coast of Georgia and South Carolina southward in the Caribbean and in Central America; migrates through the Mississippi River states and westward. *Plant food* (75%). CHOICE: aneilema (keisak), barley, bulrush (saltmarsh), corn, cutgrass (rice), flatsedge (redroot), millet (foxtail, proso), oat (common), panicum (fall), potamogeton (sago), rye, sorghum (grain), wheat, widgeongrass. FAIR: barnyardgrass, buttonbush, chufa, cockspur (coast), duckweed, hornwort, naiad, oak (pin), sedge, smartweed (curltop, Pennsylvania), stonewort, waterlily (yellow Mexican). *Animal food.* Aquatic insects, crustaceans, fly larvae, mollusks. *Nest.* On the ground, usually in short or tall grasses. *Attracting.* Provide ponds and flooded fields with choice foods.

shrike, loggerhead (also called butcherbird, and migrant, southern, or white-rumped shrike; *Lanius ludovicianus*). Common summer resident of farmlands from southern Canada southward to the Gulf of Mexico and Florida. Northern subspecies winter with southern subspecies in southern

United States. *Animal food* (nearly 100%). Beetles, caterpillars, cicadas, fresh carrion (including birds), frogs, grasshoppers, lizards, mice, snails, wasps. Also suet. *Nest.* Frequently in apple, cottonwood, hackberry, hawthorn, honeylocust, oak (blackjack, live, pin, water, white), osageorange willow. *Attracting.* Sometimes comes to a suet feeder.

shrike, migrant. See shrike, loggerhead.

shrike, northeastern. See shrike, northern.

shrike, northern (also called butcherbird and northeastern shrike; *Lanius excubitor*). Fairly common summer resident of open lands in northern Ontario, Quebec, and central Labrador; winters southward from breeding range to Iowa, Indiana, and Washington, D.C. *Animal food* (nearly 100%). Beetles, caterpillars, grasshoppers, lizards, mice, small birds, suet, wasps *Nest.* Frequently in spruce; occasionally in thorny shrubs.

shrike, southern. See shrike, loggerhead.

shrike, white-rumped. See shrike, loggerhead.

siskin, pine (*Spinus pinus*). Common yearlong resident of forest and adjacent weedy areas from southern Canadian provinces southward to Kansas, Michigan, and New York; extends its range southward in winter to southern Texas and central Florida. *Plant food* (90% winter, 20% summer). CHOICE: alder, birch, butternut meats, chickweed, cottonthistle (Scotch), dandelion, hemlock, hemp, millet (foxtail), pine (eastern white, jack, pitch, red, shortleaf), spruce (red, white), sunflower (common), sweetgum, whitecedar (northern). FAIR: elm, maple, sycamore, tamarack. *Animal food.* Aphids, bugs, caterpillars, fly larvae, spiders. *Nest.* Frequently in pine (Austrian, Norway, Scotch), spruce (Norway, white), whitecedar; occasionally in boxelder, elm, fir, hemlock, redcedar. *Attracting.* Sometimes come to platform or window feeders for hemp, nut meats, sunflowers.

skimmer, black (also called storm gull and scissorbill; *Rynchops nigra*). Abundant summer resident along the Atlantic and Gulf coasts from New York to Florida and Texas. *Animal food* (100%). Crustaceans, fish, shrimp. *Nest.* On bare sand on Atlantic and Gulf coasts and islands.

skua. See jaeger.

skylark, Missouri or prairie. See pipit, Sprague's.

snakebird. See anhinga.

snipe, common (also called jacksnipe and Wilson's snipe; *Capella gallinago*). Common shore bird along the edges of ponds and streams, and in shallow bays and mudflats. Summer resident from Ontario and Labrador southward to Iowa, Michigan, and Pennsylvania; winters from Missouri, Indiana, northern Georgia and North Carolina southward through United States to South America. *Animal food* (more than 90%). Aquatic beetles, crustaceans, earthworms, fish, fly larvae, freshwater snails. *Nest.* In a grass-lined depression in marsh ground. *Attracting.* W. W. Neely of South Carolina developed a technique for managing fields and marshy tracts which improves the supply of food for snipe and attracts them in good numbers. His method consists of plowing vegetation into the ground in the fall and keeping the area well watered, so that it is dotted with saturated ground, shallow pools, and dry clods and ridges. The plowed vegetation supports the aquatic animal life upon which the snipe feeds.

snipe, gray, red-bellied, or red-breasted. See dowitcher, short-billed.

snipe, robin. See dowitcher, short-billed; knot.

snipe, surf or white. See sanderling.

snipe, Wilson's. See snipe, common.

snowbird. See bunting, snow; junco, slate-colored.

snowflake. See bunting, snow.

snowy, little. See egret, snowy.

solitaire, Townsend's (*Myadestes townsendi*). Accidental winter visitor from Minnesota to Illinois, Ohio, New York, and New Brunswick; resident in western North America. *Animal food* (50%). Ants, beetles, caterpillars, moths, spiders. *Plant food.* Hackberry (common), pine, redcedar, rose, serviceberry, sumac. *Nest.* Usually on the ground, sometimes on log or stump or in rubbish.

sora (also called marsh hen, Carolina rail, and common rail; *Porzana carolina*). A member of the rail family; common summer resident of fresh-water marshes from Ontario and New Brunswick southward to Missouri and Pennsylvania. Winters in freshwater ponds and saltwater bays from South Carolina and the Gulf states to Central and South America. *Animal food* (50%). Beetles, crickets, crustaceans, grasshoppers, snails, spiders. *Plant food.* CHOICE: bulrush, paspalum (bull), rice, sedge, smartweed, wildrice. FAIR: algae, barnyardgrass, cordgrass, cutgrass (rice), duckweed, panicum, signalgrass (broadleaf), spikerush. *Nest.* In freshwater marshes; frequently in bulrush, cattail.

sparrow. This book covers 25 species known as sparrows that occur in eastern North America. All of the true sparrows belong to the Fringillidae, a family which also includes grosbeaks, finches, and buntings. Like these other species, the sparrows have stout beaks which are well-suited to crack-ing seeds. In the summertime, they vary their predominantly seed diets by eating many destructive insects. They are, in the main, beneficial birds, and among them are many delightful songsters. The ubiquitous house (English) sparrow is not really a sparrow; it belongs to the weaver finch family, the Ploceidae. It is the only "sparrow" which is regarded as a pest.

sparrow, Acadian. See sparrow, sharp-tailed.

sparrow, Bachman's (also called pine woods sparrow and southern pine finch; *Aimophila aestivalis*). Fairly common summer resident of fallow fields, palmetto scrub, and open woods from southern Missouri, central Indiana and Ohio, and Maryland southward to the Gulf coast and central Florida. Winters southward from northeast Texas, Georgia, and North Carolina; casual north of the summer and winter areas. *Plant food* (75%). CHOICE: blueberry, bristlegrass, crabgrass, dropseed, goldstargrass, panicum, paspalum. FAIR: nutrush, pine. *Animal food.* Caterpillars, grasshoppers, leafhoppers, snails, spiders, wasps. *Nest.* On the ground under palmetto, a bush, or clump of grass.

sparrow, bay-winged. See sparrow, vesper.

sparrow, black-hooded. See sparrow, Harris'.

sparrow, Cape Sable (also called Cape Sable seaside sparrow; *Ammospiza mirabilis*). Local in brackish-water marsh in southwestern Florida (Ochopee Marsh near Everglade, mouth of Gum Slough to the Shark River Basin; formerly to Cape Sable). *Animal food* (nearly 100%). Insects, small mollusks, and spiders. *Nest.* Frequently in and attached to saltgrass, switchgrass.

sparrow, chipping (also called eastern chipping sparrow; *Spizella passerina*). Common to abundant summer resident of farms, open woodland, and towns from about the Canadian border southward to Louisiana and South Carolina; winters from Oklahoma, Tennessee, and Maryland southward to the Gulf of Mexico and Florida. *Plant food* (90% winter, 50% summer). CHOICE: amaranth (redroot, slim), brazilnut, bread, bristlegrass (yellow), cake crumbs, canarygrass, corn (cracked), crabgrass, dandelion, doughnuts, millet (browntop, foxtail, Japanese, pearl, proso, Texas), oat, panicum, peanut, peanutbutter, pecan, pine (eastern white), ragweed (common), sorghum (grain). FAIR: bluegrass (annual), chickweed, sesame. *Animal food.* Chiefly ants, beetles, bugs, caterpillars, grasshoppers, leafhoppers, spiders, wasps; also suet. *Nest.* Frequently in apple, arborvitae, beech, birch, blackberry, grape, hemlock, horsechestnut, larch, maple, pear, pine (jack, red, shortleaf), redcedar, rose, spruce. *Attracting.* Come readily to feeding stations for any of their choice foods, which they prefer to eat from the ground.

sparrow, clay-colored (*Spizella pallida*). Common summer resident of brushy prairie land from Michigan and northwestern Illinois westward. Rarely winters in eastern North America but wanders occasionally in migration on the Atlantic coast. *Plant food* (75%). CHOICE: amaranth, bristlegrass, crabgrass, goosefoot, panicum, thistle. *Animal food.* Beetles, leafhoppers, moths, spiders. *Nest.* Frequently near the ground in hawthorn, hazel, hemlock, maple, oak, rose, serviceberry, willow; occasionally on the ground.

sparrow, dusky seaside (also called black shore finch; *Ammospiza nigrescens*). Local resident of salt marshes of eastern Brevard and Orange counties, Florida, including Merritt Island. *Plant food.* CHOICE: Probably similar to seaside sparrow, below. *Animal food.* Probably similar to seaside sparrow, below. *Nest.* Frequently in glasswort, rush, switchgrass.

sparrow, English. See sparrow, house.

sparrow, European tree (*Passer montanus*). Introduced and established locally in St. Charles County, Missouri; also in Calhoun and St. Clair counties, Illinois. *Plant food.* CHOICE: corn, oat, wheat. *Animal food.* Flying insects, often taken over water. *Nest.* Frequently in birdhouses and cavities in trees, roofs, quarries. Occasionally they build bulky nests in trees, as house sparrows do.

sparrow, field (also called eastern field sparrow; *Spizella pusilla*). Common summer resident of brushy grassland from Minnesota, Quebec, and Maine southward to central Texas and southern Georgia. Winters from Missouri, West Virginia, and Massachusetts southward to the Gulf of Mexico, Florida to Texas. *Plant food* (nearly 100% winter, 50% summer). CHOICE: amaranth (redroot), barnyardgrass, blackberry, bluegrass (annual), bread (white), bristlegrass (Faber's, yellow), butternut, canarygrass (common, reed), corn (cracked, ground), cornbread, crabgrass (hairy), dandelion, dropseed, Hardinggrass, hickory, millet (browntop, foxtail, Japanese, pearl, proso, Texas), oat, panicum (Dominican, hiddenseed, shoredune), peanut, peanutbutter, pecan bits, raspberry, rice, sudangrass, switchgrass, wheat. FAIR: chickweed, goosefoot, raisins, sesame, sorgo, timothy, walnut (black). *Animal food.* Ants, beetles, bugs, caterpillars, grasshoppers, leafhoppers, spiders; also suet. *Nest.* Frequently in blackberry, hawthorn, raspberry, rose (multiflora). *Attracting.* They come to feeding stations for any of the choice foods, especially if fed on the ground.

sparrow, fox (also called eastern fox sparrow; *Passerella iliaca*). Commonly breeds in Ontario and Newfoundland northward as far as trees grow. Winters in brushy woodlands of eastern United States from the Canadian border southward to the southern states. *Plant food* (90% winter, 50% summer). CHOICE: barley (cultivated), blackberry, bread (white), bristlegrass, canarygrass, corn (cracked, ground), grape (wild), millet (browntop, pearl, proso), oat, peanut, ragweed, raspberry, smartweed, sorghum (grain), sudangrass, wheat. FAIR: amaranth, creeper (Virginia), euonymus, hackberry, hawthorn, pokeberry (common), pyracantha, redcedar, rose (multiflora), sesame, sorgo. *Animal food.* Beetles, millipedes; also suet. *Nest.* Usually on the ground, occasionally low in a shrub or tree. *Attracting.* Feed well on the ground where any of the choice foods are offered.

sparrow, grasshopper (also called eastern grasshopper sparrow; *Ammodramus savannarum*). Common summer resident of brushy grassland from about the Canadian border southward to Oklahoma, Arkansas, Georgia, and South Carolina. Winters in the southern edge of the breeding area and southward to Central America. *Plant food* (70% or more fall and winter, 40% spring and summer). CHOICE: amaranth (redroot), bristlegrass, oat, panicum, ragweed (common). FAIR: sheepsorrel, smartweed, sunflower. *Animal food.* Chiefly grasshoppers; also ants, bugs, caterpillars, snails, spiders. *Nest.* On the ground, built of grass.

sparrow, Harris' (also called black-hooded sparrow; *Zonotrichia querula*). Breeds in north central Canada. Winters commonly from Iowa to Oklahoma, and central Texas; rare or casual eastward. *Plant food* (95% winter). CHOICE: bread, bristlegrass, corn, elm, hemp, millet (browntop), oat, ragweed, smartweed, sorghum (grain), sunflower, wheat. FAIR: amaranth, blueberry, bulrush, cranberry, crowberry (black), goosefoot, Johnsongrass, panicum. *Animal food.* Insects, snails, spiders. *Nest.* On the ground. *Attracting.* They come to feeders for any of the choice foods, placed on the ground or a window shelf.

sparrow, Henslow's (also called eastern Henslow's sparrow, and stink bird by bobwhite hunters; *Passerherbulus henslowii*). Fairly common summer resident of meadows and weedy fields from Minnesota, southern Ontario, and New Hampshire southward to Missouri, Kentucky, and North Carolina. Winters in the coastal plain from South Carolina and northern Florida to Texas. *Plant food* (perhaps 50% or more). Blackberry, bristlegrass, panicum, ragweed. *Animal food.* Ants, beetles, bugs, caterpillars, grasshoppers, leafhoppers. *Nest.* On the ground, under tufts of grass.

sparrow, house (also called English sparrow; *Passer domesticus*). Abundant to common yearlong resident of towns and farms from southern Canadian provinces to the Gulf of Mexico. Introduced into America from Europe in 1850 and 1852. *Plant food* (100% winter, 90% summer). CHOICE: bread, bristlegrass (green, yellow), canarygrass (canariensis, reed), Columbusgrass, corn (cracked, ground), crabgrass (hairy, smooth), dandelion, fig, grape, Hardinggrass, hemp, Johnsongrass, lettuce, millet (browntop, foxtail, Japanese, pearl, proso, Texas), oat, oatmeal, paspalum (bull), peanut, ragweed (common, giant), rice, rye, sorghum (grain, reed), sudangrass, wheat, wildrice. FAIR: amaranth, bahiagrass, barley (cultivated), barnyardgrass, bittersweet, bluegrass (annual), cantaloup seed, chickencorn, chickweed, crackers, crapemyrtle, dogwood (flowering), elm, flatsedge (poorland), goosefoot, palmetto (cabbage), papermulberry, peach, peanutbutter, pear, pecan, pyracantha, sesame, smartweed (Pennsylvania), sorgo, sunflower (common, cultivated, prairie). *Animal food.* Ants, bees, beetles, bugs, caterpillars, fly larvae, grasshoppers, moths, wasps; suet is a fair food. *Nest.* In eaves, barns, birdhouses, and often in trees and on ivy-covered walls when buildings furnish insufficient nesting sites. *Attracting.* They come to choice foods at feeders (except swinging feeders, of which they are wary). House sparrows are widely regarded as pests because of their noisy chatter, because they flock in great numbers in grain fields and at feeding stations, and because they compete with bluebirds for housing. To discourage house sparrows from nesting leave no nesting nooks at the eaves or elsewhere about building. A grill excludes them if its spaces measure 1 inch or less. Tear down their nests if you wish, from trees and above drain spouts.

House sparrows love to nest in the ivy growing on walls of buildings. Although flocks may do considerable damage to grain crops, especially rice, much of their food is waste seed and destructive insects, so they do have good traits.

sparrow, Ipswich (*Passerculus princeps*). Breeds locally in small numbers on Sable Island, Nova Scotia; winters along the Atlantic coast to Georgia, casually inland in Massachusetts. *Plant food* (90% winter, 20% summer). CHOICE: beachgrass (American). FAIR: blueberry, lovegrass, panicum, saltbush (fat-hen). *Animal food.* Beetles, bugs, caterpillars, flies, snails, spiders. *Nest.* On the ground in grassy places.

sparrow, Labrador savannah. See sparrow, savannah.

sparrow, large-billed. See sparrow, savannah.

sparrow, lark (also called eastern lark sparrow; *Chondestes grammacus*). Common summer resident of open brush and woodland farms from Minnesota, southern Michigan, and New York southward to southern Texas and North Carolina. Winters from the Gulf coast, Texas to Florida, and southwestward. *Plant food* (100% winter, 50% summer). CHOICE: bristlegrass, corn, knotgrass, oats, panicum, ragweed, sorghum (grain), sunflower, wheat. FAIR: amaranth. *Animal food.* Chiefly grasshoppers; also beetles, caterpillars. *Nest.* Frequently on the ground and in shrubs and trees—apple, cottonwood, mulberry, privet (Japanese), redcedar, rose (sweetbrier).

sparrow, Le Conte's (*Passerherbulus caudacutus*). Common summer resident of bogs and swamps in north central Canada, Minnesota, Wisconsin, and Michigan. Winters commonly to sparingly southward from Oklahoma, Arkansas, Georgia, and South Carolina to northern Florida, the Gulf coast, and Texas; usually in "broomsedge" fields and short-grass prairies (southern Louisiana). *Food.* Food habits are not well known. It feeds on insects, grass, and weed seeds. *Nest.* In dead grass on the ground.

sparrow, Lincoln's (*Melospiza lincolnii*). Common summer resident of bogs, marshes, and willow thickets from northern Ontario and central Labrador southward to Minnesota, New York, and Maine. Winters from Oklahoma and Georgia southward to Louisiana and central Florida. *Plant food* (90% fall and winter, 30% spring). CHOICE: amaranth, barley (cultivated), bread, bristlegrass, corn, crabgrass, goosefoot, panicum, ragweed, sedge, sunflower. FAIR: barnyardgrass, knotgrass, polypogon (rabbitfoot). *Animal food.* Ants, beetles, bugs, grasshoppers, millipedes, spiders. *Nest.* On the ground in marsh.

sparrow, Nelson's. See sparrow, sharp-tailed.

sparrow, pine woods. See sparrow, Bachman's.

sparrow, savannah (also called large-billed sparrow and eastern or Labrador savannah sparrow; *Passerculus sandwichensis*). Common summer resident of fields, grassland, and salt-grass shores from northern Canada southward to southern Minnesota, Wisconsin, Michigan, Ohio, West Virginia, and Maryland, Winters from mid-United States to Florida and Central America. *Plant food* (90% winter, 30% summer). CHOICE: amaranth (redroot), barley (cultivated), bluegrass (annual), bristlegrass, crabgrass, oat (wild), panicum, ragweed (common). FAIR: barnyardgrass, brome, canarygrass, chickweed, dropseed, goosefoot, goosegrass, polypogon (rabbitfoot), sandverbena, sedge, sheepsorrel, smartweed, sunflower, wheat. *Animal food.* Ants, beetles, bugs, caterpillars, crabs, flies, grasshoppers, snails, spiders. *Nest.* On the ground, concealed in tall grass.

sparrow, seaside (*Ammospiza maritima*). Four subspecies are called Fisher's or Louisiana, Macgillivray's, Scott's, and Texas seaside sparrow. Common yearlong resident of saltmarshes of the Atlantic and Gulf coasts from Massachusetts to Texas. *Animal food* (probably dominant). Bugs, small crabs, flies, leafhoppers, sandfleas. *Plant food.* Bristlegrass, cordgrass, saltbush (fat-hen), smartweed. *Nest.* On the ground in saltmarsh or meadow, just above normal high tide, in baccharis (eastern), cordgrass (smooth), dropseed (seashore), paspalum (seashore), rush (needlegrass).

sparrow, sharp-tailed. (*Ammospiza caudacuta*). Two subspecies are called Acadian and Nelson's sparrow. Common to abundant summer resident of salt and brackish marshes from Quebec and New Brunswick southward to North Carolina, mostly on the Atlantic coast. Winters from New York to Florida and along the Gulf coast to Texas. *Animal food* (probably dominant). Bugs, flies, leafhoppers, sandfleas. *Plant food.* Cordgrass, panicum, saltbush (fat-hen), wildrice. *Nest.* On the ground, in saltmarsh or meadow.

sparrow, song (also called Atlantic, eastern, and Mississippi song sparrow; *Melospiza melodia*). Widespread but never abundant resident of brush, marshes, and thickets from northern Canada to the Gulf of Mexico and Florida. Some from the far north migrate southward in winter as far as Mexico. *Plant food* (90% winter, 60% summer). CHOICE: amaranth (redroot, slim), barnyardgrass, bread, bristlegrass, canarygrass, corn, crabgrass (hairy), dandelion, dogwood (tatarian), elder, Hardinggrass, hemp, millet (browntop, foxtail, Japanese, pearl, proso, Texas), mulberry, oat, panicum, peanut, peanutbutter, pecan meats, pine (Virginia), ragweed (common), smartweed (Pennsylvania), sorghum (grain), sudangrass, sunflower (common), walnut meats, wheat. FAIR: goosefoot, nightshade, pyracantha, ragweed (giant), rose (multiflora), sorgo. *Animal food.* Ants, beetles, bugs, caterpillars, crickets, grasshoppers. *Nest.* Frequently on the ground in alfalfa or other fields; also in barberry, blackberry, redcedar, spirea, spruce (red), willow. *Attracting.* One or two usually come to choice foods offered on the ground.

sparrow, swamp (*Melospiza georgiana*). Common summer resident of bogs, brushy marshes, and swamps from northern Ontario and Newfound-

land southward to Missouri, West Virginia, and Maryland. Winters from
Iowa, southern Great Lakes, and Massachusetts southward to Florida and
the Gulf coast of Texas, in swamps, cattail marshes, and fields of tall grass.
Plant food (85% summer and fall, 45% winter, 15% spring). CHOICE: bristlegrass, panicum, sedge, smartweed, verbena. FAIR: crabgrass (hairy), cutgrass
(rice), ragweed (giant), strawberry. *Animal food.* Ants, beetles, caterpillars,
crickets, grasshoppers. *Nest.* On or near the ground in marsh.

sparrow, tree (also called eastern tree sparrow; *Spizella arborea*). Abundant summer resident of willow thickets in northern Canada and Alaska;
winters from about the Canadian border southward to central Texas, Arkansas, Tennessee, and North Carolina. *Plant food* (95% fall, winter, and spring;
percent uncertain in summer). CHOICE: amaranth (redroot), bread, bristlegrass, corn (cracked), cornmeal, crabgrass, hemp, millet (browntop, foxtail,
proso), oat, panicum, peanutbutter, pumpkin seed, sedge, sorghum (grain),
switchgrass, weigela (hybrid), wheat. FAIR: bluestem (little), cutgrass
(rice), dropseed, goosefoot, ragweed (common), rose (multiflora), St. Johnswort (shrubby), sheepsorrel. *Animal food.* Ants, beetles, bugs, caterpillars,
grasshoppers, spiders, suet. *Nest.* In a low tree, shrub, or on the ground.
Attracting. Come readily to choice foods at feeders.

sparrow, vesper (also called bay-winged sparrow and eastern vesper
sparrow; *Pooecetes gramineus*). Common to abundant summer resident of
fields, dry meadows, and brushy grasslands from Ontario and Nova Scotia
to Missouri, Tennessee, and North Carolina. Winters from Arkansas, Kentucky, and Pennsylvania southward to Mexico, the Gulf coast, and central
Florida. Often seen singing on fences in the spring. *Plant food* (90% winter,
60% spring and fall, 40% summer). CHOICE: amaranth (prostrate, redroot),
bluegrass, bristlegrass, millet (foxtail), oat, panicum (fusiform), ragweed,
smartweed, wheat. FAIR: brome, goosefoot, sunflower. *Animal food.* Ants,
beetles, bugs, caterpillars, grasshoppers. *Nest.* On the ground in grassland.

sparrow, white-crowned (*Zonotrichia leucophrys*). Fairly common summer resident of fields, pastures, and brushy cover from Ontario to Labrador
and Newfoundland. Winters from Missouri, Kentucky, western North Carolina, Georgia, and Louisiana westward and south to Mexico. *Plant food*
(nearly 100% fall and winter, 75% spring, 65% summer). CHOICE: amaranth
(redroot), bluegrass (annual), bread, bristlegrass, corn, dandelion, goosefoot, hemp, oat (common), panicum, peanut, ragweed, rice, smartweed,
sorghum (grain), sunflower, walnut meats. FAIR: barley (cultivated), chickweed, cowpea, dropseed, fig, pyracantha, raisins, raspberry, sweetgum. *Animal food.* Ants, beetles, bugs, caterpillars, grasshoppers, spiders, wasps. *Nest.*
Frequently on the ground or in arborvitae, spruce, thimbleberry. *Attracting.*
Feeds readily on choice foods offered on the ground.

sparrow, white-throated (also called Canada bird, Canada white-throat, and Peabody bird; *Zonotrichia albicollis*). Common to abundant summer resident of woodland thickets from Ontario and southern Labrador southward to Minnesota, Ohio, and New York. Winters from its southern summer range southward to northern Florida, the Gulf coast, and south Texas; casually north to southern Canada. *Plant food* (90% fall and winter, 50% spring and summer). CHOICE: amaranth (redroot), barnyardgrass, beech (staminate flowers), birdeye, blackberry, blueberry (lowbush), brazilnut, bread (white), bristlegrass (Faber's, giant, green, yellow), canarygrass (*canariensis*, reed), cherry (black), corn (cracked, ground), cornbread, crabgrass (hairy), croton (oneseed, woolly), dandelion, doughnut, elder (American), grape, Hardinggrass, hemp, millet (browntop, foxtail, Japanese, pearl, proso, Texas), oat, panicum (Dominican, hiddenseed), paspalum (bull), peanut, pecan, pine (eastern white, loblolly, shortleaf, slash), ragimillet, ragweed (common), rice, rye, seaoats, smartweed (Pennsylvania), sorghum (grain), spruce (white), strawberry, sudangrass, sunflower (common, cultivated, prairie), sweetgum, switchgrass, walnut (Persian), wheat. FAIR: amaranth (slim), buckwheat, chickencorn, dogwood (alternateleaf, flowering, redosier), lespedeza (Kobe), mountainash (American), mulberry, pokeberry (common), ragweed (giant), sesame, signalgrass (broadleaf), sorgo, spicebush (common), viburnum (European). *Animal food.* Ants, beetles, bugs, caterpillars, flies, millipedes, snails, spiders, suet. *Nest.* Usually on the ground; occasionally in a shrub. *Attracting.* They come to bread, scratchfeed, and other choice foods, fed on the ground.

speckle-belly. See goose, white-fronted.

spoonbill. See shoveler.

spoonbill, roseate (also called rosy spoonbill and pink curlew; *Ajaia ajaja*). A few hundred spoonbills are yearlong residents of shallow ponds, marshes, and mangrove swamps in southern Florida, Louisiana, and Texas; rarely wanders northward. *Animal food* (100%). Aquatic insects, fish, shrimp. *Nest.* Frequently in baldcypress, hackberry (spiny), mangrove (red), oak (willow); occasionally on the ground.

spooney. See shoveler.

sprig or **sprig-tail.** See pintail.

stake driver. See bittern, American.

starling (*Sturnus vulgaris*). Abundant naturalized resident of cities, towns, and rural areas from central Canadian provinces southward throughout eastern North America. Introduced from Europe to New York City in 1890. *Animal food* (90% spring, 60% summer, 40% fall, 70% winter). Chiefly beetles, caterpillars, grasshoppers, millipedes; also bacon grease, fresh carrion, meat, suet. *Plant food.* CHOICE: apple slices, blackgum, blueberry, bread (white), camphortree, cherry (black, mazzard, sour), creeper (Virginia), dogwood (flowering, roughleaf), elaeagnus (cherry), elder (American, European red), hackberry (common, sugar), mulberry, papermulberry (common), pecan, pokeberry (common), potato chips, privet (Chinese, Japanese), strawberry, sweetgum. FAIR: bittersweet, blackberry, buckwheat (common), cantaloup, corn, crabapple, elaeagnus (autumn), grape (cultivated, wild), lettuce, magnolia (southern), oak, oat, pea (garden), peach, pear, ragweed, raspberry, redcedar, rice, sumac (shining, smooth, staghorn), tallowtree, viburnum (nannyberry), waxmyrtle (northern), wheat. *Nest.* In holes, in cavities of trees, woodpecker holes, eaves of buildings, cliffs, and in birdboxes with openings of 2 inches or larger. *Attracting.* Most people are more concerned with discouraging than with attracting starlings, because they frequently expropriate the nests of more desirable species and compete with them for food. They are a mixed blessing to farmers, for although they eat many kinds of destructive insects, they are also fond of berries, cherries, and other fruits. Starlings congregate in large, noisy flocks in shade trees and about buildings in cities, where many kinds of warfare have been waged against them with little apparent success. Significant reduction in their numbers may not be possible unless some natural parasite selects them as a host. To discourage their attendance about the backyard or lawn, offer food only in swinging or enclosed feeders (as for the bluebird); do not scatter foods such as fruit, bread, and table scraps, on the ground. Erect birdhouses for only small bird species, with openings no larger than 1½ inches. These measures, of course, may also deprive some desirable species of food and shelter.

stilt, black-necked (*Himantopus mexicanus*). Fairly common yearlong resident of saltwater and freshwater marshes and mudflats of the Gulf coast in Texas and Louisiana; lesser numbers occur in South Carolina and Florida (Merritt Island). Casual migrant north and eastward, in migration between South America and their breeding areas in western United States. *Animal food* (100%). Beetles, caddisfly nymphs, crustaceans, dragonfly nymphs, mayflies, mollusks, snails, waterbugs. *Nest.* In a depression in sand, sometimes hidden in weeds.

stint, American. See sandpiper, least.

stork, American wood. See ibis, wood.

striker. See tern, common; and hawk, Cooper's.

swallow, bank (*Riparia riparia*). Abundant to common summer resident near marshes, streams, and ponds from Ontario and Labrador southward to Texas, northern Alabama, and Virginia. Migrant through southern United States; winters in South America. *Animal food* (100%). Ants, beetles, flies. *Nest.* Frequently in deep burrows dug into vertical banks of clay, sand, or gravel, always near water; occasionally in a sawdust pile or a hollow tree.

swallow, barn (also called American barn swallow; *Hirundo rustica*). Abundant and widely distributed summer resident of barns and farm buildings, feeding over fields and waters from Ontario and Newfoundland southward to Oklahoma, northern Alabama, Tennessee, and North Carolina. Migrant through southern United States; winters in South America. *Animal food* (100%). Ants, bees, beetles, bugs, flies, wasps. *Nest.* Built of mud and straw and attached to the face of rocky cliffs, on beams or rafters inside buildings, on the outside under eaves, or, like the phoebe, on a platform with a sloping roof, nailed to the side of a building.

swallow, chimney. See swift, chimney.

swallow, cliff (also called eave swallow; *Petrochelidon pyrrhonota*). Abundant local summer resident in colonies about cliffs, canyons, and rivers from southern Ontario and New Brunswick southward to northeastern Oklahoma, southern Illinois, the mountains of North Carolina and Virginia, and New Jersey. Winters in South America. *Animal food* (100%). Chiefly ants, beetles, bugs; also spiders. *Nest.* A mud nest, often called a mud bottle or jug, is attached to vertical walls of cliffs, concrete dams and locks, and under eaves of barns or houses. *Attracting.* A board nailed up horizontally near the eaves of a building attracts cliff swallows. They also need a nearby supply of mud and straw for building their nests. Destroy the old nests each fall or winter, to discourage house sparrows from taking over, as they begin nesting before the cliff swallows return from South America later in the spring.

swallow, eave. See swallow, cliff and tree.

swallow, rough-winged (*Stelgidopteryx ruficollis*). Common summer resident near lakes and streams from the Canadian border southward to eastern Texas and central Florida. Winters in southern Louisiana and Central America; casual in Florida. *Animal food* (almost 100%). Chiefly ants, beetles, bugs, flies. *Nest.* Frequently in river-bank burrows of clay, sand, or gravel as bank swallows do; occasionally in holes or crannies of buildings. *Attracting.* Start a few holes in a steep bank, and the swallows frequently finish them for nesting.

swallow, tree (also called eave swallow, and white-bellied or white-breasted swallow; *Iridoprocne bicolor*). Abundant local summer resident of cliffs and open country near water from northern Ontario and southern Labrador southward to Missouri and Virginia. Winters from the Gulf coast to Central America; occasionally on the Atlantic coast as far north as Massachusetts. *Animal food* (100% spring, 70% fall and winter). Ants, bees, beetles, bugs, flies, grasshoppers, moths, spiders, wasps. *Plant food.* CHOICE: elaeagnus (autumn), waxmyrtle (northern). FAIR: creeper (Virginia), red-cedar. *Nest.* In birdboxes near marshes or water, in drainpipes, under eaves of buildings, or in holes in trees. *Attracting.* Place a gourd or a wooden nesting house from 3 to 6 feet off the ground. The house should be 6 inches deep, with a 5x5-inch floor and a 1½-inch entrance hole, cut 1–5 inches above the floor. If house sparrows pre-empt your tree-swallow birdhouse, you can drive the sparrows away by removing their nesting materials and by other forms of harassment.

swallow, white-bellied or **white-breasted.** See swallow, tree.

swamp robin. See thrush, wood.

swan, mute (*Cygnus olor*). This is the domestic ornamental swan from European stock. *Plant food* (nearly 100%). Chiefly green forage and grains such as barley, corn, and wheat. *Nest.* On the ground.

swan, whistling (also called American whistling swan; *Olor columbianus*). Fairly common summer resident in the arctic tundra. Winters commonly on large lakes near the Atlantic coast from Maryland to North Carolina, rarely southward to Florida and Gulf coast or northward to Maine. *Plant food* (95% or more). CHOICE: arrowhead (common, duckpotato), corn, grasses, horsetail, potamogeton (sago), rye, smartweed (spotted), wheat, wildcelery. FAIR: burreed, spikerush (squarestem). *Animal food.* Larvae of aquatic beetles and dragonflies, fish, frogs, tadpoles. *Nest.* On the ground in or near marsh.

swift, American. See swift, chimney.

swift, chimney (also called chimney swallow and American swift; *Chaetura pelagica*). Abundant summer resident in towns from Ontario and Nova Scotia southward to the Gulf of Mexico and central Florida; winters in South America. *Animal food* (100%). Flying insects: winged ants, bees, beetles, bugs, craneflies, mayflies, other flies, and wasps. *Nest.* Built on inside wall of unused chimney, a cave, hollow tree, inside a barn, or in an open well.

tanager, Canada. See tanager, scarlet.

tanager, Cooper's. See tanager, summer.

tanager, scarlet (also called firebird, black-winged redbird, and Canada tanager; *Piranga olivacea*). Fairly common summer resident of hardwood forests from Ontario and New Brunswick southward to eastern Oklahoma, northern Georgia mountains, and Maryland. Migrates through southern United States; winters in South America. *Animal food* (possibly 90% in summer). Ants, bees, beetles, bugs, caterpillars, moths, wasps. *Plant food.* CHOICE: blackberry, blueberry, cherry (mazzard), grape, mulberry, service-berry (downy). *Nest.* Frequently in apple, beech, hemlock, maple, oak (black, scarlet, white); occasionally in blackgum, cherry (black), elm, oak (post), redcedar, tuliptree, walnut (black). *Attracting.* Grow fruit trees, shrubs, and vines which produce their choice fleshy fruits.

tanager, summer (also called summer redbird and Cooper's tanager; *Piranga rubra*). Fairly common summer resident of river woodlands from central Oklahoma, eastern Kansas, northwestern Missouri, central Illinois and Ohio, and Delaware, southward to the Gulf coast and southern Florida.

Winters in Central and South America, rarely in extreme southern Texas; casual in other eastern United States and Canadian areas. *Plant food* (probably 50% summer). CHOICE: blackberry, blackgum, bread (white), cherry (black), dogwood (flowering), elaeagnus (cherry), elder, grape (muscadine), mulberry, peanutbutter, pokeberry (common), raisins, sugar water. FAIR: cantaloup seed, plum (garden). *Animal food.* Ants, bees, beetles, bugs, caterpillars, wasps. Suet is a choice food; butter is fair. *Nest.* Frequently in dogwood (flowering), oak (blackjack, live, post, scarlet, turkey, white), pine (loblolly, shortleaf), sweetgum, willow. *Attracting.* Peanutbutter and suet are eaten regularly at feeders. Grow their choice summer fruits in your yard.

teacher. See ovenbird.

teal, blue-winged (*Anas discors*). Surface-feeding duck; common summer resident of freshwater marshes and ponds from southern Ontario and New Brunswick southward to Missouri, Illinois, and New Jersey, rarely to Louisiana and North Carolina. Migrates early in the fall and late in spring through southern United States; winters from South Carolina and Texas to Central and South America, occasionally northward. *Plant food* (70% summer and fall, 80% winter, 55% spring). CHOICE: barley, barnyardgrass, bulrush (alkali, river, saltmarsh, softstem), corn, cutgrass (rice), flatsedge (redroot), junglerice, lovegrass (teal), millet (browntop, foxtail, Texas), naiad (northern), panicum (fall), potamogeton (sago), rice, smartweed (bigroot, Pennsylvania), wheat, widgeongrass, wildrice. FAIR: beakrush (horned), bristlegrass (yellow), chufa, cockspur (coast), duckweed, hornwort, naiad (spiny), paspalum (brownseed), sedge, spikerush (squarestem), stonewort, waterhemp (tall), waterlily (yellow Mexican), watershield. *Animal food.* Chiefly snails and other mollusks; also aquatic insects and crustaceans. *Nest.* On the ground, often in alfalfa, bluegrass (Kentucky), cordgrass (marshhay, prairie), quackgrass, rivergrass. *Attracting.* Grow choice foods in ponds or fields that can be flooded; and protect marsh nesting cover in the North.

teal, green-winged (*Anas carolinensis*). Surface-feeding duck; nests commonly in northwestern United States and Canada and sparingly across the northern states and southern Canada. Winters commonly in brackish marshes, bays, ponds, and lakes from Oklahoma and South Carolina southward to Central America, occasionally northward in United States. *Plant food* (90%). CHOICE: aneilema (keisak), barley (cultivated), barnyardgrass, buckwheat (common), bulrush (alkali, American, saltmarsh), corn, flatsedge (redroot), junglerice, lovegrass (teal), millet (foxtail, Japanese, proso), naiad (northern), oat (common), panicum (fall), paspalum (brownseed), potamogeton (sago), rice, rye, smartweed (bigroot, curltop, dotted, Pennsylvania), sorghum (grain), wheat, widgeongrass, wildrice. FAIR: arrowhead (common), beakrush (horned), bristlegrass (green, yellow), bulrush, chufa, cockspur (coast), duckweed (common), hornwort, longtom, oak (pin), podgrass (shore), poolmat, sedge, signalgrass (broadleaf), spikerush, stonewort, waterhemp (tall), wildcelery. *Animal food.* Aquatic insects, crustaceans, snails. *Nest.* On the ground, in thick grass, or among willows. *Attracting.* Widgeongrass, in brackish and saltwater ponds, attracts them; also any of the other choice foods.

teeter; teeterer; teeter-tail. See sandpiper, spotted.

tell-tale, greater and **lesser.** See yellowlegs, greater and lesser.

tern, arctic (*Sterna paradisaea*). Common summer resident of arctic regions, extreme northern Ontario and Newfoundland northward, and sparingly along the Atlantic coast southward to Massachusetts; rare in other states. Winters in the antarctic. *Animal food* (100%). Chiefly small crustaceans and fish. *Nest.* In an unlined hollow in sand, gravel, sphagnum, or rocks.

tern, black (also called American black tern; *Chlidonias niger*). Common summer resident of interior sloughs and marshes from central Ontario and Maine southward to Missouri, Ohio, and New York; migrant on the Atlantic coast and through interior southern states. Winters in South America. *Animal food* (100%). Chiefly fish and insects (dragonflies, grasshoppers, moths); also crayfish, mollusks, spiders. *Nest.* In marshes, frequently in cattails or reed.

tern, bridled (*Sterna anaethetus*). Rare wanderer from the West Indies to Florida and South Carolina shores at times of hurricanes. *Animal food* (100%). Fish, squid, and other marine animals. *Nest.* Usually among rocks or in the entrance of a burrow, in colonies of sooty terns in the West Indies.

tern, Cabot's. See tern, sandwich.

tern, Caspian (*Hydroprogne caspia*). Common summer resident of interior lakes, coastal bays, and sandy shores from Lake Michigan to Labrador and southward to Texas and South Carolina; winters along the shores of the Gulf of Mexico; migrant on the Atlantic coast. *Animal food* (100%). Chiefly small fish, also bird eggs and mussels. *Nest.* In dry sand, shell beds, gravel, or among driftwood.

tern, common (also called mackerel gull, medrick, striker, and Wilson's tern; *Sterna hirundo*). Abundant summer resident from Ontario and the Gulf of St. Lawrence southward to Minnesota, Ohio, and New York; also on the Atlantic coast to Cape Hatteras, North Carolina, and on the Florida and Texas coasts. Winters from South Carolina and Florida southward to South America. *Animal food* (100%). Almost entirely small fish. *Nest.* In a slight hollow in sand, rocks, or pebbles of a beach, usually lined with stems of beach grasses.

tern, Forster's (*Sterna forsteri*). Common summer resident on the Atlantic and Gulf coasts from Virginia to Texas, also on inland marshes in parts of

Iowa, Minnesota, and Wisconsin. Winters from Texas to northern Florida and Virginia on the coasts. *Animal food* (100%). Fish, frogs, insects (dragonflies). *Nest.* Usually on rafted masses of grasses or seaweed; occasionally on the ground lined with grass.

tern, gull-billed (*Gelochelidon nilotica*). Common resident of lakes, marshes, islands, and the coast from Florida to Texas; accidental northward. *Animal food* (100%). Chiefly insects and spiders. *Nest.* In a depression on the ground, usually among shells or pebbles above high tide; occasionally in short-grass marshes.

tern, least (also called little tern; *Sterna albifrons*). Common summer resident of beaches and bays along the Atlantic and Gulf coasts from Massachusetts to Florida and Texas. Also inland along the Mississippi River system in Iowa, Missouri, Kentucky, and Tennessee. Winters off the coast of Brazil; occasional on Louisiana coast. *Animal food* (100%). Chiefly fish (minnows); also crustaceans and insects. *Nest.* Usually on flat sandy beaches above high tide, in an unlined depression among shells and small stones.

tern, little. See tern, least.

tern, noddy (also called noddy and brown noddy; *Anous stolidus*). Abundant breeder on Bird Key of the Dry Tortugas, off the coast of southern Florida. Winters in the sea about the breeding area, casual to Florida, Louisiana, and South Carolina. *Animal food* (100%). Almost entirely fish. *Nest.* Usually built off the ground in baycedar; occasionally on the ground.

tern, roseate (*Sterna dougallii*). Common local summer resident of small rocky or sandy islands along the Atlantic coast from Nova Scotia to Virginia (most abundant Maine to Massachusetts); also nests on Bush Key, Dry Tortugas, off south Florida. Winters south of United States. *Animal food* (100%). Almost entirely small fish. *Nest.* On the ground, in open sands or rocks, or concealed in thick growth: frequently in beachgrass (American) or poisonivy.

tern, royal (*Thalasseus maximus*). Abundant resident in colonies on sandy islands along the Atlantic from Maryland to Georgia, and the Gulf coast from Louisiana to Texas. Winters from South Carolina southward; wanders north to Massachusetts. *Animal food* (100%). Mostly small fish, but also shrimp. *Nest.* In a slight depression in the sand of island sandbars slightly above high tide.

tern, sandwich (also called Cabot's tern; *Thalasseus sandvicensis*). Abundant summer resident in colonies on island sandbars along the Atlantic coast from Virginia to South Carolina, and the Gulf coast from Texas to Louisiana. Winters from Florida southward. *Animal food* (100%). Chiefly small fish. *Nest.* Without lining, on bare island sandbars above high tide.

tern, sooty (also called eastern sooty tern; *Sterna fuscata*). Abundant breeder on islands of the Dry Tortugas, off Florida's southern tip; accidental or rare elsewhere in United States. *Animal food* (100%). Chiefly small fish. *Nest.* Frequently in a slight depression in bare sand, among rocks, or on coral; occasionally in bermudagrass, glasswort, or tall grasses.

tern, Wilson's. See tern, common.

thistlebird. See goldfinch, American.

thrasher, brown (also called brown thrush; *Toxostoma rufum*). Common summer resident of brushy woodlands from the Canadian border southward in all the states in eastern North America. Winters from Arkansas, Tennessee, and North Carolina to the Gulf coast; casually northward. State bird of Georgia. *Plant food* (75% fall and winter, 50% summer, 30% spring). CHOICE: ampelopsis (heartleaf), beautyberry (American), blackberry (highbush), blackgum, blueberry, bread, cherry (black, mahaleb, mazzard, sour), corn, (cracked, ground), creeper (Virginia), currant, dogwood (flowering, silky, tatarian), elaeagnus (cherry), elder (American, European red), fig, grape (cultivated, summer), honeysuckle (Belle, Manchurian), magnolia (southern), mountainash (American, European), mulberry, oak (Arkansas, water, white), papermulberry (common), peach, peanut, peanutbutter, plum (American, garden), poisonivy, pokeberry (common), pyracantha, raisins, serviceberry (Allegheny, downy), strawberry, sugar water. FAIR: blueberry, gooseberry, moonseed, pine, plum (American), redcedar, rose (multiflora), sumac (smooth, staghorn), tallowtree, waxmyrtle (northern). *Animal food.* Chiefly beetles; also ants, caterpillars, crickets, cutworm, dragonfly, earthworm, frogs, grasshoppers, lizards, mayflies, moths, salamanders, spiders, wireworms; also cheese, suet. *Nest.* Frequently in apple, barberry (Japanese), crabapple, elaeagnus (thorny), gooseberry, hawthorn, honeysuckle (Amur, Japanese, winter), laurelcherry, osageorange, plum (American), privet (Chinese, Japanese), redcedar, rose (multiflora), spirea (bridalwreath, Vanhoutte), spruce, willow. *Attracting.* Come regularly to bird feeders for bread, cheese, corn, nut meats, peanuts, raisins, suet, and wheat. They are fond of water, usually bathing twice a day in warm weather. You can attract brown thrashers where you want them with plantings of choice nesting shrubs, especially thorny elaeagnus, multiflora rose, and rose vines.

thrush, Bicknell's. See thrush, gray-cheeked.

thrush, brown. See thrasher, brown.

thrush, golden-crowned. See ovenbird.

thrush, gray-cheeked (also called Bicknell's thrush; *Hylocichla minima*). Common summer resident of shrubby forests from near northern tree limit in Canada southward to New York and Massachusetts. Migrates southward through all the eastern United States; winters in Central and South America. *Plant food* (65% fall, 20% summer, negligible spring). CHOICE: blackgum, blueberry, cherry (black), dogwood (flowering, roughleaf), elder (American), grape. FAIR: blackberry, sassafras, spicebush. *Animal food.* Chiefly ants, beetles, caterpillars, weevils; also crayfish, earthworms, sowbugs. *Nest.* Frequently in low trees, occasionally on the ground. *Attracting.* Save or plant choice fruit shrubs and trees.

   thrush, hermit (also called eastern hermit thrush; *Hylocichla guttata*). Common summer resident of woodlands and thickets from northern Ontario, central Quebec, and southern Labrador southward to central Minnesota and eastward to New York. Winters southward to the Gulf coast, Texas to Florida. State bird of Vermont. *Plant food* (60% fall and winter, 10% spring and summer). CHOICE: blueberry, cherry (black), dogwood (flowering), elaeagnus (autumn), grape (frost), holly (American), honeysuckle (Amur), nut meats, pokeberry (common), raisins, serviceberry (downy). FAIR: blackgum, creeper (Virginia), currant, dogwood (roughleaf), elder (American, scarlet), gallberry, hackberry (common), honeysuckle (Japanese), huckleberry (black), pyracantha, raspberry, redcedar (eastern), sassafras, spicebush (common), sumac (shining, smooth, staghorn), supplejack (Alabama), viburnum (nannyberry), waxmyrtle (northern). *Animal food.* Ants, beetles, bugs, caterpillars; also suet. *Nest.* Frequently in fir (balsam), huckleberry, or on the ground near fir or hemlock. *Attracting.* Grow choice fruit plants. They sometimes come to nut meats and suet at feeders.

   thrush, olive-backed. See thrush, Swainson's.

   thrush, Swainson's (also called olive-backed thrush; *Hylocichla ustulata*) Common summer resident of Canadian spruce forest from northern Manitoba and Newfoundland southward to Michigan, New York, and in Appalachian mountains to West Virginia. Migrates through southern United States; winters in Central America. *Plant food* (65% fall, 45% summer, 10% spring). CHOICE: barberry (Japanese), cherry (black, pin, sour), creeper (Virginia), dogwood (flowering, gray, redosier, silky), elder (American, scarlet), hackberry (common), serviceberry. FAIR: blackberry, blackgum, fig, grape (frost), mulberry, pokeberry (common), raspberry, rose, sassafras. *Animal food.* Chiefly ants, beetles, and caterpillars; also bugs, earthworms, flies, grasshoppers, millipedes, snails, sowbugs, spiders. *Nest.* Frequently in fir, hemlock, maple, spruce (red); occasionally in alder, bamboo, birch (gray).

   thrush, willow. See veery.

   thrush, Wilson's. See veery.

   thrush, wood (also called swamp robin; *Hylocichla mustelina*). Common summer resident of river woods from Minnesota and New Hampshire southward throughout the eastern United States (except south Florida). Winters in Central America, occasionally in Southern Florida and Texas. Official bird of the District of Columbia. *Plant food* (75% fall, 35% summer, 5% spring). CHOICE: ampelopsis (heartleaf), barberry (Japanese), beautyberry (American), blackberry, blackgum, blueberry, cherry (black, choke, mazzard, sour), dogwood (alternateleaf, flowering, silky), elder (American, European red), grape (frost), honey syrup, magnolia (southern), mulberry, peanutbutter, peppervine, pokeberry (common), serviceberry (downy), spicebush (common), strawberry, sumac (smooth), sweetbay. FAIR: creeper (Virginia), mountainash (American), pyracantha, sarsaparilla (wild). *Animal food.* Ants, beetles, caterpillars, earthworms, flies, grasshoppers, snails, spiders; also suet. *Nest.* Frequently in beech, dogwood (flowering, gray), hawthorn, maple, oak (blackjack, post, white), rhododendron; occasionally in ailanthus (tree-of-heaven), apple, arborvitae (eastern), birch, boxelder, candlenuttree, elm (American), fir, grape, hemlock, hickory, honeysuckle (Japanese), peach, privet, sweetgum, viburnum. *Attracting.* Occasionally come to a feeder for bread, cornmeal, honey syrup, peanutbutter, and suet. Grow their choice fruit plants and shrubby cover. A birdbath attracts them.

thunder pumper. See bittern, American.

timber doodle. See woodcock, American.

tinker. See razorbill.

tip-up. See sandpiper, spotted.

tip-up, yellow. See warbler, palm.

tit, tufted. See titmouse, tufted.

titlark. See pipit, water.

titmice. See titmouse, tufted.

titmouse, crested. See titmouse, tufted.

titmouse, tufted (also called tomtit, tufted tit, titmice, and crested titmouse; *Parus bicolor*). Common yearlong resident of woodlands from Iowa, Lake Erie, and New Jersey southward to Florida and the Gulf of Mexico; uncommon farther north in the United States. *Plant food* (75% winter, 15% summer). CHOICE: almond, beech, brazilnut, bread (white), butternut, cantaloup seed, cashew, cookie crumbs, cornbread, filbert (commercial), hickory (mockernut, shagbark), oak (live, post, turkey, water, willow), peanut, peanutbutter, pecan, piecrust, pine (eastern white, loblolly, longleaf, slash), pistachionut, sunflower (common, cultivated), walnut (black, Persian). FAIR: locust (black), safflower. *Animal food.* Chiefly caterpillars and wasps; also ants, beetles, scale insects, spiders; suet also choice. *Nest.* In birdboxes and holes or cavities in trees. *Attracting.* They will come to a feeding station the year around for bread, cracked nuts, peanuts, peanutbutter, pie crust, safflower, suet, sunflower seed. They will eat from a freely swinging feeder and, like the bluebirds, will enter an enclosed feeder (see figure 2.4). They nest readily in a birdhouse placed on a tree trunk, 4 or 5 feet above ground, using the same type of box as bluebirds, with a 4x4-inch floor, 1¼- or 1½-inch entrance, 6 or 8 inches above the floor.

tomtit. See titmouse, tufted.

towhee, eastern or red-eyed. See towhee, rufous-sided.

towhee, rufous-sided (also called chewink, joree, and eastern or red-eyed towhee; *Pipilo erythrophthalmus*). Common summer resident of brushy woodlands near small towns and in rural areas from southern Ontario to southern Maine and southward to Oklahoma, central Louisiana, the eastern Gulf coast and Florida. Winters from Iowa, the Great Lakes, and Massachusetts southward in the United States. *Plant food* (50% summer, 80% winter). CHOICE: almond, blackberry, blueberry, bread (white), bristlegrass, canarygrass, corn, elaeagnus (cherry), elder (American), grape (muscadine), hickorynut meats, millet (browntop, pearl, proso, Texas), nettlespurge (bellyache), oak (bluejack, turkey), oat (common), panicum, peanut, pecan, pine (eastern white, loblolly), ragweed (common), raspberry, sorghum (grain), sudangrass, sunflower (cultivated), walnut (Persian), watermelon seed, wheat. FAIR: barley (cultivated), buckwheat, cherry (black), dock, elder (blueberry), fig, gooseberry, hemp, huckleberry (black), moonseed, mulberry, paspalum, peach, peanutbutter, peppertree (Brazil), plum (garden), rice, serviceberry, sorgo, strawberry, sweetgum, waxmyrtle (southern). *Animal food.* Ants, bees, beetles, bugs, caterpillars, crickets, flies, grasshoppers, moths, spiders, wasps. *Nest.* Frequently on the ground or in abelia, blackberry, elaeagnus (thorny), hawthorn, hemlock, honeysuckle (Japanese), redcedar, rose (multiflora and others), yaupon. *Attracting.* Come to feeding stations all year to eat white bread, corn, cracker crumbs, doughnuts, peanuts and nut meats, grain sorghums, sunflower seeds, watermelon seeds, and wheat. They nest in the vicinity where you feed them if choice shrubs are available.

turkey (also called American, eastern, Florida, and wild turkey; *Meleagris gallopavo*). Common woodland game bird on large preserves, ranches, and refuges from Oklahoma and Texas eastward to Florida and Pennsylvania; formerly native in states farther north. *Plant food* (85%). CHOICE: bahiagrass, barley, beech, blackberry, blackgum, blueberry, bluegrass (Kentucky), brome (rescue, smooth), buckwheat (common), burclover, buttercup, carpetgrass, chinkapin, chufa, clover (crimson, white), corn, cottonseed cake, cowpeas, croton (woolly), dewberry (southern), dogwood (flowering), gallberry, gooseberry, grape (muscadine, summer), hackberry (sugar), magnolia (southern), millet (browntop, foxtail, proso), mulberry, oak acorns (bear, black, blackjack, chestnut, laurel, live, northern red, overcup, pin, post, runner, scarlet, Shumard, southern red, swamp chestnut, turkey, water, white, willow), oat (common), oatgrass (tall), palmetto (cabbage), panicum (beaked, bosc, flexile, redtop, roundseed), paspalum (bull), peanut, pecan, pine (loblolly, longleaf, shortleaf, slash), redroot (blood), rice, rye, ryegrass, sawpalmetto, sorghum (grain), · soybean, sprangletop, strawberry (wild), sweetgum, wheat, yelloweyegrass. FAIR: aster, beggartick (bearded), bristlegrass, bumelia (gum), cherry (black), chokeberry, crabgrass (hairy, smooth), creeper (Virginia), dogwood (gray, silky, stiffcornel), dropseed, elder (American), elm, goldeneye, goosefoot, goosegrass, hawthorn, hickory, hogpeanut (southern), holly (American), hophornbeam, huckleberry (dwarf), locust (black), maple, moonseed, mushroom, pawpaw, persimmon (common), ragweed, rose (multiflora), sassafras, sheepsorrel, sumac (shining, smooth, staghorn), sunflower, supplejack (Alabama), tickclover, vetch (American, Carolina, narrowleaf), witchgrass (common), witchhazel. *Animal food.* Ants, bees, beetles, centipedes, cicadas, crayfish, crickets, flies, grasshoppers, salamanders, snails, spiders, stinkbugs, walkingsticks, wasps. *Nest.* On the ground. *Attracting.* Grow winter grazing crops such as clovers and small grains; maintain choice woodland foods, and provide permanent watering places. See USDA Leaflet 526, "Wild Turkeys," for management details.

turnstone, ruddy (also called common turnstone, and calico bird or calico plover; *Arenaria interpres*). Arctic breeder; migrant through eastern North America. Winters on the Gulf coast and on the Atlantic coast from Florida to South Carolina, occasionally north to Massachusetts. Nonbreeding birds in small numbers summer in the wintering area. *Animal food* (100%). Crustaceans, insects, mollusks. *Nest.* In a slight depression on the ground, lined with grass.

veery (also called cathedral bird, willow thrush, and Wilson's thrush; *Hylocichla fuscescens*). Uncommon (or seldom seen) bird of dark, damp, hardwood areas; member of the thrush family. A summer resident of brushy woodlands from southern Ontario to central Newfoundland and southward to southern Minnesota, northern Indiana, and the Appalachian mountains of Pennsylvania and northward; also breeds southward in the higher Appalachian mountains to northern Georgia. Winters in Central and South America, migrating through all the eastern states. *Plant food* (65% fall, 35% summer, 5% spring). CHOICE: blackberry, blueberry, cherry (black, pin), dogwood (alternateleaf, roughleaf), elder (American, scarlet), mulberry, pokeberry (common), raspberry, serviceberry (downy), spicebush (common). FAIR: cherry (choke), mountainash (American), strawberry. *Animal food.* Ants, beetles, bugs, caterpillars, flies, grasshoppers, mayflies, snails, sowbugs, spiders. *Nest.* Frequently in beech, blackberry, mountainlaurel, winterberry; occasionally in dogwood (redosier), fir, hemlock, honeysuckle (Japanese), rhododendron, spruce, yew, and on the ground or on a stump.

vireo. The vireo family, Vireonidae, has eight members that occur in eastern North America: Bell's, black-whiskered, Philadelphia, red-eyed, solitary, warbling, white-eyed, and yellow-throated. They are also widely known as greenlets. These small, warblerlike birds are tree-living species that inhabit orchards, shade trees, and brushy woodlands. They are seen most often during spring migration, at about the same time as the migrating warblers. About 90% of their food is insects gleaned from tree foliage. Berries and fruit are the only vegetable matter they eat. Their beautiful little nests of woven fibers are hung from forked branches of trees.

vireo, Bell's (also called least vireo and Bell's greenlet; *Vireo bellii*). Common summer resident of brush, briers, hedgerows, and willow thickets in prairie districts from northern Illinois westward and south to eastern Texas. Winters in Central America. *Animal food* (nearly 100%). Ants, bees, beetles, caterpillars, flies, moths, spiders, wasps. *Nest.* Frequently in apple, baccharis, blackberry, cherry (black), elder, elm, filbert, hackberry, hawthorn, hydrangea, lilac, maple (sugar), osageorange, persimmon (common), sassafras, viburnum, willow.

vireo, black-whiskered (*Vireo altiloquus*). Rather uncommon summer resident of mangrove swamps in south Florida and the Florida Keys; winters in South America and West Indies (sparingly). *Animal food* (probably 100%). Insects. *Nest.* In mangrove.

vireo, blue-headed. See vireo, solitary.

vireo, Key West. See vireo, white-eyed.

vireo, least. See vireo, Bell's.

vireo, Maynard's. See vireo, white-eyed.

vireo, mountain. See vireo, solitary.

vireo, Philadelphia (also called Philadelphia greenlet; *Vireo philadelphicus*). Rarest of the vireos in eastern North America; uncommon summer resident of willow thickets from Ontario and northern Minnesota eastward on both sides of the U.S.-Canadian border. Winters in Central America and migrates commonly through the Mississippi river basin. Seen east of the Appalachians mainly in the fall. *Animal food* (about 90%). Ants, bees, beetles, bugs, caterpillars, flies, moths, spiders, wasps. *Plant food.* Fruits of dogwood, grape, rose. *Nest.* Frequently in alder, aspen (quaking), maple (sugar), poplar, spirea, willow.

vireo, red-eyed (also called preacher bird and red-eyed greenlet; *Vireo olivaceus*). Common to abundant summer resident of woodlands, shade trees, and orchards in eastern North America from northern Ontario and Nova Scotia to central Texas, the Gulf coast, and Florida; winters in South America. *Animal food* (75% fall, 99% spring). Ants, bees, beetles, bugs, caterpillars, flies, grasshoppers, moths, spiders, wasps. *Plant food.* CHOICE: blackberry, cherry (black, mazzard, pin), creeper (Virginia), dogwood (tatarian), elder, grape, magnolia (southern), mulberry, sassafras, serviceberry (downy), spicebush (common), sweetbay. *Nest.* Frequently in aspen, beech, birch, dogwood (flowering, redosier), linden, maple, oak (northern red, white), sweetgum; occasionally in apple, arborvitae (eastern), baldcypress, crabapple, hemlock, kalmia (mountainlaurel), pine, sassafras, witchhazel. *Attracting.* Favor their choice fruit plants in and at the edge of woodlands, since they eat no vegetable items except fruits.

vireo, solitary (also called mountain vireo, and blue-headed vireo or greenlet; *Vireo solitarius*). Fairly common summer resident of woodlands from Ontario to New Brunswick southward to Minnesota, New Jersey, and in the mountains from West Virginia to Georgia. Winters in the coastal plains from South Carolina and Florida to Louisiana and to Central America. *Animal food* (nearly 100%). Insects such as caterpillars. *Nest.* Frequently in alder, apple, ash, beech, birch, hemlock, hornbeam, maple, oak (bear, black, white), pine (eastern white), redcedar, sycamore.

vireo, warbling (also called warbling greenlet and eastern warbling vireo; *Vireo gilvus*). Common summer resident of woodlands from Ontario, southern Quebec, Nova Scotia, and Maine southward to central Texas, southern Louisiana, northern Alabama, western North Carolina, and Virginia; rarely in the higher Appalachian mountains and on the Atlantic coastal plain from New Jersey to Virginia. Winters in Central America. *Animal food* (more than 90%). Beetles, bugs, caterpillars, snails, spiders. *Plant food.* Cherry (black), grape, pokeberry. *Nest.* Frequently in alder, apple, aspen (quaking), cottonwood, elm (American), maple, oak (black), poplar, sycamore.

vireo, white-eyed (also called white-eyed greenlet, small white-eyed vireo, and Key West or Maynard's vireo; *Vireo griseus*). Fairly common summer resident of brushy woodland habitat from Iowa, central Ohio, and Rhode Island southward to Texas and northern Florida. Winters from the Gulf coast area to Mexico and Central America. *Animal food* (about 90%). Ants, bees, beetles, caterpillars, flies, moths, spiders, wasps. *Plant food.* Blackberry, elder, magnolia (southern), mulberry, raspberry, waxmyrtle (southern). *Nest.* Frequently in alder, birch, blackberry, camellia, hawthorn, maple, spicebush, sweetgum, waxmyrtle.

vireo, yellow-throated (also called yellow-throated greenlet; *Vireo flavifrons*). Fairly common summer resident of shade trees and woodlands from central Minnesota, southern Ontario and Quebec, and northern New Hampshire southward to central Texas, the Gulf coast, and central Florida. Winters in Central America. *Animal food* (predominant). Chiefly beetles, caterpillars, flies, grasshoppers. *Plant food.* Small berries, perhaps similar to those eaten by red-eyed and white-eyed vireos. *Nest.* Frequently in apple, beech, blackberry, elm, hickory, maple, oak (white), sweetgum, tuliptree.

vulture, black (also called black buzzard; *Coragyps atratus*). Common yearlong resident from Texas northeastward to southern Illinois and Maryland, and southward to Florida and Central America; casual elsewhere in eastern North America. *Animal food* (nearly 100%). Carrion. *Plant food.* May very rarely include sweet potatoes. *Nest.* On the ground, in the base of a hollow tree or log, or on rocks.

vulture, turkey (also called turkey buzzard; *Cathartes aura*). Common summer resident from Minnesota and New York southward to the Gulf of Mexico and Central America; less common northward. Winters in the same area except seldom farther north than the Ohio valley and Maryland. *Animal food* (nearly 100%). Carrion. *Nest.* In a cavern, a cavity between rocks, or a hollow tree or log.

wagtail or **wood wagtail.** See ovenbird.

warbler. The family Parulidae—"wood warblers" or "American wood warblers"—includes 40 secies that occur in the East. Of these, 34 have the name warbler; the other 6 are the yellow-breasted chat, ovenbird, American redstart, Louisiana and northern waterthrushes, and yellowthroat. A thorough treatise on the warblers is the book *The Warblers of North America,* by Ludwig Griscom and Alexander Sprunt (New York: Devin-Adair, 1957).

warbler, Bachman's (*Vermivora bachmanii*). Perhaps the rarest warbler of eastern North America, a summer resident of swamps and lowland thickets from southeastern Missouri to Virginia and southward to Alabama and Georgia. Winters in Cuba, rarely northward to southern Mississippi, Georgia, and Florida. *Animal food* (perhaps 100%). Ants, caterpillars. *Nest.* Frequently in blackberry, palmetto, switch cane.

warbler, bay-breasted (*Dendroica castanea*). Fairly common summer resident of brushy growth in evergreen woodlands from southern Canada southward to northern Minnesota and northeastern New York. Winters in Central and South America. Migrates in spring up through the Mississippi River drainage; rare from Florida to Virginia. *Animal food* (nearly 100%). Ants, beetles, caterpillars, flies, grasshoppers. *Plant food.* Creeper (Virginia), mulberry. *Nest.* Frequently in birch, fir, hemlock, magnolia, myrtle, spruce (red, white).

warbler, black-and-white (also called black-and-white creeper; *Mniotilta varia*). Common summer resident of woodlands and orchards, seen feeding on the trunks and large limbs of trees, from northern Ontario and Newfoundland southward to central Texas, Alabama and Georgia, and southeastern North Carolina. Winters from central Florida and central Texas southward to South America, casually to Georgia and South Carolina. *Animal food* (nearly 100%). Bark beetles, caterpillars, insect eggs and larvae, moths, wood-boring insects. *Nest.* Frequently in slight depression in the ground; occasionally in crevice at the base of a stump, under a log, or about the roots of a tree.

warbler, black-and-yellow. See warbler, magnolia.

warbler, Blackburnian (also called orange-throated warbler; *Dendroica fusca*). Fairly common summer resident of evergreen woodlands from Ontario and the Gulf of St. Lawrence southward to Minnesota, southeastern New York, and in the higher Appalachian mountains to Georgia; winters in Central and South America. *Animal food* (100%). Chiefly winged insects. *Nest.* Frequently in fir, hemlock, pine (eastern white), spruce (red, white); occasionally in larch, oak, redcedar.

warbler, black-capped. See warbler, Wilson's.

warbler, blackpoll (also called black-poll, and black-polled warbler; *Dendroica striata*). Perhaps the most common warbler of far-north forests from northern Ontario and Labrador southward to the Adirondacks in Vermont and New Hampshire. Winters in Central America and may be seen commonly in migration in eastern states from the Gulf of Mexico, northward. *Animal food* (100%). Chiefly mosquitoes and termites; also ants, beetles, gnats, grasshoppers, plantlice. *Nest.* Frequently in spruce; rarely on the ground.

warbler, black-throated blue (also called northern black-throated blue, and Cairn's warbler; *Dendroica caerulescens*). Common summer resident of small trees and tall shrubs (such as laurel) from Ontario and Nova Scotia southward to Minnesota, northern Ohio, and New Jersey, and in the higher Appalachians as far south as Georgia. Winters in the West Indies and Central America; migrates chiefly east of the Appalachians. *Animal food* (75%). Ants, caterpillars, dragonflies, mayflies, moths, slugs, white cabbage butterflies; also suet. *Plant food.* Bread, and sap of beech and birch. *Nest.* Frequently in beech, hemlock, kalmia (mountainlaurel), maple (sugar), rhododendron, yew (Canada); occasionally in a dozen other kinds of shrubs, or on a fallen log.

warbler, black-throated gray (*Dendroica nigrescens*). Rare winter visitor in southern Florida, Louisiana, and Texas.

warbler, black-throated green (also called Wayne's warbler; *Dendroica virens*). Common summer resident of evergreen woods from southern Canadian provinces southward to Minnesota, Pennsylvania, and New Jersey, also southward in the mountains to Alabama and Georgia, and in river swamps of coastal Virginia to South Carolina. Winters from southern Florida and Texas to West Indies and Central America; migrates commonly through southern states. *Animal food* (100%). Ants, caterpillars, flies, mayflies, moths, spiders. *Nest.* Frequently in beech, birch, fir, hemlock, maple, pine (red), spruce; occasionally in alder, barberry, elm, grape, magnolia (southern), oak (live, white).

warbler, blue. See warbler, cerulean.

warbler, blue-winged (also called blue-winged yellow warbler; *Vermivora pinus*). Common summer resident of deciduous woods from southern Minnesota and Massachusetts southward to Arkansas, Tennessee, and Virginia. Uncommon migrant in South; winters in Central America. *Animal food* (100%). Ants, beetles, caterpillars, spiders. *Nest.* Frequently on the ground; occasionally in coralberry.

warbler, Cairn's. See warbler, black-throated blue.

warbler, Canada (also called Canadian flycatcher and Canadian flycatching warbler; *Wilsonia canadensis*). Common summer resident of swampy woods from northern Ontario and Newfoundland southward to central Minnesota, northern Ohio, and New Jersey, and also in the Appalachian mountains to North Carolina, Tennessee, and Georgia. Winters in South America; rather uncommon migrant in southern states. *Animal food* (100%). Insects. *Nest.* In clump of weeds or grass, in swampy woods.

warbler, Cape May (*Dendroica tigrina*). Uncommon to rare summer resident of woodlands, orchards, and parks from northern Ontario and New Brunswick southward to Minnesota and northeastern New York; migrates along the Atlantic coast and Florida, to winter in the West Indies. *Animal food* (nearly 100%). Beetles, caterpillars, flies, moths, spiders, wasps, weevils. *Plant food.* Grape juice, honey syrup. *Nest.* In spruce (black), or other low evergreen trees.

warbler, cerulean (also called blue warbler; *Dendroica cerulea*). Common summer resident of swampy woodlands from southern Minnesota to southeastern New York southward to eastern Texas and central North Carolina; winters in South America. *Animal food* (100%). Ants, beetles, caterpillars, wasps, weevils. *Nest.* Frequently in linden, oak (white).

warbler, chestnut-sided (*Dendroica pensylvanica*). Common summer resident of roadside thickets and woodlands, both deciduous and coniferous, from Ontario to Nova Scotia southward to Minnesota and Maryland, and through the higher Appalachians to Tennessee, Georgia, and South Carolina. Winters in Central America; common in migration through southern states. *Animal food* (100%). Chiefly ants, borers, caterpillars, flying insects, leaf-hoppers, moths, plantlice. *Nest.* Frequently in azalea, beech, blackberry, hornbeam, huckleberry, maple, raspberry.

warbler, Connecticut (*Oporornis agilis*). Uncommon summer resident of low thickets in swamps, from northern Ontario and Quebec southward to northern Minnesota, Wisconsin, and Michigan. Migrates in spring through the Mississippi valley, and in fall through the Atlantic coast states; winters in South America. *Animal food* (nearly 100%). Usually feeds on the ground, on insects. *Nest.* On the ground, in swampy woods.

warbler, golden-winged (*Vermivora chrysoptera*). Fairly common summer resident of the edge of deciduous woods from Minnesota, the Great Lakes, and Massachusetts southward to Iowa and Pennsylvania, and in the higher Appalachian mountains to Tennessee, Georgia, and South Carolina. Winters in Central America. *Animal food* (100%). Bugs, cankerworms, caterpillars, spiders. *Nest.* Frequently on or close to the ground; occasionally in blackberry, dogwood.

warbler, hooded (*Wilsonia citrina*). Abundant summer resident of shrubby bottomland woods from Iowa, the Great Lakes, and Rhode Island southward to the Gulf coast, Texas to northern Florida. Winters in Central America. *Animal food* (nearly 100%). Caterpillars, crickets, grasshoppers, plantlice. *Plant food.* Elder, pokeberry (common). *Nest.* Frequently in alder, beech, cane, huckleberry, maple, rhododendron.

warbler, jack-pine. See warbler, Kirtland's.

warbler, Kentucky (*Oporornis formosus*). Common summer resident of deciduous woodland thickets from Iowa to New Jersey and southward to eastern Texas, central Georgia, and South Carolina. Winters chiefly in Central America; occasionally on Florida Keys. *Animal food* (100%). Ants, beetles, grasshoppers, moths (larvae), plantlice. *Nest.* On the ground in grass.

warbler, Kirtland's (also called jack-pine warbler; *Dendroica kirtlandii*). Local summer resident in jack-pine woods of an area of roughly 60x100 miles in central Michigan. Winters in the Bahamas; migratory in states between Florida and Michigan. *Animal food* (probably 100%). Insects. *Nest.* On the ground, almost always under clumps of jack pine.

warbler, magnolia (also called black-and-yellow warbler; *Dendroica magnolia*). Common summer resident of lowland shrubbery and upland woods from Ontario, Quebec, and Newfoundland southward to central Wisconsin and northern Massachusetts and in the Appalachian mountains to West Virginia. Common migrant through southern states; winters in West Indies and Central America. *Animal food* (100%). Beetles, flies, plantlice. *Nest.* Frequently in fir, hemlock, spruce (black, red, white); occasionally in pine, redcedar, rhododendron, spirea.

warbler, mourning (also called Philadelphia warbler; *Oporornis philadelphia*). Uncommon summer resident of brushy hillsides and draws from northern Ontario, Quebec, and Newfoundland southward to Minnesota, southeastern New York, and New England states (except the coast), and in the higher Appalachian mountains to the Virginias. Winters in Central America and northern South America; rather uncommon migrant, chiefly west of the Allegheny mountains. *Animal food* (100%). Beetles, spiders. *Nest.* Frequently on the ground, but occasionally in blackberry, oak (bear), snapweed, thistle.

warbler, myrtle (also called eastern myrtle warbler and yellow-rumped warbler; *Dendroica coronata*). Common to abundant summer resident of varied habitats (upland and stream-side woodlands, fields, and brushy areas and gardens) from tree limit of northern Canada southward to northern

Minnesota, the Great Lakes, and Massachusetts. Winters commonly from Kansas, northeastern Illinois, New York, and the coastal area north to Maine, and southward to Mexico and the West Indies. *Plant food* (perhaps 90% winter, 20% summer). CHOICE: almond, brazilnut, bread (white), butternut, cake, cashew, cornbread, cornmeal, creeper (Virginia), dogwood (flowering), filbert (commercial), hackberry bits (common), hickory (mockernut), peanut, peanutbutter, pecan, pistachionut, poisonivy, redcedar, walnut (black, Persian), waxmyrtle (northern, southern). FAIR: euonymus (European, Maack, Siebold), fig (dried), sumac (smooth), tallowtree. *Animal food.* Ants, aphids, beetles, caterpillars, flies, plantlice, scale insects, spiders; suet is a favorite. *Nest.* Frequently in birch, fir, hemlock, pine (eastern white, jack), redcedar, spruce (red, white). *Attracting.* They come to feeders for bread, cornmeal, nut meats, peanutbutter, suet, and are said to winter in the Great Lakes region when the waxy berries of bayberries (waxmyrtle) are plentiful.

warbler, Nashville (also called eastern Nashville warbler and red-capped warbler; *Vermivora ruficapilla*). Uncommon summer resident of open woodland and nearby grassy areas from central Ontario, southern Quebec, and Nova Scotia southward to southern Minnesota, northern Ohio, and Pennsylvania. Winters from southern Florida and southern Texas to Central and South America. Their chief migration route is through the Mississippi drainage, rarely on the Atlantic slope. *Animal food* (nearly 100%). Beetles, caterpillars, flies, leafhoppers, and the egg and larval stages of insects. *Nest.* On the ground.

warbler, orange-crowned (also called common orange-crowned warbler; *Vermivora celata*). Fairly common migrant, especially in the Mississippi valley; breeds in northern Quebec, Ontario, and westward. Winters commonly from South Carolina to Florida, the Gulf coast to Texas, and in Central America, usually in live oak, magnolia, or other evergreen trees. *Animal food* (perhaps 100% summer, 60% winter). Ants, beetles, caterpillars, flies, plantlice, scale insects, wasps. *Plant food.* Bread, cornbread, peanut, peanutbutter. *Nest.* Usually on the ground; occasionally in shrubs. *Attracting.* Sometimes come to feeders for bread, nut meats, suet.

warbler, orange-throated. See warbler, Blackburnian.

warbler, palm (also called tip-up warbler and yellow tip-up; *Dendroica palmarum*). Two subspecies are the western and yellow palm warblers. Common summer resident of shrubby woodlands and their borders from Minnesota and Ontario eastward on both sides of the United States–Canadian border to Maine and Nova Scotia. Winters commonly from northern Louisiana, Tennessee, and North Carolina southward through the United States to Central America and West Indies; casually northward to Oklahoma, Ohio, and Massachusetts. *Animal food* (perhaps 90%). Ants, beetles, bugs, caterpillars, flies. *Plant food.* Small fruits such as raspberries, and some seeds. *Nest.* Frequently on the ground; occasionally in a small spruce.

warbler, parula (also called northern and southern parula warbler; *Parula americana*). Common summer resident of streams and swampy woods from southern Ontario, Quebec, and New Brunswick southward to southern Texas, Gulf states, and central Florida. Winters from Florida to Central America; occasionally on the Gulf coast of Alabama and Louisiana. *Animal food* (100%). Beetles, caterpillars, flies, insect eggs and larvae, moths, spiders; also suet. *Nest.* In Spanishmoss (*Tillandsia usneoides*) and in any kind of tree in which "hanging mosses" grow.

warbler, Philadelphia. See warbler, mourning.

warbler, pileated. See warbler, Wilson's.

warbler, pine (also called Florida pine warbler and northern pine warbler; *Dendroica pinus*). Common summer resident of open pine woodlands from Ontario, Quebec, and New Brunswick southward to the Gulf states, Texas to Florida. Winters from southern Virginia to Illinois, and Florida to Texas and Mexico. *Plant food* (percentage uncertain but significant in winter). CHOICE: almond, bread (white), butternut, cookie crumbs, cornbread, cornmeal, filbert (commercial), hickory (mockernut, shagbark), peanut, peanutbutter, pecan, pie crust, walnut (black, Persian). FAIR: dogwood (flowering), pine (loblolly). *Animal food.* Chiefly insects in summer—ants, beetles, bugs, caterpillars, flies, grasshoppers, moths, scale insects, spiders, and rendered pork fat; suet is choice. *Nest.* Frequently in pine (jack, loblolly, red); occasionally in baldcypress, oak (post), pine (eastern white), redcedar. *Attracting.* They come readily to feeders for bread, cornmeal, nut meats, peanutbutter, pie crust, and suet.

warbler, prairie (also called Florida prairie warbler and northern prairie warbler; *Dendroica discolor*). Fairly common summer resident of shrubby hillside woodlands from the northern states (except northern New England) southward to Louisiana and Florida. Winters from central Florida to the West Indies and Central America; occasionally in northern states. *Animal food* (100%). Beetles, bugs, moths (larvae and adults). *Nest.* Frequently in apple, blueberry, dogwood (flowering), hackberry (common), huckleberry, kalmia (mountainlaurel), maple, redbud, rose, walnut (black); occasionally in barberry, blackberry, locust (black), mangrove, oak (post), pear, pine, sweetgum.

warbler, prothonotary (also called swamp yellowbird; *Protonotaria citrea*). Common but seldom seen summer resident of river swamps from Wisconsin, western New York, and New Jersey southward to Texas and central Florida. Winters in Central and South America and the West Indies. *Animal food* (100%). Ants, bees, caterpillars, flies, snails and other aquatic animals, spiders. *Nest.* Frequently in tin cans, woodpecker holes, and tree cavities, usually in swamps or over water; occasionally under bridges or in buildings. The prothonotary is the only warbler that nests in holes, and it will also nest in a birdhouse that has a 4x4-inch floor (or a bit smaller), and a 1½-inch entrance, 5 inches up. It should be placed 4–7 feet above water in a swamp (at the edge of the swamp, if you want to observe its activities).

warbler, red-capped. See warbler, Nashville.

warbler, ruby-crowned. See kinglet, ruby-crowned.

warbler, Swainson's (*Limnothlypis swainsonii*). A rare warbler, summer resident of rhododendron, cane, and vine-tangled thickets in lowlands (such as the Dismal Swamp) from Virginia to northern Florida, southeastern Louisiana, and river bottoms northward to southern Missouri and Ohio. Winters in West Indies and Central America. *Animal food* (100%). Ants, bees, caterpillars, spiders, and other small insect life. *Nest.* Frequently in cane, palmetto; occasionally in blackberry, hemlock, holly (American), honeysuckle, kalmia (mountainlaurel), oak, rhododendron, spicebush.

warbler, sycamore. See warbler, yellow-throated.

warbler, Tennessee (*Vermivora peregrina*). Common summer resident of woodland habitat from northern Ontario, southern Quebec, and New Brunswick southward to Minnesota, Michigan, New York, and New Hampshire. Winters in Central and South America. Migrates chiefly through the Mississippi River system; less numerous east of the Appalachians. As common as myrtle warblers in Alabama, Mississippi, and Louisiana. *Animal food* (perhaps 90%). Winged insects, caterpillars, and other leaf-eating insects. *Plant food.* Grapes (juice). *Nest.* On the ground, usually damp mossy situations.

warbler, tip-up. See warbler, palm.

warbler, Wayne's. See warbler, black-throated green.

warbler, Wilson's (also called black-capped and pileated warbler and Wilson's flycatcher; *Wilsonia pusilla*). Common summer resident of dense thickets bordering woodlands, or in open woods, from the arctic region of Canada southward to the U.S.-Canadian border; sparingly in United States. Migrates down the Appalachian mountains; rather uncommon in southern states. Winters in Cental America, rarely on the Gulf coast and in Florida. *Animal food* (nearly 100%). Chiefly winged insects. *Nest.* On the ground.

warbler, worm-eating (*Helmitheros vermivorus*). Fairly common summer resident of shaded low-bush habitat (often seen walking on the ground) from Missouri, Ohio, and New York southward to Arkansas and South Carolina. Migrates through more southern states; winters in Central America and, rarely, in Florida. *Animal food* (100%). Ants, beetles, caterpillars, grasshoppers, spiders. *Nest.* On the ground, in woods.

warbler, yellow (also called eastern yellow warbler, yellowbird, and yellow-rump, and miscalled wild canary; *Dendroica petechia*). Widespread common summer resident of shrubs and small trees near water in all states and provinces of North America; winters in Central and South America and on the Florida Keys. *Animal food* (nearly 100%). Chiefly beetles, cankerworms, caterpillars, plantlice, weevils. *Plant food.* Raspberry. *Nest.* Frequently in alder, cottonwood, elder, grape, honeysuckle, hornbeam, larch, lilac, maple, ninebark, sassafras, spicebush, willow; occasionally in about 20 other species of trees and shrubs.

warbler, yellow-rumped. See warbler, myrtle.

warbler, yellow-throated (also called sycamore warbler; *Dendroica dominica*). Rather uncommon summer resident in the tops of evergreen trees from Iowa to New Jersey and southward to the Gulf coast and northern Florida. Winters from southern Texas and South Carolina to West Indies and Central America. *Animal food* (perhaps 90%). Beetles, bugs, crickets, flies, grasshoppers, moths, scale insects, spiders. *Plant food.* Cornbread, cornmeal, and nut meats at feeders. *Nest.* Frequently in baldcypress, pine, Spanishmoss, sycamore.

water chicken. See gallinule, common.

waterthrush, Grinnell's. See waterthrush, northern.

waterthrush, large-billed. See waterthrush, Louisiana.

waterthrush, Louisiana (also called large-billed waterthrush; *Seiurus motacilla*). A member of the wood warbler family; a shy, ground-frequenting bird, seldom seen but fairly common summer resident of wet areas along wooded streams and brushy swamp from Minnesota, Michigan, and New Hampshire southward to eastern Texas and South Carolina. Winters mostly in Central America. *Animal food* (100%). Chiefly aquatic insect larvae and small aquatic animals found in wet ground; also ants, beetles, snails, spiders, worms. *Nest.* Among tree roots, or in a crevice in a rocky, wooded bank near a stream, or in a swamp.

waterthrush, northern (also called Grinnell's waterthrush; *Seiurus noveboracensis*). A member of the wood warbler family; fairly common and bold summer resident in swamps, around ponds, and along streams from northern Ontario and Labrador southward to northern Minnesota, Ohio, and Massachusetts. Winters in Central and South America; common on the Gulf coast in migration, and occasional in South Carolina and northward. *Animal food* (100%). Chiefly crustaceans, aquatic insects. *Nest.* On or near the ground in a bed of moss, often under a large root, in swampy woods or bogs.

water turkey. See anhinga; cormorants.

water witch. See grebe, pied-billed.

waxwing, Bohemian (also called wandering chatterer; *Bombycilla garrula*). Breeds in northwestern Canada and Alaska; wanders irregularly in winter as far east as Nova Scotia, occasionally into the New England and the Great Lakes states. *Plant food* (90%). CHOICE: apple (frozen), asparagus, barberry (Japanese), cotoneaster, crabapple, currant, fig, grape, hackberry (common), hawthorn, mountainash (American, European), plum (garden), raisins, raspberry, redcedar, viburnum (American cranberrybush, European cranberrybush). FAIR: bread, cherry (choke), garbage, holly (American), hollyhock, rose; also buds of cherry and elm (Siberian). *Animal food.* Chiefly insects, meat scraps. *Nest.* Frequently in fir, hemlock, larch, pine (jack), spruce (northwestern North America). *Attracting.* Dried fruits left hanging in the trees attract Bohemian waxwings when food supplies become more scarce in their normal range. Sometimes they come to feeders for bread and meat scraps.

waxwing, Carolina. See waxwing, cedar.

waxwing cedar (also called Carolina waxwing, cedar bird, and cherry bird; *Bombycilla cedrorum*). Common summer resident of orchards and open woodlands from northern Ontario and Newfoundland southward to Missouri, Kentucky, and northern Georgia. Winters in large flocks in the breeding area and southward to the Gulf coast, except rarely in southern Florida. *Plant food* (90% or more fall and winter, 75% spring and summer). CHOICE: fruits of apple, arborvitae (oriental), asparagus, barberry (Japanese), bilberry (bog), blackberry, blackgum, blueberry (highbush), camphortree, cherry (black, mahaleb, mazzard, pin, sour), chokeberry (red), cotoneaster, crabapple (Japanese flowering), dogwood (flowering), elaeagnus (autumn, thorny), elder (American, European red), gallberry, grape (cultivated, frost), hackberry (common, sugar), hawthorn, holly (American, Burford, Chinese), honeysuckle (Amur, Japanese), laurelcherry, mistletoe (Christmas), mountainash (American, European), mulberry, peppertree (Brazil), photinia (Chinese), pokeberry (common), possumhaw, privet (Amur, Chinese, glossy, Japanese), pyracantha, raspberry (blackcap, red), redcedar, rose (multiflora), serviceberry (Allegheny, downy), strawberry, viburnum (American, European cranberrybush); also bread and raisins. FAIR: apple blossoms, birch (yellow), bittersweet, bumelia (gum), cherry (choke), coralberry (Indiancurrant), date, dogwood (roughleaf), gooseberry, liriope, moonseed, nandina, nightshade, pear, pitanga, sumac (staghorn), viburnum (blackhaw, nannyberry), yaupon. *Animal food.* Chiefly ants, beetles, bugs, cankerworms, caterpillars, crickets, flies, grasshoppers, mayflies. Often catches insects in the air as flycatchers do. *Nest.* Frequently in apple, arborvitae (eastern), fir, larch, maple, pine (eastern white, red, Virginia), redcedar, spruce (black), willow. *Attracting.* Plant and leave choice fruit plants. Cedar waxwings drink frequently from ponds and streams and bathe in bird baths and pools.

whimbrel (also called American whimbrel, jack curlew, and Hudsonian curlew; *Numenius phaeopus*). Arctic breeder; common migrant on the Atlantic shores south from New Jersey and along the coasts of Louisiana and Texas; less common from the Great Lakes through the Mississippi valley.

Winters chiefly to South America, rarely on the Gulf coast. *Animal food* (nearly 100%). Chiefly beetles, crabs, crustaceans, grasshoppers, insect larvae, spiders. *Plant food.* Blueberries (and other berries in tundra). *Nest.* On the ground, in a depression or grass tussock.

whip-poor-will (also called eastern whip-poor-will and goatsucker; *Caprimulgus vociferus*). Fairly common summer resident of woodland areas from southern Canada southward to northern Louisiana, Georgia, and South Carolina. Winters from South Carolina, Florida, and the Gulf states southward to West Indies and Central America. *Animal food* (100%). Night-flying insects such as ants, beetles, gnats, mosquitoes, moths. *Nest.* On the ground, in a nest of dry leaves.

whisky jack. See jay, gray.

whistler. See goldeneye, common.

widgeon, American (also called baldpate and widgeon; *Mareca americana*). Common to abundant surface-feeding duck of marshes, ponds, and bays; summer resident chiefly in the western states, Canada, and Alaska. Winters in eastern North America from the Canadian border southward, chiefly in Atlantic and Gulf coastal areas. *Plant food* (95% fall, winter, and spring; perhaps 75% summer). CHOICE: alfalfa, arrowhead (common), barley, bulrush (American, river saltmarsh), cabbage, clover (white), corn, eelgrass, lettuce, millet (foxtail, Japanese, proso), naiad (northern, southern), oat, potamogeton (leafy), redroot, rice, rye, ryegrass, sorghum (grain), stonewort, turnip, wheat, widgeongrass. FAIR: algae (filamentous), anacharis, asparagus, barnyardgrass, buckwheat, burreed, buttonbush, chufa, cutgrass (rice), duckweed (common), hornwort, poolmat, smartweed (bigroot, curltop, water), spikerush, wildcelery, wildrice, witchgrass (common). *Animal food.* Aquatic insects, crickets, crustaceans, grasshoppers, mollusks. *Nest.* On dry ground, some distance from water, in tall grasses. *Attracting.* Widgeongrass in brackish-water ponds, tender green forage of pastures, and water-covered grain in fields attract the American widgeon.

willet (*Catoptrophorus semipalmatus*). Includes two subspecies, eastern and western willet. Common summer resident of brackish tidal marshes along the Atlantic coast from New Jersey to Florida and along the Gulf coast to Texas (also locally in Nova Scotia). Common to abundant in winter in the tidal areas on the Gulf coast, and on the Atlantic from Virginia to Florida, and southward on Caribbean shores. *Animal food* (100%). Aquatic insects, crabs, fish, marine worms, mollusks. *Nest.* On the ground, in a tussock of grass.

windhover. See hawk, sparrow.

woodcock, American (also nicknamed timber doodle; *Philohela minor*). Common summer resident of wet meadows and brushy swamps from Ontario and Newfoundland southward to Louisiana and central Florida.

Winters mainly in Arkansas, Louisiana, and Mississippi, less commonly in other southern states from eastern Oklahoma to Virginia. *Animal food* (more than 90%). Mostly earthworms; also beetles, caterpillars, centipedes, crustaceans, flies, millipedes, snails, and spiders. *Plant food.* Corn. *Nest.* On the ground, made of leaves and grass, in wooded bottomlands.

woodpecker. The birds known collectively as woodpeckers belong to the family Picidae. Nine of the eleven eastern species are named woodpecker: black-backed three-toed, downy, hairy, ivory-billed, northern three-toed, pileated, red-bellied, red-cockaded, and red-headed. The other two species are the yellow-shafted flicker and the yellow-bellied sapsucker.

woodpecker, American three-toed. See woodpecker, northern three-toed.

woodpecker, arctic three-toed. See woodpecker, black-backed three-toed.

woodpecker, banded-backed. See woodpecker, northern three-toed.

woodpecker, black-backed three-toed (also called arctic three-toed woodpecker; *Picoides arcticus*). Uncommon yearlong resident of woodlands from northern Ontario and Quebec southward to northern Minnesota, New York, and the New England states; occasionally farther south in winter. *Animal food* (perhaps 75%). Chiefly larvae of beetles and moths; also ants, beetles, spiders. *Plant food.* Nuts, wild fruits. *Nest.* In a hole in living or dead trees.

woodpecker, downy (also called southern downy woodpecker; *Dendrocopos pubescens*). Common yearlong resident of hardwood or mixed woodlands, especially along rivers, throughout eastern North America from Canadian tree limit southward. *Animal food* (80% summer, 70% winter). Chiefly ants, beetles, and larvae of beetles and moths; also aphids, caterpillars, scale insects, snails, spiders. Suet (beef, mutton) is extra-choice food. Will eat pork fat. *Plant food.* CHOICE: bread, cherry (black), creeper (Virginia), honey syrup, mulberry, oak, pecan, poisonivy, walnut (black, Persian). FAIR: corn, peanut, sugar water, sumac, sunflower (cultivated). *Nest.* In a a hole in dead or dying wood; also in birdhouses. *Attracting.* Downy woodpeckers feed regularly on suet at feeders placed on a tree; and use rustic-type birdhouses for nesting. The house should be 8–10 inches deep, with a 1¼-inch entrance hole, 6 or 8 inches above a floor that measures 4x4 inches. It should be placed on a tree 6–20 feet above ground. About 2 inches of wood shavings or sawdust should be placed in the bottom each time the birdhouse is cleaned.

woodpecker, hairy (also called northern hairy woodpecker; *Dendrocopos villosus*). Fairly common yearlong resident of woodlands from southern Canadian provinces southward to central Texas, the Gulf coast, and Florida. *Animal food* (75%). Ants, aphids, beetles, caterpillars, millipedes, spiders; also suet. *Plant food.* CHOICE: beech, blackgum, cherry (black), corn, creeper (Virginia), dogwood (flowering, roughleaf), filbert (American), mulberry, oak, peanutbutter, serviceberry (downy), syrup and juice (sugarcane), tupelo (water), walnut (Persian). FAIR: apple, blackberry, cherry (choke), poisonivy, pokeberry (common), sunflower (cultivated). *Nest.* In a hole in a tree; occasionally in a birdhouse. *Attracting.* They come to feeders for nut meats, peanutbutter, and suet. Leave dead stubs for their nesting. They sometimes use a rustic-type birdhouse placed 12–16 feet above the ground. It should have a 1½-inch entrance, 9–12 inches above a 6-inch square floor. Put 2–3 inches of wood shavings or sawdust in the bottom each time the nest is cleaned.

woodpecker, ivory-billed (*Campephilus principalis*). Very rare, almost extinct resident of virgin swamps in southeastern states. *Animal food* (probably 90%). Chiefly wood-boring insects—beetles, large grubs, larvae. *Plant food.* Grape, hackberry, magnolia (southern), pecan, persimmon (common). *Nest.* In holes in large (mature) trees.

woodpecker, northern three-toed (also called banded-backed woodpecker and American or eastern three-toed woodpecker; *Picoides tridactylus*). Year-long resident of evergreen forests from tree limit in Canada southward to Minnesota, northern New York, and New Hampshire. *Animal food* (100%). Chiefly larvae of beetles and moths; also ants, beetles, spiders. *Nest.* In a hole in a tree.

woodpecker, pileated (also called cock of the wood and logcock; *Dryocopus pileatus*). Three subspecies are called northern, southern, and Florida pileated woodpecker. Fairly common yearlong resident of heavy, mature woodland areas from northern Ontario and New Brunswick southward to central Texas, the Gulf coast, and Florida. *Animal food* (95% spring, 80% summer, 45% fall and winter). Chiefly ants, beetles; also pork fat, hamburger, meat rind, pork rind, suet. *Plant food.* CHOICE: beech, blackgum, camphortree, cherry (black, choke), corn, creeper (Virginia), dogwood (alternateleaf, flowering), elder (American), grape (frost), magnolia (southern), oak, pecan, pyracantha, sassafras, tupelo (water), walnut (black). FAIR: dahoon, hackberry (common), persimmon (common), poisonivy, sumac. *Nest.* In holes in large trees in deep woods. *Attracting.* Come to feeders occasionally for nut meats and suet. Have been known to nest in birdhouses with 3- to 4-inch entrance cut 10–12 inches above an 8-inch square floor, and placed 12 or more feet high in a large tree in the woods.

woodpecker, red-bellied (also called chad, and nicknamed zebra woodpecker; *Centurus carolinus*). Common yearlong resident of woodlands, orchards, and rural towns from northern United States (except New England) southward to the Gulf coast and Florida. *Plant food* (80% fall and winter, 50% spring and summer). CHOICE: almond, apple, beech, blackberry, blackgum, blueberry, brazilnut, bread (white), butternut, cashew, cherry (black), corn (cracked or whole grain), creeper (Virginia), dogwood (flowering, roughleaf), elaeagnus (cherry), elder (American, scarlet), fig, filbert (commercial), grape (fox, frost, muscadine, summer), hickory, magnolia (southern), mulberry, oak (chinkapin, laurel, live, pin, Shumard, turkey, water, white), orange juice, peanut, peanutbutter, pecan, poisonivy, strawberry, sunflower (cultivated), syrup (sugarcane), walnut (black, Persian). FAIR: holly (American), pokeberry (common), possumhaw, raspberry, sawpalmetto, waxmyrtle (northern, southern). *Animal food.* Chiefly ants; also beetles, bugs, caterpillars, crickets, grasshoppers, lizards. Suet (beef, mutton) is choice; also pork fat. *Nest.* Frequently in a hole in a tree; occasionally in a stump, post, or pole. *Attracting.* They come to feeders for bread, corn, cracked hickorynuts, peanuts, peanutbutter, pecans, pork fat, suet, and walnuts. They will nest in a birdhouse with 2½-inch entrance cut 10 or 12 inches above a 6-inch-square floor, and placed 12 or more feet up in a tree.

woodpecker, red-cockaded (*Dendrocopos borealis*). A rather uncommon species found in small local areas of overmature pine woods from eastern Oklahoma, Tennessee, and Virginia southward to eastern Texas, the Gulf coast, and Florida. *Animal food* (about 80%). Chiefly ants and larvae of beetles; also caterpillars, crickets, grasshoppers, roaches' eggs, spiders, termites. *Plant food.* CHOICE: corn, grape, pine. FAIR: magnolia (southern), oak, poisonivy, pokeberry (common). *Nest.* In a hole in living pine trees. They must have overmature pines, with a fungus disease known as "red heart," for nesting. Therefore, save groups of such pines for them.

woodpecker, red-headed (*Melanerpes erythrocephalus*). Common yearlong resident of scattered trees in rural areas and towns from about the Canadian border southward to central Texas, the Gulf coast, and Florida. *Plant food* (80% fall and winter, 40% spring and summer). CHOICE: apple, beech, blackberry, blackgum, blueberry, bread (white), cherry (black, choke, pin, sour), chinkapin, corn, cornbread, dogwood (alternateleaf, flowering, roughleaf), elder (American, scarlet), fig, grape (frost), huckleberry, magnolia (southern), mountainash (American, European), mulberry, oak (chinkapin, laurel, live, pin, post, shingle), peanut, peanutbutter, pecan, plum (American), potato chips, raspberry, strawberry. FAIR: poisonivy, sumac (shining, smooth). *Animal food.* Ants, beetles, bugs, caterpillars, grasshoppers; also suet. *Nest.* Frequently in a hole in tree, telephone pole, stub, or stump; occasionally in a birdhouse. *Attracting.* These woodpeckers are subject to serious loss from hunting by children; they are, on the whole, beneficial birds which should be protected. They will sometimes nest in a birdhouse placed on a pole or in a tree, 12–15 feet above ground. It should have a 2-inch entrance hole, cut 9–12 inches above a 6-inch-square floor. They regularly come for bread, corn, cracked nuts, peanuts, and suet placed on the ground, or to a feeder in a tree.

woodpecker, yellow-bellied. See sapsucker, yellow-bellied.

woodpecker, zebra. See woodpecker, red-bellied.

wood pewee, eastern (also called pewee and pewee flycatcher; *Contopus virens*). Common summer resident of open woodlands and orchards from southern Canada to the Gulf coast and central Florida; winters in Central America. *Animal food* (100%). Chiefly beetles, bugs, flies; also grasshoppers, spiders. *Nest.* Frequently in apple, ash, elm, hickory, locust (black), maple (sugar), oak (post, water, white), pine (loblolly), poplar, redcedar.

wren, Bewick's (also called eastern Bewick's wren; *Thryomanes bewickii*). Common yearlong resident of brushy thickets and gardens from Nebraska, Ohio, and Pennsylvania southward to southern Texas, central Alabama, and South Carolina. *Animal food* (95%). Beetles, bugs, plantlice, scale insects, spiders, suet, weevils. *Plant food.* Bread, nuts, peanutbutter. *Nest.* In birdhouses, gourds, tin cans, metal newspaper boxes, cylinders, mailboxes, porch ledges, crevices of buildings, and holes in trees. *Attracting.* As suggested in the "nest" paragraph above, Bewick's wrens use many odd places to build their nests. A birdhouse for them should have the same dimensions as those given for the house wren, below.

wren, Carolina (also called jenny wren and mocking wren; *Thryothorus ludovicianus*). The Florida wren is a subspecies. Common yearlong resident of brushy areas in heavy woodlands from Nebraska and Connecticut southward to the Gulf coast and Florida. State bird of South Carolina. *Animal food* (95%). Ants, beetles, flies, grasshoppers, millipedes, moths, suet, weevils. *Plant food.* Almond, brazilnut, bread (white), butternut, cashew, filbert (commercial), peanut, peanutbutter, pecan, walnut (black, Persian). *Nest.* In a birdbox, basket, can, crevice, or hole, often near a house, barn, or other building. *Attracting.* Carolina wrens will come to a feeding station on a windowsill or a tree, for peanuts, pecan and walnut meats, suet, and, it is reliably reported, for raw hamburger. They will nest in man-made birdhouses, which should have an entrance hole of 1¼x2½ inches cut 6–8 inches above the floor, which should measure 4x4 inches. The house should be placed 5–10 feet from the ground on a shade tree or the side of a building. A woven basket, placed under the eaves of a porch or carport, is also suitable for nesting. It should be about 8 inches deep, open at the top, and with a 4-inch bottom. In cold weather Carolina wrens will use roosting boxes.

wren, Florida. See wren, Carolina.

wren, house (also called jenny wren and eastern house wren; *Troglodytes aedon*). Common to abundant summer resident of roadside thickets, open woods, and town gardens from central Ontario and New Brunswick southward to northern Texas, Tennessee, and Georgia. Winters from Florida, the Gulf coast, and Texas to southern Mexico. *Animal food* (100%). Chiefly beetles, bugs, caterpillars, grasshoppers, spiders. *Nest.* In tree cavities, woodpecker holes, birdhouses, and under eaves of buildings. *Attracting.* The birdhouses shown in figure 3.2 are suitable for Bewick's, house, and winter wrens.

Any of them may be hung in a shady spot, or attached to a tree or building from 5 to 10 feet above the ground. The house should be 6–8 inches deep, with a 1-inch round or a 1x2½-inch oblong entrance hole cut 4–6 inches above a 4-inch floor.

wren, jenny. See wren, house and Carolina.

wren, long-billed marsh (also called eastern marsh wren and prairie marsh wren; *Telmatodytes palustris*). Includes six eastern North American subspecies; long-billed, Louisiana, Marian's, prairie, Wayne's and Worthington's marsh wrens. Common to abundant yearlong residents of wet cattail marshes and mangrove swamps from southern Canada southward through all eastern states to Mexico, the Gulf coast, and Florida. *Animal food* (100%). Ants, beetles, bugs, caterpillars, dragonflies, green larvae, spiders; also small mollusks. *Nest.* Frequently in cattail, sedge; occasionally in mangrove, reed, rush (needlegrass).

wren, marsh. See wren, long-billed and short-billed marsh.

wren, mocking. See wren, Carolina.

wren, short-billed marsh (*Cistothorus platensis*). Fairly common but shy summer resident of grassy marshes from Ontario, Quebec, and New Brunswick southward to Arkansas and Virginia. Winters from Maryland southward along the Atlantic coast to Florida, the Gulf coast to Texas and Mexico, and inland to central Virginia and Reelfoot Lake, Tennessee. Usually found in little colonies. *Animal food* (100%). Ants, bugs, grasshoppers, spiders, weevils. *Nest.* A foot or less above the ground in dense broomsedge, rushes, saltgrass, sedges.

wren, winter (also called eastern winter wren; *Troglodytes troglodytes*). Rather uncommon summer resident of swamp and deep woods from northern Ontario and Newfoundland southward to Minnesota, New York, Massachusetts, and in the Appalachians to northern Georgia. Winters from Iowa, southern Ontario, New York, and Massachusetts southward to Texas, the Gulf coast, and southern Florida; casually northward in its breeding range. *Animal food* (100%). Ants, beetles, bugs, caterpillars, leafhoppers, snails, white grubs, worms. *Nest.* In a hole or crevice of a log or stump, near water. *Attracting.* This smallest of the eastern wrens is reported to nest in a birdhouse of the same dimensions specified for the house wren.

yellowbird. See warbler, yellow.

yellowbird, swamp. See warbler, prothonotary.

yellowhammer. See flicker, yellow-shafted.

yellowlegs, greater (also called greater yellowshank and greater tell-tale; *Totanus melanoleucus*). Common summer resident of beaches, mudflats, and ponds from northern Ontario and Labrador southward to southeastern Quebec and Newfoundland; nonbreeding birds summer along the Atlantic coast. Winters from central Texas, Gulf states, and South Carolina southward to Central and South America; occasionally in the Tennessee valley; migrates along the Atlantic coast.

yellowlegs, lesser (also called lesser yellowshank and lesser tell-tale; *Totanus flavipes*). Common summer resident of marshy shores and mudflats in Ontario and Quebec. Winters from South Carolina, Florida, Louisiana, and Texas southward through the West Indies and Central America to South America; migrates in fall along the Atlantic coast. *Animal food* (100%). Chiefly ants, flies, and grasshoppers; also crustaceans, fish, snails, and worms. *Nest.* In a slight depression in the ground, sometimes lined with leaves or grass.

yellow-rump. See warbler, yellow.

yellowshank, greater. See yellowlegs, greater.

yellowshank, lesser. See yellowlegs, lesser.

yellowthroat (also called common, Florida, Maryland, northern, and southern yellowthroat; *Geothlypis trichas*). A member of the wood warbler family; common summer resident of brushy thickets and swamps from Ontario and Newfoundland southward to Florida, the Gulf coast, and Mexico. Winters commonly in the Gulf states, the West Indies, and Central America. *Animal food* (100%). Ants, aphids, caterpillars, crickets, grasshoppers, spiders, and suet. *Nest.* Usually on or near the ground, in grass and weeds, or shrubby growth; occasionally in trees and shrubs.

zebra. See woodpecker, red-bellied.

Plants and Other Foods—
How Birds Use Them

This section provides an up-to-date appraisal of the usefulness of plant species as food, shelter, and nesting sites for birds. It contains essentially the same information that is provided in section 4 but arranges it by plants and foods instead of by birds, and specifies which parts of a plant are eaten by which species. It includes more than 700 entries, including most of the farm and garden crops and weeds; significant woodland trees, shrubs, and vines; many pasture grasses and legumes; plants and flowers commonly used in landscaping; and foods you can buy for bird feeding.

This listing of the important foods that attract and support birds adds numerous items omitted from books. It is not cluttered wih entries for the many plants that birds seldom eat beyond "tasting," but does include a few common plants such as ailanthus and redbud to inform the reader that these have little or no value to birds.

The entries are arranged in alphabetical order by the common name of each plant or food, which is printed in **boldface type.** The approved common names for trees and grasses are drawn for the most part from the *Check List of Native and Naturalized Trees of the United States,* by Elbert J. Little, Jr. (Washington, D.C.: U.S. Department of Agriculture, Forest Service, Agricultural Handbook No. 41, 1953) and the *Manual of the Grasses of the United States,* by A. S. Hitchcock (2d ed., revised by Agnes Chase; Washington, D.C.: U.S. Department of Agriculture, Miscellaneous publication No. 200, 1950). For other plants, the common names usually are those established by *Standardized Plant Names,* prepared by the editorial committee of the American Joint Committee on Horticultural Nomenclature (2d ed.; Harrisburg, Pa.: J. Horace McFarland Co., 1942). In a few cases the author took exception to his sources' use of a name that seemed confusing, and used instead the technical name or a widely accepted common name.

Most often the entries bear the titles of individual plant species. Occasionally, when information could not be ascertained for separate species, generic-name entries are used, and the birds known to use undetermined species of the genus are listed. The birds named in the entry for a plant genus are not repeated in entries for separate species. When a plant is represented solely by a generic entry, it may be assumed that information about the use of species is unavailable, uncertain, or of minor significance. The data for blackberries, blueberries, dewberries, and hawthorns, for example, is given for their generic names, because many of the records do not break down the information by species. Similarly, information about alders and birches is given under their generic names because records of stomach analyses and direct observations of feeding birds are often uncertain about the identification of the numerous species and hybrid forms.

In parentheses following the accepted common name of the plant you will find its other vernacular names, if any; also its scientific name, printed in in *italic type*. The unstandardized vernacular names of plants will also be found in their alphabetical places with a reference to the common name used in this book (e.g., "pigweed. See amaranth"). If you know a plant's technical Latin name only, you can find its common name by turning to the alphabetical listing of scientific plant names in section 7.

Each plant entry begins with an identification—ornamental shrub, common fruit tree, hay plant, garden or field weed, perennial marsh plant, submersed waterweed, cultivated grain, or some other brief designation. Further description and information on methods of growing the plant can be found in botanical books and agricultural and horticultural bulletins.

Each entry continues with information about the plant's general usefulness as a nesting site, if any, and appraises it as a food for the various species of birds. Wherever possible, the food is evaluated as a "choice food" for the bird species which it attracts readily and regularly, or as an important "fair food" which is eaten in significant quantity when choice foods are unavailable. For more complete definitions of the terms "choice" and "fair," as used in this book, see section 1, "Food Preferences."

Birds' relation to agriculture

Most of the birds in eastern North America live in environments in which plant and animal life are governed chiefly by man's agricultural, industrial, residential, political, and recreational needs. Much of the acreage available for bird habitat—cropland, orchard, pasture and rangeland, woodland, pond, stream, and marshland—is privately owned. Agricultural lands and waters and thoughtfully landscaped residential areas usually support higher populations of birds than nature alone ever did.

Food is the most important single influence on bird populations. It provides the energy for health, self-preservation, and reproduction. A nearby source of choice foods suitable for offspring often appears to be a deciding factor in birds' selection of nesting places.

Fortunately, those who own or manage land can maintain and increase foods that attract and support enjoyable birds in marshes, ponds, fields, pastures, swamps, woodlands, orchards, parks, landscaped homes, and feeding stations. The chief problem lies in the selection of plants to be retained, planted, or otherwise favored in accordance with their qualities as food for individual species of birds. Are they "choice," "fair" but still important, or of insignificant value for birds? To favor a better food plant, the owner must sacrifice plants of lesser value, since the available sunlight, moisture, plant nutrients, and space for growth are already fully utilized in most plant communities. The entries in this section will help guide such decisions.

Many choice foods can be grown on farms and around homes to provide a dependable source of nutritious foods for birds that eat seeds, fruits, acorns, or nuts. Insects and earthworms also become available to many birds on improved pastures, good lawns, golf courses, and other short-grass lands. Fertilizer stimulates the growth of grasses and legumes, thereby increasing the number of insects and worms available. Farm ponds produce the larvae which later escape as flying insects that attract martins, swifts, and other birds which feed almost exclusively on insects in flight. Furthermore, the insects from farms and gardens provide much of the food that supports beneficial birds, and many species of upland birds feed almost wholly on insects or similar foods, eating few or no seeds and fruits.

On the other hand, insects often damage crops. Birds may control destructive insects to some extent, but their aid is seldom if ever sufficient alone. To protect crops, fruits, and ornamentals against insects you may need to apply insecticides, but you'll want to use chemicals sparingly and cautiously to avoid killing your winged friends.

Some species of birds, of course, are widely regarded as pests because they descend in large flocks upon fall crops. Sorghums, millets, and rice are particularly vulnerable to marauding hordes of blackbirds, bobolinks, cowbirds, crows, grackles, and house sparrows. Since repellents and frightening devices seldom work successfully, the best protection against loss is to harvest the crop without delay as soon as it is ripe enough. After the crop is harvested, the waste grain left on the ground is a substantial contribution to the lives of these and many other upland-feeding birds.

Several species of birds eat figs, grapes, oats, and wheat as they ripen, but damage usually is minor since ripening occurs during nesting time, when birds do not feed in large flocks. Only a few pairs and their young are feeding in any single field or orchard at that season.

Woody plants—shrubs, trees and vines—produce bird foods, nesting sites, shade, wood products, living fences, ornamental and landscape values, and protection to the soil against erosion. Section 5 will help a landowner select the kinds of plants that each bird prefers for food and nesting.

The exact details of these land-management practices are not provided in this book, because plant-and-soil conditions in eastern North America vary greatly. Standards, specifications, and guides to the management of plants, soils, water, and birds are available in the Soil Conservation Service offices in nearly every county in the eastern United States. Assistance can be obtained from the soil-conservation technicians.

Birdwatching becomes more enjoyable as we learn to appreciate the food preferences in each bird's daily diet. A person who knows bird-plant relationships will have more luck spotting birds where choice food plants occur, particularly when their seeds, fruits, and nuts are attractively ripe or mature. It is well to remember that choice foods are always more attractive than those that a bird recognizes as only fair.

WHAT TO PLANT. If you intend to plant some ornamentals, or grow grain crops that will feed your favorite birds, you should consult the entries for the plants you have in mind. You may find that although the plants you've selected are indeed appealing to the birds you like, they are even more attractive to the species you regard as pests. Don't fret; turn to the entries in section 4 for your favorite birds and see what other plants they prefer. Using both sections in this fashion, you probably can find alternatives to your first selections that will feed the birds you like and are not especially attractive to pests.

WHAT TO FEED AT FEEDING STATIONS. If disturbing numbers of unwanted birds visit your feeding station regularly, study the alternative foods that your favorite birds like and the undesirable ones do not. You should be able to select foods that encourage the birds you want, and discourage unwelcome visitors.

Can a person confidently expect to attract and hold a specific kind of bird by providing it choice foods? The fact that one can is the delightful promise of the information in this book. This promise, of course, is limited by some reasonable conditions. The place of feeding must be within the natural, geographic, seasonal, and climatic range of the bird and be in a suitable environment. The best of foods may fail to dissuade a migratory species from going south in the fall and winter season, or from returning to its northern nesting grounds when the spring mating urge arrives. But within these limits, you can depend on the local birds and winter visitors coming to your food each day, year after year. A few examples may make this point more understandable.

Bluebirds and mocking birds cannot remain in northern wintering areas nor survive severe periods of storms unless they find daily rations to supplement their principal foods—insects. Robins are similarly dependent upon earthworms. While these three will eat limited amounts of bread in winter, they cannot be expected to eat grains. All three can survive periods when the ground is frozen or covered with snow and no worms or insects are available if you provide them with attractive berries or fruits such as raisins, currants, and pyracantha.

Nuts, peanutbutter, and suet are outstanding winter foods for the birds that like these fat-rich items, but many birds will not eat them. Sunflower seed is another choice food—for those species which like sunflower seeds. On the other hand, the mourning dove is almost exclusively a weed-and grain-seed eater and will not be attracted by fruits, nuts, peanutbutter, or suet.

For winter roosting cover, of course, evergreen shrubs and trees are ideal whether you live in the North or the South. Birds that build their first nests early in the spring on branches of trees also prefer evergreens to deciduous species that bring forth their shade-producing leaves at a later date.

PLANTS AND OTHER FOODS — How Birds Use Them

abelia, glossy (*Abelia grandiflora*). Ornamental shrub; occasional nest plant.

ailanthus (also called tree-of-heaven; *Ailanthus altissima.*) Naturalized tree; rarely a nest site; seeds not eaten.

albizzia, silktree (also called flowering mimosa, and silktree; *Albizzia julibrissin*). Ornamental; seldom a nest tree; seeds not eaten. Nectar is a choice food of ruby-throated hummingbird.

alder (*Alnus* species). Native tree; frequently nest plant. Seeds or buds are a choice food of ruffed grouse, common redpoll, pine siskin; fair food of snow bunting, American goldfinch, sharp-tailed grouse.

alfalfa (*Medicago sativa*). Hay plant; occasional nest plant. Green leaves are a choice food of coot, fulvous tree duck, Canada goose, sharp-tailed grouse, American widgeon; fair food of sandhill crane, mallard, gray partridge, ring-necked pheasant.

algae, filamentous (*Spirogyra* and related species). Aquatic plant. Vegetative parts are a fair food of coot, gadwall, redhead, sora, American widgeon.

alligator-pear. See avocado.

almond (*Prunus amygdalus*). Cultivated nut tree, occasional nest site. Nut meat is a choice food of cardinal, Carolina chickadee, red crossbill, common crow, nuthatch (brown-headed, red-breasted), tufted titmouse, towhee, warbler (myrtle, pine), red-bellied woodpecker, Carolina wren.

almond, earth or **ground.** See chufa.

althea. See shrubalthea.

amaranth (also called pigweed; *Amaranthus* species). Annual weed. Seeds of undetermined species are a choice food of lark bunting, ground dove, longspur (chestnut-collared, Lapland), water pipit, common redpoll, sparrow (clay-colored, Lincoln's); fair food of ring-necked pheasant, sparrow (fox, Harris', house, lark).

amaranth, green. See amaranth, redroot.

amaranth, prostrate (also called spreading pigweed; *Amaranthus blitoides*). Annual weed. Seed is a choice food of bobwhite, mourning dove, horned lark, vesper sparrow.

amaranth, redroot (also called green amaranth, beetroot, or redroot pigweed; *Amaranthus retroflexus*). Annual weed. Seed is a choice food of snow bunting, mourning dove, slate-colored junco, horned lark, sparrow (chipping, field, grasshopper, savannah, song, tree, vesper, white-crowned, white-throated); fair food of bobwhite, gray partridge.

amaranth, slim (also called pigweed; *Amaranthus hybridus*). Annual weed. Seed is a choice food of mourning dove, horned lark, sparrow (chipping, song); fair food of white-throated sparrow.

amaranth, spiny (also called spiny pigweed or thorny amaranth; *Amaranthus spinosus*). Annual weed. Seed is fair food of bobwhite.

amaryllis (*Amaryllis*). Ornamental flowering plant. Nectar is a choice food of ruby-throated hummingbird.

American-mistletoe. See mistletoe.

ampelopsis, heartleaf (also called heartleaf ivy; *Ampelopsis cordata*). Vine. Fruit is a choice food of yellow-shafted flicker, brown thrasher, wood thrush.

anacharis (also called waterweed and Canada waterweed; *Anacharis canadensis*). Submersed waterweed. Leafy stems are a fair food of coot, American widgeon.

Aneilema, keisak (*Aneilema keisak*). Wetland annual herb of south Atlantic coastal area. Seed is a choice food of bobwhite, duck (black, wood), mallard, pintail, shoveler, green-winged teal.

Aneilema nudiflorum. Annual herb, escaped in southern Florida. Seed is choice food of mourning dove.

apple (*Malus pumila*). Fruit tree; favorite nesting site of several bird species. Blossoms are fair food of purple finch, cedar waxwing. Buds are fair food of pine grosbeak, greater prairie chicken. Dried apple is fair food of cardinal. Seeds are a choice food of pine grosbeak; fair food of red crossbill. Apple, frozen, sliced, or whole, is a choice food of catbird, grosbeak (evening, pine), ruffed grouse, yellow-bellied sapsucker, starling, waxwing (Bohemian, cedar), woodpecker (red-bellied, red-headed); fair food of common crow, common grackle, jay (blue, gray, scrub), mockingbird, Baltimore oriole, ring-necked pheasant, robin, hairy woodpecker. Apple blossom is the state flower of Arkansas and Michigan.

apricot (*Prunus armeniaca*). Fruit tree; occasional nest tree. Fruit or flowers are a choice food of common crow, black-headed grosbeak; fair food of robin, yellow-bellied sapsucker.

arborvitae, Chinese. See arborvitae, oriental.

arborvitae, eastern or **northern.** See white-cedar, northern.

arborvitae, oriental (also called Chinese arborvitae; *Thuja orientalis*). Introduced ornamental; seldom a nest plant. Seed is a choice food of cardinal, cedar waxwing; fair food of mockingbird.

arbutus, trailing. See trailing-arbutus.

ardisia, Christmas (*Ardisia crenulata*). Ornamental shrub. Fruit is fair food of mockingbird.

arrowarum, redfruit (*Peltandra glauca*) and **Virginia** (*P. virginica*). Marsh plants. Seeds are fair food of coot, duck (black, wood), mallard.

arrowgrass. See podgrass, shore.

arrowhead (also called duckpotato and wapato; *Sagittaria* species). Marsh plant. Tubers are a choice food of canvasback, sandhill crane, duck (black, ring-necked, wood), gadwall, mallard, pintail, king rail, lesser scaup, whistling swan, American widgeon; fair food of duck (mottled, ruddy), greater scaup, green-winged teal.

ash, Biltmore. See ash, white.

ash, white (also called Biltmore ash; *Fraxinus americana* and probably other species). Native tree; occasional nest site. Seeds are a choice food of blackbird (red-winged, rusty), purple finch, grosbeak (evening, pine); fair food of bobwhite, cardinal, wood duck.

asparagus, garden (*Asparagus officinalis*). Garden vegetable. Fruit is a choice food of mockingbird, waxwing (Bohemian, cedar); fair food of eastern bluebird, ring-necked pheasant, American widgeon (sprouts).

aspen, bigtooth (also called largetooth aspen, popple, poplar; *Populus grandidentata*). Native tree. Buds are a choice food of ruffed grouse.

aspen, golden or **mountain.** See aspen, quaking.

aspen, quaking (also called popple; golden, mountain, or trembling aspen; *Populus tremuloides*). Native tree. Buds are a choice food of ruffed grouse; fair food of sharp-tailed grouse, Baltimore oriole, greater prairie chicken.

aspen, trembling. See aspen, quaking.

aster (*Aster* species). Native perennial herbs. Occasional nest plant of American goldfinch. Seed is fair food of turkey.

Australian-pine. See beefwood.

avocado (also called alligator-pear; *Persea americana*). Introduced tree. Pulp of the fruit is a choice food of spotted-breasted oriole.

azalea (*Azalea* species). Ornamental shrubs; occasional nest plant; good cover for ground birds. Nectar is a choice food of ruby-throated hummingbird.

baccharis (also called groundselbush; *Baccharis* species). Shrub; often a nest plant; not a food.

bahiagrass (*Paspalum notatum*). Pasture grass. Seed is a choice food of brown-headed cowbird, house sparrow, turkey; fair food of cardinal, mourning dove.

baldcypress (also called cypress, and gulf, red, southern, white, or yellow cypress; *Taxodium distichum*). Swamp tree; frequent nest plant of anhinga, cormorant, bald eagle, egrets, hawk (red-shouldered, short-tailed), herons, ibis, kites, osprey, spoonbill, and a few smaller birds. Little value as a food plant. State tree of Louisiana.

balsam or **Canada balsam.** See fir, balsam.

bamboo (*Bambusa* and *Phyllostachys* species). Wood or treelike grasses of the tropics and semitropics. Occasional nest plants; good cover.

banana (*Musa*). Fruit tree; seldom a nest plant. Fruit is a choice food of purple gallinule, gray jay, mockingbird, spotted-breasted oriole.

Barbadoscherry (*Malpighia glabra*). Ornamental tropical shrub. Red fruit is a choice food of bulbul, spotted-breasted oriole.

barberry, European (*Berberis vulgaris*). Ornamental shrub. Berries are fair food of mockingbird, ring-necked pheasant, robin.

barberry, Japanese (*Berberis thunbergi*). Ornamental shrub; occasional nest plant. Berries are a choice food of rose-breasted grosbeak, robin, thrush (Swainson's, wood), waxwing (Bohemian, cedar); fair food of ruffed grouse, mockingbird, ring-necked pheasant.

barberry, wintergreen (*Berberis julianae*). Ornamental shrub. Seldom used by birds.

barley, cultivated (*Hordeum vulgare*). Cultivated grain. Seed is a choice food of red-winged blackbird, bobolink, brant, snow bunting, canvasback, cardinal, coot, sandhill crane, common crow, white-winged dove, duck (black, wood), gadwall, goose (Canada, white-fronted), mallard, oldsquaw, gray partridge, ring-necked pheasant, pintail, greater prairie chicken, redhead, shoveler, sparrow (fox, Lincoln's, savannah), teal (blue-winged, green-winged), turkey, American widgeon; fair food of blackbird (Brewer's, yellow-headed), mourning dove, scrub jay, slate-colored junco, sparrow (house, white-crowned), rufous-sided towhee.

barley, wild (*Hordeum* species). Wild grass. Seeds are fair food of goose (Canada, snow).

barnyardgrass (also called duck or wild millet; *Echinochloa crusgalli*). Native grass, usually in wet soils. Seed is a choice food of red-winged blackbird, bobolink, cardinal, brown-headed cowbird, mourning dove, gadwall, goose (Canada, white-fronted), slate-colored junco, mallard, eastern meadowlark, pintail, sparrow (field, song, white-throated), teal (blue-winged, green-winged); fair food of Brewer's blackbird, canvasback, duck (black, fulvous tree, mottled, ring-necked, wood), Smith's longspur, redhead, lesser scaup, shoveler, sora, sparrow (house, Lincoln's, savannah), American widgeon.

basswood, American (also called American linden; *Tilia americana*). Native tree; occasional nest site.

bayberry. See waxmyrtle, northern and southern.

baycedar (also called thatch-leaf; *Suriana maritima*). Shrub; frequent nest plant of noddy tern.

beachgrass, American (*Ammophila breviligulata*). Native grass. Seed is a choice food of Ipswich sparrow; fair food of snow bunting.

beadruby, Canada (*Maianthemum canadense*). Low native perennial herb. Berry is a choice food of ruffed grouse.

beakrush, horned (*Rhynchospora corniculata*). Marsh plant. Seed is fair food of duck (black, mottled), mallard, pintail, teal (blue-winged, green-winged).

bean, mung (also called mungbean and mungo; *Phaseolus aureus*). Cultivated annual legume. Seed is fair food of bobwhite.

bean, scarlet runner (*Phaseolus coccineus*). Cultivated legume. Nectar is a choice food of ruby-throated hummingbird.

bean, trailing. See wildbean.

beard-grass, See polypogon, rabbitfoot.

beautyberry, American (*Callicarpa americana*). Native shrub; occasional nest plant. Fruit is a choice food of bulbul, cardinal, mockingbird, brown thrasher, wood thrush; fair food of bobwhite, catbird, robin.

beautyberry, Japanese (*Callicarpa japonica*). Introduced ornamental shrub. Fruit is a choice food of cardinal.

beebalm, oswego (*Monarda didyma*). Native aromatic herb. Nectar is a choice food of ruby-throated hummingbird.

beech, American (*Fagus grandifolia*). Native tree; frequent nest plant. Nut is a choice food of bobwhite, common crow, duck (black, wood), yellow-shafted flicker, common grackle, grosbeak (evening, rose-breasted), ruffed grouse, blue jay, white-breasted nuthatch, white-throated sparrow (food is staminate flowers), tufted titmouse, turkey, woodpecker (hairy, pileated, red-bellied, red-headed); fair food of blackbird (red-winged, rusty), red crossbill, purple finch, spruce grouse.

beech, blue. See hornbeam, American.

beefwood (also called casuarina, Australian-pine, and horsetail beefwood; *Casuarina equisetifolia*). Introduced tree. Seeds are a choice food of ground dove.

beggar's-lice. See tickclover.

beggarticks (also called bur-marigold, Spanishneedles, stick-tights, and tick-seed; *Bidens* species). Annual weeds. Seeds are a choice food of pine grosbeak; fair food of duck (black, wood), American goldfinch, mallard, ring-necked pheasant, turkey.

beggarweed, Florida (*Desmodium polycarpum*). Annual legume of cultivated fields. Seed is a choice food of bobwhite.

bellyache-bush. See nettlespurge, bellyache.

benne. See sesame.

Bermudagrass (*Cynodon dactylon*). Lawn and pasture grass. Underground runners are fair food of goose (blue, Canada, snow).

bilberry, bog (*Vaccinium uliginosum*). Native shrub. Fruit is a choice food of Canada goose, horned lark, cedar waxwing.

birch (*Betula* species). Native tree; frequent or occasional nest site of several birds. Seeds or buds are a choice food of red crossbill, purple finch, American goldfinch, grouse (ruffed, sharp-tailed, spruce), red-breasted nuthatch, common redpoll, pine siskin; fair food of cardinal, black-capped chickadee, greater prairie chicken, cedar waxwing. "Paper" (white) birch is the state tree of New Hampshire.

birdcherry. See cherry, European bird.

birdeye (*Caperonia castaneaefolia*). Subtropical wetland annual weed. Seed is a choice food of cardinal, mourning dove, white-throated sparrow; fair food of red-winged blackbird, slate-colored junco.

bittersweet. See nightshade, bitter.

bittersweet, American (also called false bittersweet; *Celastrus scandens*). Native ornamental climbing vine. Fruit is fair food of eastern bluebird, cardinal, catbird, pine grosbeak, ruffed grouse, mockingbird, robin, house sparrow, starling, cedar waxwing.

blackberry (*Rubus* species). Native and cultivated varieties of blackberries, dewberries, and their hybrids. The shrubby blackberry species provide good thorny nesting sites and escape cover for several birds that eat the berries. Fruits are a choice food of eastern bluebird, bobwhite, indigo bunting, cardinal, catbird, yellow-breasted chat, fish crow, grosbeak (blackheaded, pine), ruffed grouse, eastern kingbird, mockingbird, oriole (Baltimore, orchard), ring-necked pheasant, greater prairie chicken, robin, sparrow (field, fox, Henslow's, white-throated), tanager (scarlet, summer), brown thrasher, wood thrush, rufous-sided towhee, turkey, veery, vireo (redeyed, white-eyed), cedar waxing, woodpecker (red-bellied, red-headed); fair food of blackbird (Brewer's, rusty), common crow, yellow-shafted flicker, flycatcher (Acadian, great crested, Traill's), common grackle, grosbeak (blue, evening, rose-breasted), blue jay, slate-colored junco, starling, thrush (gray-cheeked, Swainson's), hairy woodpecker.

blackgum (also called black and swamp tupelo; *Nyssa sylvatica*). Native tree. Fruit is a choice food of eastern bluebird, catbird, yellow-shafted flicker, eastern kingbird, mockingbird, robin, starling, summer tanager, brown thrasher, thrush (gray-cheeked, wood), turkey, cedar waxwing, woodpecker (hairy, pileated, red-bellied, red-headed).

blackhaw. See viburnum.

blacklocust. See locust, black.

blackmangrove (also called blackwood; *Avicennia nitida*). Shrub of coastal swamps; frequent nest site of red-winged blackbird, double-crested cormorant, common egret, common grackle, herons, osprey, brown pelican; occasionally bald eagle.

blackwood. See blackmangrove.

bladderwort, common (*Utricularia vulgaris*). Submersed waterweed. Seed is fair food of coot.

blazing-star. See tritonia.

blueberry (*Vaccinium* species). Native and cultivated shrub; occasional nesting site; fruit is a choice food of eastern bluebird, catbird, yellow-breasted chat, yellow-shafted flicker, Canada goose, grouse (ruffed, sharp-tailed, spruce), herring gull, blue jay, eastern kingbird, orchard oriole, willow ptarmigan, robin, sparrow (Bachman's, white-throated), starling, scarlet tanager, brown thrasher, thrush (gray-cheeked, hermit, wood), rufous-sided towhee, turkey, veery, cedar waxwing, whimbrel, woodpecker (red-bellied, red-headed); fair food of bobwhite, cardinal, black-capped chickadee, sandhill crane, fish crow, long-billed curlew, great crested flycatcher, scrub jay, Baltimore oriole, sparrow (Harris', Ipswich).

blue-curls. See selfheal, common.

bluegrass, annual (*Poa annua*). Annual winter grass often in lawns. Seed is a choice food of mourning dove, sparrow (field, savannah, vesper, white-crowned); fair food of sparrow (chipping, house).

bluegrass, Kentucky (*Poa pratensis*). Perennial lawn and pasture grass. Leaves are a choice food of ruffed grouse, turkey.

blue-sailors. See chicory.

bluestem (*Andropogon* species). Native grasses. Root stems are fair food of goose (blue, snow).

bluestem, big (*Andropogon gerardi*). Native grass. Seed is a choice food of indigo bunting.

bluestem, little (also called broomsedge; *Andropogon scoparius*). Native grass. Seed is fair food of tree sparrow.

bodark. See osageorange.

bogbean, common (*Menyanthes trifoliata*). Native perennial herb. Seed is fair food of dowitchers, Hudsonian godwit, lesser scaup.

bois d'arc. See osageorange.

bottlebrush (*Callistemon* species). Tropical ornamental shrubs. Fruit is a choice food of bulbul, spotted-breasted oriole.

bottletree (*Brachychiton*). Ornamental shrub. Fruit is a choice food of mockingbird.

bougainvillea (*Bougainvillea*). Ornamental vine; little used by birds.

bowwood. See osageorange.

box, common (*Buxus sempervirens*). Ornamental shrub; occasional nest plant.

boxelder (*Acer negundo*). Native tree; occasional nest site. Seed is a choice food of purple finch, grosbeak (evening, pine).

brazilnut (*Bertholletia excelsa*). South American tree. Commercial nut meat is a choice food of cardinal, Carolina chickadee, brown-headed nuthatch, sparrow (chipping, white-throated), tufted titmouse, myrtle warbler, red-bellied woodpecker, Carolina wren.

bread, corn. See cornbread.

bread, white. White bread, biscuits, and crackers are choice foods of blackbird (Brewer's, red-winged), painted bunting, cardinal, catbird, chickadee (black-capped, Carolina), brown creeper, rock dove, black duck, purple gallinule, grackle (boat-tailed, common), black-headed grosbeak, jay (blue, gray, scrub), slate-colored junco, mockingbird, white-breasted nuthatch, spotted-breasted oriole, common raven, robin, sparrow (chipping, field, fox, Harris', house, Lincoln's, song, tree, white-crowned, white-throated), starling, summer tanager, brown thrasher, tufted titmouse, rufous-sided towhee, warbler (black-throated blue, myrtle, orange-crowned, pine), cedar wax-wing, woodpecker (downy, red-bellied, red-headed), wren (Bewick's, Carolina); fair foods of eastern bluebird, harlequin duck, sparrow hawk, oriole (Baltimore, orchard), ring-necked pheasant, Bohemian waxwing.

bristlegrass, including **Faber's** (*Setaria faberii*), **giant** (S. *magna*), **green** (*S. viridis*), **yellow** (S. *lutescens*). Annual grasses, Seeds are a choice food of blackbird (red-winged, rusty, yellow-headed), bobolink, bobwhite, bunting (indigo, painted, snow), cardinal, brown-headed cowbird, dickcissel, dove (ground, mourning, white-winged), mottled duck, blue grosbeak, slate-colored junco, horned lark, longspur (chestnut-collared, Lapland, McCown's, Smith's), meadowlark (eastern, western), gray partridge, ring-necked pheasant, sparrow (Bachman's, chipping, clay-colored, field, fox, grasshopper, Harris', Henslow's, house, lark, Lincoln's, savannah, seaside, song, swamp, tree, vesper, white-crowned, white-throated), rufous-sided towhee; fair food of Brewer's blackbird, canvasback, goose (blue, snow), grackle (boat-tailed, common), sharp-tailed grouse, pintail, water pipit, greater prairie chicken, yellow rail, redhead, common redpoll, scaup (greater, lesser), teal (blue-winged, green-winged), turkey.

brome (also called bromegrass and rescuegrass; (*Bromus* species). Pasture grasses. Green leaves are a choice food of Canada goose, greater prairie chicken, turkey. Seeds are fair food of horned lark, gray partridge, sparrow (savannah, vesper).

broomsedge. See bluestem, little.

browntopmillet. See millet, browntop.

buckeye, Ohio (*Aesculus glabra*). Native tree. Nectar is a choice food of ruby-throated hummingbird. State tree of Ohio.

buckwheat, common (*Fagopyrum sagittatum*). Annual field grain. Seed is a choice food of cardinal, common crow, black duck, evening grosbeak, ruffed grouse, horned lark, gray partridge, ring-necked pheasant, greater prairie chicken, green-winged teal, turkey; fair food of bobwhite, mourning dove, purple finch, blue jay, mallard, pintail, white-throated sparrow, starling, towhee, widgeon.

bugle, carpet (also called bugle-weed; *Ajuga reptans*). Creeping ornamental perennial. Nectar is a choice food of ruby-throated hummingbird.

bugle-weed. See bugle, carpet.

bulrush (*Scirpus* species). Perennial marsh plants. Frequent or occasional nest site of American bittern, red-winged blackbird, coot, many ducks, egrets, geese, boat-tailed grackle, grebes, herons, white-faced ibis, clapper rail, sora. Seeds or rootstocks of fresh-water species are eaten by coot, crane (sandhill, whooping), dowitchers, most ducks, geese, godwits, Smith's longspur, rail (Virginia, yellow), sora, Harris' sparrow.

bulrush, alkali. See bulrush, saltmarsh.

bulrush, saltmarsh (also called alkali bulrush; *Scirpus robustus*). Brackish-water or saltmarsh perennial. Seed is a choice food of duck (black, mottled), gadwall, goose (blue, snow), pintail, scaup (greater, lesser), shoveler, teal (blue-winged, green-winged); fair food of purple finch.

bumelia, gum. (also called woollybucket bumelia, and chittam-wood; *Bumelia lanuginosa*). Native tree; occasional nest site. Fruit is a fair food of bobwhite, turkey, cedar waxwing.

burclover (*Medicago hispida*). Annual pasture legume. Green leaves are a choice food of turkey.

burdock, smaller (*Arctium minus*). Bristly biennial weed. Seed is a choice food of American goldfinch.

bur-marigold. See beggarticks.

burreed (*Sparganium* species). Marsh plants. Seeds probably should be classified as fair food of canvasback, coot, duck (black, ring-necked, wood), goose, mallard, redhead, scaup (greater, lesser), whistling swan, American widgeon.

bushhoneysuckle. See honeysuckle, dwarf bush.

butter. Fair food of cardinal, mockingbird, summer tanager.

buttercup (*Ranunculus* species). Marsh plants. Seeds or vegetative parts are a choice food of ring-necked duck, turkey; fair food of snow bunting.

butterflypea, coastal (*Centrosema virginianum*). Native vining legume. Seed is fair food of bobwhite.

butternut (also called white walnut, and oilnut; *Juglans cinerea*). Native tree; nest site of broad-winged hawk. Nut meat is a choice food of chickadee (black-capped, Carolina), purple finch, nuthatch (brown-headed, red-breasted, white-breasted), field sparrow, tufted titmouse, warbler (myrtle, pine), red-bellied woodpecker, Carolina wren.

buttonball-tree. See sycamore, American.

buttonbush (also called buttonwillow; *Cephalanthus occidentalis*). Native wetland shrub; frequent nesting site of anhinga, red-winged blackbird, egrets, grackles, herons, white ibis. Seed is fair food of mallard, lesser scaup, shoveler, American widgeon.

buttonwillow. See buttonbush.

cabbage (*Brassica oleracea*). Garden plant. Young leaves are a choice food of American widgeon; fair food of goose (blue, Canada, snow, white-fronted).

cabbage-palm. See palmetto, cabbage.

cake. Crumbs of cake and cookies are choice foods of eastern bluebird, catbird, Carolina chickadee, scrub jay, mockingbird, brown-headed nuthatch, chipping sparrow, tufted titmouse, warbler (myrtle, pine), and probably other birds that eat biscuits and bread.

camellia (*Camellia japonica*). Ornamental shrub. Useful bird cover, and frequent or occasional nest site of cardinal, mockingbird, robin, brown thrasher, white-eyed vireo. State flower of Alabama.

camphortree (*Cinnamomum camphora*). Subtropical landscape tree. Fruit is a choice food of eastern bluebird, cardinal, fish crow, rock dove, ring-billed gull, mockingbird, robin, starling, cedar waxwing.

campion. See silene.

canarygrass (*Phalaris canariensis*). Annual, introduced grass. Seed, commonly used in bird-food mixtures, is a choice food of red-winged blackbird, bobwhite, cardinal, mourning dove, purple finch, American goldfinch, slate-colored junco, sparrow (chipping, field, fox, house, song, white-throated), rufous-sided towhee; fair food of common grackle, water pipit, savannah sparrow.

canarygrass, reed (*Phalaris arundinacea*). Native perennial grass. Seed is a choice food of mourning dove, slate-colored junco, sparrow (field, house, white-throated).

candle-berry. See waxmyrtle, northern and southern.

cane. See sorgo.

cantaloup (*Cucumis melo*). Garden melon. Seed is a choice food of cardinal, common crow, white-winged dove, nuthatch (red-breasted, white-breasted), tufted titmouse; fair food of mourning dove, house sparrow, starling, summer tanager.

cape-jasmine. See gardenia.

cardinalflower (*Lobelia cardinalis*). Flowering herb. Nectar is a choice food of ruby-throated hummingbird.

carissa, natalplum (also called natalplum; *Carissa grandiflora*). Spiny tropical shrub. Fruit is a choice food of bulbul.

Carolinajessamine (also called yellow jessamine; *Gelsemium sempervirens*). Native southern vine; no records. State flower of South Carolina.

carpetgrass (*Axonopus* species). Native grass. Seed is a choice food of turkey; fair food of bobwhite.

carrot, garden (*Daucus carota sativa*). No eastern records of bird use.

carrot, wild (*Daucus carota*). Native herb. Seed is fair food of American goldfinch.

cashew (*Anacardium occidentale*). Cultivated tree. Nut meat is a choice food of Carolina chickadee, brown-headed nuthatch, tufted titmouse, myrtle warbler, red-bellied woodpecker, Carolina wren.

cassena. See dahoon; yaupon.

castorbean (*Ricinus communis*). Ornamental plant. Seed is seldom eaten.

casuarina. See beefwood.

catalpa (also called catawba; *Catalpa* species). Ornamental shade tree; occasional nest site. Seed is a fair food of evening grosbeak.

catawba. See catalpa.

catchfly. See silene.

catmint. See catnip.

catnip (also called catmint; *Nepeta cataria*). Perennial weed; seed is a choice food of American goldfinch, common redpoll.

cattail (also called tules; *Typha* species). Marsh plants; frequent nest site of bitterns, blackbirds, ducks, grackles, grebes, rails, sora, and long-billed marsh wren. Roots are a choice food of goose (blue, snow, white-fronted).

cattailmillet. See millet, pearl.

cedar, red. See redcedar, eastern.

cedar, southern red. See redcedar, southern.

cedar, white. See white-cedar.

celery, wild. See wildcelery.

chastetree, lilac (also called hemp-tree, Monk's peppertree, and blue vitex; *Vitex agnuscastus*). Ornamental shrub; occasional nest site of mockingbird. Seed not eaten by birds.

cheese. American cheese and cottage cheese are choice foods of catbird, Carolina chickadee, mockingbird, brown thrasher.

cherry, Barbados. See Barbadoscherry.

cherry, bessey (*Prunus besseyi*). Native fruiting shrub. Fruit is fair food of ring-necked pheasant, and possibly other birds.

cherry, bird. See cherry, pin; cherry, European bird.

cherry, black (also called mountain black cherry; *Prunus serotina*). Native tree; occasional nest site. Fruit is a choice food of eastern bluebird, bobwhite, cardinal, catbird, common crow, yellow-shafted flicker, grosbeak (evening, rose-breasted), ruffed grouse, blue jay, eastern kingbird, mockingbird, oriole (Baltimore, orchard), robin, yellow-bellied sapsucker, white-throated sparrow, starling, summer tanager, brown thrasher, thrush (gray-cheeked, hermit, Swainson's, wood), veery, vireo (red-eyed, warbling), cedar waxwing, woodpecker (downy, hairy, pileated, red-bellied, red-headed), fair food of red-winged blackbird, great crested flycatcher, common grackle, sharp-tailed grouse, ring-necked pheasant, greater prairie chicken, rufous-sided towhee, turkey.

cherry, choke (also called common chokecherry; *Prunus virginiana*). Native shrub or small tree; occasional nest site. Fruit is a choice food of eastern bluebird, grosbeak (evening, rose-breasted), grouse (ruffed, sharp-tailed), eastern kingbird, robin, wood thrush, woodpecker (pileated, red-headed); fair food of common crow, yellow-shafted flicker, great crested flycatcher, blue jay, ring-necked pheasant, greater prairie chicken, veery, waxwing (Bohemian, cedar), hairy woodpecker.

cherry, European bird (also called birdcherry; *Prunus padus*). Introduced and naturalized shrub. Fruit is a choice food of robin.

cherry, fire. See cherry, pin.

cherry-laurel. See laurelcherry.

cherry, mahaleb (also called mahaleb; *Prunus mahaleb*). European cherry tree stock. Fruit is a choice food of eastern bluebird, catbird, yellow-shafted flicker, blue jay, eastern kingbird, robin, brown thrasher, cedar waxwing.

cherry, mazzard (also called sweet cherry; *Prunus avium*). Orchard tree. Fruit is a choice food of eastern bluebird, cardinal, catbird, common crow, yellow-shafted flicker, grosbeak (black-headed, evening, pine, rose-breasted), ruffed grouse, blue jay, eastern kingbird, mockingbird, oriole (Baltimore, orchard), robin, starling, scarlet tanager, brown thrasher, wood thrush, red-eyed vireo, cedar waxwing.

cherry, mountain black. See cherry, black.

cherry, northern pin. See cherry, pin.

cherry, pie. See cherry, sour.

cherry, pigeon. See cherry, pin.

cherry, pin (also called bird, fire, northern pin, red, wild red, and pigeon cherry; *Prunus pensylvanica*). Native tree. Fruit is a choice food of eastern bluebird, yellow-shafted flicker, grosbeak (evening, rose-breasted), grouse (ruffed, sharp-tailed), eastern kingbird, robin, Swainson's thrush, veery, red-eyed vireo, cedar waxwing, red-headed woodpecker; fair food of great crested flycatcher, ring-necked pheasant, greater prairie chicken.

cherry, red or **wild red.** See cherry, pin.

cherry, sand (*Prunus pumila*). Low shrub. Fruit is a choice food of ruffed grouse; fair food of greater prairie chicken.

cherry, sour (also called pie cherry; *Prunus cerasus*). Orchard tree, "pie" cherries. Fruit is a choice food of eastern bluebird, cardinal, catbird, purple finch, grosbeak (black-headed, evening, pine, rose-breasted), ruffed grouse, blue jay, eastern kingbird, mockingbird, oriole (Baltimore, orchard), robin, starling, brown thrasher, thrush (Swainson's, wood), cedar waxwing, red-headed woodpecker.

cherry, Surinam. See pitanga.

cherry, sweet. See cherry, mazzard.

cherry, wild red. See cherry, pin.

chestnut, American (*Castanea dentata*). Native forest tree. Nut meat is a choice food of wood duck, common grackle, ruffed grouse, blue jay, white-breasted nuthatch.

chickencorn (*Sorghum vulgare drummondi*). Cultivated sorghum; seed is fair food of cardinal, mourning dove, common grackle, blue jay, slate-colored junco, sparrow (house, white-throated).

chickweed (also called common chickweed; *Stellaria media*). Garden, lawn, and field weed. Seed is a choice food of bobwhite, dove (ground, mourning), American goldfinch, pine siskin; fair food of cardinal, water pipit, sparrow (chipping, field, house, savannah, white-crowned).

chicory (also called blue-sailors and common chicory; *Cichorium intybus*). Naturalized European plant, attractive blue flowers, coffee adulterant. Seed is a choice food of American goldfinch.

chinaberry (also called chinatree, umbrella chinaberry, or umbrella-tree; *Melia azedarach*). Naturalized Asian ornamental and shade tree; occasional nest site. Nectar is a choice food of ruby-throated hummingbird. Fruit is occasionally eaten by mockingbird, robin.

chinalaurel (*Antidesma bunius*). Tropical tree. Berry is a choice food of bulbul, spotted-breasted oriole.

chinatree. See chinaberry.

chinkapin, also spelled chinquapin (*Castanea* species). Native tree or shrub. Nut is a choice food of blue jay, turkey, red-headed woodpecker.

chittam-wood. See bumelia, gum.

chocolate-weed. See melochia, cluster.

chokeberry, red (*Aronia arbutifolia*). Native shrub. Fruit is a choice food of cedar waxwing; fair food of eastern bluebird, common grackle, ruffed grouse, ring-necked pheasant, robin, turkey.

chokecherry. See cherry, choke.

Christmasberry. See yaupon.

Christmasfern (also called dagger fern; *Polystichum acrostichoides*). Native fern. Tender stem is a choice food of ruffed grouse.

chufa (also called earth or ground almond, nutgrass, and chufa flatsedge; *Cyperus esculentus*). Annual sedge. Tubers are a choice food of sandhill crane, mottled duck, Canada goose, mallard, pintail, turkey; fair food of common crow, duck (black, ring-necked, wood), gadwall, boat-tailed grackle, lesser scaup, shoveler, teal (blue-winged, green-winged), American widgeon.

clover, alsike (*Trifolium hybridum*). Perennial legume. Leaves are a choice food of ruffed grouse.

clover, bur. See burclover.

clover, crimson (*Trifolium incarnatum*). Annual pasture legume. Leaves are a choice food of bobwhite, Canada goose, turkey.

clover, Ladino. See clover, white.

clover, red (*Trifolium pratense*). Perennial legume. Leaves are a choice food of ruffed grouse. State flower of Vermont.

clover, sweet (*Melilotus* species). Introduced biennial legumes. Green leaves are a choice food of sharp-tailed grouse.

clover, white (also called Ladino clover and white Dutch clover; *Trifolium repens*). Lawn and pasture perennial legume. Leaves are a choice food of bobwhite, coot, sandhill crane, mottled duck, Canada goose, grouse (ruffed, sharp-tailed), greater prairie chicken, turkey, American widgeon.

cockspur, coast (also called duck, Walter's, and wild millet; *Echinochloa walteri*). Native grass. Seed is a choice food of red-winged blackbird, fulvous tree duck, purple gallinule, white-fronted goose, mallard, pintail; fair food of cardinal, duck (mottled, ring-necked), redhead, shoveler, teal (blue-winged, green-winged).

columbine, American (*Aquilegia canadensis*). Garden flower. Nectar is a choice food of ruby-throated hummingbird. "Columbine" is the state flower of Colorado.

Columbusgrass (*Sorghum almum*). A sorghum. Seed is a choice food of cardinal, mourning dove, house sparrow.

coneflower (*Rudbeckia* species). Native flower. Seed is fair food of American goldfinch.

cookie crumbs. See cake.

coontail. See hornwort.

copperleaf (*Acalypha* species). Herbs. Seeds are fair food of mourning dove, water pipit.

coral-bead. See snailseed, Carolina.

coralberry (*Symphoricarpos orbiculatus*). Native shrub. Nectar is a choice food of ruby-throated hummingbird; fruit is fair food of cardinal, purple finch, robin, cedar waxwing.

coralvine, mountainrose (*Antigonon leptopus*). Tendril-climbing vine. Flower nectar is a choice food of ruby-throated hummingbird.

cordgrass (*Spartina* species). Perennial grasses. Seeds are a choice food of sparrow (seaside, sharp-tailed); fair food of black duck, rail (clapper, Virginia), sora. Tender sprouts are a choice food of brant, whooping crane, goose (blue, Canada, snow).

cordia, Geiger-tree (also called Geiger-tree; *Cordia sebestena*). Tropical tree. Seeds or fruits are choice foods of gray kingbird, white-crowned pigeon.

coreopsis (*Coreopsis* species). Garden flowers. Seeds are a choice food of American goldfinch.

corktree, Chinese (*Phellodendron chinense*). Ornamental tree. Fruit is a choice food of mockingbird.

corn (also called maize; *Zea mays*). Cultivated crop. Cracked corn is a choice food of blackbird (Brewer's, red-winged, rusty, yellow-headed), bobwhite,* brant,* bunting (indigo, snow), canvasback,* cardinal,* coot, brown-headed cowbird, crane (sandhill,* whooping*), crow (common,* fish*), dove (ground, mourning,* rock,* white-winged), duck (black,* fulvous tree,* mottled,* ring-necked,* ruddy,* wood*), purple finch, gadwall,* common goldeneye,* American goldfinch, Canada goose,* grackle (boat-tailed,* common*), grosbeak (blue, rose-breasted), grouse (ruffed, sharp-tailed), jay (blue,* scrub), slate-colored junco, horned lark, Lapland longspur, mallard,* meadowlark (eastern, western), hooded merganser,* oldsquaw, gray partridge, ring-necked pheasant, pintail,* greater prairie chicken,* common raven,* redhead,* scaup (greater,* lesser*), shoveler,* sparrow (chipping, European tree, field, fox, Harris', house, lark, Lincoln's, song, tree, white-crowned, white-throated), whistling swan,* teal

---

* Also eat whole grains of corn.

(blue-winged, green-winged), brown thrasher, rufous-sided towhee,* turkey,* American widgeon,* American woodcock, woodpecker (hairy, pileated, red-bellied,* red-cockaded, red-headed); fair food of brown creeper, dickcissel, yellow-shafted flicker, evening grosbeak, white-breasted nuthatch, water pipit, robin, starling, downy woodpecker.

cornbread. A choice food of red-winged blackbird, cardinal, purple finch, American goldfinch, common grackle, blue jay, slate-colored junco, robin, sparrow (field, white-throated), tufted titmouse, warbler (myrtle, orange-crowned, pine, yellow-throated), red-headed woodpecker.

cornflower (*Centaurea cyanus*). Garden flower. Seed is a choice food of American goldfinch; fair food of mourning dove.

cornmeal. A choice food of painted bunting, tree sparrow, warbler (myrtle, pine); fair food of eastern bluebird, yellow-throated warbler.

cosmos (*Cosmos* species). Garden flowers. Seeds are a choice food of American goldfinch.

cotoneaster (*Cotoneaster* species). Ornamental shrubs; fruit is a choice food of eastern bluebird, robin, waxwing (Bohemian, cedar); fair food of purple finch, mockingbird.

cotton (*Gossypium* species). Cultivated lint crop. Seed is not used by birds.

cottonseed cake. Manufactured product from cotton seed; it is a choice food of turkey; fair food of common crow.

cottonthistle, Scotch (also called Scotch thistle; *Onopordum acanthium*). Ornamental biennial. Seed is a choice food of pine siskin.

cottonwood, eastern (also called eastern poplar and southern cottonwood; *Populus deltoides*). Native tree; frequent nest plant of many birds. Buds are fair food of evening grosbeak and ruffed grouse. "Cottonwood" is the state tree of Kansas.

cowberry (*Vaccinium vitis-idaea*). Native red-berried low shrub. Fruit is a choice food of spruce grouse, willow ptarmigan.

cowlily (also called spatterdock; *Nuphar* species). Aquatic plants. Seeds are a choice food of ring-necked duck; fair food of duck (black, mottled), mallard, pintail.

cowpea, common (*Vigna sinensis*). Cultivated legume. Seeds of many varieties are a choice food of bobwhite, turkey; fair food of cardinal, mourning dove, white-throated sparrow.

crabapple, wild (*Malus* species). Small native trees, including southern, sweet, and prairie crabapples. Fruit is a choice or fair food of red crossbill, grosbeak (black-headed, evening, pine), mockingbird, ring-necked pheasant, robin, starling, waxwing (Bohemian, cedar).

crabgrass, hairy (*Digitaria sanguinalis*) and **smooth** (*D. ischaemum*). Weedy grasses of lawns, gardens, fields, and pastures. Seeds are a choice food of indigo bunting, slate-colored junco, Lapland longspur, water pipit, sparrow (chipping, field, house, song, white-throated, and probably Bachman's, clay-colored, Lincoln's, savannah, swamp, tree); fair food of dove (ground, mourning), turkey, and possibly blackbirds, cowbirds, blue grosbeak, and other small seed-eating birds.

crackers. See bread, white.

cranberry (*Vaccinium macrocarpum*). Native shrub; common market cranberry. Fruit is a choice food of robin; fair food of common crow, sharptailed grouse, Harris' sparrow.

cranberry, highbush. See viburnum, American cranberrybush; viburnum, European cranberrybush.

cranberry, small (*Vaccinium oxycoccos*). Fruiting shrub. Fruit is a choice food of Hudsonian godwit, robin.

cranberrybush. See viburnum, American cranberrybush; viburnum, European cranberrybush.

cranesbill. See geranium, Carolina.

crapemyrtle (*Lagerstroemia indica*). Ornamental flowering shrub; occasional nest site. Seed is fair food of house sparrow.

creeper, Japanese (also called Boston ivy; *Parthenocissus tricuspidata*). Climbing vine introduced from Asia; frequent nest site of house sparrow. Fruit is a choice food of catbird.

creeper, Virginia (also called American or five-leaf ivy, and woodbine; *Parthenocissus quinquefolia*). Native climbing vine; frequent nest site of house sparrow. Fruit is a choice food of eastern bluebird, catbird, common crow, yellow-shafted flicker, great crested flycatcher, eastern kingbird, mockingbird, robin, yellow-bellied sapsucker, starling, brown thrasher, Swainson's thrush, red-eyed vireo, warbler (bay-breasted, myrtle), woodpecker (downy, hairy, pileated, red-bellied); fair food of black-capped chickadee, western kingbird, fox sparrow, tree swallow, thrush (hermit, wood), turkey.

crinum, Florida (*Crinum americanum*). A swamp lily. Choice food of whooping crane.

crotalaria (*Crotalaria* species). Native and introduced legume. Seeds are poisonous and not eaten by birds.

crotalaria, cape (*Crotalaria capensis*). Cultivated legume. Nectar is a choice food of orchard oriole.

croton (also called doveweed; *Croton* species). Native herbs, almost grazeproof. Seeds of undetermined species are a choice food of pipit (Sprague's, water); fair food of Brewer's blackbird, greater prairie chicken.

croton, glandular. See croton, tropic.

croton, gulf (*Croton punctatus*). Graze-proof, perennial shrub. Seed is a choice food of bobwhite, cardinal, mourning dove.

croton, linear (*Croton linearis*). Annual herb. Seed is a choice food of bobwhite.

croton, oneseed (*Croton monanthogynus*). Annual herb. Seed is a choice food of bobwhite, cardinal, mourning dove, white-throated sparrow.

croton, Texas (*Croton texensis*). Graze-proof annual herb. Seed is a choice food of bobwhite, cardinal, mourning dove.

croton, tropic (also called glandular croton; *Croton glandulosus*). Annual weed of cultivated fields. Seed is a choice food of bobwhite, cardinal, dove (ground, mourning).

croton, woolly (*Croton capitatus*). Annual weed of pasture and cropland. Seed is a choice food of bobwhite, cardinal, dove (mourning, white-winged), white-throated sparrow, turkey; fair food of red-winged blackbird, brown-headed cowbird, common grackle.

crotonopsis (also called rushfoil; *Crotonopsis* species). Annual herb. Seed is fair (possibly choice) food of bobwhite.

crowberry, black (*Empetrum nigrum*). Low ornamental evergreen shrub. Fruit is a choice food of goose (Canada, snow), spruce grouse, Iceland gull, oldsquaw, American golden plover; fair food of sandhill crane, pine grosbeak, ruffed grouse, water pipit, Harris' sparrow.

crow-foot. See goosegrass.

crown-of-thorns. See Jerusalemthorn.

currant (*Ribes* species). Wild and cultivated shrubs. Fresh fruits are a choice food of eastern bluebird, robin, brown thrasher, Bohemian waxwing; fair food of grouse (ruffed, spruce), hermit thrush. Dried fruits are a choice food of eastern bluebird, catbird, mockingbird, robin.

cutgrass, giant (also called white-marsh and southern wildrice; *Zizaniopsis miliacea*). Tall marsh grass. Tender shoots are a choice food of blue goose.

cutgrass, rice (*Leersia oryzoides*). Pond-edge grass. Seed is a choice food of brown-headed cowbird, black duck, common goldeneye, mallard, shoveler, blue-winged teal; perhaps only fair food of gadwall, pintail, lesser scaup, sora, sparrow (swamp, tree), American widgeon.

cypress. See baldcypress.

dahlia (*Dahlia* species). Tuberous-rooted garden flowers. Nectar is a choice food of ruby-throated hummingbird.

dahoon (also called cassena, Alabama dahoon, and dahoon holly; *Ilex cassine*). Native tree of the holly family. Fruit is a choice food of eastern bluebird; fair food of fish crow, yellow-shafted flicker, pileated woodpecker.

dandelion (*Taraxacum* species). Flowering weed of lawns and pastures. Seed is a choice food of indigo bunting, American goldfinch, grouse (ruffed, sharp-tailed), pine siskin, sparrow (chipping, field, house, song, white-crowned, white-throated); fair food of white-breasted nuthatch, gray partridge, ring-necked pheasant.

date (also called date palm; *Phoenix dactylifera*). Introduced tree. Fruit is a fair food of eastern bluebird, mockingbird, robin, cedar waxwing.

dayflower (*Commelina* species). Native flowering herbs. Seeds are fair food of mourning dove.

deer-plum (also called gopher-apple; *Geobalanus oblongifolius*). Low native southern shrub. Fruit is a fair food of bobwhite.

deutzia (*Deutzia* species). Ornamental shrubs; occasional nest sites.

devils-walkingstick (also called Hercules-club and prickly-ash; *Aralia spinosa*). Spiny shrub or small tree; occasional nest site of smooth-billed ani, cardinal.

devil-wood. See osmanthus.

dewberry (*Rubus* species). Trailing blackberrylike plant; not a nest site. Fruit probably eaten by the same birds that feed on blackberries.

dewdrop, golden (*Duranta repens*). Tropical shrub. Fruit is a choice food of bulbul.

dock, sour. See sorrel, sheep.

dogwood, alternateleaf (also called blue and pagoda dogwood; *Cornus alternifolia*). Native shrub. Fruit is a choice food of eastern bluebird, catbird, yellow-shafted flicker, robin, wood thrush, veery, woodpecker (pileated, red-headed); fair food of common crow, eastern kingbird, white-throated sparrow.

dogwood, American. See dogwood, flowering and redosier.

dogwood, blue. See dogwood, alternateleaf.

dogwood, flowering (also called American and Florida dogwood; *Cornus florida*). Native tree; occasional nest site. Fruit is a choice food of eastern bluebird, bobwhite, cardinal, yellow-shafted flicker, grosbeak (evening, pine), mockingbird, robin, yellow-bellied sapsucker, starling, summer tanager, brown thrasher, thrush (gray-cheeked, hermit, Swainson's, wood), turkey, myrtle warbler, cedar waxwing, woodpecker (hairy, pileated, red-bellied, red-headed); fair food of common crow, common grackle, rose-breasted grosbeak, sparrow (house, white-throated), pine warbler. State tree of Missouri; state flower of North Carolina; "American dogwood" is the state flower and unofficial tree of Virginia.

dogwood, gray (*Cornus racemosa*). Native shrub; sometimes a nest site. Fruit is a choice food of eastern bluebird, robin, Swainson's thrush; fair food of eastern kingbird, greater prairie chicken, turkey.

dogwood, pagoda. See dogwood, alternateleaf.

dogwood, redosier (also called kinnikinnik and American dogwood; *Cornus stolonifera*). Native shrub; often a nest site. Fruit is a choice food of ruffed grouse, Swainson's thrush; fair food of common crow, sharp-tailed grouse, white-throated sparrow.

dogwood, roughleaf (*Cornus drummondii*). Native shrub. Fruit is a choice food of eastern bluebird, cardinal, yellow-shafted flicker, eastern kingbird, mockingbird, robin, starling, gray-cheeked thrush, veery, woodpecker (hairy, red-bellied, red-headed); fair food of flycatcher (great crested, Traill's), rose-breasted grosbeak, greater prairie chicken, hermit thrush, cedar waxwing.

dogwood, silky (*Cornus amomum*). Native shrub. Fruit is a choice food of catbird, robin, brown thrasher, thrush (Swainson's, wood); fair food of eastern kingbird, turkey.

dogwood, stiffcornel (*Cornus stricta*). Native shrub. Fruit is fair food of robin, turkey.

dogwood, tatarian (*Cornus alba*). Ornamental shrub. Fruit is a choice food of catbird, yellow-shafted flicker, robin, song sparrow, brown thrasher, red-eyed vireo.

dollar-weed. See rhynchosia.

doughnuts. A choice food of chickadee (black-capped, Carolina), blue jay, slate-colored junco, nuthatch (red-breasted, white-breasted), sparrow (chipping, white-throated), and other birds that eat cake or cookies.

doveweed. See croton.

dropseed (*Sporobolus* species). Native grasses. Seeds are a choice food of slate-colored junco, longspur (chestnut-collared, Smith's), sparrow (Bachman's, field); fair food of snow bunting, goose (blue, snow), Lapland longspur, sparrow (savannah, tree, white-crowned), turkey.

duck-millet. See barnyardgrass; cockspur, coast; junglerice.

duckpotato. See arrowhead.

duckweed (*Lemna* species). Tiny floating aquatic weeds. Plants are a fair food of bufflehead, coot, duck (black, mottled, ring-necked, ruddy), gadwall, purple gallinule, Franklin's gull, mallard, pintail, redhead, lesser scaup, shoveler, sora, teal (blue-winged, green-winged), American widgeon.

eelgrass (*Zostera marina*). Aquatic plant. Leaves and stems are a choice food of brant, black duck, dunlin, Canada goose, oldsquaw, American widgeon; fair food of coot, ruddy duck, king eider, mallard, pintail, scaup (greater, lesser).

elaeagnus, autumn (also called autumn olive; *Elaeagnus umbellata*). Introduced small tree. Fruit is a choice food of eastern bluebird, cardinal, catbird, mockingbird, robin, tree swallow, hermit thrush, cedar waxwing; fair food of bobwhite, black-capped chickadee, purple finch, ruffed grouse, slate-colored junco, ring-necked pheasant, starling.

elaeagnus, cherry (also called summer elaeagnus; *Elaeagnus multiflora*). Introduced shrub. Fruit is a choice food of eastern bluebird, cardinal, catbird, yellow-breasted chat, common grackle, ruby-throated hummingbird, blue jay, mockingbird, robin, starling, summer tanager, brown thrasher, red-bellied woodpecker.

elaeagnus, evergreen. See elaeagnus, thorny.

elaeagnus, summer. See elaeagnus, cherry.

elaeagnus, thorny (also called evergreen elaeagnus, *Elaeagnus pungens*). Ornamental evergreen shrub; frequent nest site of mockingbird, thrasher, towhee. Fruit is a choice food of eastern bluebird, mockingbird, robin, cedar waxwing.

elder (also called elderberry; *Sambucus* species). Native and introduced shrubs. Fruits of undetermined species are a choice food of indigo bunting, grosbeak (black-headed, evening), scrub jay, orchard oriole, song sparrow, vireo (red-eyed, white-eyed), hooded warbler, pileated woodpecker; fair food of rusty blackbird, yellow-billed cuckoo, gray jay, western kingbird, Baltimore oriole.

elder, American (also called common or black-berry elder, and elderberry; *Sambucus canadensis*). Native flowering shrub. Black berries are a choice food of eastern bluebird, cardinal, catbird, yellow-breasted chat, rose-breasted grosbeak, blue jay, mockingbird, robin, yellow-bellied sapsucker, white-throated sparrow, starling, brown thrasher, thrush (gray-cheeked, Swainson's, wood), rufous-sided towhee, veery, cedar waxwing, woodpecker (red-bellied, red-headed); fair food of yellow-shafted flicker, flycatcher (great crested, Traill's), common grackle, eastern kingbird, hermit thrush, turkey.

elder, black-berry or **common.** See elder, American.

elder, European red (*Sambucus racemosa*). Introduced shrub. Attractive red berries are a choice food of eastern bluebird, catbird, rose-breasted grosbeak, robin, starling, brown thrasher, wood thrush, cedar waxwing.

elder, scarlet (also called scarlet elderberry; *Sambucus pubens*). Native shrub. Red berries are a choice food of rose-breasted grosbeak, ruffed grouse, robin, Swainson's thrush, veery, woodpecker (red-bellied, red-headed); fair food of yellow-shafted flicker, ring-necked pheasant, hermit thrush.

elderberry. See elders.

elm (*Ulmus* species). Native and introduced trees; undetermined species, probably American elms, provide nesting sites for many eastern birds. Seeds or buds are eaten by black-capped chickadee, wood duck, rose-breasted grosbeak, ruffed grouse, greater prairie chicken, common redpoll, siskin, sparrow (Harris', house), turkey.

elm, American (also called soft or white elm; *Ulmus americana*). Native tree; frequent nest site. Seed is a choice food of purple finch, American goldfinch, evening grosbeak, ruffed grouse; fair food of cardinal. State tree of Massachusetts, Nebraska, and North Dakota.

elm, Chinese (*Ulmus parvifolia*) and **Siberian** (*U. pumila*). Introduced shade trees; frequent nest sites. Seeds are a choice food of American goldfinch; buds are fair food of Bohemian waxwing.

elm, soft or **white.** See elm, American.

euonymus (*Euonymus* species). Native and introduced ornamental shrubs or vines. Fruits are fair food of eastern bluebird, mockingbird, fox sparrow, myrtle warbler.

euphorbia (also called spurge; *Euphorbia* species). Field weeds. Seeds of many species are a choice food of mourning dove, pipit (Sprague's, water); fair food of greater prairie chicken.

eveningprimrose (*Oenothera* species). Flowering herbs. Nectar is a choice food of ruby-throated hummingbird.

false-cypress. See white-cedar, Atlantic.

falsegarlic, yellow (*Nothoscordum bivalve*). Naturalized wild herb. Choice food of whooping crane.

fanwort, Carolina (*Cabomba caroliniana*). Submersed waterweed. Plant is a fair food of mottled duck.

farkleberry, See sparkleberry.

fat-hen. See saltbush, fat-hen.

fern, dagger. See Christmasfern.

fescue (*Festuca* species). Pasture grass. Seeds are seldom eaten; leaves are fair food of goose (blue, Canada, snow).

fig, common (*Ficus carica*). Small fruit tree. Fruit or its juice is a choice food of catbird, fish crow, boat-tailed grackle, black-headed grosbeak, ruby-throated hummingbird, jay (blue, scrub), mockingbird, oriole (Baltimore, orchard), robin, house sparrow, brown thrasher, Bohemian waxwing, woodpecker (red-bellied, red-headed); fair food of red-winged blackbird, eastern bluebird, cardinal, common crow, common grackle, white-crowned sparrow, Swainson's thrush, rufous-sided towhee, myrtle warbler.

filbert, American (also called American hazel or hazelnut; *Corylus americana*). Native shrub. Nut is a choice food of ruffed grouse, blue jay, hairy woodpecker.

filbert, beaked (also called beaked hazel or hazelnut; *Corylus cornuta*). Native shrub. Nut is a choice food of grouse (ruffed, sharp-tailed), blue jay; fair food of greater prairie chicken.

filbert, European (*Corylus avellana*) and **giant** (*C. maxima*) and their varieties. Commercial nut meat is a choice food of cardinal, Carolina chickadee, blue jay, slate-colored junco, mockingbird, brown-headed nuthatch, tufted titmouse, warbler (myrtle, pine), red-bellied woodpecker, Carolina wren.

fir, balsam (also called balsam, Canada balsam, and eastern fir; *Abies balsamea*). Native forest tree; frequent nest site of many birds. Seed is a choice food of boreal chickadee, crossbill (red, white-winged), purple finch, grosbeak (evening, pine), spruce grouse; fair food of black-capped chickadee, white-breasted nuthatch.

fir, eastern. See fir, balsam.

firethorn. See pyracantha.

flamevine (*Pyrostegia ignea*). Flowering tropical vine; occasional nest site of cardinal.

flatsedge, chufa. See chufa.

flatsedge, poorland (*Cyperus compressus*). Grass-like herb. Seed is fair food of dove (ground, mourning), house sparrow.

flatsedge, redroot (*Cyperus erythrorhizos*). Grass-like herb. Seeds are a choice food of duck (black, wood), mallard, shoveler, teal (blue-winged, green-winged); fair food of ring-necked duck, gadwall, pintail, lesser scaup.

flax, common (*Linum usitatissimum*). Agricultural crop. Seed is fair food of cardinal, mourning dove.

fleabane, daisy (*Erigeron strigosus* and possibly other fleabanes). Native weed. Seed is a choice food of American goldfinch.

floweringquince, Japanese (*Chaenomeles japonica*). Flowering ornamental shrub; nesting site of mockingbird, brown thrasher.

foamflower, Allegheny (*Tiarella cordifolia*). Perennial herb. Fair food of ruffed grouse.

forestiera, Texas. See swamp-privet.

forsythia (*Forsythia* species). Flowering shrubs; occasional nest sites of yellow-billed cuckoo, blue jay, field sparrow, brown thrasher.

four-o'clock, common (*Mirabilis jalapa*). Garden flower. Nectar is a choice food of ruby-throated hummingbird; seed is fair food of bobwhite, cardinal.

fuchsia (*Fuchsia* species). Ornamental flowering shrub. Nectar is a choice food of ruby-throated hummingbird.

gallberry (also called inkberry; *Ilex glabra*). Native evergreen shrub. Fruit is a choice food of robin, turkey, cedar waxwing; fair food of eastern bluebird, bobwhite, mockingbird, hermit thrush.

gallberry, large (also called sweet gallberry; *Ilex coriacea*). Native evergreen shrub. Fruit is a choice food of eastern kingbird, mockingbird.

gallberry, sweet. See gallberry, large.

gardenia (also called cape-jasmine; *Gardenia jasminoides*). Ornamental evergreen flowering shrub. Little used by birds.

Geiger-tree. See cordia, Geiger-tree.

geranium, Carolina (also called cranesbill; *Geranium carolinianum*). Annual weed. Early summer-ripening seed is a choice food of mourning dove.

gladiolus (*Gladiolus* species). Garden flower. Nectar is a choice food of ruby-throated hummingbird.

glasswort (also called samphire and saltwort; *Salicornia* species). Herb of saline soil. Stems are fair food of gadwall, goose (Canada, snow), pintail.

goldeneye (*Viguiera* species). Native annual flowering herbs. Seed is fair food of turkey.

goldenrod (*Solidago* species). Native wildflower. Seed is fair food of American goldfinch, ruffed grouse, greater prairie chicken. State flower of Kentucky and Nebraska.

goldstargrass (also called stargrass; *Hypoxis* species). Native grass. Seed is a choice food of Bachman's sparrow; fair food of bobwhite.

goldthread, common (*Coptis groenlandica*). Perennial herb of wet soils. Fair food of ruffed grouse.

gooseberry (*Ribes* species). Thorny wild or garden shrubs; frequent nest sites. Fruit is a choice food of catbird, black-headed grosbeak, robin, turkey; fair food of brown thrasher, rufous-sided towhee, cedar waxwing.

goosefoot (also called pigweed; *Chenopodium* species). Annual weeds of gardens and fields. Seed is a choice food of snow bunting, American goldfinch, slate-colored junco, horned lark, common redpoll, sparrow (clay-colored, Lincoln's, white-crowned); fair food of dove (ground, mourning), longspur (chestnut-collared, McCown's), sparrow (field, Harris', house, savannah, song, tree, vesper), turkey.

goosegrass (also called crowfoot and yardgrass; *Eleusine indica*). Weedy grass in fields and dooryards. Seed is a fair food of red-winged blackbird, cardinal, mourning dove, savannah sparrow, turkey.

gopher-apple. See deer-plum.

gourd, lagenaria (*Lagenaria vulgaris*). A cultivated vine, many varieties of which produce hard-shelled fruiting forms that are used for ornaments, utensils, and birdhouses. Dry, mature lagenaria gourds (also referred to as siphon, African pipe, dipper, Anaconda, bottle, calabash, Hercules club, powder horn, and sugar trough gourds), are commonly hung for nesting of purple martins. Other birds that will use them are the eastern bluebird, great crested flycatcher, white-breasted nuthatch, house sparrow, starling, tree swallow, tufted titmouse, downy woodpecker, and wrens. The size of the entrance hole and its height above the base of the gourd ought to be as close as possible to the dimensions given in the birdhouse table (section 3) for each of the above species. The gourds should have a diameter of 5–7 inches. They need no ventilation holes at the top, but must have small holes in the lowest part of the base, to drain off rainwater that may blow in through the entrance hole. Since purple martins prefer to live in sunny spots, gourds meant for their use should be hung 15 feet high, in direct sunlight; a finish of white paint will serve to keep them cool and protect them from the elements. These martin homes must be hung far enough apart to prevent their knocking together on windy days. Gourds for the other species may be nailed up in almost any location where they will be shaded for most of the day; they may be finished with spar varnish, lacquer, or shellac. Before any finish is applied, however, soak the outside of the gourd and scrape the skin from it with a dull knife; otherwise the skin will peel after weathering and become unsightly.

grape (*Vitis* species). Native wild and cultivated vines, species undetermined. Fruits are a choice food of eastern bluebird, scrub jay, mockingbird, ovenbird, American redstart, sparrow (fox, golden-crowned, house, white-throated), scarlet tanager, gray-cheeked thrush, red-eyed vireo, Cape May warbler, waxwing (Bohemian, cedar), red-cockaded woodpecker; fair food of rusty blackbird, yellow-breasted chat, crow (common, fish), yellow-billed cuckoo, purple finch, great crested flycatcher, boat-tailed grackle, oriole (Baltimore, orchard), ring-necked pheasant, roadrunner, starling, vireo (Philadelphia, warbling), ivory-billed woodpecker.

grape, cultivated (*Vitis* species). Vines are occasional nest sites. Fruits are a choice food of cardinal, catbird, jay (blue, gray), mockingbird, robin, brown thrasher, cedar waxwing; fair food of starling. Juice is fair food of Tennessee warbler. See also raisins.

grape, fox (also called plum grape; *Vitis labrusca*). Fruit is a choice food of eastern kingbird, robin, red-bellied woodpecker.

grape, frost (also called riverside and winter grape; *Vitis vulpina*). Fruit is a choice food of cardinal, catbird, ruffed grouse, eastern kingbird, robin, thrush (hermit, wood), cedar waxwing, woodpecker (pileated, red-bellied, red-headed); fair food of yellow-shafted flicker, yellow-bellied sapsucker, Swainson's thrush.

grape, muscadine (also called scuppernong; *Vitis rotundifolia*). Large native grape. Fruit is a choice food of cardinal, common grackle, blue jay, summer tanager, rufous-sided towhee, turkey, red-bellied woodpecker.

grape, pigeon. See grape, summer.

grape, plum. See grape, fox.

grape, riverside. See grape, frost.

grape, scuppernong. See grape, muscadine.

grape, summer (also called pigeon grape; *Vitis aestivalis*). Fruit is a choice food of cardinal, catbird, ruffed grouse, robin, brown thrasher, turkey, red-bellied woodpecker.

grape, winter. See grape, frost.

grapefruit (*Citrus paradisi*). Citrus fruit. Seldom a bird plant.

greenbrier (also called horsebrier, sawbrier, and smilax; *Smilax* species). Native vines. Fruit is a choice food of ruffed grouse; fair food of cardinal, catbird, fish crow, yellow-shafted flicker, common grackle, mockingbird.

groundcherry (*Physalis* species). Annual or perennial weed-like herbs. Fruit is fair food of sharp-tailed grouse.

groundnut. See potatobean, American.

groundselbush. See baccharis.

guava (*Psidium guajava*). Escaped shrub. Fruit is a choice food of mottled duck; fair food of mockingbird.

hackberry, common (*Celtis occidentalis*) and **sugar** (*C. laevigata*). Native trees; frequent nest sites. Fruits are a choice food of eastern bluebird, cardinal, yellow-shafted flicker, mockingbird, robin, yellow-bellied sapsucker, starling, Swainson's thrush, turkey, waxwing (Bohemian, cedar);

fair food of bobwhite, catbird, crow (common, fish), rock dove, common grackle, evening grosbeak, Townsend's solitaire, fox sparrow, hermit thrush, woodpecker (ivory-billed, pileated).

hackmatack. See tamarack.

Hardinggrass (*Phalaris tuberosa stenoptera*). Select strain of canarygrass. Seed is a choice food of bobwhite, cardinal, mourning dove, slate-colored junco, sparrow (field, house, song, white-throated).

haw. See hawthorn.

hawthorn (also called haw, redhaw, and thorn; *Crataegus* species). Thorny shrubs; frequent nest sites. Some fruits are a choice food of ruffed grouse, waxwing (Bohemian, cedar); fair food of cardinal, yellow-shafted flicker, grosbeak (evening, pine), sharp-tailed grouse, blue jay, mockingbird, ring-necked pheasant, yellow-bellied sapsucker, fox sparrow, turkey. State flower of Missouri.

hazel or **hazelnut.** See filbert, American and beaked.

heal-all. See selfheal, common.

he-balsam. See spruce, red.

hegari. See sorghum, grain.

hemlock, eastern (also called hemlock and Canada hemlock; *Tsuga canadensis*). Native forest tree; frequent nest site. Seed is a choice food of boreal chickadee, crossbill (red, white-winged), American goldfinch, pine siskin; fair food of black-capped chickadee. State tree of Pennsylvania.

hemp (*Cannabis sativa*). Large annual weedy herb, the "marijuana" plant. Sterlized seeds are sold and are a choice food of bobwhite, indigo bunting, cardinal, black-capped chickadee, dove (mourning, white-winged), purple finch, American goldfinch, grosbeak (evening, pine, rose-breasted), slate-colored junco, white-breasted nuthatch, common redpoll, pine siskin, sparrow (Harris', house, song, tree, white-crowned, white-throated); fair food of Carolina chickadee, common grackle, ring-necked pheasant, rufous-sided towhee.

hemp-tree. See chastetree, lilac.

hepatica, roundlobe (*Hepatica americana*). Low-growing herb; fair food of ruffed grouse.

Hercules-club. See devils-walkingstick.

hibiscus (also called rosemallow; *Hibiscus* species). Ornamental flowering shrub. Nectar is a choice food of ruby-throated hummingbird. State flower of Hawaii.

hickory (*Carya* species). Native tree. Nut meats of most species are a choice food of cardinal, Carolina chickadee, nuthatch (brown-headed, white-breasted), field sparrow, tufted titmouse, rufous-sided towhee, warbler (myrtle, pine), red-bellied woodpecker; fair food of grosbeak (pine, rose-breasted), turkey.

hickory, swamp. See hickory, water.

hickory, water (also called bitter pecan and swamp hickory; *Carya aquatica*). Native tree. Bitter, small nut may be fair food of wood duck, mallard.

hogpeanut, southern (*Amphicarpa bracteata*). Woodland legume, vine. Tuber is a choice food of ruffed grouse; fair food of bobwhite, turkey.

holly, American (*Ilex opaca*). Native evergreen tree. Red fruit is a choice food of eastern bluebird, mockingbird, cedar waxwing; fair food of cardinal, yellow-shafted flicker, robin, yellow-bellied sapsucker, hermit thrush, turkey, Bohemian waxwing, red-bellied woodpecker. State tree of Delaware.

holly, Chinese (*Ilex cornuta*). Introduced evergreen shrub or tree; an excellent ornamental; occasional nest site of mockingbird, brown thrasher, towhee. Red fruit is a choice food of cedar waxwing; fair food of eastern bluebird, mockingbird, robin.

holly, dahoon. See dahoon.

holly, deciduous. See possumhaw.

holly, English (*Ilex aquifolium*). Ornamental landscape shrub; occasional nest site of mockingbird, brown thrasher, towhee. Red fruit seldom eaten.

holly, evergreen. See yaupon.

holly, Japanese (*Ilex crenata*). Low ornamental shrub. Black fruit is a choice food of mockingbird, robin; fair food of eastern bluebird.

holly, mountain. See mountainholly.

hollyhock (*Althaea rosea*). Showy garden flower. Seed is fair food of Bohemian waxwing.

honey. Both honey and honey syrup are choice foods of catbird, black-capped chickadee, purple finch, rose-breasted grosbeak, ruby-throated hummingbird, oriole (Baltimore, orchard), wood thrush, Cape May warbler, downy woodpecker. Honey syrup usually is made by adding one part of honey to three parts of water. It may be fed in jars or in the attractive commercial feeders especially made for hummingbirds.

honeylocust (*Gleditsia triacanthos*). Native tree; thorny or thornless variety of this tree is often a nest site. Seeds not eaten by birds.

honeysuckle, Amur (*Lonicera maacki*). Ornamental shrub; frequent nest site. Red berries are a choice food of eastern bluebird, purple finch, mockingbird, robin, yellow-bellied sapsucker, hermit thrush, cedar waxwing.

honeysuckle, Belle (*Lonicera bella*). Ornamental shrub. Berries are a choice food of catbird, robin, brown thrasher.

honeysuckle, dwarf bush (also called bushhoneysuckle; *Diervilla lonicera*). Shrub; occasional nest site. Nectar is a choice food of ruby-throated hummingbird; fruit is a choice food of eastern kingbird.

honeysuckle, Japanese (*Lonicera japonica*) Twining evergreen vine; frequent nest site. Black fruit is a choice food of eastern bluebird, cedar waxwing; fair food of catbird, hermit thrush. Nectar is an attractive choice food of ruby-throated hummingbird.

honeysuckle, limber (*Lonicera dioica*). Shrubby vine. Nectar is a choice food of ruby-throated hummingbird.

honeysuckle, Manchurian (*Lonicera ruprechtiana*). Shrub. Fruit is a choice food of robin, brown thrasher.

honeysuckle, Morrow (*Lonicera morrowi*). Shrub. Fruit is a choice food of robin.

honeysuckle, tatarian (*Lonicera tatarica*). Ornamental shrub; frequent nest site. Fruit is a choice food of catbird, robin; fair food of American goldfinch.

honeysuckle, winter (*Lonicera fragrantissima*). Ornamental shrub; frequent nest site. Fruit is a choice food of catbird, mockingbird.

honeysuckle, woodbine (*Lonicera periclymenum*). Climbing vine. Fruit is a choice food of evening grosbeak; fair food of yellow-shafted flicker.

hophornbeam, eastern (also called ironwood and American hophornbeam; *Ostrya virginiana*). Native tree. Seed is a choice food of ruffed grouse; fair food of purple finch, mockingbird, turkey.

hornbeam, American (also called blue beech; *Carpinus caroliniana*). Native tree; frequent nest site. Seed is a choice food of cardinal, American goldfinch, evening grosbeak.

horned-pondweed. See poolmat, common.

hornwort (also called coontail; *Ceratophyllum demersum*). Submersed waterweed. Stems probably are only fair food of buffledhead, canvasback, coot, duck (black, mottled, ring-necked, wood), gadwall, mallard, pintail, redhead, scaup (greater, lesser), shoveler, teal (blue-winged, green-winged), American widgeon.

horsebrier. See greenbrier.

horsechestnut, common (*Aesculus hippocastanum*). Introduced ornamental shade tree. Nectar is a choice food of ruby-throated hummingbird.

horsetail (*Equisetum* species). Wetland herb. Roots and stems are a choice food of goose (blue, snow), whistling swan.

huckleberry (*Gaylussacia* species). Shrubs; frequent nest sites. Fruits of undetermined species are choice foods of ruffed grouse, blue jay, red-headed woodpecker; fair foods of fish crow, yellow-shafted flicker, scrub jay, orchard oriole.

huckleberry, black (*Gaylussacia baccata*). Shrub. Fruit is a choice food of catbird, robin; fair food of eastern bluebird, pine grosbeak, hermit thrush, rufous-sided towhee.

huckleberry, dwarf (*Gaylussacia dumosa*). Shrub. Fruit is fair food of turkey.

huckleberry, tree or winter. See sparkleberry.

hydrangea (*Hydrangea* species). Ornamental shrubs. Little used by birds.

inkberry. See gallberry.

ironwood. See hophornbeam, eastern.

ivy, American. See creeper, Virginia.

ivy, Boston. See creeper, Japanese.

ivy, English (*Hedera helix*). Ornamental evergreen vine. Fruit is fair food of robin.

ivy, five-leaf. See creeper, Virginia.

ivy, heartleaf. See ampelopsis, heartleaf.

Japanclover. See lespedeza, common.

Jerusalemcherry (*Solanum pseudocapsicum*). Ornamental fruiting shrub. Fruit is fair food of mockingbird, robin.

Jerusalemthorn (also called crown-of-thorns and retama; *Parkinsonia aculeata*). Small thorny ornamental, introduced tree; occasional nest site of scissor-tailed and vermilion flycatchers.

jessamine, yellow. See Carolinajessamine.

jewel-weed. See snapweed, spotted.

joepyeweed, spotted (also called smokeweed; *Eupatorium maculatum*). Native weed. Seed is a choice food of American goldfinch.

Johnsongrass (*Sorghum halepense*). A grassy sorghum. Seed is a choice food of indigo bunting, cardinal, blue grosbeak, house sparrow; fair food of bobwhite, mourning dove, Harris' sparrow.

jointgrass. See knotgrass.

Judas-tree. See redbud, eastern.

juneberry. See serviceberry, Allegheny.

junglerice (also called duck millet and wild millet; *Echinochloa colonum*). Native weedy grass in fields. Seed is a choice food of blackbird (Brewer's, red-winged), bobolink, painted bunting, brown-headed cowbird, duck (fulvous tree, mottled), mallard, pintail, teal (blue-winged, green-winged).

juniper (*Juniperus* species). Includes two native junipers, Ashe and common, and several introduced ornamental evergreen trees and shrubs that have little food value, are only occasional nesting sites, but have fair value as shelter for birds.

juniper, red. See redcedar, eastern.

kaffir. See sorghum, grain.

kinnikinnik. See dogwood, redosier.

knotgrass (also called jointgrass; *Paspalum distichum*). Native grass of wet soils. Seed is a choice food of mourning dove, fulvous tree duck, purple gallinule, mallard, pintail, lark sparrow; fair food of bobolink, Lincoln's sparrow.

kudzu (also called kudzu-vine; *Pueraria lobata*). Vigorous leguminous vine. Little used by birds.

lady-of-the-night (*Brunfelsia americana*). Tropical shrub or tree. Berry is fair food of bulbul.

lady's-thumb. See smartweed, spotted.

larch, American, black, or eastern. See tamarack.

larch, European (*Larix decidus*). Introduced ornamental tree. Seed is a choice food of American goldfinch, common redpoll.

larch, Japanese (*Larix leptolepsis*). Introduced ornamental tree. Seed is a choice food of American goldfinch, common redpoll.

laurel. See mountainlaurel.

laurel, china. See chinalaurel.

laurelcherry (also called cherry-laurel; *Prunus caroliniana*). Broadleaf evergreen, ornamental trees; occasional nest sites. Fruits are a choice food of eastern bluebird, mockingbird, robin, cedar waxwing; fair food of ring-billed gull.

lemon (*Citrus limon*). Citrus fruit tree; frequent nest plant of ani (groove-billed, smooth-billed).

lespedeza, bicolor (*Lespedeza bicolor*). Perennial legume, shrub. Seed is a choice food of bobwhite; little competition from other birds.

lespedeza, common (also called Japanclover; *Lespedeza striata*). Annual legume. Seed is a choice food of bobwhite, rock dove.

lespedeza, japonica (*Lespedeza japonica*). Perennial legume, shrub. Seed is a choice food of bobwhite.

lespedeza, Kobe (*Lespedeza striata*, var. *Kobe*). An improved strain of common lespedeza. Seed is a choice food of bobwhite; fair food of mourning dove, slate-colored junco, white-throated sparrow.

lespedeza, Korean (*Lespedeza stipulacea*). Annual legume. Seed is a choice food of bobwhite; fair food of mourning dove. Leaves are fair food of greater prairie chicken.

lespedeza, sericea (*Lespedeza cuneata*). Perennial herbaceous legume. Seed is fair food of slate-colored junco.

lespedeza, Thunberg (*Lespedeza thunbergii*). Perennial legume, shrub. Seed is a choice food of bobwhite.

lettuce, blue (*Lactuca spicata*). Annual or biennial herb. Seed is a choice food of American goldfinch.

lettuce, garden (*Lactuca sativa*). Garden salad green. Tender leaves are a choice food of pintail, house sparrow, American widgeon; fair food of starling.

lettuce, prickly (*Lactuca serriola*). Annual or biennial weedy herb. Seed is fair food of gray partridge, ring-necked pheasant.

lilac (also called common lilac; *Syringa vulgaris*). Ornamental shrub; occasional nest site. State flower of New Hampshire.

lily, Easter (also called Japanese Easter lily, long-tubed white lily, and trumpet lily; *Lilium longiflorum*). Garden flower. Buds and flowers are a choice food of bulbul.

lily, swamp. See lily, turkscap.

lily, tiger (*Lilium tigrinum*). Garden flower. Nectar is a choice food of ruby-throated hummingbird.

lily, torch. See torchlily.

lily, trumpet. See lily, Easter.

lily, turkscap (also called American Turk's-cap lily, lily-royal, and swamp lily; *Lilium superbum*). Garden flower. Nectar is a choice food of ruby-throated hummingbird.

lily, water. See waterlily.

lily-royal. See lily, turkscap.

linden, or American linden. See basswood, American.

liriope, creeping (*Liriope spicata*). Border plant in garden. Fruit is a choice food of eastern bluebird; fair food of cedar waxwing.

lizardtail, common (*Saururus cernuus*). Marsh plant. Unimportant to birds.

locust, black (also called yellow locust; *Robinia pseudoacacia*). Native eastern tree; often a nest site. Nectar is a choice food of ruby-throated hummingbird; seed is fair food of bobwhite, Carolina chickadee, ring-necked pheasant, tufted titmouse, turkey.

locust, yellow. See locust, black.

longtom (*Paspalum lividum*). Native grass. Seed is fair food of pintail, green-winged teal.

loquat (*Eriobotrya japonica*), Broadleaf evergreen ornamental tree. Fruit is a choice food of bulbul, mockingbird.

lovegrass (*Eragrostis* species). Annual or perennial grasses. Seeds of undetermined species are fair food of goose (blue, snow), Ipswich sparrow.

lovegrass, teal (*Eragrostis hypnoides*). Wet-ground annual grass. Seed is a choice food of pintail, teal (blue-winged, green-winged); fair food of ring-necked duck, gadwall.

lovevine (also called woe-vine; *Cassytha filiformis*). Parasitic vine. Seed is fair food of bobwhite.

lupine, bicolor (*Lupinus bicolor*). Winter annual legume. Seed is a choice food of bobwhite.

magnolia, flowering. See magnolia, southern.

magnolia, laurel. See sweetbay.

magnolia, southern (also called flowering magnolia; *Magnolia grandiflora*). Native tree. Fruit is a choice food of catbird, fish crow, yellow-shafted flicker, eastern kingbird, mockingbird, robin, brown thrasher, wood thrush, turkey, vireo (red-eyed, white-eyed), woodpecker (ivory-billed, pileated, red-bellied, red-headed); fair food of cardinal, starling, red-cockaded woodpecker. State flower of Louisiana and Mississippi; state tree of Mississippi.

magnolia, swamp, swampbay, and **sweetbay.** See sweetbay.

mahaleb. See cherry, mahaleb.

maize. See corn; sorghum, grain.

mango (also called common mango; *Mangifera indica*). Tropical tree. Fruit is a choice food of bulbul.

mangrove (also called American and red mangrove; *Rhizophora mangle*). Coastal swamp shrub; frequent nest site of anhinga, egrets, herons, ibis, brown pelican.

mangrove, black. See blackmangrove.

mangrove, red. See mangrove.

mannagrass, fowl (*Glyceria striata*). Meadow grass. Seed is fair food of wood duck.

maple (*Acer* species). Shade and lumber trees; undetermined species are frequent nest sites. Seeds, buds, or flowers are fair food of purple finch, grouse (ruffed, sharp-tailed), pine siskin, turkey. "Red maple" is the state tree of Rhode Island.

maple, sugar (*Acer saccharum*). Native tree; frequent nest site. Seed is fair food of grosbeak (evening, pine). State tree of New York, Vermont, West Virginia, and Wisconsin.

marestail (*Hippuris vulgaris*). Perennial aquatic herb. Fair food of mallard, greater scaup.

marigold, bur. See beggarticks.

marijuana. See hemp.

marshcress, bog (*Rorippa palustris*). Aquatic herb. Choice food of blue goose; fair food of Canada goose.

matrimonyvine (*Lycium halimifolium*). Ornamental shrub. Fruit is a choice food of robin.

mayflower. See trailing-arbutus.

melochia, cluster (also called chocolate-weed and teaweed; (*Melochia corchorifolia*). Southern field weed. Seed is low-fair food of mourning dove.

milkpea (*Galactia* species). Native vining legume. Seed is a choice food of bobwhite.

milkweed, butterfly (*Asclepias tuberosa*). Native flowering perennial herb. Nectar is a choice food of ruby-throated hummingbird.

millet, browntop (*Panicum ramosum*). Annual cultivated grass. Seed is a choice food of red-winged blackbird, bobwhite, indigo bunting, cardinal, brown-headed cowbird, dove (mourning, rock, white-winged), duck (black, mottled, ring-necked, wood), purple finch, slate-colored junco, mallard, eastern meadowlark, pintail, sparrow (chipping, field, fox, Harris', house, song, tree, white-throated), blue-winged teal, rufous-sided towhee, turkey; fair food of Canada goose.

millet, cattail. See millet, pearl.

millet, duck. See barnyardgrass; coast cockspur; junglerice; millet, Japanese.

millet, foxtail (also called German and Italian millet; *Setaria italica*). Annual hay and bird-seed plant. Seed is a choice food of bobwhite, cardinal, mourning dove, wood duck, purple finch, gadwall, American goldfinch, Canada goose, slate-colored junco, Lapland longspur, mallard, redhead, redpoll, shoveler, pine siskin, sparrow (chipping, field, house, song, tree, vesper, white-throated), teal (blue-winged, green-winged), turkey, American widgeon; fair food of greater prairie chicken.

millet, German. See millet, foxtail.

millet, hog. See millet, proso.

millet, Italian. See millet, foxtail.

millet, Japanese (also called duck millet; *Echinochloa crusgalli frumentacea*). Annual, cultivated strain of barnyardgrass. Seed is a choice food of bobolink, bobwhite, indigo bunting, cardinal, brown-headed cowbird, mourning dove, duck (black, ring-necked), gadwall, blue grosbeak, slate-colored junco, mallard, pintail, sparrow (field, house, song, white-throated), green-winged teal, American widgeon; fair food of wood duck.

millet, pearl (also called cattail millet; *Pennisetum glaucum*). Annual grass, grown for hay and grazing. Seed is a choice food of red-winged blackbird, bobwhite, cardinal, mourning dove, American goldfinch, blue grosbeak, slate-colored junco, sparrow (chipping, field, fox, house, song, white-throated), rufous-sided towhee; fair food of common grackle.

millet, proso (also called hog millet; *Panicum miliaceum*). Cultivated grass. Seed, often in bird-seed mixtures, is a choice food of bobwhite, painted bunting, cardinal, coot, brown-headed cowbird, dickcissel, dove (mourning, white-winged), wood duck, purple finch, gadwall, Canada goose, slate-colored junco, mallard, redhead, shoveler, sparrow (chipping, field, fox, house, song, tree, white-throated), green-winged teal, rufous-sided towhee, turkey, American widgeon; fair food of common grackle, blue jay, ring-necked pheasant.

millet, Texas (also called Texas panicum; *Panicum texanum*). Annual reseeding grass. Seed is a choice food of bobwhite, indigo bunting, cardinal, brown-headed cowbird, mourning dove, slate-colored junco, mallard, sparrow (chipping, field, house, song, tree, white-throated), blue-winged teal, rufous-sided towhee.

millet, Walter's. See cockspur, coast.

millet, wild. See barnyardgrass; junglerice; cockspur, coast.

milo. See sorghum, grain.

mimosa, flowering. See albizzia, silktree.

mistletoe, Christmas (also called American-mistletoe; *Phoradendron flavescens*). Parasitic evergreen plant that grows on trees. Fruit is a choice food of cedar waxwing; fair food of eastern bluebird, fish crow. Mistletoe is the state flower of Oklahoma.

miterwort, common (*Mitella diphylla*). Low perennial herb. Leaf is a fair food of ruffed grouse.

mockorange (also called syringa; *Philadelphus* species). Flowering ornamental shrubs; occasional nest plants. State flower of Idaho is Lewis mockorange.

moonseed, Carolina. See snailseed, Carolina.

moonseed, common (*Menispermum canadense*). Native woody vine. Bluish-black fruit is fair food of robin, brown thrasher, rufous-sided towhee, turkey, cedar waxwing.

moonseed, red. See snailseed, Carolina.

morningglory (*Ipomoea* species). Annual flowering vines of garden and waste places. Nectar is a choice food of ruby-throated hummingbird; seeds are not eaten.

moss, Florida, long, or Spanish. See Spanishmoss.

mountainash, American (*Sorbus americana*). Ornamental woody plant. Fruit is a choice food of eastern bluebird, catbird, common grackle, grosbeak (evening, pine), grouse (ruffed, sharp-tailed), Baltimore oriole, robin, brown thrasher, waxwing (Bohemian, cedar), red-headed woodpecker; fair food of western kingbird, white-throated sparrow, wood thrush, veery.

mountainash, European (also called rowan-tree; *Sorbus aucuparia*). Introduced ornamental tree. Fruit is a choice food of catbird, common grackle, pine grosbeak, Baltimore oriole, robin, brown thrasher, waxwing (Bohemian, cedar), red-headed woodpecker.

mountainholly (*Nemopanthus mucronata*). Native shrub. Dull red fruit is a choice food of ruffed grouse.

mountainlaurel (also called laurel; *Kalmia latifolia*). Evergreen shrub. Buds and leaves are a choice food of ruffed grouse. State flower of Connecticut and Pennsylvania.

mulberry, black, red, white, Russian (*Morus* species). Native and introduced trees; occasional nest sites. Fruit of all species appears to be equally sought by birds: a choice food of red-winged blackbird, eastern bluebird, bobwhite, bulbul, indigo bunting, cardinal, catbird, crow (common, fish), purple finch, great crested flycatcher, American goldfinch, grosbeak (black-headed, rose-breasted), blue jay, eastern kingbird, mockingbird, oriole (Baltimore, orchard), robin, song sparrow, starling, tanager (scarlet, summer), brown thrasher, wood thrush, turkey, veery, vireo (red-eyed, white-eyed), bay-breasted warbler, cedar waxwing, woodpecker (downy, hairy, red-bellied, red-headed); fair food of cuckoo (black-billed, yellow-billed), yellow-shafted flicker, common grackle, white-throated sparrow, Swainson's thrush, rufous-sided towhee.

mungbean or mungo. See bean, mung.

mushrooms. Fungi. Flesh is a choice food of grouse (ruffed, spruce); fair food of turkey.

muskgrass. See stonewort.

naiad, northern (also called bushy pondweed; *Najas flexilis*). Submersed waterweed. Stems, leaves, and seeds are a choice food of bufflehead, coot, duck (ring-necked, ruddy), gadwall, scaup (greater, lesser), teal (blue-winged, green-winged), American widgeon; fair food of canvasback, black duck, mallard, pintail, redhead.

naiad, southern (*Najas guadalupensis*). Submersed waterweed. Stems, leaves, and seeds are a choice food of coot, duck (black, mottled, ruddy), gadwall, Canada goose, American widgeon; fair food of canvasback, mallard, redhead, scaup (greater, lesser).

naiad, spiny (*Najas mariana*). Submersed weed of brackish water. Stems and leaves are fair food of ruddy duck, redhead, blue-winged teal.

nandina (*Nandina domestica*). Ornamental shrub. Fruit is fair food of mockingbird, robin, yellow-bellied sapsucker, cedar waxwing.

nannyberry. See viburnum.

nasturtium (*Tropaeolum majus*). Garden flower. Nectar is a choice food of ruby-throated hummingbird.

natalplum. See carissa.

needlegrass (*Stipa* species). Native grass. Seed is a choice food of lark bunting, longspur (chestnut-collared, McCown's, Smith's).

nettlespurge, bellyache (also called bellyache-bush; *Jatropha gossypifolia*). Woody shrub, naturalized in Florida. Choice food of cardinal, mourning dove, rufous-sided towhee.

nightshade, bitter (also called bittersweet; *Solanum dulcamara*). Shrubby climber. Fruit is fair food of common crow, robin.

nightshade, black (*Solanum nigrum*). Weedy annual herb. Fruit is a choice food of cardinal.

ninebark (*Physocarpus* species). Shrubs; occasional nest site of Traill's flycatcher, American goldfinch, yellow warbler.

nutgrass. See chufa.

nutrush (also called razorsedge; *Scleria* species). Annual sedge. Seeds of undetermined species are fair food of ground dove, yellow rail, Bachman's sparrow.

nutrush, fringed (*Scleria ciliata*). Annual sedge. Seed is a choice food of bobwhite.

nutrush, sloughgrass (*Scleria Muhlenbergii*). Annual sedge. Seed is a choice food of bobwhite, mourning dove.

oak (*Quercus* species). Shade and timber trees; frequent nest sites. One or more kinds of acorns are a choice food of rusty blackbird, common crow, duck (black, fulvous tree, ring-necked), gray jay, lesser scaup, woodpecker (downy, hairy, pileated); fair food of black-capped chickadee, yellow-shafted flicker, evening grosbeak, pintail, starling, red-cockaded woodpecker. State tree of Iowa.

oak, Arkansas (also called Arkansas water oak; *Quercus arkansana*). Native tree. Acorn is a choice food of bobwhite, brown thrasher.

oak, basket. See oak, swamp chestnut.

oak, bear (also called scrub oak; *Quercus ilicifolia*). Native tree; often a nest site. Acorn is a choice food of ruffed grouse, turkey.

oak, black (also called smooth-bark and yellowbark oak; *Quercus veluntina*). Native tree; often a nest site. Acorn is a choice food of common grackle, scrub jay, turkey.

oak, blackjack (*Quercus marilandica*). Native tree; often a nest site. Acorn is a choice food of whooping crane, wood duck, common grackle, blue jay, turkey.

oak, bluejack (*Quercus incana*). Native tree. Acorn is a choice food of bobwhite, rufous-sided towhee.

oak, bur (also called mossycup or mossy-overcup oak; *Quercus marcrocarpa*). Native tree; occasional nest site. Acorn is a choice food of wood duck, common grackle. State tree of Illinois.

oak, chestnut (*Quercus prinus*). Native tree. Acorn is a choice food of ruffed grouse, turkey.

oak, chinkapin (*Quercus Muhlenbergii*). Native tree. Acorn is a choice food of blue jay, woodpecker (red-bellied, red-headed).

oak, cow. See oak, swamp chestnut.

oak, fork-leaf. See oak, white.

oak, laurel (also called laurel-leaved oak; *Quercus laurifolia*). Native shade tree; often a nest site. Acorn is a choice food of common grackle, blue jay, turkey, woodpecker, (red-bellied, red-headed).

oak, live (also called Virginia live oak; *Quercus virginiana*). Native shade tree; often a nest site. Acorn is a choice food of bobwhite, whooping crane, blue jay, tufted titmouse, turkey, woodpecker, (red-bellied, red-headed). State tree of Georgia.

oak, mossycup or mossy-overcup. See oak, bur.

oak, northern pin (*Quercus ellipsoidalis*). Native ornamental and timber tree. Acorn is a choice food of common grackle, ruffed grouse.

oak, northern red (also called eastern red and mountain red oak; *Quercus rubra*). Native timber and shade tree. Acorn is a choice food of bobwhite, common grackle, ruffed grouse, turkey. "Red oak" is the state tree of New Jersey.

oak, Nuttall (*Quercus nuttallii*). Native timber tree. Acorn is a choice food of mallard.

oak, overcup (*Quercus lyrata*). Lowland native tree; occasional nest site of orioles. Acorn is a choice food of turkey.

oak, pin (*Quercus palustris*). Native shade and timber tree; often a nest site. Acorn is a choice food of bobwhite, whooping crane, duck (black, wood), common grackle, blue jay, mallard, white-breasted nuthatch, turkey, woodpecker (red-bellied, red-headed); fair food of shoveler, green-winged teal.

oak, possum. See oak, water.

oak, post (*Quercus stellata*). Native tree; often a nest site. Acorn is a choice food of bobwhite, common grackle, blue jay, tufted titmouse, turkey, red-headed woodpecker.

oak, red. See oak, northern red.

oak, ridge. See oak, white.

oak, runner (*Quercus pumila*). Native shrub. Acorn is a choice food of bobwhite, common grackle, turkey.

oak, sawtooth (*Quercus acutissima*). Introduced shade and timber tree. Acorn is a choice food of bobwhite.

oak, scarlet (*Quercus coccinea*). Native shade and timber tree; occasional nest site. Acorn is a choice food of common grackle, sharp-tailed grouse, blue jay, greater prairie chicken, turkey; fair food of evening grosbeak. Official tree of District of Columbia.

oak, scrub. See oak, bear.

oak, shingle (*Quercus imbricaria*). Native timber tree. Acorn is a choice food of common grackle, blue jay, red-headed woodpecker.

oak, Shumard (*Quercus shumardii*). Native timber tree. Acorn is a choice food of bobwhite, turkey, red-bellied woodpecker.

oak, smooth-bark. See oak, black.

oak, southern red (*Quercus falcata*). Native timber tree; often a nest site. Acorn is a choice food of bobwhite, wood duck, common grackle, jay (blue, scrub), turkey.

oak, stave. See oak, white.

oak, swamp chestnut (also called basket oak and cow oak; *Quercus michauxii*). Native swamp tree; occasional nest site of hawks. Acorn is a choice food of turkey.

oak, swamp white (*Quercus bicolor*). Native swamp tree; occasional nest site of hawks and herons.

oak, turkey (*Quercus laevis*). Native tree. Acorn is a choice food of tufted titmouse, turkey, red-bellied woodpecker; broken bits are a choice food of rufous-sided towhee.

oak, Virginia live. See oak, live.

oak, water (also called possum oak; *Quercus nigra*). Native shade and timber tree; often a nest site. Acorn is a choice food of bobwhite, wood duck, common grackle, blue jay, mallard, brown thrasher, tufted titmouse, turkey, red-bellied woodpecker.

oak, white (also called fork-leaf, ridge, and stave oak; *Quercus alba*). Native shade and timber tree; often a nest tree. Acorn is a choice food of bobwhite, duck (black, wood), ruffed grouse, blue jay, mallard, brown thrasher, turkey, red-bellied woodpecker. State tree of Connecticut and Maryland.

oak, willow (*Quercus phellos*). Native shade and timber tree; occasional nest site. Acorn is a choice food of bobwhite, common grackle, blue jay, tufted titmouse, turkey.

oak, yellowbark. See oak, black.

oat, common (*Avena sativa*). Cropland grain and hay plant. Seed is a choice food of blackbird (Brewer's, red-winged, rusty, yellow-headed), bobolink, bobwhite, bunting (indigo, lark, snow), cardinal, coot, brown-headed cowbird, crane (sandhill, whooping), common crow, dickcissel, dove (rock, white-winged), duck (black, wood), purple finch, gadwall, American goldfinch, goose (Canada, white-fronted), common grackle, grosbeak (blue, rose-breasted), jay (gray, scrub), slate-colored junco, horned lark, mallard, western meadowlark, oldsquaw, gray partridge, ring-necked pheasant, greater prairie chicken, raven, redhead, shoveler, sparrow (chipping, European tree, field, fox, grasshopper, Harris', house, lark, song, tree, vesper, white-crowned, white-throated), green-winged teal, rufous-sided towhee, turkey, American widgeon; fair food of fish crow, mourning dove, yellow-shafted flicker, boat-tailed grackle, grouse (ruffed, sharp-tailed), Franklin's gull, blue jay, eastern meadowlark, pintail, water pipit, starling.

oat, wild (*Avena fatua*). Annual grass. Seeds are a choice food of Brewer's blackbird, Canada goose, scrub jay, horned lark, Lapland longspur, mallard, savannah sparrow; fair food of white-fronted goose, ring-necked pheasant.

oatgrass, tall (*Arrhenatherum elatius*). Perennial grass. Leaf blades are a choice food of turkey.

oatmeal. Sometimes fed at feeders. A choice food of gray jay, slate-colored junco, house sparrow.

oilnut. See butternut.

olea, Florida. See osmanthus.

oleander (*Nerium oleander*). Ornamental. No important bird use.

olive, autumn. See elaeagnus, autumn.

orange, mock. See mockorange.

orange, osage. See osageorange.

orange, sweet (*Citrus sinensis*). Common commercial citrus fruit; occasional nest site. Juice is a choice food of bulbul, oriole (Baltimore, spotted-breasted), red-bellied woodpecker; seeds are fair food of dove (mourning, white-winged). Orange blossom is the state flower of Florida.

orchardgrass (*Dactylis glomerata*). Perennial grass. Green leaves are fair food of Canada goose.

osageorange (also called bodark, bois-d'arc, and bowwood; *Maclura pomifera*). Native thorny tree; often a nest plant. Seed is a choice food of purple finch, American goldfinch, evening grosbeak; fair food of bobwhite.

osmanthus (also called devil-wood and Florida olea; *Osmanthus* species). Ornamental shrubs or small trees, fragrant flowers; nest site of scrub jay. Not a food.

paintedcup (*Castilleja* species). Flowering herbs. Nectar is a choice food of ruby-throated hummingbird.

palm, date. See date.

palm, sabal. See palmetto, cabbage.

palmetto, cabbage (also called sabal palm and cabbage-palm; *Sabal palmetto*). Native tree; often a nest site. Seed is a choice food of ring-billed gull, scrub jay, turkey; fair food of red-winged blackbird, bobwhite, fish crow, grackle (boat-tailed, common), herring gull, blue jay, mockingbird, robin, house sparrow. "Cabbage palm" is the state tree of Florida and South Carolina.

panicgrass. See panicum.

panicum (also called panicgrass; *Panicum* species). Native grasses. Seeds of one or more undetermined species are a choice food of bobolink, bobwhite, bufflehead, painted bunting, cardinal, brown-headed cowbird, dove (ground, mourning, white-winged), duck (black, mottled), gadwall, white-fronted goose, blue grosbeak, slate-colored junco, horned lark, longspur (chestnut-collared, Lapland, Smith's), pintail, shoveler, sparrow (Bachman's, chipping, clay-colored, field, grasshopper, lark, Lincoln's, savannah, song, swamp, tree, vesper, white-crowned, white-throated), teal (blue-winged, green-winged), rufous-sided towhee, turkey; fair food of blackbird (Brewer's, rusty), bunting (snow), dickcissel, wood duck, purple gallinule, goose (blue, Canada, snow), mallard, eastern meadowlark, Sprague's pipit, sora, sparrow (Harris', Henslow's, Ipswich, sharp-tailed). See the specific panicums listed below; also browntop, proso and Texas millet; switchgrass, and witchgrass.

panicum, Bartow (*Panicum bartowense*). Native grass. Seed is a choice food of mottled duck.

panicum, beaked (*Panicum anceps*). Native grass. Seed is a choice food of turkey; fair food of bobwhite, mourning dove.

panicum, bosc (*Panicum bosci*). Native grass. Seed is a choice food of turkey.

panicum, browntop (*Panicum fasciculatum*). Native grass. Seed is a choice food of bobwhite, brown-headed cowbird.

panicum, bulb (*Panicum bulbosum*). Native grass. Seed is fair food of mallard.

panicum, Dominican (*Panicum adspersum*). Native grass. Seed is a choice food of mourning dove, slate-colored junco, sparrow (field, white-throated); fair food of bobwhite.

panicum, fall (*Panicum dichotomiflorum*). Native grass. Seed is a choice food of bufflehead, mourning dove, duck (black, mottled), gadwall, pintail, shoveler, teal (blue-winged, green-winged); fair food of bobwhite, Canada goose, mallard.

panicum, flexile (*Panicum flexile*). Native grass. Seed is a choice food of turkey; fair food of bobwhite.

panicum, fusiform (*Panicum fusiforme*). Native grass. Seed is a choice food of bobwhite, vesper sparrow.

panicum, hiddenseed (*Panicum clandestinum*). Native grass. Seed is a choice food of cardinal, mourning dove, slate-colored junco, sparrow (field, white-throated); fair food of bobwhite.

panicum, longleaf (*Panicum longifolium*). Native grass. Seed is fair food of bobwhite.

panicum, needleleaf (*Panicum aciculare*). Native grass. Seed is fair food of bobwhite.

panicum, redtop (*Panicum agrostoides*). Native grass. Seed is a choice food of mottled duck, turkey; fair food of wood duck.

panicum, roundseed (*Panicum sphaerocarpon*). Native grass. Seed is a choice food of turkey; fair food of bobwhite.

panicum, shoredune (*Panicum amarulum*). Native grass. Seed is a choice food of mourning dove, slate-colored junco, field sparrow.

panicum, Tennessee (*Panicum tennesseense*). Native grass. Seed is fair food of bobwhite.

panicum, Texas. See millet, Texas.

panicum, torpedo (*Panicum repens*). Native grass. Tender shoots are a choice food of blue goose.

panicum, velvet (*Panicum scoparium*). Native grass. Seed is a choice food of mourning dove; fair food of bobwhite.

panicum, warty (*Panicum verrucosum*). Native grass. Seed is a choice food of black duck; fair food of bobwhite.

panicum, woolly (*Panicum lanuginosum*). Native grass. Seed is fair food of bobwhite, mallard.

Panicum neuranthum. Native grass. Seed is fair food of bobwhite.

Panicum oligosanthes. Native grass. Seed is fair food of bobwhite.

papaya (*Carica papaya*). Herbaceous tropical tree. Melonlike fruit is a choice food of spotted-breasted oriole.

papermulberry, common (*Broussonetia papyrifera*). Introduced tree. Fruit is a choice food of cardinal, catbird, mockingbird, robin, starling, brown thrasher; fair food of blue jay, house sparrow.

parrotfeather (also called watermilfoil; *Myriophyllum* species). Troublesome waterweeds. Seeds are fair food of canvasback, coot, mallard, pintail, greater scaup.

partridgeberry (also called twin-berry; *Mitchella repens*). Native shrub of moist woods. Red fruit is a choice food of ruffed grouse; fair food of eastern bluebird, mockingbird.

partridgepea, sensitive (*Chamaecrista procumbens*). Native annual legume. Seed is a choice food of bobwhite.

partridgepea, showy (*Chamaecrista fasciculata*). Native annual legume. Seed is a choice food of bobwhite.

paspalum, barestem (*Paspalum longepedunculatum*). Native grass. Seed is a choice food of bobwhite.

paspalum, brownseed (*Paspalum plicatulum*). Native grass. Seed is a choice food of mallard, pintail, green-winged teal; fair food of blue-winged teal.

paspalum, bull (*Paspalum boscianum*). Annual grass of cultivated fields. Seed is a choice food of red-winged blackbird, bobwhite, brown-headed cowbird, mourning dove, fulvous tree duck, pintail, sora, sparrow (house, white-throated), turkey; fair food of Canada goose, slate-colored junco, mallard.

paspalum, Florida (*Paspalum floridanum*). Native perennial grass. Seed is a choice food of red-winged blackbird, brown-headed cowbird; fair food of bobwhite.

paspalum, fringeleaf (*Paspalum ciliatifolium*). Native grass. Seed is a choice food of mottled duck.

paspalum, giant (*Paspalum giganteum*). Native perennial grass. Seed is a choice food of mourning dove.

paspalum, mudbank (*Paspalum dissectum*). Native grass. Seed is a choice food of mottled duck; fair food of blue goose.

paspalum, seashore (*Paspalum vaginatum*). Native grass; frequent nest site of seaside sparrow.

pasqueflower (also called American pasque; *Anemone patens*). Perennial herb. Choice food of sharp-tailed grouse. "American pasque" is the state flower of South Dakota.

paulownia, royal (also called princess-tree; *Paulownia tomentosa*). Ornamental tree. Not important to birds.

pawpaw (*Asimina* species). Native shrubs. Fruit is fair food of fish crow, turkey.

pea, garden (*Pisum sativum*). Green peas are a choice food of cardinal, common crow, common grackle, grosbeak (black-headed, rose-breasted), mallard, ring-necked pheasant, greater scaup; fair food of starling.

peach (*Prunus persica*). Common orchard fruit; occasional nest site. Juice and pulp are a choice food of bulbul, catbird, purple finch, blue jay, mockingbird, robin, brown thrasher; fair food of house sparrow, starling, rufous-sided towhee. Peach blossom is the state flower of Delaware.

peanut (*Arachis hypogaea*). Cultivated legume. Underground nut is a choice food of red-winged blackbird, indigo bunting, cardinal, catbird, chickadee (black-capped, Carolina), crow (common, fish), rock dove, purple finch, American goldfinch, Canada goose, evening grosbeak, jay (blue, scrub), slate-colored junco, ruby-crowned kinglet, eastern meadowlark, nuthatch (brown-headed, red-breasted, white-breasted), ovenbird, pintail, sparrow (chipping, field, fox, house, song, white-crowned, white-throated), brown thrasher, tufted titmouse, rufous-sided towhee, turkey, warbler (myrtle, orange-crowned, pine), woodpecker (red-bellied, red-headed), Carolina wren; fair food of eastern bluebird, bobwhite, mockingbird, robin, downy woodpecker.

peanutbutter. A choice food of cardinal, chickadee (black-capped, Carolina), brown creeper, dickcissel, common grackle, jay (blue, scrub), mockingbird, nuthatch (red-breasted, white-breasted), ovenbird, yellow-bellied sapsucker, sparrow (chipping, field, song, tree), summer tanager, brown thrasher, wood thrush, tufted titmouse, warbler (myrtle, orange-crowned, pine), woodpecker (hairy, red-bellied, red-headed), wren (Bewick's, Carolina); fair food of eastern bluebird, purple finch, slate-colored junco, nuthatch (brown-headed, red-breasted, white-breasted), robin, house sparrow, rufous-sided towhee.

pear (also called common pear; *Pyrus communis*). Orchard fruit tree; often a nest site. Juice and pulp are a choice food of catbird; fair food of purple finch, ruffed grouse, jay (blue, scrub), Baltimore oriole, robin, house sparrow, starling, cedar waxwing.

pecan (includes papershell, Stewart's, and other varieties; *Carya illinoensis*). Native tree, also cultivated to produce pecan nuts commercially. Nut meat is a choice food of bobwhite, cardinal, catbird, Carolina chickadee, common crow,* wood duck,* American goldfinch, grackle (boat-tailed,* common*), blue jay,* nuthatch (brown-headed, white-breasted), sparrow (chipping, field, song, white-throated), starling,* tufted titmouse, rufous-sided towhee, turkey,* warbler (myrtle, pine), woodpecker (downy, ivory-billed, pileated, red-bellied,* red-headed), Carolina wren; fair food of eastern bluebird, mockingbird, house sparrow. State tree of Texas.

---

* Also take whole pecans.

pecan, bitter. See hickory, water.

penstemon (*Penstemon* species). Flowering herbs. Nectar is a choice food of ruby-throated hummingbird.

peppertree, Brazil (*Schinus terebinthifolia*). Introduced subtropical tree. Fruit is a choice food of mockingbird, cedar waxwing; fair food of robin, rufous-sided towhee.

peppertree, Monk's. See chastetree, lilac.

peppervine (*Ampelopsis arborea*). Native vine. Fruit is a choice food of catbird, mockingbird, wood thrush.

persea, redbay or swampbay. See redbay.

persimmon, common (also called eastern persimmon; *Diospyros virginiana*). Native tree; occasional nest site. Fruit is a choice food of mockingbird; fair food of catbird, robin, turkey, pileated woodpecker.

persimmon, Japanese or Chinese. See persimmon, kaki.

persimmon, kaki (*Diospyros kaki*). Introduced cultivated subtropical tree. Fruit is a choice food of blue jay, mockingbird.

petunia (*Petunia* species). Garden flowers. Nectar is a choice food of ruby-throated hummingbird; seed is a choice food of slate-colored junco.

phlox (*Phlox* species). Garden flowers. Nectar is a choice food of ruby-throated hummingbird.

photinia, Chinese (*Photinia serrulata*). Ornamental shrub. Fruit is a choice food of cedar waxwing; fair food of eastern bluebird, mockingbird, robin.

pickerelweed (*Pontederia cordata*). Marsh plant; occasional nest site of gallinules. Seed unimportant to birds.

pie crust. A choice food of Carolina chickadee, slate-colored junco, tufted titmouse, pine warbler.

pigweed. See amaranth; goosefoot.

pine (*Pinus* species). Evergeen timber and ornamental tree; often nesting site. Seeds of one or more undetermined species are a choice food of boreal chickadee, brown creeper, blue jay, eastern meadowlark, Townsend's solitaire, hermit warbler, red-cockaded woodpecker; fair food of Bachman's sparrow, brown thrasher. State flower of Maine is "pine cone and tassel"; state tree of North Carolina is "pine."

pine, Australian. See beefwood.

pine, Banksiana. See pine, jack.

pine, eastern white (also called northern white pine and soft pine; *Pinus strobus*). Native evergreen tree; often a nest site. Seed is a choice food of cardinal, Carolina chickadee, crossbill (red, white-winged), dove (mourning, rock), common grackle, evening grosbeak, slate-colored junco, brown-headed nuthatch, pine siskin, sparrow (chipping, white-throated), tufted titmouse, rufous-sided towhee. State tree of Maine; "white pine" is the state tree of Michigan.

pine, hard or **heart.** See pine, longleaf.

pine, jack (also called Banksiana pine; *Pinus banksiana*). Native evergreen tree; often a nest site. Seed is a choice food of pine grosbeak, spruce grouse, pine siskin.

pine, loblolly (also called oldfield pine; *Pinus taeda*). Native evergreen tree; often a nest site. Seed is a choice food of red-winged blackbird, bobwhite, cardinal, Carolina chickadee, dove (mourning, rock), purple finch, American goldfinch, evening grosbeak, slate-colored junco, brown-headed nuthatch, white-throated sparrow, tufted titmouse, towhee, turkey; fair food of pine warbler.

pine, longleaf (also called hard and heart pine, and longleaf yellow pine; *Pinus palustris*). Native evergreen tree; often a nest site. Seed is a choice food of red-winged blackbird, bobwhite, cardinal, mourning dove, slate-colored junco, brown-headed nuthatch, tufted titmouse, turkey. State tree of Alabama.

pine, marsh. See pine, pond.

pine, northern white. See pine, eastern white.

pine, Norway. See pine, red.

pine, oldfield. See pine, loblolly.

pine, pitch (*Pinus rigida*). Native evergreen tree; often a nest site. Seed is a choice food of bobwhite, black-capped chickadee, red crossbill, slate-colored junco, red-breasted nuthatch, pine siskin.

pine, pocosin. See pine, pond.

pine, pond (also called marsh and pocosin pine; *Pinus serotina*). Native evergreen tree. Seed is a choice food of mourning dove.

pine, red (also called Norway pine; *Pinus resinosa*); often a nest site. Seed is a choice food of pine siskin. State tree of Minnesota.

pine, sand (*Pinus clausa*). Native evergreen tree; nest site of scrub jay.

pine, Scotch (*Pinus sylvestris*). Introduced ornamental tree; occasional nest site. Seed is a choice food of red crossbill.

pine, scrub. See pine, Virginia.

pine, shortleaf (also called shortleaf, and yellow pine; *Pinus echinata*). Native evergreen tree; frequent nest site. Seed is a choice food of red-winged blackbird, bobwhite, cardinal, Carolina chickadee, red crossbill, mourning dove, purple finch, American goldfinch, evening grosbeak, slate-colored junco, brown-headed nuthatch, pine siskin, white-throated sparrow, turkey. State tree of Arkansas.

pine, slash (also called swamp pine and South Florida slash pine; *Pinus elliotti*). Native evergreen tree; occasional nest site. Seed is a choice food of red-winged blackbird, bobwhite, cardinal, mourning dove, purple finch, American goldfinch, evening grosbeak, slate-colored junco, brown-headed nuthatch, white-throated sparrow, tufted titmouse, turkey.

pine, soft. See pine, eastern white.

pine, spruce (*Pinus glabra*). Seed is a choice food of bobwhite, mourning dove.

pine, swamp. See pine, slash.

pine, Virginia (also called scrub pine; *Pinus virginiana*). Native evergreen tree; often a nest site. Seed is a choice food of bobwhite, cardinal, Carolina chickadee, red crossbill, mourning dove, evening grosbeak, brown-headed nuthatch, song sparrow.

pine, yellow. See pine, longleaf and shortleaf.

pinkweed. See smartweed, Pennsylvania.

pipewort (*Eriocaulon* species). Wetland perennial herbs. A choice food of black duck; fair food of ring-necked duck.

pistachionut (*Pistacia vera*). Commercial nut, chiefly imported from Mediterranean area. Nut meat is a choice food of cardinal, Carolina chickadee, tufted titmouse, myrtle warbler; fair food of brown-headed nuthatch.

pitanga (also called Surinam cherry; *Eugenia uniflora*). Tropical evergreen shrub. Fruit is a choice food of bulbul, spotted-breasted oriole; fair food of mockingbird, cedar waxwing.

planertree. See waterelm.

planetree, American. See sycamore, American.

plum, American (also called wild plum; *Prunus americana*). Native shrub; occasional nest site. Fruit is a choice food of bobwhite, blue jay, robin, red-headed woodpecker; fair food of sharp-tailed grouse, ring-necked pheasant, brown thrasher.

plum, Damson. See plum, garden.

plum, garden (also called Damson plum; *Prunus domestica*). Small tree. Fruit of this and other cultivated plums are choice foods of catbird, black-headed grosbeak, blue jay, mockingbird, robin, brown thrasher, Bohemian waxwing; fair foods of cardinal, yellow-shafted flicker, yellow-bellied sapsucker, summer tanager, rufous-sided towhee. See also prunes.

plum, sapodilla. See sapodilla.

plum, wild. See plum, American.

podgrass, shore (also called arrowgrass; *Triglochin maritima*). Perennial marsh plant. Fruit is a choice food of black duck, mallard, pintail; fair food of blue goose, green-winged teal.

poisonivy (*Toxicodendron radicans*). Native vine. Wax of the fruit is a choice food of catbird, Carolina chickadee, yellow-shafted flicker, yellow-bellied sapsucker, brown thrasher, myrtle warbler, woodpecker (downy, red-bellied); fair food of eastern bluebird, black-capped chickadee, common crow, sharp-tailed grouse, mockingbird, woodpecker (hairy, pileated, red-cockaded, red-headed).

poisonsumac (*Toxicodendron vernix*). Native shrub. Fruit is fair food of common crow, yellow-shafted flicker, evening grosbeak, ring-necked pheasant.

pokeberry, common (also called pokeweed; *Phytolacca americana*). Native perennial plant. Fruit is a choice food of eastern bluebird, cardinal, catbird, common crow, eastern kingbird, mockingbird, robin, starling, summer tanager, brown thrasher, thrush (hermit, wood), veery, warbling vireo, hooded warbler, cedar waxwing; fair food of yellow-shafted flicker, flycatcher (great crested, scissor-tailed), yellow-bellied sapsucker, sparrow (fox, white-throated), Swainson's thrush, woodpecker (hairy, red-bellied, red-cockaded). Seed is a choice food of cardinal, mourning dove; fair food of bobwhite.

pokeberry, stiff (also called pokeweed; *Phytolacca rigida*). Native (Florida) perennial plant. Fruit or seed is a choice food of cardinal, mourning dove, mockingbird.

pokeweed. See pokeberry, common and stiff.

polypogon, rabbitfoot (also called rabbitfoot and beard-grass; *Polypogon monspeliensis*). Annual grass. Seed is a choice food of pintail; fair food of Canada goose, sparrow (Lincoln's, savannah).

pomegranate (also called common pomegranate; *Punica granatum*). Small tree, cultivated for its flowers and fruit. Fruit is a choice food of mockingbird.

pondweed. See potamogeton.

pondweed, bushy. See naiad, northern.

pondweed, horned. See poolmat, common.

poolmat (also called horned-pondweed; *Zannichellia palustris*). Submersed waterweed. Seed, stem, and leaves are a choice food of black duck, gadwall, mallard, oldsquaw, lesser scaup; fair food of pintail, redhead, green-winged teal, American widgeon.

poplar (*Populus* species other than aspens and cottonwoods). Native trees; occasional nest sites. Buds are a choice food of sharp-tailed grouse; fair food of purple finch, evening grosbeak, greater prairie chicken. "Cottonwood" (balsam poplar) is the state tree of Wyoming.

poplar, eastern. See cottonwood, eastern.

poplar, trembling. See aspen, quaking.

popple. See aspen, bigtooth and quaking.

poppy, Carolina. See poppy, white prickly.

poppy, Mexican prickly (*Argemone mexicana*). Annual prickly weed. Seed is a choice food of dove (mourning, white-winged).

poppy, white prickly (also called Carolina poppy; *Argemone alba*). Annual prickly weed. Seed is a choice food of mourning dove.

pork fat

pork fat. A choice food of blue jay, mockingbird, brown-headed nuthatch, pine warbler, woodpecker (downy, red-bellied).

portulaca (also called purslane; *Portulaca oleracea*). Annual herb, garden flower. Seed is a choice food of lark bunting; fair food of dove (ground, mourning), horned lark, Lapland longspur.

possumhaw (also called deciduous holly and winterberry; *Ilex decidua*). Native deciduous shrub or tree. Fruit is a choice food of eastern bluebird, robin, cedar waxwing; fair food of purple finch, yellow-shafted flicker, mockingbird, red-bellied woodpecker.

potamogeton (also called pondweed; *Potamogeton* species). Submersed waterweeds. Undetermined species are eaten by avocet, dowitcher.

potamogeton, baby (*Potamogeton pusillus*). Submersed waterweed. Seed and tender stems are a choice food of duck (black, ring-necked), gadwall, common goldeneye, mallard, redhead, greater scaup.

potamogeton, fennelleaf. See potamogeton, sago.

potamogeton, flatstem (*Potamogeton zosteriformis*). Submersed waterweed. A fair food of mallard.

potamogeton, floatingleaf (*Potamogeton natans*). Submersed waterweed. Seed is a choice food of duck (black, ring-necked, wood), common goldeneye, mallard, lesser scaup.

potamogeton, Illinois (*Potamogeton illinoensis*). Submersed waterweed. A choice food of ring-necked duck.

potamogeton, largeleaf (*Potamogeton amplifolius*). Submersed waterweed. A choice food of duck (black, ring-necked); fair food of mallard.

potamogeton, leafy (*Potamogeton foliosus*). Submersed waterweed. A choice food of canvasback, ring-necked duck, mallard, redhead, American widgeon; fair food of coot.

potamogeton, longleaf (*Potamogeton americanus*). Submersed waterweed. A choice food of canvasback, duck (black, ring-necked), redhead; fair food of coot, mottled duck, mallard, pintail.

potamogeton, ribbonleaf (*Potamogeton epihydrus*). Submersed waterweed. A choice food of duck (black, ring-necked).

potamogeton, sago (*Potamogeton pectinatus*). Submersed waterweed. The sago is the most useful specie of all potamogeton. Seed, leaves, and stem are a choice food of bufflehead, canvasback, coot, duck (ring-necked, ruddy), marbled godwit, goldeneye (Barrow's, common), Canada goose, mallard, redhead, scaup (greater, lesser), shoveler, whistling swan, teal (blue-winged, green-winged); fair food of ring-billed gull, pintail.

potamogeton, stiff leaf (*Potamogeton strictifolius*). Submersed waterweed. A choice food of mallard.

potamogeton, thorowort (*Potamogeton perfoliatus*). Submersed waterweed. A choice food of bufflehead, canvasback, duck (ring-necked, ruddy), common goldeneye, mallard, redhead.

potamogeton, variableleaf (*Potamogeton gramineus*). Submersed water-weed. A choice food of ring-necked duck.

potato (*Solanum tuberosum*). Garden food-plant. Tubers are reported to be a choice food of sandhill crane, harlequin duck; fair food of ring-necked pheasant.

potato, sweet. See sweetpotato.

potatobean, American (also called groundnut; *Apios americana*). Native legume. Seed and tubers are fair food of bobwhite.

potato chips. A choice food of common grackle, starling, red-headed woodpecker.

prickly-ash. See devils-walkingstick.

primrose. See eveningprimrose.

princess-tree. See paulownia, royal.

privet, Amur (*Ligustrum amurense*). Ornamental shrub. Fruit is a choice food of mockingbird, cedar waxwing; fair food of eastern bluebird, robin.

privet, Chinese (*Ligustrum sinense*). Ornamental shrub; often a nest site. Fruit is a choice food of purple finch, mockingbird, starling, cedar waxwing; fair food of eastern bluebird, bobwhite, cardinal, robin.

privet, glossy (*Ligustrum lucidum*). Ornamental shrub. Fruit is a choice food of purple finch, mockingbird, cedar waxwing; fair food of eastern bluebird, cardinal, robin.

privet, Japanese (*Ligustrum japonicum*). Ornamental shrub. Fruit is a choice food of purple finch, mockingbird, cedar waxwing; fair food of eastern bluebird, cardinal, robin, starling.

privet, swamp. See swamp-privet.

proso. See millet, proso.

prunes. The dried fruit of garden plum varieties. Fair food of eastern bluebird, robin.

pumpkin (*Cucurbita pepo*). Garden plant. Seed is a choice food of cardinal, chickadee (black-capped, Carolina), purple finch, blue jay, slate-colored junco, white-beasted nuthatch, tree sparrow.

purslane. See portulaca.

pyracantha (also called firethorn; *Pyracantha* species). Ornamental shrubs; often a nest plant. Fruits of some varieties are a choice food of eastern bluebird, mockingbird, brown thrasher, cedar waxwing, pileated woodpecker; fair food of bobwhite, cardinal, catbird, purple finch, blue jay, robin, sparrow (fox, house, song, white-crowned), thrush (hermit, wood).

quackgrass (*Agropyron repens*). Perennial grass. Seed is a choice food of horned lark.

queen's delight. See stillingia.

quince, common (*Cydonia oblonga*). Shrub or small tree, grown for its fruits; occasional nest site of cardinal and mockingbird.

rabbitfoot. See polypogon, rabbitfoot.

ragimillet (*Eleusine coracana*). Introduced annual grass. Seed is fair food of cardinal, mourning dove, white-throated sparrow.

ragweed (*Ambrosia* species, including ragweeds other than "giant"). Annual weeds. Seeds of undetermined species are a choice food of indigo bunting, common redpoll, sparrow (fox, Harris', Henslow's, lark, Lincoln's, vesper, white-crowned), rufous-sided towhee; fair food of Brewer's blackbird, black-capped chickadee, white-winged crossbill, ground dove, grosbeak (pine, rose-breasted), starling, turkey.

ragweed, common (*Ambrosia artemisifolia*). Annual weed. Seed is a choice food of blackbird (red-winged, rusty), bobwhite, snow bunting, cardinal, red crossbill, mourning dove, duck (mottled, ring-necked), American goldfinch, slate-colored junco, horned lark, Lapland longspur, gray partridge, ring-necked pheasant, greater prairie chicken, sparrow (chipping, grasshopper, house, savannah, song, tree, white-throated), rufous-sided towhee; fair food of yellow-headed blackbird, bobolink, brown-headed cowbird, yellow-shafted flicker, common grackle, Smith's longspur, eastern meadowlark, pipit (Sprague's, water).

ragweed, giant (also called great ragweed; *Ambrosia trifida*). Tall annual weed. Seed is a choice food of red-winged blackbird, cardinal, purple finch, house sparrow; fair food of sparrow (song, swamp, white-throated).

ragweed, lanceleaf (*Ambrosia bidentata*). Annual weed. Seed is a choice food of bobwhite.

ragweed, western (*Ambrosia psilostachya*). Annual weed. Seed is a choice food of bobwhite; fair food of yellow-headed blackbird, greater prairie chicken.

raisins (*Vitis*). Dried cultivated grapes. A choice food of eastern bluebird, catbird, mockingbird, robin, summer tanager, brown thrasher, hermit thrush, waxwing (Bohemian, cedar); fair food of cardinal, harlequin duck, sparrow (field, white-crowned).

rape (*Brassica napus*). Annual herb of the mustard family. The seed, sometimes in bird-feed mixtures, is a choice food of bobwhite, mourning dove, American goldfinch, common redpoll; fair food of purple finch, slate-colored junco.

raspberry (*Rubus* species). Wild or cultivated shrubs. Fruit is a choice food of cardinal, catbird, black-headed grosbeak, ruffed grouse, scrub jay, mockingbird, robin, sparrow (field, fox), rufous-sided towhee, veery, white-eyed vireo, yellow warbler, waxwing (Bohemian, cedar), red-headed woodpecker; fair food of eastern bluebird, bobwhite, common crow, yellow-shafted flicker, flycatcher (Acadian, great crested, Traill's), grouse (sharp-tailed, spruce), slate-colored junco, gray partridge, ring-necked pheasant, white-crowned sparrow, starling, thrush (hermit, Swainson's), red-bellied woodpecker.

raspberry, flowering. See thimbleberry, fragrant.

rattanvine. See supplejack, Alabama.

razorsedge. See nutrush.

redbay (also called swampbay, and redbay or swampbay persea; *Persea borbonia*). Native shrub. Fruit is a choice food of eastern bluebird; fair food of bobwhite, fish crow.

redbud, eastern (also called Judas-tree; *Cercis canadensis*). Native ornamental tree. Unimportant to birds. State tree of Oklahoma.

redcedar, eastern (also called red juniper; *Juniperus virginiana*). Native evergreen tree; often a nest site. Fruit is a choice food of eastern bluebird, purple finch, grosbeak (evening, pine), mockingbird, robin, Townsend's solitaire, myrtle warbler, waxwing (Bohemian, cedar); fair food of cardinal, catbird, white-winged crossbill, crow (common, fish), yellow-shafted flicker, Traill's flycatcher, ruffed grouse, yellow-bellied sapsucker, fox sparrow, starling, tree swallow, brown thrasher, hermit thrush.

redcedar, southern (*Juniperus silicicola*). Native evergreen tree. Few records of bird use.

redgum. See sweetgum.

redhaw. See hawthorn.

red-hot-poker. See torchlily.

redroot, blood (*Lachnanthes tinctoria*). Wetland plant of organic soils. Root is a choice food of wood duck, Canada goose, mallard, pintail, turkey, American widgeon.

reed (also called common reed; *Phragmites communis*). Wetland tall grass; often a nest site. Tender shoots are fair food of goose (blue, snow).

rescuegrass. See brome.

retama. See Jerusalemthorn.

rhododendron (also called rosebay; *Rhododendron* species). Evergreen shrubs; occasional nest site. Not a bird food. State flower of West Virginia is rosebay rhododendron (*R. maximum*); coast rhododendron (*R. macrophyllum*) is the state flower of Washington.

rhynchosia (*Rhynchosia* species, one called dollarweed). Annual native legumes. Seeds are fair food of bobwhite.

rice (*Oryza sativa*). Cultivated grain. Seed is a choice food of blackbird (Brewer's, red-winged, rusty), bobolink, painted bunting, cardinal, coot, sandhill crane, dove (ground, rock), duck (black, fulvous tree, mottled), gadwall, purple gallinule, goose (blue, Canada, snow, white-fronted), grackle (boat-tailed, common), slate-colored junco, mallard, pintail, king rail, greater scaup, sora, sparrow (field, house, white-crowned, white-throated), teal (blue-winged, green-winged), turkey, American widgeon; fair food of bobwhite, brown-headed cowbird, mourning dove, duck (ring-necked, wood), eastern meadowlark, starling, rufous-sided towhee.

rice, jungle. See junglerice.

rice, wild. See wildrice.

rivergrass (also called whitetop; *Fluminea festucacea*). Native grass; frequent nest site of ruddy duck, mallard, blue-winged teal.

rose (*Rosa* species). Native shrubs; undetermined species provide occasional nest sites. Fruit is fair food of sharp tailed grouse, Townsend's solitaire, Swainson's thrush, Philadelphia vireo, Bohemian waxwing. State flower of Georgia is "Cherokee rose"; Iowa's is "wild rose"; New York's is simply "rose"; North Dakota's is "wild prairie rose." District of Columbia's official flower is "American beauty rose."

rose, multiflora (*Rosa multiflora*). Living-fence shrub; often a nest site. Fruit is a choice food of mockingbird, cedar waxwing; fair food of eastern bluebird, cardinal, American goldfinch, evening grosbeak, ruffed grouse, slate-colored junco, ring-necked pheasant, greater prairie chicken, robin, sparrow (fox, song, tree), brown thrasher, turkey.

rosebay. See rhododendron.

rosemallow. See hibiscus.

rowan-tree. See mountainash, European.

ruellia (*Ruellia* species). Native herbs. Seed is a choice food of greater prairie chicken.

rush, brown-fruited (*Juncus pelocarpus*). Marsh plant. Roots are a choice food of ring-necked duck.

rush, needlegrass (*Juncus roemerianus*). Saltwater marsh plant; nest site of red-winged blackbird, clapper rail, seaside sparrow, long-billed marsh wren.

rushfoil. See crotonopsis.

rye (*Secale cereale*). Cultivated grain. Seeds or green leaves are a choice food of bobwhite, indigo bunting, coot, rock dove, wood duck, gadwall, mallard, greater prairie chicken, redhead, shoveler, sparrow (house, white-throated), whistling swan, green-winged teal, turkey, American widgeon; fair food of Brewer's blackbird, cardinal, mourning dove, purple finch, yellow-shafted flicker, common grackle, blue jay, slate-colored junco, ring-necked pheasant.

ryegrass, Italian (*Lolium multiflorum*). Annual winter grass. Blades are a choice food of coot, duck (black, wood), goose (blue, Canada), turkey, American widgeon.

safflower (*Carthamus tinctorius*). Cultivated herb. Seed is a choice food of cardinal, white-winged dove, purple finch, evening grosbeak; fair food of mourning dove, blue jay, ring-necked pheasant, tufted titmouse.

sage, lyreleaf (*Salvia lyrata*). Native winter annual. Seed is fair food of cardinal, mourning dove.

sage, red garden (*Salvia officinalis rubriflora*). Garden flower. Nectar is a choice food of ruby-throated hummingbird.

sage, scarlet (*Salvia splendens*). Garden flower. Nectar is a choice food of ruby-throated hummingbird.

St. Augustinegrass (*Stenotaphrum secundatum*). Lawn grass. Blades are fair food of coot.

St. Johnswort, shrubby (*Hypericum prolificum*). Native shrub. Seed is fair food of slate-colored junco, tree sparrow.

salsify, meadow (also called goatsbeard; *Tragopogon pratensis*). Introduced weed. Seed is a choice food of American goldfinch.

saltbush, fat-hen (*Atriplex patula*). Saltmarsh plant. Seed is fair food of pintail, sparrow (Ipswich, seaside, sharp-tailed).

saltgrass, seashore (*Distichlis spicata*). Saline marsh grass. A choice food of goose (blue, Canada, snow); fair food of coot, pintail.

saltwort. See glasswort.

samphire. See glasswort.

sandgrass, purple (*Triplasis purpurea*). Native annual grass. Seed is a choice food of snow bunting.

sandverbena (*Abronia* species). Native herbs. Seed is fair food of savannah sparrow.

sapgum. See sweetgum.

sapodilla (also called sapote and sapodilla plum; *Achras zapota*). Tropical tree. Fruit is a choice food of bulbul.

sapote. See sapodilla.

sarsaparilla, wild (also called small spinard; *Aralia nudicaulis*). Perennial herb. Fruit is fair food of wood thrush. See also snailseed, Carolina.

sassafras (also called common sassafras; *Sassafras albidum*). Native tree; occasional nest site. Fruit is a choice food of eastern bluebird, bobwhite, catbird, great crested flycatcher, eastern kingbird, robin, red-eyed vireo, pileated woodpecker; fair food of mockingbird, yellow-bellied sapsucker, thrush (gray-cheeked, hermit, Swanson's), turkey.

sawbrier. See greenbrier.

sawgrass, Jamaica (*Cladium jamaicensis*). Native grass; frequent nest site. Seed unimportant to birds, though found frequently in ducks' gizzards.

sawpalmetto (*Serenoa repens*). Low-growing shrub. Seed is a choice food of turkey; fair food of fish crow, red-bellied woodpecker.

saxifrage, lettuce (*Saxifraga micranthidifolia*). Perennial herb; a choice food of ruffed grouse in winter.

scarlet-runner. See bean, scarlet-runner.

scratch-feed. A commercial mixture of cracked corn, with grain sorghum and wheat seeds, usually prepared for poultry. See corn, sorghum, and wheat for birds that like scratch-feed.

seabuckthorn, common (*Hippophae rhamnoides*). Ornamental woody plant. Fruit is fair food of robin.

sealettuce (*Ulva lactuca*). Seaweed-alga. Reported to be a choice food of brant, Canada goose, scaup (greater, lesser).

seaoats (*Uniola paniculata*). Native grass. Seed is a choice food of red-winged blackbird, cardinal, white-throated sparrow; fair food of mourning dove.

sedge (Cyperaceae). The word "sedge" has two meanings: specifically, it designates more than 100 species of the genus *Carex;* and generally, it applies to more than 300 species of the "sedge" family, Cyperaceae. These are grass- or rushlike plants that usually grow in wet meadows and shallow margins of lakes, ponds, and streams. The sedge family includes *Carex* (sedge), *Cladium* (sawgrass), *Cyperus* (flatsedge), *Eleocharis* (spikerush), *Rhynchospora* (beakrush), *Scirpus* (bulrush), *Scleria* (nutrush), and a few other genera not mentioned in this book. The bird-food value of most members in the sedge family appears to be nearly negligible or somewhat obscured in the liturature, except for the specific entries in sections 4 and 5. Food studies that are published from analyses of gizzard contents (especially of waterfowl) contain considerable bias because the sedge seeds digest very slowly. More comprehensive studies of the sedge-family values may be desirable.

sedge (*Carex* species). Wetland sedges. Seed is perhaps a choice food of snow bunting, Lapland longspur, yellow rail, sora, sparrow (Lincoln's, swamp, tree); fair food of coot, duck (black, ring-necked, ruddy), goose (blue, snow), grouse (ruffed, sharp-tailed, spruce), mallard, pintail, greater prairie chicken, redhead, scaup (greater, lesser), shoveler, savannah sparrow, teal (blue-winged, green-winged).

selfheal, common (also called blue-curls and heal-all; *Prunella vulgaris*). Native herb. A choice food of ruffed grouse.

serviceberry (also called juneberry, *Amelanchier* species). Native shrubs or trees. Fruits of undetermined species are a choice food of common crow, grosbeak (black-headed, evening), American redstart, Swainson's thrush; fair food of eastern bluebird, black-capped chickadee, sharp-tailed grouse, jay (blue, gray), robin, Townsend's solitaire, rufous-sided towhee.

serviceberry, Allegheny (also called juneberry and shadbush; *Amelanchier laevis*). Native tree. Fruit is a choice food of catbird, American goldfinch, rose-breasted grosbeak, Baltimore oriole, robin, brown thrasher, cedar waxwing; fair food of scrub jay.

serviceberry, downy (also called shadblow serviceberry; *Amelanchier arborea*). Native tree. Fruit is a choice food of cardinal, rose-breasted grosbeak, ruffed grouse, eastern kingbird, mockingbird, Baltimore oriole, robin, scarlet tanager, brown thrasher, thrush (hermit, wood), veery, red-eyed vireo, cedar waxwing, hairy woodpecker; fair food of yellow-shafted flicker, common grackle.

serviceberry, shadblow. See serviceberry, downy.

sesame (also called benne; *Sesamum indicum*). Cultivated annual plant. Seed is fair food of red-winged blackbird, bobwhite, cardinal, mourning dove, slate-colored junco, sparrow (chipping, field, fox, house, white-throated).

sesbania, hemp (*Sesbania exalti*). Tall annual legume. Seed is fair food of bobwhite.

shadblow. See serviceberry, downy.

shadbush. See serviceberry, Allegheny.

sheepsorrel (also called common field sorrel, sourgrass, and sour-dock; *Rumex acetosella*). Native weedy perennial herb. Seed is fair food of ruffed grouse, sparrow (grasshopper, savannah, tree), turkey.

shoalgrass, marine (also called Cuban shoalweed; *Halodule wrightii*). Small submersed herb. A choice food of Canada goose.

shoalweed, Cuban. See shoalgrass, marine.

shortleaf. See pine, shortleaf.

shrimp-plant (*Beloperone guttata*). Tropical ornamental herb. Seed is a choice food of bulbul, spotted-breasted oriole.

shrubalthea (also called althea; *Hibiscus syriacus*). Ornamental shrub. Unimportant to birds.

signalgrass, broadleaf (*Brachiaria platyphylla*). Native grass. Seed is a choice food of red-winged blackbird, bobwhite, mourning dove, fulvous tree duck, purple gallinule; fair food of blackbird (Brewer's, rusty), bobolink, slate-colored junco, mallard, sora, white-throated sparrow, green-winged teal.

silktree. See albizzia.

smartweed (*Polygonum* species). Marsh and aquatic plants. Seeds are perhaps a choice food of yellow rail, common redpoll, sora, sparrow (fox, Harris', seaside, swamp, vesper, white-crowned); fair food of Brewer's blackbird, bobolink, canvasback, fulvous tree duck, Hudsonian godwit, goose (blue, snow), grosbeak (blue, rose-breasted), slate-colored junco, horned lark, water pipit, greater prairie chicken, sparrow (grasshopper, savannah).

smartweed, bigroot (*Polygonum coccineum*). Perennial marsh and shallow-water plant. Seed is a choice food of duck (black, ring-necked), common goldeneye, mallard, pintail, redhead, teal (blue-winged, green-winged); fair food of gadwall, American widgeon.

smartweed, curltop (*Polygonum lapathifolium*). Annual wetland plant.

Seed is a choice food of common goldeneye, mallard, redhead, green-winged teal; fair food of gadwall, pintail, lesser scaup, shoveler, American widgeon.

smartweed, dotted (*Polygonum punctatum*). Perennial marsh and shallow-water plant. Seed is a choice food of red-winged blackbird, duck (black, mottled, ring-necked), green-winged teal; fair food of mallard, lesser scaup.

smartweed, marshpepper (also called water-pepper; *Polygonum hydropiper*). Perennial marsh and shallow-water plant. Seed is a choice food of duck (black, ring-necked), mallard; fair food of lesser scaup.

smartweed, Pennsylvania (also called pinkweed; *Polygonum pensylvanicum*). Annual wetland plant. Seed is a choice food of black duck, common goldeneye, mallard, pintail, redhead, sparrow (song, white-throated), teal (blue-winged, green-winged); fair food of bufflehead, ruddy duck, gadwall, Canada goose, ring-necked pheasant, lesser scaup, shoveler, house sparrow.

smartweed, Puerto Rico (*Polygonum portoricense*). Perennial aquatic plant. Seed is a choice food of mottled duck; fair food of mallard.

smartweed, spotted (also called lady's-thumb; *Polygonum persicaria*). Annual marsh plant. Seed is a choice food of whistling swan; fair food of mallard, greater scaup.

smartweed, swamp (also called mild water-pepper; *Polygonum hydropiperoides*). Perennial marsh and shallow-water plant. Seed is a choice food of duck (mottled, ring-necked, wood), mallard, pintail, redhead; fair food of gadwall, lesser scaup.

smartweed, water (*Polygonum natans*). Perennial aquatic plant. Seed is a choice food of wood duck, mallard, pintail; fair food of greater scaup, American widgeon.

smilax. See greenbrier.

smoketree (*Cotinus obovatus*). Shrub or tree. Seed is a choice food of purple finch, American goldfinch.

smokeweed. See joepyeweed, spotted.

snailseed, Carolina (also called coral-bead, and Carolina or red moonseed, and miscalled wild sarsaparilla; *Cocculus carolinus*). Slender, climbing perennial vine. Red fruit is a choice food of eastern bluebird, mockingbird, robin.

snapdragon (*Antirrhinum* species). Garden flowers. Nectar is a choice food of ruby-throated hummingbird.

snapweed, spotted (also called jewel-weed; *Impatiens biflora*). Native annual herb. Seed is a choice food of bobwhite, ruffed grouse; nectar is a choice food of ruby-throated hummingbird.

sorghum, grain (also called maize; *Sorghum vulgare*). Cultivated grain, including milo, kaffir, hegari, and many other varieties. Seed is a choice food of blackbird (Brewer's, red-winged, yellow-headed), bobwhite, indigo bunting, cardinal, coot, brown-headed cowbird, crane (sandhill, whooping), common crow, dove (ground, mourning, white-winged), wood duck, gadwall, Canada goose, common grackle, blue grosbeak, blue jay, slate-colored junco, mallard, meadowlark (eastern, western), ring-necked pheasant, pintail, greater prairie chicken, redhead, lesser scaup, shoveler, sparrow (chipping, fox, Harris', house, lark, song, tree, white-crowned, white-throated), green-winged teal, rufous-sided towhee, turkey, American widgeon; fair food of American goldfinch, horned lark.

sorghum, reed (*Sorghum arundinacea*). Sorghum species. Seed is a choice food of cardinal, mourning dove, house sparrow.

sorgo (also called sweet or saccharine sorghum, and cane; *Sorghum vulgare saccharatum*). Variety of sorghum used principally to make syrup. Seed is a choice food of mourning dove; fair food of cardinal, slate-colored junco, sparrow (field, fox, house, song, white-throated), rufous-sided towhee.

sorrel. See sheepsorrel.

sorrel-tree. See sourwood.

sourgrass or **sour-dock.** See sheepsorrel.

sourwood (also called sorrel-tree; *Oxydendrum arboreum*). Native tree. Seed is fair food of American goldfinch.

sowthistle (*Sonchus* species). Weed of old fields. Seeds are fair food of cardinal, American goldfinch.

soybean (*Glycine soja*). Cultivated annual legume. Seed is a choice food of greater prairie chicken, turkey; fair food of bobwhite, dove (mourning, rock), Canada goose, mallard, ring-necked pheasant, pintail.

spadeleaf (*Centella asiatica*). Perennial aquatic herb. May be fair food of mottled duck.

Spanishmoss (also called Florida or long moss; *Tillandsia usneoides*). Southern epiphytic plant that hangs from trees; often nest site of warblers (parula and yellow-throated).

Spanishneedles. See beggarticks.

sparkleberry (also called farkleberry, and tree and winter huckleberry; *Vaccinium arboreum*). Native woodland shrub. Fruit is a choice food of mockingbird; fair food of bobwhite.

spatterdock. See cowlily.

spicebush, common (*Lindera benzoin*). Native shrub. Fruit is a choice food of eastern kingbird, robin, wood thrush, veery, red-eyed vireo; fair food of catbird, yellow-shafted flicker, great crested flycatcher, white-throated sparrow, thrush (gray-cheeked, hermit).

spiderflower (*Cleome* species). Weeds of cultivated places. Seed is fair food of mourning dove.

spikerush (also called spikesedge; *Eleocharis* species). Shallow-water sedge. Seeds of several undetermined species are fair food of Brewer's blackbird, coot, ducks, purple gallinule, goose, Virginia rail, sora, green-winged teal, American widgeon.

spikerush, squarestem (*Eleocharis quadrangulata*). Shallow-water sedge.

Seed is fair food of coot, goose (blue, snow), mallard, whistling swan, blue-winged teal.

spikesedge. See spikerush.

spinach (*Spinacia oleracea*). Garden vegetable. Tender sprouts are fair food of goose (blue, Canada, snow, white-fronted).

spinard, small. See sarsaparilla, wild.

spirea (*Spiraea* species). Ornamental shrubs; occasional nest sites. Unimportant as food.

spirogyra. See algae, filamentous.

sprangletop, Amazon (*Leptochloa panicoides*). A grass. Seed is a choice food of turkey.

springbeauty (*Claytonia* species). Perennial flower. Seed is fair food of gray partridge.

spruce (*Picea* species). Evergreen trees; often nest sites. Seeds of one or more undetermined species are a choice food of boreal chickadee, crossbill (red, white-winged), American goldfinch, grosbeak (evening, pine), spruce grouse, pine siskin, white-throated sparrow; fair food of black-capped chickadee, mourning dove.

spruce, black (also called bog, eastern, shortleaf black, and swamp spruce; *Picea mariana*). Native evergreen tree; often a nest site. Seed is a choice food of red-breasted nuthatch.

spruce, bog. See spruce, black.

spruce, Canadian. See spruce, white.

spruce, eastern. See spruce, black, red, and white.

spruce, Norway (*Picea abies*). Introduced ornamental evergreen tree; often a nest site. Seed is a choice food of red crossbill, pine grosbeak.

spruce, red (also called eastern and yellow spruce, and he-balsam; *Picea rubens*). Native evergreen tree; often a nest site. Seed is a choice food of crossbill (red, white-winged), pine siskin.

spruce, shortleaf black. See spruce, black.

spruce, swamp. See spruce, black.

spruce, white (also called Canadian and eastern spruce; *Picea glauca*). Native evergreen tree; often a nest site. Seed is a choice food of crossbill (red, white-winged), purple finch, evening grosbeak, spruce grouse, pine siskin, white-throated sparrow; fair food of mourning dove.

spruce, yellow. See spruce, red.

spurge. See euphorbia.

spurge-nettle. See treadsoftly, risky.

squash, winter (*Cucurbita maxima*). Garden vegetable. Seed is a choice food of cardinal, chickadee (black-capped, Carolina), blue jay, white-breasted nuthatch.

stargrass. See goldstargrass.

stick-tights. See beggarticks.

stillingia (also called queen's-delight; *Stillingia* species). Native perennial herbs. Seeds probably are fair food of bobwhite.

stonewort (also called muskgrass; *Chara* species). Submersed aquatics. Plant is a choice food of coot, duck (ring-necked, ruddy), redhead, scaup (greater, lesser), American widgeon; fair food of bufflehead, canvasback, duck (black, wood), gadwall, mallard, pintail, shoveler, teal (blue-winged, green-winged).

strawberry, cultivated and wild (*Fragaria* species). Fruit is a choice food of bobwhite, cardinal, catbird, common crow, grosbeak (black-headed, evening, rose-breasted), ruffed grouse, blue jay, eastern kingbird, mockingbird, robin, yellow-bellied sapsucker, white-throated sparrow, starling, brown thrasher, wood thrush, turkey, cedar waxwing, woodpecker (red-bellied, red-headed); fair food of Brewer's blackbird, yellow-breasted chat, yellow-shafted flicker, pine grosbeak, ring-necked pheasant, swamp sparrow, rufous-sided towhee, veery.

strawberry-bush. See wahoo, eastern.

sudangrass (*Sorghum sudanense*). Cultivated grass. Seed is a choice food of bobwhite, cardinal, mourning dove, purple finch, American goldfinch, slate-colored junco, mallard, pintail, sparrow (field, fox, house, song, white-throated), rufous-sided towhee; fair food of common grackle, blue jay, greater prairie chicken.

suet, beef. This animal food is often fed to birds in a suet feeder. Suet can be chopped or ground and molded into suet cakes, with or without the addition of peanutbutter, bits of pecan meats, syrup, or seeds. There is little advantage to the addition of seeds but the other mixes are good. Mrs. Ruth Thomas, columnist of the Little Rock, Arkansas, *Gazette*, prepares a "magic-mix" by adding ¼ to ½ cup of syrup to ½ cup of melted suet. Miss Perna M. Stine, Zephyrhills, Florida, varies the recipe by adding about 1 cup of corn-meal or bread crumbs to make the final mixture as thick as bread dough. She stores it in pint-sized cans and feeds it to warblers, summer tanagers, and cardinals. She says, "Only in summer is it necessary to refrigerate the magic-mix for keeping." Suet or a suet-mix is a choice food of catbird, chickadee (black-capped, Carolina), brown creeper, common crow, purple finch, yellow-shafted flicker, common grackle, rose-breasted grosbeak, jay (blue, gray, scrub), slate-colored junco, kinglet (golden-crowned, ruby-crowned), mockingbird, nuthatch (brown-headed, red-breasted, white-breasted), Baltimore oriole, redstart, yellow-bellied sapsucker, shrike (loggerhead, northern), sparrow (chipping, field, fox, tree, white-throated), starling, summer tanager, brown thrasher, thrush (hermit, wood), tufted titmouse, warbler (black-and-white, black-throated blue, myrtle, orange-crowned, parula, pine), woodpecker (downy, hairy, pileated, red-bellied, red-headed), wren

(Bewick's, Carolina), yellowthroat; fair food of eastern bluebird, cardinal, hawk (Cooper's, red-shouldered), robin, house sparrow.

suet, mutton. A choice food of woodpecker (downy, red-bellied).

sugar. Water sweetened with sucrose, dextrose, and levulose. A choice food of catbird, ruby-throated hummingbird, ruby-crowned kinglet, mockingbird, orchard oriole, summer tanager, brown thrasher; fair food of blue jay, Baltimore oriole, downy woodpecker. Sugar syrup is made by adding one part sugar to about three parts water, boiling the mix about 3 minutes to avoid spoilage. Feed in small jars, or for hummingbirds in commercially made vials.

sumac (*Rhus* species). Native shrubs; seldom nest sites. Fruits of undetermined species are fair food of cardinal, yellow-breasted chat, fish crow, gray jay, Townsend's solitaire, woodpecker (downy, pileated).

sumac dwarf. See sumac, shining.

sumac, poison. See poisonsumac.

sumac, scarlet. See sumac, smooth.

sumac, shining (also called dwarf sumac; *Rhus copallina*). Native shrub. Fruit is a choice food of catbird; fair food of eastern bluebird, mockingbird, robin, starling, hermit thrush, turkey, red-headed woodpecker.

sumac, smooth (also called scarlet sumac; *Rhus glabra*). Native shrub. Fruit is a choice food of eastern bluebird, catbird, common crow, mockingbird, wood thrush; fair food of bobwhite, purple finch, ruffed grouse, blue jay, ring-necked pheasant, greater prairie chicken, robin, starling, brown thrasher, hermit thrush, turkey, myrtle warbler, red-headed woodpecker.

sumac, staghorn (also called velvet sumac; *Rhus typhina*). Native shrub. Fruit is fair food of eastern bluebird, catbird, black-capped chickadee, common crow, grosbeak (evening, pine), ruffed grouse, blue jay, robin, starling, brown thrasher, hermit thrush, turkey, cedar waxwing.

sumac, velvet. See sumac, staghorn.

sumpweed, bigleaf (*Iva frutescens*). Weed of waste places. Unimportant to birds.

sumpweed, seacoast (*Iva ciliata*). A weed seldom used by birds. Possibly fair food of bobwhite.

sunflower (*Helianthus* species). Native annual or perennial flowering plants. Seeds of undetermined species are a choice food of lark bunting, boreal chickadee, white-winged dove, grosbeak (black-headed, blue, rose-breasted), sharp-tailed grouse, scrub jay, slate-colored junco, longspur (chestnut-collared, McCown's), sparrow (Harris', house, lark, Lincoln's, white-crowned), rufous-sided towhee; fair food of blackbird (Brewer's, yellow-headed), bobolink, common crow, horned lark, meadowlark (eastern, western), gray partridge, ring-necked pheasant, greater prairie chicken, sparrow (grasshopper, savannah, vesper), turkey.

sunflower, blackhead (*Helianthus scaberrimus*). Native perennial flowering plant. Seed is a choice food of American goldfinch.

sunflower, common (*Helianthus annuus*). Annual, flowering plant. Seed is a choice food of bobwhite, cardinal, Carolina chickadee, mourning dove, purple finch, slate-colored junco, pine siskin, sparrow (song, white-throated), tufted titmouse; fair food of red-winged blackbird, house sparrow. State flower of Kansas.

sunflower, cultivated (*Helianthus annuus*). Annual plant, large-seeded, cultivated varieties. Seed is an extra-choice food of cardinal, chickadee (black-capped, Carolina), crossbill (red, white-winged), purple finch, American goldfinch, common grackle, evening grosbeak, blue jay, nuthatch (brown-headed, red-breasted, white-breasted), white-throated sparrow, tufted titmouse, rufous-sided towhee, red-bellied woodpecker; fair food of red-winged blackbird, house sparrow, woodpecker (downy, hairy).

sunflower, prairie (*Helianthus petiolaris*). Annual plant of fields. Seed is a choice food of cardinal, mourning dove, American goldfinch, slate-colored junco; fair food of house sparrow.

supplejack, Alabama (also called rattanvine; *Berchemia scandens*). Native shrubby vine. Fruit is fair food of mockingbird, robin, hermit thrush, turkey.

swampbay. See redbay and sweetbay.

swamp-cedar. See white-cedar, northern.

swamp-privet (also called Texas forestiera; *Forestiera acuminata*). Swampland shrub; occasional nest plant. Fruit is a choice food of wood duck and mallard.

sweetbay (also called swamp, sweetbay, and laurel magnolia, and swamp-bay; *Magnolia virginiana*). Fruit is a choice food of eastern kingbird, mockingbird, robin, wood thrush, red-eyed vireo.

sweetgum (also called redgum, sapgum and American sweetgum; *Liquidambar styraciflua*). Native tree. Heavy producer of seed that is a choice food of red-winged blackbird, bobwhite, cardinal, dove (mourning, rock), purple finch, American goldfinch, evening grosbeak, slate-colored junco, common redpoll, pine siskin, white-throated sparrow, starling, turkey; fair food of chickadee (black-capped, Carolina), mallard, white-crowned sparrow, rufous-sided towhee.

sweetpotato (*Ipomoea batatas*). Cultivated garden plant. Potatoes are a choice food of crane (sandhill, whooping); also eaten ocasionally by black vulture.

sweetshrub (also called Carolina allspice; *Calycanthus* species). Sweet-scented flowering shrubs. Apparently unused by birds.

switchgrass (*Panicum virgatum*). Tall native perennial grass. Seed is a choice food of bobwhite, mourning dove, slate-colored junco, sparrow (field, tree, white-throated); fair food of cardinal, brown-headed cowbird.

sycamore, American (also called American planetree and buttonball-tree; *Platanus occidentalis*) Native tree; often a nest site. Seed is fair food of purple finch, American goldfinch, pine siskin.

syringa. See mockorange.

syrup, sugarcane. A choice food of woodpecker (hairy, red-bellied). See also honey and sugar, from which syrups are made.

tallowtree, Chinese (*Sapium sebiferum*). Introduced shade tree. Waxy fruit is fair food of red-winged blackbird, cardinal, fish crow, yellow-shafted flicker, boat-tailed grackle, blue jay, starling, brown thrasher, myrtle warbler.

tamarack (also called American, black, and eastern larch, and hackmatack; *Larix laricina*). Native tree, often a nest site. Seed from its cones is a choice food of crossbill (red, white-winged), purple finch; fair food of pine siskin. Buds and leaves are a choice food of spruce grouse.

tangerine (*Citrus reticulata*). Cultivated citrus-fruit tree. No records of bird use.

tearthumb, arrowleaf (*Tracaulon sagittatum*). Native marsh plant. Seed is a choice food of duck (black, mottled), mallard; fair food of pintail.

teasel, venuscup (also called venuscup; *Dipsacus sylvestris*). Cultivated plant or escaped weed. Seed is a choice food of white-winged crossbill; fair food of American goldfinch.

teaweed. See melochia, cluster.

thatch-leaf. See baycedar.

thimbleberry, fragrant (also called flowering raspberry; *Rubus odoratus*). A native raspberry; occasional nest site. Fruit is a choice food of yellow-breasted chat, spruce grouse.

thistle (*Cirsium* species). Annual or perennial prickly herbs. Seeds are a choice food of American goldfinch, clay-colored sparrow; nectar is a choice food of ruby-throated hummingbird.

thistle, Scotch. See cottonthistle, Scotch.

thistle, sow. See sowthistle.

thorn. See hawthorn.

threeawn (*Aristida* species). Native grasses. Seed is fair food of longspur (chestnut-collared, Smith's).

tickclover (also called beggar's lice; *Desmodium* species). Native perennial legumes. Seed is a choice food of bobwhite; fair food of ruffed grouse, turkey.

tick-seed. See beggarticks.

timothy (*Phleum pratense*). Cultivated hay and pasture grass. Seed is a choice food of Canada goose, common redpoll; fair food of brown-headed cowbird, slate-colored junco, Smith's longspur.

torchlily (also called red-hot-poker; *Kniphofia* species). Garden flowers. Nectar is a choice food of ruby-throated hummingbird.

trailing-arbutus (also called mayflower; *Epigaea repens*). Creeping evergreen of acid soils. Leaves are a choice food of ruffed grouse. Mayflower is the state flower of Massachusetts.

treadsoftly, risky (also called spurge-nettle; *Cnidoscolus stimulosus*). Native herb. Seed is fair food of bobwhite, mourning dove.

tree-of-heaven. See ailanthus.

tritonia (also called blazing-star; *Tritonia* species). Garden flowers. Nectar is a choice food of ruby-throated hummingbird.

trumpetcreeper, common (*Campsis radicans*). Native vine. Nectar is a choice food of ruby-throated hummingbird; seed is fair food of American goldfinch.

trumpettree, silverleaf (*Cecropia palmata*). Tropical tree; fruit is fair food of mockingbird.

tules. See cattail.

tuliptree or **tulip-poplar.** See yellow-poplar.

tungoiltree (*Aleurites fordi*). Introduced tree; often a nest site. No importance as a food plant.

tupelo, black. See blackgum.

tupelo, swamp. See blackgum; tupelo, water.

tupelo, water (also called swamp tupelo and tupelo-gum; *Nyssa aquatica*). Native swamp tree. Fruit is a choice food of yellow-shafted flicker, robin, woodpecker, (hairy, pileated); fair food of blue jay.

tupelo-gum. See tupelo, water.

turnip (*Brassica rapa*). Garden vegetable. Seed is a choice food of American goldfinch, American widgeon.

twin-berry. See partidgeberry.

umbrella-tree. See chinaberry.

vaseygrass (*Paspalum urvillei*). Introduced perennial grass. Seed is a choice food of painted bunting.

velvetgrass, common (*Holcus lanatus*). Introduced grass. Seed is a choice food of American goldfinch.

venuscup. See teasel, venuscup.

verbena (also called vervain; *Verbena* species). Native and cultivated flowering herbs. Nectar is a choice food of ruby-throated hummingbird; seeds are fair food of cardinal, swamp sparrow.

vervain. See verbena.

vetch (*Vicia* species). Annual legumes, usually cultivated. Green leaves and seeds are a choice food of bobwhite; fair food of dove (mourning, rock), turkey.

viburnum (also called blackhaw and nannyberry; *Viburnum* species). Native and introduced shrubs grown for their flowers. Fruits of undetermined species are a choice food of eastern bluebird, waxwing (Bohemian, cedar); fair food oof cardinal, pine grosbeak, grouse (ruffed, spruce), gray jay, mockingbird, robin, white-throated sparrow, starling, hermit thrush.

viburnum, American cranberrybush (also called highbush cranberry and American cranberrybush; *Viburnum trilobum*). Native shrub. Fruit is a choice food of waxwing (Bohemian, cedar); fair food of grouse (ruffed, spruce).

viburnum, European cranberrybush (also called highbush cranberry and European cranberrybush; *Viburnum opulus*). Introduced shrub. Fruit is a choice food of mockingbird, waxwing (Bohemian, cedar); fair food of ruffed grouse, white-throated sparrow.

violet (*Viola* species). Flowering herbs. Seeds are a choice food of ruffed grouse, water pipit; fair food of ground dove, slate-colored junco. State flower of Rhode Island. "Native violet" is the state flower of Illinois, "purple violet," of New Jersey, and "butterfly violet," of Wisconsin.

vitex, blue. See chastetree, lilac.

wahoo, eastern (also called strawberry-bush; *Euonymus atropurpureus*). Small native shrub. Berries little eaten.

walnut, black (also called American and eastern black walnut; *Juglans nigra*). Native nut tree; occasional nest site. Nut meat is a choice food of cardinal, catbird, Carolina chickadee, common crow, blue jay, slate-colored junco, ruby-crowned kinglet, brown-headed nuthatch, sparrow (song, white-crowned), tufted titmouse, warbler (myrtle, pine), woodpecker (downy, pileated, red-bellied), Carolina wren; fair food of field sparrow.

walnut, English. See walnut, Persian.

walnut, Persian (also called English walnut; *Juglans regia*). Cultivated commercial nut tree. Nut meat is a choice food of cardinal, chickadee (black-capped, Carolina), blue jay, nuthatch (brown-headed, red-breasted, white-breasted), white-throated sparrow, tufted titmouse, rufous-sided towhee, warbler (myrtle, pine), woodpecker (downy, hairy, red-bellied), Carolina wren.

walnut, white. See butternut.

wapato. See arrowhead.

water. One of the most important elements of bird habitat is water, and many species that cannot be enticed to a backyard feeding station may be lured to bathe or drink at a shallow birdbath. Dripping water or a spray has been found to be an even more effective attractant than still water. Species which feed almost exclusively on seeds drink more often than those that eat moisture-laden foods such as berries, green forage, fruits, and insects. Doves (an extreme example) usually drink twice daily, and cannot survive without water more than 4 or 5 days; but bobwhites can live without drinking water. Normally, birds find sufficient water in rain puddles, ponds, and streams, but in prolonged summer dry spells or in freezing weather they are deprived of many of these natural supplies and may be forced to range over wide areas to find usable water. The homeowner who keeps fresh water in his yard in the summer and who sets out warm water several times a day in the winter will be rewarded with a great number (and often a surprising variety) of bird visitors. In northern areas, many bird lovers buy electric warming devices, which they instill in the birdbath at the onset of the first cold spell.

watercress (*Rorippa nasturtium-aquaticum*). Green vegetable. Fair food of mallard.

waterelm (also called planertree; *Planera aquatica*). Native swamp tree. Fruit is a choice food of duck (black, ring-necked, wood), mallard.

waterhemp (*Acnida* species). Tall marsh plants. Seeds are fair food of black duck, mallard, pintail, teal (blue-winged, green-winged).

waterlily (*Nymphaea* species). Aquatic flowering plants. Seeds of undetermined species are fair food of sandhill crane, wood duck, pintail, lesser scaup.

waterlily, yellow Mexican (*Nymphaea mexicana*). Aquatic plant. Tender vegetative parts and seed are a choice food of canvasback, duck (black, ring-necked), redhead; fair food of duck (mottled, wood), mallard, scaup (greater, lesser), shoveler, blue-winged teal.

watermelon (*Citrullus vulgaris*). Garden and field crop. Seed is a choice food of cardinal, common crow, dove (mourning, white-winged), black-headed grosbeak, rufous-sided towhee.

watermilfoil. See parrotfeather.

water-pepper. See smartweed, marshpepper.

water-pepper, mild. See smartweed, swamp.

waterprimrose, creeping (*Jussiaea repens*). Aquatic plant. Seed may be fair food of mallard.

watershield (*Brasenia schreberi*). Aquatic plant. Seed is fair food of bufflehead, canvasback, duck (black, fulvous tree, mottled, ring-necked, ruddy, wood), mallard, pintail, redhead, scaup (greater, lesser), blue-winged teal.

waterweed. See anacharis.

waxmyrtle, northern (also called bayberry, northern bayberry, and candle-berry; *Myrica pensylvanica*). Native shrub; sometimes a nest plant. Waxy fruit is a choice food of tree swallow, myrtle warbler; fair food of eastern bluebird, bobwhite, catbird, black-capped chickadee, yellow-shafted flicker, robin, starling, brown thrasher, hermit thrush, red-bellied woodpecker.

waxmyrtle, southern (also called bayberry and candle-berry; *Myrica cerifera*). Native shrub; often a nest plant. Waxy fruit is a choice food of white-eyed vireo, myrtle warbler; fair food of bobwhite, common grackle, scrub jay, rufous-sided towhee, red-bellied woodpecker.

weigela (*Weigela* species). Flowering shrubs. Nectar is a choice food of ruby-throated hummingbird; seed is a choice food of tree sparrow.

wheat (*Triticum aestivum*). Cultivated grain. Seed or leaf blades are a choice food of blackbird (Brewer's, red-winged, rusty, yellow-headed), bobolink, bobwhite, bunting (indigo, lark, snow), cardinal, coot, brown-headed cowbird, sandhill crane, crow (common, fish), dove (mourning, rock, white-winged), duck (ring-necked, wood), gadwall, goose (Canada, snow, white-fronted), common grackle, grosbeak (blue, rose-breasted), sharp-tailed grouse, jay (blue, scrub), slate-colored junco, horned lark, longspur (chestnut-collared, Lapland, McCown's, Smith's), mallard, meadowlark (eastern, western), oldsquaw, gray partridge, ring-necked pheasant, pintail, water pipit, greater prairie chicken, redhead, greater scaup, shoveler, sparrow (European tree, field, fox, Harris', house, lark, song, tree, vesper, white-throated), whistling swan, teal (blue-winged, green-winged), rufous-sided towhee, turkey, American widgeon; fair food of whooping crane, dickcissel, ground dove, yellow-shafted flicker, black-headed grosbeak, Franklin's gull, savannah sparrow, starling.

wheatgrass (*Agropyron* species). Native grass. Seed is a choice food of gray partridge.

white-cedar, Atlantic (also called false-cypress and southern white-cedar; *Chamaecyparis thyoides*). Native evergreen tree; occasional nesting site. Seed is a choice food of pine siskin.

white-cedar, eastern. See white-cedar, northern.

white-cedar, northern (also called eastern and northern arborvitae, eastern white-cedar, swamp-cedar; *Thuja occidentalis*). Native evergreen tree; sometimes a nest tree. Seed is a choice food of pine siskin.

white-cedar, southern. See white-cedar, Atlantic.

white-marsh. See cutgrass, giant.

whitetop. See rivergrass.

whortleberry, ovalleaf (*Vaccinium ovalifolium*). Native shrub. Fruit is a choice food of spruce grouse.

widgeongrass (*Ruppia maritima*). Submersed brackish-water plant. Stem, leaf, and seed are a choice food of brant, bufflehead, coot, duck (black, ring-necked, ruddy), gadwall, Canada goose, knot, oldsquaw, redhead, scaup (greater, lesser), shoveler, teal (blue-winged, green-winged), American widgeon; fair food of canvasback, mottled duck, king eider, purple gallinule, mallard, pintail.

wildbean (also called trailing bean; *Strophostyles* species). Native legumes. Seeds are fair food of bobwhite, mourning dove.

wildcelery (*Vallisneria spiralis*). Submersed fresh-water aquatic. Plant is a choice food of canvasback, coot, duck (black, ring-necked, ruddy), common goldeneye, redhead, scaup (greater, lesser), whistling swan; fair food of bufflehead, wood duck, mallard, green-winged teal, American widgeon.

wildrice, annual (*Zizania aquatica*). Tall marsh grass. Seed is a choice food of blackbird (red-winged, rusty), bobolink, canvasback, coot, duck (black, ring-necked, wood), snow goose, blue grosbeak, mallard, pintail, Virginia rail, redhead, scaup (greater, lesser), sora, sparrow (house, sharp-tailed), teal (blue-winged, green-winged); fair food of bufflehead, fish crow, American widgeon.

wildrice, southern. See cutgrass, giant.

wildrye (*Elymus* species). Native grass. Seed is fair food of snow bunting.

willow (*Salix* species). Native wetland trees; often nest sites of many birds. Buds of several undetermined species are choice foods of grouse (sharp-tailed, spruce); fair foods of grosbeak (evening, pine).

willow, pussy (also called silver pussy willow; *Salix discolor*). Native shrub. Buds are a choice food of ruffed grouse.

windmillgrass, tumble (*Chloris verticillata*). Native grass. Seed is a choice food of purple gallinule.

winterberry. See possumhaw; winterberry, common.

winterberry, common (*Ilex verticillata*). Native shrub; frequent veery nest site. Fruit is a choice food of mockingbird; fair food of common crow, black duck, yellow-shafted flicker, robin.

wistaria. See wisteria.

wisteria (*Wisteria* species). Ornamental twining vines; occasional nest site. No importance as food.

witchgrass, common (*Panicum capillare*). Native annual grass. Seed is a choice food of water pipit; fair food of red-winged blackbird, mourning dove, turkey, American widgeon.

witchhazel (also called common and southern witchhazel; *Hamamelis virginiana*). Native shrub or small tree; occasional nest site. Seed is a choice food of cardinal, ruffed grouse; fair food of turkey.

woe-vine. See lovevine.

woodbine. See creeper, Virginia.

yardgrass. See goosegrass.

yaupon (also called cassena, Christmasberry, and evergreen holly; *Ilex vomitoria*). Native evergreen tree; often a nest site. Fruit is a choice food of mockingbird, cedar waxwing.

yelloweyegrass (*Xyris* species.) Native grasses. Seed is a choice food of turkey.

yellow-poplar (also called tuliptree and tulip-poplar; *Liriodendron tulipifera*). Native tree; often a nest plant. Nectar is a choice food of ruby-throated hummingbird; seed is a fair food of cardinal, purple finch, grosbeak (evening, pine). "Tuliptree" is the state tree of Indiana, Kentucky; "tulip-poplar" of Tennessee.

yew, Canada (*Taxus canadensis*). Prostrate evergreen shrub; occasional nest site.

zinnia, common (*Zinnia elegans*). Annual garden flower. Seeds are a choice food of American goldfinch; nectar is a choice food of ruby-throated hummingbird.

Technical Index to the Common Names of Birds

This index, presented for the convenience of those who are more familiar with the scientific names of birds, is an alphabetical list of Latin binomials for all the species treated in this book. The vernacular forms at right are the names by which the species are entered in section 4.

Acanthis, redpoll
 flammea, common r.
 hornemanni, hoary r.

Accipiter, hawk
 cooperii, Cooper's h.
 gentilis, goshawk
 striatus, sharp-shinned h.

Actitis, sandpiper
 macularia, spotted s.

Aechmophorus, grebe
 occidentalis, western g.

Aegolius, owl
 acadicus, saw-whet o.
 funereus, boreal o.

Agelaius, blackbird
 phoeniceus, red-winged b.

Aimophila, sparrow
 aestivalis, Bachman's s.

Aix, duck
 sponsa, wood d.

Ajaia, spoonbill
 ajaja, roseate s.

Alca torda, razorbill

Ammodramus, sparrow
 savannarum, grasshopper s.

Ammospiza, sparrow
 caudacuta, sharp-tailed s.
 maritima, seaside s.
 mirabilis, Cape Sable s.
 nigrescens, dusky seaside s.

Anas, duck
 acuta, pintail
 carolinensis, green-winged teal
 discors, blue-winged teal
 fulvigula, mottled d.
 platyrhynchos, mallard
 rubripes, black d.
 strepera, gadwall

Anhinga anhinga, anhinga

Anous, tern
 stolidus, noddy t.

Anser, goose
  albifrons, white-fronted g.

Anthus, pipit
  spinoletta, water p.
  spragueii, Sprague's p.

Aphelocoma, jay
  coerulescens, scrub j.

Aquila, eagle
  chrysaëtos, golden e.

Aramus guarauna, limpkin

Archilochus, hummingbird
  colubris, ruby-throated h.

Ardea, heron
  herodias, great blue h.
  occidentalis, great white h.

Arenaria, turnstone
  interpres, ruddy t.

Asio, owl
  flammeus, short-eared o.
  otus, long-eared o.

Aythya, duck
  affinis, lesser scaup
  americana, redhead
  collaris, ring-necked d.
  marila, greater scaup
  valisineria, canvasback

Bartramia, plover
  longicauda, upland p.

Bombycilla, waxwing
  cedrorum, cedar w.
  garrula, Bohemian w.

Bonasa, grouse
  umbellus, ruffed g.

Botaurus, bittern
  lentiginosus, American b.

Branta, goose
  bernicla, brant
  canadensis, Canada g.

Bubo, owl
  virginianus, great horned o.

Bubulcus, egret
  ibis, cattle e.

Bucephala, duck
  albeola, bufflehead
  clangula, common goldeneye
  islandica, Barrow's goldeneye

Buteo, hawk
  albicaudatus, white-tailed h.
  brachyurus, short-tailed h.
  harlani, Harlan's h.
  jamaicensis, red-tailed h.
  lagopus, rough-legged h.
  lineatus, red-shouldered h.
  platypterus, broad-winged h.
  swainsoni, Swainson's h.

Buteogallus, hawk
  anthracinus, black h.

Butorides, heron
  virescens, green h.

Calamospiza, bunting
  melanocorys, lark b.

Calcarius, longspur
  lapponicus, Lapland l.
  ornatus, chestnut-collared l.
  pictus, Smith's l.

Calidris canutus, knot

Campephilus, woodpecker
  principalis, ivory-billed w.

Canachites, grouse
  canadensis, spruce g.

Capella, snipe
  gallinago, common s.

Caprimulgus
  carolinensis, chuck-will's-widow
  vociferus, whip-poor-will

Caracara cheriway, caracara

Carpodacus, finch
  purpureus, purple f.

Casmerodius, egret
  albus, common e.

Cassidix, grackle
  mexicanus, boat-tailed g.

Cathartes, vulture
  aura, turkey v.

Catoptrophorus semipalmatus, willet

Centurus, woodpecker
  carolinus, red-bellied w.

Cepphus, guillemot
  grylle, black g.

Certhia, creeper
  familiaris, brown c.

Chaetura, swift
  pelagica, chimney s.

Charadrius, plover
  alexandrinus, snowy p.
  melodus, piping p.
  semipalmatus, semipalmated p.
  vociferus, killdeer
  wilsonia, Wilson's p.

Chen, goose
  caerulescens, blue g.
  hyperborea, snow g.

Chlidonias, tern
  niger, black t.

Chondestes, sparrow
  grammacus, lark s.

Chordeiles, nighthawk
  minor, common n.

Circus, hawk
  cyaneus, marsh h.

Cistothorus, wren
  platensis, short-billed marsh w.

Clangula hyemalis, oldsquaw

Coccyzus, cuckoo
  americanus, yellow-billed c.
  erythropthalmus, black-billed c.
  minor, mangrove c.

Colaptes, flicker
  auratus, yellow-shafted f.

Colinus virginianus, bobwhite

Columba, dove
  leucocephala, white-crowned pigeon
  livia, rock d.

Columbigallina, dove
  passerina, ground d.

Contopus, wood pewee
  virens, eastern w.p.

Coragyps, vulture
  atratus, black v.

Corvus, crow
  brachyrhynchos, common c.
  corax, common raven
  ossifragus, fish c.

Coturnicops, rail
  noveboracensis, yellow r.

Coturnix, quail
  coturnix, coturnix q.

Crocethia alba, sanderling

Crotophaga, ani
  ani, smooth-billed a.
  sulcirostris, groove-billed a.

Cyanocitta, jay
  cristata, blue j.

Cygnus, swan
  olor, mute s.

Dendrocopos, woodpecker
  borealis, red-cockaded w.
  pubescens, downy w.
  villosus, hairy w.

Dendrocygna, duck
  bicolor, fulvous tree d.

Dendroica, warbler
  caerulescens, black-throated blue w.
  castanea, bay-breasted w.
  cerulea, cerulean w.
  coronata, myrtle w.
  discolor, prairie w.
  dominica, yellow-throated w.
  fusca, Blackburnian w.
  kirtlandii, Kirtland's w.
  magnolia, magnolia w.
  nigrescens, black-throated gray w.
  palmarum, palm w.
  pensylvanica, chestnut-sided w.
  petechia, yellow w.
  pinus, pine w.
  striata, blackpoll w.
  tigrina, Cape May w.
  virens, black-throated green w.

Dichromanassa, egret
  rufescens, reddish e.

Dolichonyx oryzivorus, bobolink

Dryocopus, woodpecker
  pileatus, pileated w.

Dumetella carolinensis, catbird

Elanoides, kite
  forficatus, swallow-tailed k.

Elanus, kite
  leucurus, white-tailed k.

Empidonax, flycatcher
  flaviventris, yellow-bellied f.
  minimus, least f.
  traillii, Traill's f.
  virescens, Acadian f.

Eremophila, lark
  alpestris, horned l.

Ereunetes, sandpiper
  mauri, western s.
  pusillus, semipalmated s.

Erolia, sandpiper
  alpina, dunlin
  bairdii, Baird's s.
  fuscicollis, white-rumped s.
  maritima, purple s.
  melanotos, pectoral s.
  minutilla, least s.

Eudocimus, ibis
  albus, white i.

Euphagus, blackbird
  carolinus, rusty b.
  cyanocephalus, Brewer's b.

Falco, hawk
  columbarius, pigeon h.
  peregrinus, peregrine falcon
  rusticolus, gyrfalcon
  sparverius, sparrow h.

Florida, heron
  caerulea, little blue h.

Fratercula, puffin
  arctica, common p.

Fregata, frigate-bird
  magnificens, magnificent f.

Fulica, coot
  americana, American c.

Gallinula, gallinule
  chloropus, common g.

Gavia, loon
  immer, common l.
  stellata, red-throated l.

Gelochelidon, tern
  nilotica, gull-billed t.

Geococcyx californianus, roadrunner

Geothlypis trichas, yellowthroat

Grus, crane
  americana, whooping c.
  canadensis, sandhill c.

Guiraca, grosbeak
  caerulea, blue g.

Haematopus, oystercatcher
  palliatus, American o.

Haliaeetus, eagle
  leucocephalus, bald e.

Helmitheros, warbler
  vermivorus, worm-eating w.

Hesperiphona, grosbeak
  vespertina, evening g.

Himantopus, stilt
  mexicanus, black-necked s.

Hirundo, swallow
  rustica, barn s.

Histrionicus, duck
  histrionicus, harlequin d.

Hydranassa, heron
  tricolor, Louisiana h.

Hydroprogne, tern
  caspia, Caspian t.

Hylocichla, thrush
  fuscescens, veery
  guttata, hermit t.
  minima, gray-cheeked t.
  mustelina, wood t.
  ustulata, Swainson's t.

Icteria, chat
  virens, yellow-breasted c.

Icterus, oriole
  galbula, Baltimore o.
  pectoralis, spotted-breasted o.
  spurius, orchard o.

Ictinia, kite
  misisippiensis, Mississippi k.

Iridoprocne, swallow
  bicolor, tree s.

Ixobrychus, bittern
  exilis, least b.

Junco, junco
  hyemalis, slate-colored j.

Lagopus, ptarmigan
  lagopus, willow p.
  mutus, rock p.

Lanius, shrike
  excubitor, northern s.
  ludovicianus, loggerhead s.

Larus, gull
  argentatus, herring g.
  atricilla, laughing g.
  delawarensis, ring-billed g.
  glaucoides, Iceland g.
  hyperboreus, glaucous, g.
  marinus, great black-backed g.
  minutus, little g.
  philadelphia, Bonaparte's g.
  pipixcan, Franklin's g.

Laterallus, rail
  jamaicensis, black r.

Leucophoyx, egret
  thula, snowy e.

Limnodromus, dowitcher
  griseus, short-billed d.
  scolopaceus, long-billed d.

Limnothlypis, warbler
  swainsonii, Swainson's w.

Limosa, godwit
  fedoa, marbled g.
  haemastica, Hudsonian g.

Lobipes, phalarope
  lobatus, northern p.

Lophodytes, merganser
  cucullatus, hooded m.

Loxia, crossbill
  curvirostra, red c.
  leucoptera, white-winged c.

Mareca, widgeon
  americana, American w.

Megaceryle, kingfisher
  alcyon, belted k.

Melanerpes, woodpecker
  erythrocephalus, red-headed w.

Melanitta, scoter
  deglandi, white-winged s.
  perspicillata, surf s.

Meleagris gallopavo, turkey

Melospiza, sparrow
  georgiana, swamp s.
  lincolnii, Lincoln's s.
  melodia, song s.

Mergus, merganser
  merganser, common m.
  serrator, red-breasted m.

Micropalama, sandpiper
  himantopus, stilt s.

Mimus polyglottos, mockingbird

Mniotilta, warbler
  varia, black-and-white w.

Molothrus, cowbird
  ater, brown-headed c.

Morus bassanus, gannet

Muscivora, flycatcher
  forficata, scissor-tailed f.

Myadestes, solitaire
  townsendi, Townsend's s.

Mycteria, ibis
  americana, wood i.

Myiarchus, flycatcher
  crinitus, great crested f.

Numenius, curlew
  americanus, long-billed c.
  borealis, Eskimo c.
  phaeopus, whimbrel

Nuttallornis, flycatcher
  borealis, olive-sided f.

Nyctanassa, heron
  violacea, yellow-crowned night h.

Nyctea, owl
  scandiaca, snowy o.

Nycticorax, heron
  nycticorax, black-crowned night h.

Oidemia, scoter
  nigra, common s.

Olor, swan
   columbianus, whistling s.

Oporornis, warbler
   agilis, Connecticut w.
   formosus, Kentucky w.
   philadelphia, mourning w.

Otus, owl
   asio, screech o.

Oxyura, duck
   jamaicensis, ruddy d.

Pagophila, gull
   eburnea, ivory g.

Pandion haliaetus, osprey

Parabuteo, hawk
   unicinctus, Harris' h.

Parula, warbler
   americana, parula w.

Parus, chickadee
   atricapillus, black-capped c.
   bicolor, tufted titmouse
   carolinensis, Carolina c.
   hudsonicus, boreal c.

Passer, sparrow
   domesticus, house s.
   montanus, European tree s.

Passerculus, sparrow
   princeps, Ipswich s.
   sandwichensis, savanna s.

Passerella, sparrow
   iliaca, fox s.

Passerherbulus, sparow
   caudacutus, Le Conte's s.
   henslowii, Henslow's s.

Passerina, bunting
   ciris, painted b.
   cyanea, indigo b.

Pedioecetes, grouse
   phasianellus, sharp-tailed g.

Pelecanus, pelican
   erythrorhynchos, white p.
   occidentalis, brown p.

Perdix, partridge
   perdix, gray p.

Perisoreus, jay
   canadensis, gray j.

Petrochelidon, swallow
   pyrrhonota, cliff s.

Phalacrocorax, cormorant
   auritus, double-crested c.
   carbo, great c.
   olivaceus, olivaceous c.

Phalaropus, phalarope
   fulicarius, red p.

Phasianus, pheasant
   colchicus, ring-necked p.

Pheucticus, grosbeak
   ludovicianus, rose-breasted g.
   melanocephalus, black-headed g.

Philohela, woodcock
   minor, American w.

Picoides, woodpecker
   arcticus, black-backed three-
     toed w.
   tridactylus, northern three-toed w.

Pinicola, grosbeak
   enucleator, pine g.

Pipilo, towhee
   erythrophthalmus, rufous-sided t.

Piranga, tanager
   olivacea, scarlet t.
   rubra, summer t.

Plautus alle, dovekie

Plectrophenax, bunting
  nivalis, snow b.

Plegadis, ibis
  chihi, white-faced i.
  falcinellus, glossy i.

Pluvialis, plover
  dominica, American golden p.

Podiceps, grebe
  auritus, horned g.
  caspicus, eared g.
  dominicus, least g.
  grisegena, red-necked g.

Podilymbus, grebe
  podiceps, pied-billed g.

Polioptila, gnatcatcher
  caerulea, blue-gray g.

Pooecetes, sparrow
  gramineus, vesper s.

Porphyrula, gallinule
  martinica, purple g.

Porzana carolina, sora

Progne, martin
  subis, purple m.

Protonotaria, warbler
  citrea, prothonotary w.

Pycnonotus, bulbul
  jocosus, red-whiskered b.

Pyrocephalus, flycatcher
  rubinus, vermilion f.

Quiscalus, grackle
  quiscula, common g.

Rallus, rail
  elegans, king r.
  limicola, Virginia r.
  longirostris, clapper r.

Recurvirostra, avocet
  americana, American a.

Regulus, kinglet
  calendula, ruby-crowned k.
  satrapa, golden-crowned k.

Rhynchophanes, longspur
  mccownii, McCown's l.

Richmondena cardinalis, cardinal

Riparia, swallow
  riparia, bank s.

Rissa, kittiwake
  tridactyla, black-legged k.

Rostrhamus, kite
  sociabilis, Everglade k.

Rynchops, skimmer
  nigra, black s.

Sayornis, phoebe
  phoebe, eastern p.

Seiurus, waterthrush
  aurocapillus, ovenbird
  motacilla, Louisiana w.
  noveboracensis, northern w.

Selasphorus, hummingbird
  rufus, rufous h.

Setophaga, redstart
  ruticilla, American r.

Sialia, bluebird
  sialis, eastern b.

Sitta, nuthatch
  canadensis, red-breasted n.
  carolinensis, white-breasted n.
  pusilla, brown-headed n.

Somateria, eider
  mollissima, common e.
  spectabilis, king e.

Spatula clypeata, shoveler

Speotyto, owl
cunicularia, burrowing o.

Sphyrapicus, sapsucker
varius, yellow-bellied s.

Spinus
pinus, pine siskin
tristis, American goldfinch

Spiza americana, dickcissel

Spizella, sparrow
arborea, tree s.
pallida, clay-colored s.
passerina, chipping s.
pusilla, field s.

Squatarola, plover
squatarola, black-bellied p.

Steganopus, phalarope
tricolor, Wilson's p.

Stelgidopteryx, swallow
ruficollis, rough-winged s.

Stercorarius, jaeger
longicaudus, long-tailed j.
parasiticus, parasitic j.
pomarinus, pomarine j.

Sterna, tern
albifrons, least t.
anaethetus, bridled t.
dougallii, roseate t.
forsteri, Forster's t.
fuscata, sooty t.
hirundo, common t.
paradisaea, arctic t.

Streptopelia, dove
risoria, ringed turtle d.

Strix, owl
nebulosa, great gray o.
varia, barred o.

Sturnella, meadowlark
magna, eastern m.
neglecta, western m.

Sturnus vulgaris, starling

Sula, booby
dactylatra, blue-faced b.
leucogaster, brown b.

Surnia ulula, owl, hawk

Telmatodytes, wren
palustris, long-billed marsh w.

Thalasseus, tern
maximus, royal t.
sandvicensis, Sandwich t.

Thryomanes, wren
bewickii, Bewick's w.

Thryothorus, wren
ludovicianus, Carolina w.

Totanus, yellowlegs
flavipes, lesser y.
melanoleucus, greater y.

Toxostoma, thrasher
rufum, brown t.

Tringa, sandpiper
solitaria, solitary s.

Troglodytes, wren
aedon, house w.
troglodytes, winter w.

Tryngites, sandpiper
subruficollis, buff-breasted s.

Turdus migratorius, robin

Tympanuchus, prairie chicken
cupido, greater p.c.

Tyrannus, kingbird
dominicensis, gray k.
tyrannus, eastern k.
verticalis, western k.

Tyto, owl
  alba, barn o.

Uria, murre
  aalge, common m.
  lomvia, thick-billed m.

Vermivora, warbler
  bachmanii, Bachman's w.
  celata, orange-crowned w.
  chrysoptera, golden-winged w.
  peregrina, Tennessee w.
  pinus, blue-winged w.
  ruficapilla, Nashville w.

Vireo, vireo
  altiloquus, black-whiskered v.
  bellii, Bell's v.
  flavifrons, yellow-throated v.
  gilvus, warbling v.
  griseus, white-eyed v.

  olivaceus, red-eyed v.
  philadelphicus, Philadelphia v.
  solitarius, solitary v.

Wilsonia, warbler
  canadensis, Canada w.
  citrina, hooded w.
  pusilla, Wilson's w.

Xanthocephalus, blackbird
  xanthocephalus, yellow-headed b.

Zenaida, dove
  asiatica, white-winged d.

Zenaidura, dove
  macroura, mourning d.

Zonotrichia, sparrow
  albicollis, white-throated s.
  leucophrys, white-crowned s.
  querula, Harris' s.

Technical Index to the Common Names of Plants

This index is offered for the convenience of those who know plants most familiarly by their scientific names. It lists, in alphabetical order, the Latin names of all the species mentioned in this book, and gives the common name by which they are entered in section 5.

Abelia, abelia
  grandiflora, glossy a.

Abies, fir
  balsamea, balsam f.

Abronia, sandverbena

Acalypha, copperleaf

Acer, maple
  negundo, boxelder
  saccharum, sugar m.

Achras zapota, sapodilla

Acnida, waterhemp

Aesculus
  glabra, Ohio buckeye
  hippocastanum, common
    horsechestnut

Agropyron, wheatgrass
  repens, quackgrass

Ailanthus altissima, ailanthus

Ajuga, bugle
  reptans, carpet b.

Albizzia, albizzia
  julibrissin, silktree a.

Aleurites fordi, tungoiltree

Alnus, alder

Althaea rosea, hollyhock

Amaranthus, amaranth
  blitoides, prostrate a.
  hybridus, slim a.
  retroflexus, redroot a.
  spinosus, spiny a.

Amaryllis, amaryllis

Ambrosia, ragweed
  artemisifolia, common r.
  bidentata, lanceleaf r.
  psilostachya, western r.
  trifida, giant r.

Amelanchier, serviceberry
  arborea, downy s.
  laevis, Allegheny s.

Ammophila, beachgrass
  breviligulata, American b.

Ampelopsis, ampelopsis
  arborea, peppervine
  cordata, heartleaf a.

Amphicarpa, hogpeanut
  bracteata, southern h.

Anacardium occidentale, cashew

Anacharis canadensis, anacharis

Andropogon, bluestem
  gerardi, big b.
  scoparius, little b.

Aneilema, aneilema
  keisak, keisak a.
  nudiflorum, (no common name)

Anemone patens, pasqueflower

Antidesma bunius, chinalaurel

Antigonon, coralvine
  leptopus, mountainrose c.

Antirrhinum, snapdragon

Apios, potatobean
  americana, American p.

Aquilegia, columbine
  canadensis, American c.

Arachis hypogaea, peanut

Aralia nudicaulis, wild sarsaparilla
  spinosa, devils-walkingstick

Arctium, burdock
  minus, smaller b.

Ardisia, ardisia
  crenulata, Christmas a.

Argemone, prickly poppy
  alba, white p.p.
  mexicana, Mexican p.p.

Aristida, threeawn

Aronia, chokeberry
  arbutifolia, red c.

Arrhenatherum, oatgrass
  elatius, tall o.

Asclepias, milkweed
  tuberosa, butterfly m.

Asimina, pawpaw

Asparagus, asparagus
  officinalis, garden a.

Aster, aster

Atriplex, saltbush
  patula, fat-hen s.

Avena, oat
  fatua, wild o.
  sativa, common o.

Avicennia nitida, blackmangrove

Axonopus, carpetgrass

Azalea, azalea

Baccharis, baccharis

Bambusa, bamboo

Beloperone guttata, shrimp-plant

Berberis, barberry
  julianae, wintergreen b.
  thunbergi, Japanese b.
  vulgaris, European b.

Berchemia, supplejack
  scandens, Alabama s.

Bertholletia excelsa, brazilnut

Betula, birch

Bidens, beggarticks

Bougainvillea, bougainvillea

Brachiaria, signalgrass
platyphylla, broadleaf s.

Brachychiton, bottletree

Brasenia schreberi, watershield

Brassica
napus, rape
oleracea, cabbage
rapa, turnip

Bromus, brome

Broussonetia, papermulberry
papyrifera, common p.

Brunfelsia americana, lady-of-the-night

Bumelia, bumelia
lanuginosa, gum b.

Buxus, box
sempervirens, common b.

Cabomba, fanwort
caroliniana, Carolina f.

Callicarpa, beautyberry
americana, American b.
japonica, Japanese b.

Callistemon, bottlebrush

Calycanthus, sweetshrub

Camellia japonica, camellia

Campsis, trumpetcreeper
radicans, common t.

Cannabis sativa, hemp

Caperonia castaneaefolia, birdeye

Carex, sedge

Carica papaya, papaya

Carissa, carissa
grandiflora, natalplum c.

Carpinus, hornbeam
caroliniana, American h.

Carthamus tinctorius, safflower

Carya, hickory
aquatica, water h.
illinoensis, pecan

Cassytha filiformis, lovevine

Castanea, chestnut; chinkapin
dentata, American chestnut

Castilleja, paintedcup

Casuarina equisetifolia, beefwood

Catalpa, catalpa

Cecropia, trumpettree
palmata, silverleaf t.

Celastrus, bittersweet
scandens, American b.

Celtis, hackberry
laevigata, sugar h.
occidentalis, common h.

Centaurea cyanus, cornflower

Centella asiatica, spadeleaf

Centrosema, butterflypea
virginianum, coastal b.

Cephalanthus occidentalis, buttonbush

Ceratophyllum demersum, hornwort

Cercis, redbud
canadensis, eastern r.

Chaenomeles, floweringquince
  japonica, Japanese f.

Chamaecrista, partridgepea
  fasciculata, showy p.
  procumbens, sensitive p.

Chamaecyparis thyoides, Atlantic
  white-cedar

Chara, stonewort

Chenopodium, goosefoot

Chloris, windmillgrass
  verticillata, tumble w.

Cichorium intybus, chicory

Cinnamomum camphora, camphortree

Cirsium, thistle

Citrullus vulgaris, watermelon

Citrus, citrus
  limon, lemon
  paradisi, grapefruit
  reticulata, tangerine
  sinensis, sweet orange

Cladium, sawgrass
  jamaicensis, Jamaica s.

Claytonia, springbeauty

Cleome, spiderflower

Cnidoscolus, treadsoftly
  stimulosus, risky t.

Cocculus, snailseed
  carolinus, Carolina s.

Commelina, dayflower

Coptis, goldthread
  groenlandica, common g.

Cordia, cordia
  sebestena, Geiger-tree c.

Coreopsis, coreopsis

Cornus, dogwood
  alba, tatarian d.
  alternifolia, alternateleaf d.
  amomum, silky d.
  drummondii, roughleaf d.
  florida, flowering d.
  racemosa, gray d.
  stolonifera, redosier d.
  stricta, stiffcornel d.

Corylus, filbert
  americana, American f.
  avellana, European f.
  cornuta, beaked f.
  maxima, giant f.

Cosmos, cosmos

Cotinus obovatus, smoketree

Cotoneaster, cotoneaster

Crataegus, hawthorn

Crinum, crinum
  americanum, Florida c.

Crotalaria, crotalaria
  capensis, cape c.

Croton, croton
  capitatus, woolly c.
  glandulosus, tropic c.
  linearis, linear c.
  monanthogynus, oneseed c.
  punctatus, gulf c.
  texensis, Texas c.

Crotonopsis, crotonopsis

Cucumis melo, cantaloup

Cucurbita
  maxima, winter squash
  pepo, pumpkin

Cydonia, quince
  oblonga, common q.

Cynodon dactylon, Bermudagrass

Cyperus, flatsedge
  compressus, poorland f.
  erythrorhizos, redroot f.
  esculentus, chufa

Dactylis glomerata, orchardgrass

Dahlia, dahlia

Daucus, carrot
  carota, wild c.
  carota sativa, garden c.

Desmodium, tickclover
  polycarpum, beggarweed, Florida

Deutzia, deutzia

Diervilla lonicera, honeysuckle,
  dwarf bush

Digitaria, crabgrass
  ischaemum, smooth c.
  sanguinalis, hairy c.

Diospyros, persimmon
  kaki, kaki p.
  virginiana, common p.

Dipsacus, teasel
  sylvestris, venuscup t.

Distichlis, saltgrass
  spicata, seashore s.

Duranta repens, dewdrop, golden

Echinochloa, cockspur
  colonum, junglerice
  crusgalli, barnyardgrass
  crusgalli frumentacea, Japanese
    millet
  walteri, coast c.

Elaeagnus, elaeagnus
  multiflora, cherry e.
  pungens, thorny e.
  umbellata, autumn e.

Eleocharis, spikerush
  quadrangulata, squarestem s.

Eleusine coracana, ragimillet
  indica, goosegrass

Elymus, wildrye

Empetrum, crowberry
  nigrum, black c.

Epigaea repens, trailing-arbutus

Equisetum, horsetail

Eragrostis, lovegrass
  hypnoides, teal l.

Erigeron, fleabane
  strigosus, daisy f.

Eriobotrya japonica, loquat

Eriocaulon, pipewort

Eugenia uniflora, pitanga

Euonymus, euonymus
  atropurpureus, wahoo, eastern

Eupatorium maculatum, joepyeweed,
  spotted

Euphorbia, euphorbia

Fagopyrum, buckwheat
  sagittatum, common b.

Fagus, beech
  grandifolia, American b.

Festuca, fescue

Ficus, fig
  carica, common f.

Fluminea festucacea, rivergrass

Forestiera acuminata, swamp-privet

Forsythia, forsythia

Fragaria, strawberry, cultivated and
    wild

Fraxinus, ash
    americana, white a.

Fuchsia, fuchsia

Galactia, milkpea

Gardenia jasminoides, gardenia

Gaylussacia, huckleberry
    baccata, black h.
    dumosa, dwarf h.

Gelsemium sempervirens, Carolina-
    jessamine

Geobalanus oblongifolius, deer-plum

Geranium, geranium
    carolinianum, Carolina g.

Gladiolus, gladiolus

Gleditsia triacanthos, honeylocust

Glyceria, mannagrass
    striata, fowl m.

Glycine soja, soybean

Gossypium, cotton

Halodule, shoalgrass
    wrightii, marine s.

Hamamelis virginiana, witchhazel

Hedera, ivy
    helix, English i.

Helianthus, sunflower
    annuus, common s., cultivated s.
    petiolaris, prairie s.
    scaberrimus, blackhead s.

Hepatica, hepatica
    americana, roundlobe h.

Hibiscus, hibiscus
    syriacus, shrubalthea

Hippophae, seabuckthorn
    rhamnoides, common s.

Hippuris vulgaris, marestail

Holcus, velvetgrass
    lanatus, common v.

Hordeum, barley, wild
    vulgare, cultivated b.

Hydrangea, hydrangea

Hypericum, St. Johnswort
    prolificum, shrubby St.J.

Hypoxis, goldstargrass

Ilex, holly
    aquifolium, English h.
    cassine, dahoon
    coriacea, gallberry, large
    cornuta, Chinese h.
    crenata, Japanese h.
    decidua, possumhaw
    glabra, gallberry
    opaca, American h.
    verticillata, winterberry, common
    vomitoria, yaupon

Impatiens, snapweed
    biflora, spotted s.

Ipomoea, morningglory
    batatas, sweetpotato

Iva, sumpweed
    ciliata, seacoast s.
    frutescens, bigleaf s.

Jatropha, nettlespurge
    gossypifolia, bellyache n.

Juglans, walnut
  cinerea, butternut
  nigra, black w.
  regia, Persian w.

Juncus, rush
  pelocarpus, brownfruited r.
  roemerianus, needlegrass r.

Juniperus, redcedar
  silicicola, southern r.
  virginiana, eastern r.

Jussiaea, waterprimrose
  repens, creeping w.

Kalmia latifolia, mountainlaurel

Kniphofia, torchlily

Lachnanthes, redroot
  tinctoria, blood r.

Lactuca, lettuce
  sativa, garden l.
  serriola, prickly l.
  spicata, blue l.

Lagenaria vulgaris, gourds

Lagerstroemia indica, crapemyrtle

Larix, larch
  decidua, European l.
  laricina, tamarack
  leptolepsis, Japanese l.

Leersia, cutgrass
  oryzoides, rice c.

Lemna, duckweed

Leptochloa, sprangletop
  panicoides, Amazon s.

Lespedeza, lespedeza
  bicolor, bicolor l.
  cuneata, sericea l.

japonica, japonica l.
  stipulacea, Korean l.
  striata, common l.
  striata var. Kobe, Kobe l.
  thunbergii, Thunberg l.

Ligustrum, privet
  amurense, Amur p.
  japonicum, Japanese p.
  lucidum, glossy p.
  sinense, Chinese p.

Lilium, lily
  longiflorum, Easter l.
  superbum, turkscap l.
  tigrinum, tiger l.

Lindera, spicebush
  benzoin, common s.

Linum, flax
  usitatissimum, common f.

Liquidambar styraciflua, sweetgum

Liriodendron tulipifera, yellow-
  poplar

Liriope, liriope
  spicata, creeping l.

Lobelia cardinalis, cardinalflower

Lolium, ryegrass
  multiflorum, Italian r.

Lonicera, honeysuckle
  bella, Belle h.
  dioica, limber h.
  fragrantissima, winter h.
  japonica, Japanese h.
  maacki, Amur h.
  morrowi, Morrow h.
  periclymenum, woodbine h.
  ruprechtiana, Manchurian h.
  tatarica, tatarian h.

Lupinus, lupine
  bicolor, bicolor l.

Lycium halimifolium, matrimonyvine

Maclura pomifera, osageorange

Magnolia, magnolia
  grandiflora, southern m.
  virginiana, sweetbay

Maianthemum, beadruby
  canadense, Canada b.

Malpighia glabra, Barbadoscherry

Malus, apple; crabapple
  pumila, apple

Mangifera indica, mango

Medicago
  hispida, burclover
  sativa, alfalfa

Melia azedarach, chinaberry

Melilotus, clover, sweet

Melochia, melochia
  corchorifolia, cluster m.

Menispermum, moonseed
  canadense, common m.

Menyanthes, bogbean
  trifoliata, common b.

Mirabilis, four-o'clock
  jalapa, common f.

Mitchella repens, partridgeberry

Mitella, miterwort
  diphylla, common m.

Monarda, beebalm
  didyma, Oswego b.

Morus, mulberry

Musa, banana

Myrica, waxmyrtle
  cerifera, southern w.
  pensylvanica, northern w.

Myriophyllum, parrotfeather

Najas, naiad
  flexilis, northern n.
  guadalupensis, southern n.
  mariana, spiny n.

Nandina domestica, nandina

Nemopanthus mucronata, mountainholly

Nepeta cataria, catnip

Nerium oleander, oleander

Nothoscordum, falsegarlic
  bivalve, yellow f.

Nuphar, cowlily

Nymphaea, waterlily
  mexicana, yellow Mexican w.

Nyssa, tupelo
  aquatica, water t.
  sylvatica, blackgum

Oenothera, eveningprimrose

Onopordum, cottonthistle
  acanthium, Scotch c.

Oryza sativa, rice

Osmanthus, osmanthus

Ostrya, hophornbeam
  virginiana, eastern h.

Oxydendrum arboreum, sourwood

Panicum, panicum
 aciculare, needleleaf p.
 adspersum, Dominican p.
 agrostoides, redtop p.
 amarulum, shoredune p.
 anceps, beaked p.
 bartowense, Bartow p.
 bosci, bosc p.
 bulbosum, bulb p.
 capillare, witchgrass, common
 clandestinum, hiddenseed p.
 dichotomiflorum, fall p.
 fasciculatum, browntop p.
 flexile, flexile p.
 fusiforme, fusiform p.
 lanuginosum, woolly p.
 longifolium, longleaf p.
 miliaceum, proso millet
 neuranthum (no common name)
 oligosanthes (no common name)
 ramosum, browntop millet
 repens, torpedo p.
 scoparium, velvet p.
 sphaerocarpon, roundseed p.
 tennesseense, Tennessee p.
 texanum, Texas millet
 verrucosum, warty p.
 virgatum, switchgrass

Parkinsonia aculeata, Jerusalemthorn

Parthenocissus, creeper
 quinquefolia, Virginia c.
 tricuspidata, Japanese c.

Paspalum, paspalum
 boscianum, bull p.
 ciliatifolium, fringeleaf p.
 dissectum, mudbank p.
 distichum, knotgrass
 floridanum, Florida p.

 giganteum, giant p.
 lividum, longtom
 longepedunculatum, barestem p.
 notatum, bahiagrass
 plicatulum, brownseed p.
 urvillei, vaseygrass
 vaginatum, seashore p.

Paulownia, paulownia
 tomentosa, royal p.

Peltandra, arrowarum
 glauca, redfruit a.
 virginica, Virginia a.

Pennisetum glaucum, pearl millet

Penstemon, penstemon

Persea
 americana, avocado
 borbonia, redbay

Petunia, petunia

Phalaris
 arundinacea, reed canarygrass
 canariensis, canarygrass
 tuberosa stenoptera, Hardinggrass

Phaseolus, bean
 aureus, mung b.
 coccineus, scarlet runner b.

Phellodendron, corktree
 chinense, Chinese c.

Philadelphus, mockorange

Phleum pratense, timothy

Phlox, phlox

Phoenix dactylifera, date

Phoradendron, mistletoe
 flavescens, Christmas m.

Photinia, photinia
   serrulata, Chinese p.

Phragmites communis, reed

Phyllostachys, bamboo

Physalis, groundcherry

Physocarpus, ninebark

Phytolacca, pokeberry
   americana, common p.
   rigida, stiff p.

Picea, spruce
   abies, Norway s.
   glauca, white s.
   mariana, black s.
   rubens, red s.

Pinus, pine
   banksiana, jack p.
   clausa, sand p.
   echinata, shortleaf p.
   elliotti, slash p.
   glabra, spruce p.
   palustris, longleaf p.
   resinosa, red p.
   rigida, pitch p.
   serotina, pond p.
   strobus, eastern white p.
   sylvestris, Scotch p.
   taeda, loblolly p.
   virginiana, Virginia p.

Pistacia vera, pistachionut

Pisum, pea
   sativum, garden p.

Planera aquatica, waterelm

Platanus, sycamore
   occidentalis, American s.

Poa, bluegrass
   annua, annual b.
   pratensis, Kentucky b.

Polygonum, smartweed
   coccineum, bigroot s.
   hydropiper, marshpepper s.
   hydropiperoides, swamp s.
   lapathifolium, curltop s.
   natans, water s.
   pensylvanicum, Pennsylvania s.
   persicaria, spotted s.
   portoricense, Puerto Rico s.
   punctatum, dotted s.

Polypogon, polypogon
   monspeliensis, rabbitfoot p.

Polystichum acrostichoides, Christmasfern

Pontederia cordata, pickerelweed

Populus, aspen; poplar
   deltoides, cottonwood, eastern
   grandidentata, bigtooth a.
   tremuloides, quaking a.

Portulaca oleracea, portulaca

Potamogeton, potamogeton
   americanus, longleaf p.
   amplifolius, largeleaf p.
   epihydrus, ribbonleaf p.
   foliosus, leafy p.
   gramineus, variableleaf p.
   illinoensis, Illinois p.
   natans, floatingleaf p.
   pectinatus, sago p.
   perfoliatus, thorowort p.
   pusillus, baby p.
   strictifolius, stiffleaf p.
   zosteriformis, flatstem p.

Prunella, selfheal
   vulgaris, common s.

Prunus, apricot; cherry; peach; plum
  americana, American plum
  amygdalus, almond
  armeniaca, apricot
  avium, mazzard c.
  besseyi, bessey c.
  caroliniana, laurelcherry
  cerasus, sour c.
  domestica, garden plum; prunes
  mahaleb, mahaleb c.
  padus, European bird c.
  pensylvanica, pin c.
  persica, peach
  pumila, sand c.
  serotina, black c.
  virginiana, choke c.

Psidium guajava, guava

Pueraria lobata, kudzu

Punica granatum, pomegranate

Pyracantha, pyracantha

Pyrostegia ignea, flamevine

Pyrus communis, pear

Quercus, oak
  acutissima, sawtooth o.
  alba, white o.
  arkansana, Arkansas o.
  bicolor, swamp white o.
  coccinea, scarlet o.
  ellipsoidalis, northern pin o.
  falcata, southern red o.
  ilicifolia, bear o.
  imbricaria, shingle o.
  incana, bluejack o.
  laevis, turkey o.
  laurifolia, laurel o.
  lyrata, overcup o.
  macrocarpa, bur o.
  marilandica, blackjack o.

  michauxii, swamp chestnut o.
  Muhlenbergii, chinkapin o.
  nigra, water o.
  nuttallii, Nuttall o.
  palustris, pin o.
  phellos, willow o.
  prinus, chestnut o.
  pumila, runner o.
  rubra, northern red o.
  shumardii, Shumard o.
  stellata, post o.
  velutina, black o.
  virginiana, live o.

Ranunculus, buttercup

Rhizophora mangle, mangrove

Rhododendron, rhododendron

Rhus, sumac
  copallina, shining s.
  glabra, smooth s.
  typhina, staghorn s.

Rhynchosia, rhynchosia

Rhynchospora corniculata, beakrush, horned

Ribes, currant; gooseberry

Ricinus communis, castorbean

Robinia, locust
  pseudoacacia, black l.

Rorippa, marshcress
  nasturtium-aquaticum, watercress
  palustris, bog m.

Rosa, rose
  multiflora, multiflora r.

Rubus, blackberry, dewberry; raspberry
  odoratus, thimbleberry, fragrant

Rudbeckia, coneflower

Ruellia, ruellia

Rumex acetosella, sheepsorrel

Ruppia maritima, widgeongrass

Sabal, palmetto
  palmetto, cabbage p.

Sagittaria, arrowhead

Salicornia, glasswort

Salix, willow
  discolor, pussy w.

Salvia, sage
  lyrata, lyreleaf s.
  officinalis rubriflora, red garden s.
  splendens, scarlet s.

Sambucus, elder
  canadensis, American e.
  pubens, scarlet e.
  racemosa, European red e.

Sapium sebiferum, tallowtree,
  Chinese

Sassafras albidum, sassafras

Saururus, lizardtail
  cernuus, common l.

Saxifraga, saxifrage
  micranthidifolia, lettuce s.

Schinus, peppertree
  terebinthifolia, Brazil p.

Scirpus, bulrush
  robustus, saltmarsh b.

Scleria, nutrush
  ciliata, fringed n.
  muhlenbergii, sloughgrass n.

Secale cereale, rye

Serenoa repens, sawpalmetto

Sesamum indicum, sesame

Sesbania, sesbania
  exalti, hemp s.

Setaria, bristlegrass; millet
  faberii, Faber's b.
  italica, foxtail m.
  lutescens, yellow b.
  magna, giant b.
  viridis, green b.

Smilax, greenbrier

Solanum, nightshade
  dulcamara, bitter n.
  nigrum, black n.
  pseudocapsicum, Jerusalemcherry
  tuberosum, potato

Solidago, goldenrod

Sonchus, sowthistle

Sorbus, mountainash
  americana, American m.
  aucuparia, European m.

Sorghum, sorghum
  almum, Columbusgrass
  arundinacea, reed s.
  halepense, Johnsongrass
  sudanense, sudangrass
  vulgare, grain s.
  vulgare drummondi, chickencorn
  vulgare saccharatum, sorgo

Sparganium, burreed

Spartina, cordgrass

Spinacia oleracea, spinach

Spiraea, spirea

Spirogyra, algae, filamentous

Sporobolus, dropseed

Stellaria media, chickweed

Stenotaphrum secundatum, St. Augustinegrass

Stillingia, stillingia

Stipa, needlegrass

Strophostyles, wildbean

Suriana maritima, baycedar

Symphoricarpos orbiculatus, coralberry

Syringa vulgaris, lilac

Taraxacum, dandelion

Taxodium distichum, baldcypress

Taxus, yew
   canadensis, Canada y.

Thuja, arborvitae
   occidentalis, white-cedar, northern
   orientalis, arborvitae, oriental

Tiarella, foamflower
   cordifolia, Allegheny f.

Tilia, basswood
   americana, American b.

Tillandsia usneoides, Spanishmoss

Toxicodendron
   radicans, poisonivy
   vernix, poisonsumac

Tracaulon, tearthumb
   sagittatum, arrowleaf t.

Tragopogon, salsify
   pratensis, meadow s.

Trifolium, clover
   hybridum, alsike c.
   incarnatum, crimson c.
   pratense, red c.
   repens, white c.

Triglochin, podgrass
   maritima, shore p.

Triplasis, sandgrass
   purpurea, purple s.

Triticum aestivum, wheat

Tritonia, tritonia

Tropaeolum majus, nasturtium

Tsuga, hemlock
   canadensis, eastern h.

Typha, cattail

Ulmus, elm
   americana, American e.
   parvifolia, Chinese e.
   pumila, Siberian e.

Ulva lactuca, sealettuce

Uniola paniculata, seaoats

Utricularia, bladderwort
   vulgaris, common b.

Vaccinium, blueberry; whortleberry
   arboreum, sparkleberry
   macrocarpum, cranberry
   ovalifolium, ovalleaf w.
   oxycoccos, cranberry, small
   uliginosum, bilberry, bog
   vitis-idaea, cowberry

Vallisneria spiralis, wildcelery

Verbena, verbena

Viburnum, viburnum
   opulus, European cranberrybush v.
   trilobum, American cranberrybush v.

Vicia, vetch

Vigna, cowpea
   sinensis, common c.

Viguiera, goldeneye

Viola, violet

Vitex, chastetree
    agnuscastus, lilac c.

Vitis, grape, cultivated; raisins
    aestivalis, summer g.
    labrusca, fox g.
    rotundifolia, muscadine g.
    vulpina, frost g.

Weigela, weigela

Wisteria, wisteria

Xyris, yelloweyegrass

Zannichellia palustris, poolmat

Zea mays, corn

Zinnia, zinnia
    elegans, common z.

Zizania, wildrice
    aquatica, annual w.

Zizaniopsis miliacea, cutgrass, giant

Zostera marina, eelgrass

Some Reference Books on Birds

This book does not describe birds for purposes of making identifications and does not offer exhaustive details about the distribution and seasonal concentration of each species. Readers interested in these and other aspects of bird lore may consult any of numerous excellent reference books on birds, a selection of which is given below. Some of the books are out of print, but they are often available in public libraries.

Books of National or Regional Scope

A Field Guide to the Birds [East of the Rockies], by Roger Tory Peterson. Houghton Mifflin Co., Boston, 1947.

Birds of North America: A Guide to Field Identification, by Chandler Robbins, Dr. Bertel Bruun, and Dr. Herbert S. Zim. Golden Press, Inc., New York, 1966.

Audubon Guides: All the Birds of Eastern and Central North America, by Richard H. Pough. Doubleday and Co., Inc., Garden City, N.Y., 1953.

A Pocket Guide to Birds: Eastern and Central North America, by Allan D. Cruickshank. Dodd, Mead & Co., New York, 1953.

Birds of America, edited by T. Gilbert Pearson, *et al.* Garden City Publishing Co., Garden City, N.Y., 1936.

A Guide to Bird Finding East of the Mississippi, by Olin S. Pettingill, Jr. Oxford University Press, New York, 1951.

The Book of Birds, edited by Gilbert Grosvenor and Alexander Wetmore. National Geographic Society, Washington, D.C., 1937.

The Book of Birdlife, by Arthur A. Allen. D. Van Nostrand Co. New York, 1930.

How to Know the Birds: An Introduction to Bird Recognition, by Roger Tory Peterson. Houghton Mifflin Co., Boston, 1949.

Naming the Birds at a Glance, by Lou Blachly and Randolph Jenks. Knopf, New York, 1963.

A Guide to Bird Songs, by Aretas A. Saunders. Doubleday and Co., Inc., New York, 1951.

Natural History of American Birds of Eastern and Central North America, by Edward Howe Forbush; edited by John B. May. Houghton Mifflin Co., Boston, 1955.

Birds of America, by John James Audubon. Macmillan Co., New York, 1946.
Bird Guide: Land Birds East of the Rockies, by Chester A. Reed. Doubleday & Co., Inc., Garden City, N.Y., 1951.
Handbook of Birds of Eastern North America, by Frank M. Chapman. Dover Publications, Inc., New York, 1966.
Bird Watching, Housing and Feeding, by Walter E. Schutz. Bruce Publishing Co., Milwaukee, 1963.
A Guide to Bird Watching, by Joseph J. Hickey. Garden City Publishing Co., Garden City, N.Y., 1953.
Songbirds in Your Garden, by John K. Terres. Thomas Y. Crowell Co., New York, 1953.

Books by States

Alabama *Alabama Birds*, by Thomas A. Imhof. University of Alabama Press, University, Ala., 1962.
Arkansas *Birds of Arkansas*, by W. J. Baerg. University of Arkansas, Fayetteville, 1931.
Connecticut *Birds of Connecticut*, by John H. Sage and Louis B. Bishop. Connecticut Geological and Natural History Survey, Bulletin No. 20. Hartford, 1913.
Delaware See MARYLAND.
Florida *Florida Bird Life*, by Alexander Sprunt, Jr. Coward-McCann Inc., New York, 1954.
Georgia *Georgia Birds*, by Thomas D. Burleigh. University of Oklahoma Press, Norman, 1958.
Illinois *Birds of the Chicago Region*, by Edward Russell Ford. Chicago Academy of Sciences, Special Publications No. 12, 1956.
Indiana *Common Birds of Indiana*, edited by Earl Brooks. Blatchley Nature Study Club, Noblesville, Ind., 1945.
Iowa See MINNESOTA.
Kansas *Birds in Kansas*, by A. L. Goodrich, Jr. Kansas Board of Agriculture, Topeka, 1946.
Kentucky *Birds of Kentucky*, by J. D. Figgins. University of Kentucky Press, Lexington, 1945.
Louisiana *Louisiana Birds*, by George H. Lowery. Louisiana State University Press, Baton Rouge, 1960.
Maine *Maine Birds*, by Ralph S. Palmer. Bulletin of the Museum of Comparative Zoology, Cambridge, Mass., 1949.
Maryland *Birds of Maryland and the District of Columbia*, by Robert E. Stewart and C. S. Robbins, U.S. Dept. of Interior, Fish & Wildlife Service, Washington, D.C., 1958.
Massachusetts *Birds of Cape Cod, Massachusetts*, by Norman P. Hill. William Morrow & Co., New York, 1965. *Birds of Massachusetts and Other New England States*, by Edward H. Forbush. Massachusetts Board of Agriculture, Norwood, Mass., 1925–1929.

Michigan *The Birds of Michigan,* by Norman A. Wood. University of Michigan Press, Ann Arbor, 1951.

Minnesota *A Manual for the Identification of the Birds of Minnesota and Neighboring States,* by Thomas S. Roberts. University of Minnesota Press, Minneapolis, 1955.

Mississippi *The Bird Life of the Gulf Coast Region of Mississippi,* by Thomas D. Burleigh. Louisiana State University Museum of Zoology, Occasional Papers No. 20, Baton Rouge, 1944.

Missouri *Check-List of the Birds of Missouri,* by Rudolf Bennitt. University of Missouri, Columbia, Mo., 1932.

Nebraska *Birds of North Dakota County, Nebraska,* by T. C. Stephens. Nebraska Ornithological Union, Crete, Nebr., 1957.

New Hampshire See MASSACHUSETTS.

New Jersey *Annotated List of New Jersey Birds,* by David Fables, Jr. Urner Ornithological Club, Newark, N.J., 1955.

New York *Birds of New York,* by Elon Howard Eaton. New York State Museum, Albany, 1923. *Birds of the New York Area* by John L. Bull. Harper & Row., New York, 1964. *Enjoying Birds in Upstate New York,* by Olin S. Pettingill, Jr., and Sally F. Hoyt. Cornell University Laboratory of Ornithology, Ithaca, 1963. *Enjoying Birds Around New York City,* by Robert S. Arbib Jr., Olin S. Pettingill, and Sally H. Spofford. Houghton Mifflin Co., Boston, 1966.

North Carolina *Birds of North Carolina,* by T. Gilbert Pearson, *et al.;* revised by Harry T. Davis and David L. Ray. North Carolina State Museum, Raleigh, 1959.

Ohio *Check List of the Birds of Ohio,* by D. J. Borror. *Ohio Journal of Science,* Ohio State University, Columbus, 1950.

Oklahoma *Birds of Oklahoma,* by Margaret Nice. University of Oklahoma Press, Norman, 1931.

Pennsylvania *Pennsylvania Birds,* by Earl L. Poole. Livingston Publishing Co., Narberth, Pa., 1965.

Rhode Island See CONNECTICUT and MASSACHUSETTS.

South Carolina *South Carolina Bird Life,* by Alexander Sprunt, Jr., and E. B. Chamberlin. University of South Carolina Press, Columbia, 1949.

Tennessee *Notes on the Birds of the Great Smoky Mountains National Park,* by Arthur Stupka. University of Tennessee Press, Knoxville, 1963.

Texas *A Field Guide to the Birds of Texas,* by Roger Tory Peterson. Houghton Mifflin Co., Boston, 1960.

Vermont See MASSACHUSETTS.

Virginia See WEST VIRGINIA, MARYLAND, and NORTH CAROLINA.

West Virginia *A Check-List of West Virginia Birds,* by Maurice Brooks. West Virginia University, Agric. Exper. Sta. Bulletin No. 316, Morgantown, West Virginia, 1944.

Wisconsin *Birds of Wisconsin,* by Owen J. Gromme. University of Wisconsin Press, Milwaukee, 1963.

Canadian, Caribbean, and Latin American Books

Canada *Birds of Canada,* by P. A. Taverner. Musson Book Co., Toronto, 1947. *Birds of the Labrador Peninsula and Adjacent Areas,* by W. E. C. Todd. University of Toronto Press, Toronto, 1963. *Birds of Newfoundland,* by Harold S. Peters and Thomas D. Burleigh. Houghton Mifflin Co., Boston, 1951. *The Birds of Nova Scotia,* by Robie W. Tufts. Nova Scotia Museum, Halifax, 1961. *Ontario Birds,* by Lester L. Snyder. Clarke, Irwin & Co., Toronto, 1951.

Mexico *Birds of Mexico: A Guide for Field Identification,* by Emmett R. Blake. University of Chicago Press, 1953.

West Indies *Birds of the West Indies,* by James Bond. Houghton Mifflin Co., Boston, 1960. *Birds of the Caribbean,* by Robert P. Allen. Viking Press, New York, 1961.